NEXT 79 km

# INSIGHT GUIDES
# IN THE SAME SERIES

# australia

Directed and Designed by Hans Johannes Hoefer
Edited by Phil Jarratt
Photography by Photographers of Apa Photo Agency

APA PRODUCTIONS

THE INSIGHT GUIDES SERIES RECEIVED SPECIAL AWARDS FOR EXCELLENCE FROM THE PACIFIC AREA TRAVEL ASSOCIATION.

**AUSTRALIA**
Second Edition Published by:
©APA PRODUCTIONS (HK) LTD, 1986

Printed in Korea by Pyung Hwa Dang Printing Co Ltd

Colour Separation in Singapore by Colourscan Pte Ltd

**APA PRODUCTIONS**
**Publisher and Managing Director:** Hans Johannes Hoefer
**Financial Controller:** Henry Lee
**Administrative Manager:** Alice Ng
**Editorial Manager:** Vivien Loo

**Project Editors**

Helen Abbott, Diana Ackland, Mohamed Amin, Ravindrala Anthonis, Roy Bailet, Louisa Cambell, Jon Carroll, John Eames, Janie Freeburg, Bikram Grewal, Virginia Hopkins, Samuel Israel, Jay Itzkowitz, Phil Jarratt, Tracy Johnson, Ben Kalb, Wilhelm Klein, Saul Lockhart, Slyvia Mayuga, Gordn McLauchlan, Kal Müller, Eric Oey, Daniel P. Reid, Kim Robinson, Ronn Ronck, Rolf Steinberg, Harold Stephens, Desmond Tate, Sriyani Tidbal, Lisa Van Gruisen, Merin Wexler, Made Wijaya.

**Contributing Writers**

A.D. Aird, Ruth Armstrong, T. Terence Barrow, F. Lisa Beebe, Bruce Berger, Dor Bahadur Bista, Clinton V. Black, Star Black, Frena Bloomfield, John Borthwick, Roger Boschman, Tom Brosnahan, Linda Carlock, Jerry Carroll, Tom Chaffin, Nedra Chung, Tom Cole, Orman Day, Kunda Dixit, Richard Erdoes, Guillermo Garcia-Oropeza, Ted Giannoulas, Barbara Gloudon, Harka Gurung, Sharifah Hamzah, Willard A. Hanna, Elizabeth Hawley, Sir Edmund Hillary, Tony Hillerman, Jerry Hopkins, Peter Hutton, Neil Jameson, Michael King, Michele Kort, Thomas Lucey, Leonard Lueras, Michael E. Macmillan, Derek Maitland, Buddy Mays, Craig McGregor, Reinhold Messner, Julie Michaels, Barbara Mintz, M.R. Priya Rangsit, Al Read, Elizabeth V. Reyes, Victor Stafford Reid, Harry Rolnick, E.R. Sarachchandra, Uli Schmetzer, Ilsa Sharp, Norman Sibley, Leslie Marmon Silko, Peter Spiro, Harold Stephens, Keith Stevens, Michael Stone, Colin Taylor, Deanna L. Thompson, Randy Udall, James Wade, Mallika Wanigasundara. William Warren, Cynthia Wee, Tony Wheeler, Linda White, H. Taft Wireback, Alfred A. Yuson, Paul Zach.

**Contributing Photographers**

Carole Allen, Ping Amranand, Marcello Bertinetti, Alberto Cassio, Pat Canova, Alain Compost, Ray Cranbourne, Alain Evrard, Ricard Ferro, Lee Foster, Manfred Gottschalk, Werner Hahn, Dallas and John Heaton, Brent Hesselyn, Hans Hoefer, Luca Invernizzi, Ingo Jezierski, Wilhelm Klein, Dennis Lane, Max Lawrence, Philip Little, Ian Lloyd, Bret Lundberg, Guy Marche, Antonio Martinelli, David Messent, Ben Nakayama, Vautier de Nanxe, Kal Müller, Günter Pfannmuller, Van Phillips, Ronni Pinsler, Fritz Prenzel, G.P. Reichelt, Dan Rocovits, David Ryan, Frank Salmoiraghi, Thomas Schollhammer, Blair Seitz, David Stahl, Tom Tidball, Paul Van Reil, Rolf Verres, Joe F. Viesti, Paul Von Stroheim, Bill Wassman, Rendo Yap, Hisham Youssef.

**Distributors:**

**Australia:** Lansdowne Press, 176 South Creek Road, Dee Why, N.S.W. 2099, AUSTRALIA **Benelux:** Uitgeverij Cambium, Naarderstraat 11, 1251 Aw Laren, The Netherlands. **Brazil and Portugal:** Cedibra Editora Brasileira Ltda, Rua Leonidia, 2-Rio de Janeiro, Brazil. **Denmark:** Copenhagen Book Centre Aps, Roskildeveji 338, DK-2630 Tastrup, Denmark. **Germany:**

Nelles Verlag, Schleissheimer Str. 371b, 8000 Munich 45. **Hawaii:** Pacific Trade Group Inc., P.O. Box 1227, Kailua, Oahu, Hawaii 96734, U.S.A. **Hong Kong:** Far East Media Ltd., Vita Tower, 7th Floor, Block B, 29 Wong Chuk Hang Road, Hong Kong. **India and Nepal:** India Book Distributors, 107/108 Arcadia Building, 195 Narima Point, Bombay-400-021, India. **Indonesia:** Jalan Patiunus 47, Pekalongan, Jateng, Indonesia. **Italy:** Via Ganaceto 121, 41100 Modena, Italy. **Jamaica:** Kingston Publishers, 1-A Norwood Avenue, Kingston 5, Jamaica. **Japan:** Charles E. Tuttle Co. Inc., 2-6 Suido 1-Chome, Bunkyo-ku, Tokyo, Japan. **Korea:** Korea Britannica Corporation, C.P.O. Box 690, Seoul 100, Korea, 162-1, 2-ga, Jangchung-dong, Jung-gu, Seoul, Korea. **Mexico:** Distribuidora Britannica S.A., Rio Volga 93, Col Cuauhtemoc, 06500 Mexico 5 D.F., Mexico. **New Zealand:** Lansdowne Rigby, Unit 3, 3 Marken Place, Glenfield, Auckland. **Pakistan:** Liberty Book Stall, Inverarity Road, Karachi 03, Pakistan. **Philippines:** National Book Store Inc., 701 Rizal Avenue, Manila, Philippines. **Singapore and Malaysia:** MPH Distributors (S) Pte. Ltd., 601 Sims Drive #03-21 Pan-I Warehouse and Office Complex, Singapore 1438. **Sri Lanka:** K.V.G. de Silva & Sons (Colombo) Ltd., 415 Galle Road, Colombo 4, Sri Lanka. **Spain:** Altair, Riera Alta 8, Barcelona 1, Spain. **Sweden:** Esselte Kartcentrum, Vasagatan 16, S-111 20 Stockholm, Sweden. **Switzerland:** M.P.A. Agencies-Import SA, CH. du Bochet 68, CH-1025 ST-Sulpice, Switzerland. **Taiwan:** Caves Books Ltd., 103 Chungshan N. Road, Sec. 2, Taipei, Taiwan. Republic of China. **Thailand:** Book Promotion & Service Ltd., 9/14 Soi Pipat, Silom Road, Bangkok 10500, Thailand. **United Kingdom:** Harrap Ltd., 19-23 Ludgale Hill, London EC4M 7PD, England, United Kingdom. **Mainland United States and Canada:** Prentice-Hall Inc., Englewood Cliffs, New Jersey 07632, U.S.A.

**German editions:** Nelles Verlag GmbH, Schleissheimerstrasse 371b, 8000 Munich 45, West Germany. **Italian editions:** Via Ganaceto 121, 41100 Modena, Italy.

**Advertising and Special Sales Representatives**
Advertising carried in Insight Guides gives readers direct access to quality merchandise and travel-related services. These advertisements are inserted in the Guide in Brief section of each book. Advertisers are requested to contact their nearest representatives, listed below.
Special sales, for promotion and educational purposes within the international travel industry, are also available. The advertising representatives listed here also handle special sales. Alternatively, interested parties can contact marketing director Yvan Van Outrive directly at Apa Productions, P.O. Box 219. Orchard Point Post Office, Singapore 9123.

**Thailand:** Cheney, Tan & Van Outrive, 17th Floor Rajapark Building, 163 Asoke Road, Bangkok 10110, Thailand. Tel: 2583244; Telex: 20666 RA-JAPAK TH.

**Hawaii:** Hawaiian Media Sales, 1750 Kalakau Ave., Suite 3-243, Honolulu Hawaii 96826, U.S.A. Tel: (808) 9464483.

**Hong Kong:** C Cheney & Associates, 17th Floor, D'Aguilar Place, 1-30 D'Aguilar, Central, Hong Kong. Tel: 5-213671; Telex: 63079 CCAL HX.

**India:** Dass Media Pvt. Ltd., 207 Bhandari House, 91 Nehru Place, New Delhi-110 019, India. Tel: 669772/667432; Telex: 315236 PRYA IN.

**Singapore and Malaysia:** Cheney Tan Associates, 20 McCallum Street, #17-01/02 Asia Chambers, Singapore 0106. Tel: 2222893/2222725; Telex: RS 35983 CTAL.

**Sri Lanka:** Spectrum Lanka Advertising Ltd., 56 1/2 Ward Place, Colombo 7, Sri Lanka. Tel: 5984648/596227; Telex: 21439 SPECTRM CE.

**APA PHOTO AGENCY PTE LTD**

The Apa Photo Agency is S.E. Asia's leading stock photo archive, representing the work of professional photographers from all over the world. More than 150,000 original color transparencies are available for advertising, editoral and educational uses. We are also linked with Tony Stone Worldwide, one of Europe's leading stock agencies, and their associate offices around the world:

**Singapore:** Apa Photo Agency Pte Ltd 5 Lengkong Satu Singapore 1441. **London:** Tony Stone Worldwide 28 Finchley Road St John's Nood London NW8 6ES. **New York:** Index-Stone International Inc 126 Fifth Avenue New York NY 10011 USA. **Paris:** Fotogram-Stone Agence Photographique 45 rue de Richelieu 75001 Paris France. **Barcelone:** Fototeca Torre Dels Pardais 7 Barcelona 08026 Spain **Johannesburg:** Color Library (Pty) Ltd P O Box 1659 Johannesburg South Africa 2000 **Sydney:** The Photographic Library of Australia Pty Ltd 7 Ridge Street North Sydney New South Wales 2050 Australia. **Tokyo:** Orion Press 55-1 Kanda Jimbocho Chiyoda-ku Tokyo 101 Japan.

Although it may have seemed a logical progression—from Asia to Australia—it has taken almost 15 years and a long circuitous route, through several continents, for Asia-based Apa Productions to get there. This addition to the award-winning series of *Insight Guides, Australia: Grand Tour*, was worth the long wait.

Apa Productions was established in 1970 by German-born designer and photographer **Hans Hoefer**. Hoefer, Bauhaus-trained and footloose when he arrived in Asia, sweated to produce the first of Apa's titles—*Insight Guide: Bali*. Instantly acclaimed, it presented information for travellers in a way that no publisher had done before; the pictures and text, capturing the essence of that island, combined to produce a book that inspired as it informed.

The same combination of aesthetics and accessible information became the driving force behind the subsequent titles in the series of *Insight Guides* which went on to focus on a dozen Asian and Pacific destinations over the next decade. Always, Hoefer went to great pains to see that his team of writers, photographers and editors never lost touch with their subject.

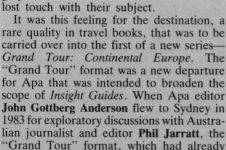

*Jarratt*

*Hoefer*

It was this feeling for the destination, a rare quality in travel books, that was to be carried over into the first of a new series—*Grand Tour: Continental Europe*. The "Grand Tour" format was a new departure for Apa that was intended to broaden the scope of *Insight Guides*. When Apa editor **John Gottberg Anderson** flew to Sydney in 1983 for exploratory discussions with Australian journalist and editor **Phil Jarratt**, the "Grand Tour" format, which had already been established and was taking shape as work on the Europe title gathered momentum, seemed ideally tailored to meet the needs of travellers in Australia.

Jarratt is one of Australia's best-known magazine journalists and about the time he accepted the Apa assignment had just finished a two-year tenure as Editor of Australia *Playboy*. Jarratt, who trained with

*Jameson*

*Anderson*

the *Sydney Morning Herald* in the late sixties and early seventies went on to work as a feature writer and sub-editor in Australia and the U.K. In the mid-seventies he threw away his coat and tie and languished in Sydney's beachside suburbs producing the surfing magazine *Tracks*. At the same time he became the laziest surf reporter ever to be heard on radio. Now married and with several children, he is working freelance as an author and journalist in addition to managing a photo/press agency. It was Jarratt who assembled a team of writers and photographers who not only knew the vast highways and backroads of the country, but who could transmit the spirit of the "wide brown land" in their words and images.

To head his team, and also to assist in the task of editing from travel logs, Jarratt chose Neil Jameson. Unable to lay claim to being from convict stock, Jameson is fourth generation Australian of British stock. Starting his journalistic career with the *Newcastle Morning Herald*, he went on to become a sportswriter and award-winning music critic. After a five-year spell as associate editor for Australian *Playboy* he joined Jarratt as a partner.

As an ancillary editor Jameson segmented the continent into tours into and out of each major city. His task involved compiling accurate and up-to-date information about outback road conditions from frequent travellers to remote areas. Jameson also contributed to the features section with a piece on the nation's sporting life.

Although many versions of Australian history have found their way into print, few are as concise and readable as the contributions which make up the history section of this book. Jarratt put the first 3,000 million years into perspective before **Patricia O'Shane** and veteran photographer, writer and advertising man Rennie Ellis wrote on Australia's Aborigines. Administrator and Aboriginal activist O'Shane, a teacher for eleven years before studying law, did a three year stint as a barrister in a private practice before involving herself in legislation relating to aborigines. She is presently head of the Ministry of Aboriginal Affairs. **John Borthwick**, a lecturer in creative writing at the Sydney College of Advanced Education and an inveterate traveller (and chronicler of travel adventures) took time out between treks in Nepal and China to pen a fast-flowing history to the end of World War Two.

The baton was then passed to **Craig McGregor**, one of Australia's most eminent social historians and authors, and an award-winning journalist to boot. McGregor wrote a compelling version of events of a traumatic period in which Australia woke from a long, apathetic slumber.

The features section also benefited from McGregor's expertise in the form of a broad view of Australian "fine" and "popular" culture.

Jarratt opened the "People" section with a look at Australians in the cities while **Richard Beckett**, now a writer in New South Wales after 27 years in journalism, followed up by deflating the myth of the rural Aussie, albeit with an affectionate tracing of the roots of the "Outback Tradition." Beckett, as Australia's foremost bush gourmet and comic writer, was responsible for explaining the national tastes in food, wine and beer.

**Steve Bunk** managed to get permanent resident status before regulations were changed in April 1982. A much-travelled full-time writer, Bunk spent a number of years working for newspapers and magazines in California and Idaho. During 1980 he was working for *Time In* magazine in Athens. Two years later he was with Australian *Playboy*. His main challenge as a traveller is to stay somewhere long enough to "find out what is going on."

Getting into Australia was, for him, "a breeze" and a seemingly endless series of cocktail party questions about how he found his way in led him to develop an interest in why he was one of the fortunate ones. Some of the answers are found in his piece on the new migrants.

**Charles Perkins** gave his views on the place of original Australians in contemporary Australia. Perkins has been professionally involved in Aboriginal affairs since 1965 and was the first aboriginal to be appointed head of a department in the Australia public service. Now Chairman of the Aboriginal Development Commission in 1980, he has always been an outspoken representative of his people.

In order to capture the feeling of the major Australian cities, the services of well-known journalists were sought. John Borthwick was asked to write again, this time on Sydney, while Rennie Ellis wrote on Melbourne. Ellis, currently Melbourne correspondent and a contributing editor to Australian *Playboy*, also writes and photographs a social column for *Mode* magazine. He has travelled widely overseas and in Australia, and authored or co-authored a number of books about his country. His most recent

O'Shane     Borthwick     McGregor

Beckett     Bunk     Perkins

Robson     Bowditch     Mann

title was *Life's a Beach*.

In Canberra the irreverent political columnist **Mungo McCallum** gave his view of the Australian capital. Before turning freelance in 1978 McCallum spent eight years with the *Nation Review* and six years with the *Australian*. He has published two books to date: *Mungo's Canberra* and *Mungo on the Zoo Plane*.

Sharp-witted author and journalist Frank Robson wrote about a love-hate relationship with his adopted home of Brisbane and then led the way on one of the tours—from Brisbane to Cairns. He spent close on ten years in newspaper journalism before turning to freelance magazine writing in 1978. His credits include a wide range of Australian periodicals and a book entitled *Dare To Be Different*.

In post-cyclone Darwin, Australia's gateway to Asia, there was only one choice—the veteran newspaperman and yarn spinner **Jim Bowditch**. Bowditch came to Darwin as managing editor of the *Northern Territory News* late in 1954; the city has been his base for his subsequent years as a journalist.

**Paul Mann**, an English-born journalist who outlined the delights of life in Adelaide, lauds the quality of life in what he calls this "magnificently provincial" city. At the other end of the continent **A.D. Aird** provided the piece on Perth and covered another of the tours—the "Long Haul" out of Perth to Darwin. The feature on how Australia's "splendid isolation" has affected its flora and fauna was also penned by Aird.

Apa editor John Gottberg Anderson, who spent several months in Sydney as a journalist in 1976, traced two routes from Sydney to Melbourne: the Hume Highway and Princes Highway. Taking over, **Sally Markham-David**, a magazine writer and author who came to live in Australia in 1970, mapped the way from Melbourne to Adelaide.

*Ellis*

*McCallum*

Bob Klima, who started his career with the *Sydney Daily Telegraph* and joined *The Australian* in 1973, was left to cover two routes between Sydney and Adelaide.

*Markham-David*

*Walter*

Meanwhile **Lewis Walter**, a veteran of the travel industry having spent close on four decades operating a travel agency, covered Tasmania; the island's capital, Hobart, was left to Grand Tour editor Jameson.

*Klima*

*Mulley*

**Alan Mulley**, a Welshman who emigrated to Australia at 18 and who now runs a successful advertising and publishing consultancy in Sydney, compiled the Guide in Brief.

The photography in this book was supplied by the Apa Photo Agency in Singapore. Special thanks are due to Landsdowne-Rigby archive in Sydney for complementing the selection on Australian history.

Phil Jarratt's photo selection in Sydney enabled the book to benefit from an even wider range of photographic talents. A full list of visual credits can be found on page 352.

Last but not least, thanks go to Apa's staff in Singapore including editor **Stuart Ridsdale** who assisted the book through its final editorial stages and gave a late-night helping hand in photo selection.

When work on a book is completed, the work of getting it to the readers begins. It would be impossible to list all of the thousands of individual bookshop owners, travel agents and special sales representatives whose multiple efforts carry this book into private homes and offices in 30 countries around the world. We wish to acknowledge with thanks their individual and collective contributions.

—Apa Productions

# TABLE OF CONTENTS

# TABLE OF CONTENTS

# A LAND CALLED "OZ"

There's no Emerald City at the end of a Yellow Brick Road. Tin woodsmen and wicked witches are in short supply in the vast island continent of Australia. But this land, known to many of its partisans simply as "Oz," contains as many surprises as young Dorothy ever found Over the Rainbow.

Instead of the Emerald City, the cultured cosmopolitan metropolises of Sydney and Melbourne display their glittering achievements of modern architecture high above blue ocean harbours. Instead of the Yellow Brick Road, there are long flat avenues of red dirt extending across hundreds of thousands of kilometres of emptiness. Cowardly lions have nothing on the unique animal life here: first reports of kangaroos as giant leaping rats which carried their babies in pouches, and of platypuses as furry, egg-laying mammals with bills like ducks and tails like beavers, were greeted in Europe with unbelieving guffaws.

Here in Australia, contradictions coexist in every corner of the land. This is the world's largest island—and smallest continent. Huge 20th Century cities with modern hotels and restaurants, and all the conveniences and diversions of affluent Western society, thrive along the coastlines of the southeast and southwest; while a few hundred kilometres inland, the dark-skinned tribal people known as Aboriginals follow a lifestyle that emerged from the Stone Age only a few decades ago.

This is a land of geographical superlatives. The hot, dry "Red Centre" is comprised of four great deserts together occupying about 2 million square kilometres of wasteland. In their midst is Ayers Rock, the largest monolith on earth. Running some 2,000 kilometres down the country's northeastern coast is the Great Barrier Reef, the largest coral reef in the world. The winter snowfields of the Great Dividing Range are greater than those of alpine Switzerland.

Surprisingly to many outsiders, Australia is a cultured nation. In fact, it can be said to be multi-cultured. There is the colourful traditional culture of the Aboriginals, with their ochre-toned bark paintings and lively *corroborees*. There is the down-to-earth cult of mateship and pioneering spirit of the bushman, the rural Aussie; and the increasingly sophisticated world of film and theatre, music and literature, focused on the large cities. Of great importance, too, is the Old World culture imported by immigrants from Greece and Italy, Lebanon and Yugoslavia, China and Malaysia, whose customs are given new meaning in a new home.

Once "Terra Australia Incognita"—the unknown southern land—this nation has emerged from humble beginnings two centuries ago as a British penal colony and has thrown off its image as being only an arid, underpopulated backwater of the Southern Hemisphere. Today it is a fascinating, vibrant land awaiting exploration by first-time visitors and lifelong residents alike.

# AUSTRALIA'S ANCIENT LANDSCAPE

If there was ever a need to furnish an explanation of the strange and delightful contradictions in which Australia abounds, one might be found in the fact that a nation so young resides in a continent so old that the stretch of its history almost defies comprehension.

Australia's topography, so forbidding to the first settlers and now so compelling to those of us who have come here these past two hundred years and become one with the land, takes us back to the earliest known history of the land forms of our world. While certain rocks have been dated back 3,000 million years, large chunks of the Australian landscape tell stories of earthly movements dating back 1,000 million years.

Whereas much of Europe and the Americas can boast the landscapes of youth— snow-covered peaks, rushing waterfalls, geysers, active volcanoes, giant gorges and mountain lakes—Australia's blunted, stunted, arid lands speak of age which has to be treated with great respect. It is a land in which even the animals and plants, developed in isolation, are different.

The last great geological shifts in Australia took place some 230 million years ago, before the Permian Period. It was then that the forces of nature convulsed the earth's crust and created alpine ranges whose peaks extended above the snow line. Since then modest convulsions on the eastern and western fringes have created low ranges we now know as tablelands, and volcanoes have occasionally erupted, but generally speaking Australia has been a sleeping giant while the rest of the world's landforms have come into being. Barring unforeseen geological circumstances it will also be the first continent to achieve equilibrium, a flattening of the land to the point where rivers cease to run, there is no further erosion and landscape becomes moonscape.

The Australia of today began to take shape some 50 million years ago when it broke away from the great southern continent known as Gondwanaland. This land mass at one time incorporated Africa, South America and India. Australia broke free and drifted north.

Preceding pages, island of the Great Barrier Reef; coast of the Great Australian Bight; Ayers Rock; Gosses Bluff Meteorite Crater; a dry lake at sunrise.

This was a time when the dinosaurs, who had ruled the animal world for 120 million years, were fast disappearing, and the Australian land mass, which had already seen great changes, was reshaping into a continent. The centre was rising from a shallow sea to unite what had been a series of islands. One of these islands, the Great Western Plateau, had been the only constant during much of this change, sometimes partly submerged but always the stable heart of the continent. Today that plateau spreads over almost half the continent, a dry and dramatic expanse of pristine beauty. It takes in the Kimberley and Hamersley Ranges, the Great Sandy Desert, Gibson Desert and the Great Victoria Desert, and although its topography has changed so much, it still houses the artefacts of ancient times. A rock found near Marble Bar yielded remains of organisms which lived 3,500 million years ago—the oldest form of life discovered. A dinosaur footprint is frozen in rock near Broome, and in the Kimberleys, once a coral reef in a shallow sea, landlocked fish have adapted to fresh water.

The central eastern lowlands, stretching south from the Gulf of Carpentaria, form a sedimentary basin which has often been encroached upon by the sea. Although this is a catchment area of 1.5 million sq km (600,000 sq miles) for rivers running inland off the eastern range, much of the water is lost through evaporation or into the vast chain of salt lakes and clay pans. Largest of the salt lakes, Lake Eyre, is also the lowest part of the continent at 15 metres (50 feet) below sea level. To man's knowledge it has filled only twice in history, but the abundance of dinosaur fossils indicates that it was once fringed with lush vegetation.

So much of the lowlands is harsh and inhospitable that it is difficult to imagine that under this surface is the Great Artesian Basin, from which bores are tapped for watering stock. The most ancient part of the basin area is the Flinders Ranges, in which rocks and remains dating back 1,000 million years are to be found.

Although, because of its great age, Australia can no longer boast a true alpine range, The Great Dividing Range which runs parallel with the east coast for more than 2,000 kilometres (1,250 miles), is as diverse as any on earth, tropical at one end and sub-alpine at the other. Mount Kosciusko,

2,228 metres (7,300 feet) is its highest point, but equally majestic are the rain forests of the north and the moors of Tasmania. The Glasshouse Mountains in southern Queensland were formed by volcanoes about 20 million years ago, while the granite belt bridging the Queensland-New South Wales border and the Warrumbungle Mountains, was born in similar circumstances a relatively short time later. In fact, Australia's last active volcano, in Victoria, died only 6,000 years ago.

In Tasmania the effects of volcanic activity and two ice ages have created a distinctive wilderness found nowhere else in Australia.

The coastline is as spectacular and as varied as the centre of Australia, ranging from the limestone cliffs at the edge of the

known example of Australian flora, the country's mammals are justly famous. The marsupials, in particular, have developed in isolation in incredible ways. Five million years ago kangaroos were three metres (10 feet) tall and a species of wombat grew as large as a rhinoceros. Now, marsupials survive in 120 different forms, from the red kangaroo to gliders that fly between trees to tiny desert mice. The platypus and echidna are the world's only egg-laying mammals; in Queensland there is a fish that can breathe above and under water.

The peopling of this continent may have begun as early as 150,000 years ago, when, anthropologists believe, small groups may have begun island-hopping southward from Southeast Asia. They could have walked

Nullabor Plain to the sharp rock formations of Tasmania and western Victoria to the mangrove swamps of the north to the spectacular beauty of the Great Barrier Reef, a lagoon which runs almost 2,000 kilometres down the Queensland coast and contains more than 2,000 coral reefs.

Australia's vegetation is dominated by the eucalypt, the humble gum tree in its more than 500 forms. One cannot escape the smell, feel and sight of this tree, often stunted, knotted and offering little shade, across the length and breadth of the continent. While its hardiness is more noteworthy than its beauty, some of its forms, such as the angophora, grow tall and attractive.

While the gum tree is perhaps the best

across the land bridge which in those times connected northern Australia with New Guinea. Certainly Aborigines have lived in Australia in considerable numbers for 40,000 years.

At Lake Mungo in western New South Wales, there is evidence of a cremation which took place some 30,000 years ago, while on the other side of the continent archaeologists have unearthed an equally old hearth. Caves on the Nullabor Plain and a Bass Strait island were occupied 20,000 years ago.

**Above, an electrical storm at Katherine Gorge. Right, Aborigines occupied caves such as this for thousands of years.**

# 40,000 YEARS OF DREAMTIME

Long before the ancient civilisations in the Middle East, Europe and the Americas flourished, there existed on the Australian continent a culture rich and complex in its customs, religions and lifestyles.

For more than 40,000 years before European navigators visited the shores of "The Great South Land," Australian Aborigines occupied this continent—its arid deserts, its tropical rainforests, and especially its major river systems and its coastal plains and mountains. Estimates by anthropologists and prehistorians put the population of Aborigines prior to 1770 at more than 300,000. They spoke 500 different languages, grouped into 31 related language families.

It is incomprehensible that Aborigines, or any other community, could have lived off the harsh, complex, fragile land for 400 centuries and not have had some adverse impact on the environment. But it is certainly true that Aboriginal harmony with the land kept environmental deterioration to a minimum. Their ancient traditions thrived in a kinship with every living thing and even with inanimate objects such as rocks and other geographical features.

Each tribe recognised the local landmarks and linked them with the rich mythology of the Dreamtime (or Dreaming). Various geological aspects were sacred sites with their own personality and significance. The aborigine considered himself, nature and the land inseparably bound and interdependent. In this state of unity, he achieved a balance with his environment.

Dreamtime is the basis of all traditional aboriginal thought and practice. It is the Aborigine's cultural, historical and ancestral heritage. In the mind of the black man it is an age that existed long ago and yet remains ever-present as a continuing, timeless experience linking past, present and future. Dreamtime was the dawn of all creation when the land, the rivers, the rain, wind and all living things were generated.

The Aborigines lived in clan groups of 10 to 50 or more people. Their economy was based on the hunting activities of the men and the fishing and gathering activities of the women. A good hunter knew intimately the habits of the creatures he stalked. He was an expert tracker and he understood the moods of the seasons and the significance of the wind. He took only what he needed to feed himself and his people and therefore kept in step with his environment. In turn, the ability of the country to support animals dictated the movements and well-being of the tribe. Conservation was the Aborigine's way of denying starvation; in a country that would kill many white pioneers, the black man was perfectly at home.

## Ceremony and Magic

Tribal elders, who possessed specialized knowledge of the community and the land, were charged with the responsibility of maintaining the clan's group identity through its totemistic religion. Groups of people formed special bonds with a totem, usually an animal or plant which acted as a protector and symbol of group identity. Through special ceremonies and other social and religious practices, the elders transmitted their knowledge.

Although there were female elders among the males, much of Aboriginal ceremonial life was secret and male-dominated. The sacred mythology which determined an individual's role in life and his tribal responsibility was passed on in complex initiation ceremonies. The tribal elders would entrust these secrets to the young boys and they in turn would not only become trustees of tribal lore but skilled hunters. Political or religious power was rarely inherited; it had to be earned.

Superstition and sorcery were common, and magic spells were used to gain power over an adversary or bring death to an enemy. Powerful sorcerers were employed to "point the bone" or chant curses over belongings of the proposed victim. Once an Aborigine was aware that he had been "sung," only the intervention of a more powerful medicine man could prevent his demise.

The Aborigines celebrated the adventures of their Dreamtime spirit heroes in paintings, songs and sacred dances. The heroes took both human and animal form; each had significance in the evolutionary cycle of the universe. The rock paintings were of special significance, bearing the strongest psychological and ritual values. As no Aboriginal language was written, these rock paintings, along with the oration of legends by tribal leaders, were responsible for passing the Dreamtime stories from one generation to the next.

The Aboriginal ceremony of celebrating with song and dance was called *corroboree*. The men dancers were expert in mimicking the movements of animals; with these skills they reconstructed legends, deeds of heroism or famous hunts. Bodies were elaborately painted and songs were chanted to the accompaniment of music sticks and boomerangs clapped together.

Basic dance themes dealt with hunting and food gathering, or sex and fertility. Sometimes they took a humorous vein but more

each person was the centre of an intricate web of relationships which gave order to the entire world and everything that might conceivably be included in it.

Totems and Dreamtime gave the individual his inherent link with the land, and thus his identity. So intricate was the Aborigine's relationship with the land that to remove him from it (and exile was indeed a punishment meted out to recalcitrants) was to spiritually kill him. Dispossession from the land meant dispossession from the Dreamtime.

often they dealt seriously with the procreation of life. Some tribes used a long, hollow piece of wood which, when blown, emitted a weird droning sound. This was the *didgerigoo*; its sound was said to resemble the calling of the spirits.

Aborigines believed a person's spirit did not die upon physical death, that ceremonies were essential to ensure the spirit left the body and became re-embodied elsewhere—in rocks, trees, animals, or perhaps in other human forms. This was important to keep the natural world on its cyclical course; thus

Preceding page, Aboriginal rock carvings at Nourlangie Rock Northern Territory. Above, a rock face bearing Aboriginal petroglyphs.

This, then, was the way of life in Australia when the sails of colliers and barques first began to be seen along the coast. The Aboriginal culture had prepared the people for everything they might expect to face in life—everything, that is, except the coming of the white man. It was the Europeans' insatiable desire for land, their guns, and their facility to spread disease (notably smallpox) that the Aborigines could not reconcile with their own beliefs. For their part, the colonists neither comprehended nor cared about the Aboriginal culture. The death rate, along with the loss of their tribal lands, left the black people confused and resentful. The dispossession was swift and utterly cruel.

# VOYAGES OF DISCOVERY

"The Great South Land": it was an idea whose time had come. When James Cook dropped anchor in 1770 in that Sydney bay, so teeming with exotic new life forms that he called it Botany Bay, he verified by flag and map an idea which for centuries Europe had craved.

"Greater Java," "Lochac," "The Golden Province of Beach," "Austrialia del Espiritu Santo," "New Holland," "Terra Australia Incognita"—this oldest of continents (yet the most recent to be discovered) was known by many names.

The Greeks, the Hindus and Marco Polo had all speculated upon its location and nature. The Arabs, the Chinese and the Malays had probably come and gone, as had the Portuguese. The Dutch came, looked and left, disappointed at not finding "uncommonly large profit." The English pirate Dampier saw the west coast as a barren reach inhabited by "the miserablest people on earth." The fertile east coast had, incredibly, been missed by a matter of kilometres by both Bougainville and Torres.

The continent's non-discovery was a history of accidents. That the land which they touched upon would not entertain or satisfy—at least at that time—the European fantasies of gold, gods and glory, makes its late "discovery" one of the great accidents of history.

Had it happened otherwise, Australia might well be writing in an Iberian tongue, or Dutch, or French, or even in the Guringai words of Sydney's first inhabitants.

Finally, it fell to a little, converted English collier and to the humbly-born genius who navigated her, to transmute the fantasies to fact and to put the stamp of Europe upon a continent which trade winds, tide, reefs, wild rumour and human frailty had so far conspired to hide from these men of maps and all who would follow them.

### Pre-European Visitors

Two thousand generations of Aborigines had roamed Australia since the first epic land and sea voyages of the Australoid migrations. Only during the last half millen-

Aborigines continued to fascinate Europeans long after the first arrivals. The sketch, left, was done by Governor John Hunter. Right, Captain Cook.

nium did the strange white sails and skins begin to appear along their coasts.

Chinese merchants seeking sandalwood and spices may have been the first. During the 13th and 14th centuries their junks penetrated the Indonesian archipelago and sailed as far as East Africa. In 1879 a small Ming Dynasty statuette of Shou Lao, the god of Long Life, was unearthed in Darwin. It was embedded four feet (more than a metre) below ground in the roots of a banyan tree, suggesting that Chinese sandalwood cutters from Timor, only 500 kilometres (310

miles) away, may have touched here.

Arab sailors, spreading the Islamic faith, had also reached Indonesia by the 13th Century. They expanded their influence at least as far as western New Guinea before being halted in the 16th Century by Dutch Protestants. They too may have reached Australia's northern coasts, only to find, like so many others, that it did not welcome them or their Allah.

The Bugis seamen of Macassar are known to have fared better. For at least a century before the white invasion of Australia, the Macassan prows were making annual excursions to the north coast in order to gather the sea creature, *trepang*, which they then sold to Chinese merchants.

By 1516 the Portuguese were spreading Catholicism and trade from their bases at Ambon in the legendary Spice Islands, the Moluccas, and at Timor. A set of documents known as the "Dieppe maps" shows that they were familiar with the whole eastern half of the continent at least 250 years before Cook's arrival. Due to the political jealousies of Spain and to the lack of gold, spices and souls agreeable to conversion, they probably suppressed the news of its location.

Pedro Fernandez de Quiros sailed west from the Spanish port of Callao in Peru in 1606. He was driven by the vision of finding the great southern continent and converting it to the "true faith" before the Protestant heretics and the Moslem infidels could taint

becoming the first European to pass through the strait between Australia and New Guinea. It now bears his name. Slumbering over the horizon, mere miles from Torres, was the Great South Land.

## Dutch Exploration

Torres had missed Australia, but already another European had taken the step which would stir the continent out of the morning of time and into Anno Domini 1606. William Jansz had sailed east from the Dutch port of Bantam, Java, and had reached the western shore of Cape York Peninsula. Failing (once again) to find nutmeg, pepper or lodes of silver or gold, and having lost several crew in an altercation with the locals, Jansz reported

it. Upon reaching the New Hebrides, Quiros mistook them for his grail and, rejoicing, offered the region to the Holy Spirit and (by a Spanish pun) to Philip III of Austria, as "Austrialia del Espiritu Santo." Upon realizing his mistake, Quiros turned back to the Americas where he died a defeated dreamer. He had not found Australia but had unwittingly provided the beginnings of its name, as well as that of Espiritu Santo, the largest island of the New Hebrides.

In 1607 his second-in-command, Luis Vaez de Torres, continued east towards the Moluccas and wrote another chapter in Australia's accident-prone history. Instead of navigating the north coast of New Guinea he was forced to the south of the island, thus

Australia to be "for the greater part desert, with wild, cruel black savages...we were constrained to return finding no good to be done there." He may have done no good, but he was the first historically verifiable European to set foot on Australia. For this he is remembered on an obscure street sign in Canberra.

For the next 35 years Java-bound ships from Holland would round the Cape of Good Hope, drop into the nautical speedway of the Roaring Forties and then "take a

**Above, white settlers came upon a people who had enjoyed a fruitful existence for thousands of years. Right, pre-dating Cook, French map of New Holland, 1644.**

left turn at Perth," so to speak. Because of difficulties in fixing longitude they often bumped into the west coast, or overshot into the Great Australian Bight.

Dirk Hartog landed on an island in Shark Bay—halfway up the coast—and left a celebrated pewter plate nailed to a tree as his calling card. Peter Nuyts missed his turn and ended up 1,600 km (1,000 miles) into the Bight. The result of all this hitting and missing was that the Dutch mapped almost two-thirds of the continent, its southern, western, and northern perimeters, and yet—because it did not fit their dream of cloves and silk, gold and fruit groves and because its barbarians knew nothing of metals or manners—they could not bring themselves to admit that this enormous territory *was* the

ers were reprieved and exiled on Australia's mainland near the present-day town of Geraldton; though nothing is known of their subsequent fate, they were no doubt Australia's first convict colonists.

The directors of the Dutch East India Company, still keen for their uncommonly large profits, despatched Abel Tasman from Java in 1642. He was told to find the Southland. Voyaging counter-clockwise around Australia he discovered Tasmania (or Van Diemansland, as he named it after the local Governor-General), the Tasman Sea, the west coast of New Zealand, and the Fiji Islands. This was the greatest voyage of discovery since Magellan, but the burghers in Batavia were not impressed.

They sent Tasman out again in 1644, but

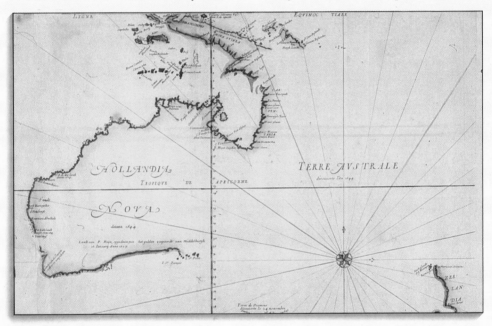

Great South Land.

The lowest moment for the dreamers of a New Holland came in 1629, when one of their treasure ships, bound for Batavia in Java, wrecked on the Abrolhos Islands (ironically, the word comes from the Portuguese "open your eyes") off the west coast. Historian Geoffrey Blainey, in his book *The Tyranny of Distance*, told how the *Batavia* "carried about 316 people, and some were drowned, and some died in the sand, and 125 were murdered by their own countrymen in a savage mutiny ashore. A few survivors reached Java in an open boat, and a ship was sent to rescue the remaining survivors, salvage treasure and cargo, and to punish the murderers." Two young murder-

again he returned without satisfying their queries on the connection (if any) between Van Diemansland, the continent and New Guinea. Worse yet, he brought no news of mines or spices, nor of people who would barter and pray. His stories of beach-roving savages confirmed the Dutch despair. They simply gave up the search.

### 'A Very Unpleasing Aspect'

In 1688 the one-time buccaneer William Dampier was searching for new British trade routes in the Pacific. The idea of using New Holland (as it was still known) as a watering place appealed to him . . . until he got there. Like the Dutch before him, he was appalled by the sere landscape of the northwest coast, the fruitless trees, naked savages and the disappointment of his well-spiced Arcadian fantasies. His account of the Aborigines epitomizes the enormous cultural gap between European expectation and antipodean fact. He saw them as the most miserable people on earth:

> ... who have no Houses and Skin Garments, Sheep, Poultry, and Fruits of the Earth ... setting aside their human shape they differ but little from Brutes ... Their Eye-lids are always half closed, to keep the Flies out of their Eyes ... They are long visaged, and of a very unpleasing aspect; having no one graceful feature in their faces ...

And so he mourned on. However, in his

when the westerlies blow offshore and the bush glitters eucalypt-green, the small barque *Endeavour* rounded the point of a bay on the southeastern coast, and things were changed forever.

## Captain Cook

The ship's captain was a 41-year-old Royal Navy lieutenant by the name of James Cook. A courageous and proud man, he was driven more by a sense of duty and personal excellence than by greed or God. All supplies of fresh food which his crew obtained he "caused to be equally divided among the whole company generally by weight, the meanest person in the Ship had an equal share with myself (Cook) or anyone on

description there was the unheralded recognition of a practice more life-sustaining and, ironically, more Christian than the drives for glory, God and gold which fired so many of his predecessors and followers. Dampier was the first to note the Australian Aborigines' communality:

> Sometimes they get as many fish as makes them a plentiful Banquet; and at other times they scarce get every one a taste: but be it little or much that they get, every one has his part, as well the young and tender, as the old and feeble, who are not able to go abroad, as the young and lusty.

The Southland lay undisturbed in its dreamtime for another century. And then on one of those bright autumn mornings

board." And as for the soul-snatching men of the cloth, he would never permit a parson to sail on his ships.

He was stern and hot-tempered; physically, he was (and the cliché be damned) tall, dark and handsome. He was also, in the parlance of his time, a "tarpaulin": an officer who had advanced to his station without the boost of aristocratic or at least "gentle" birth.

Cook was the son of a Yorkshire farm labourer and at 18 had been apprenticed onto North Sea colliers. Enlisting in the Royal Navy in 1755 he distinguished himself as a navigator and a Master, particularly on the St. Lawrence River in Quebec during the Seven Years War with France. His secular egalitarianism, pride and loyalty to the Crown, and in particular his humble origins, seem appropriate traits for the founder of a nation which has often vaunted such characteristics as its own, and has at times suffered because of them.

The Admiralty despatched Cook to Tahiti in 1768, at the request of the Royal Society, to observe a transit of the planet Venus. Among the company of 94 persons on his second-hand collier, *Endeavour*, were Daniel Carl Solander and Joseph Banks, two of the great botanists of that age.

Having fulfilled his duties in Tahiti, Cook sailed southwest to New Zealand and spent six months charting both islands. He was now free to return to England by either the Cape or the Horn. Instead, he called a

council of his officers and decided upon a route which would lead towards the unknown, then-fabled Southland. He had resolved to turn his ship "westward till we fall in with the East Coast of New Holland and then to follow that direction of the coast to the northward."

On April 28, 1770, *Endeavour* anchored in Botany Bay. Natives who had gathered on the headland and shores brandished their spears angrily, or otherwise ignored the barque. It was a scene to be often repeated

Left, Cook and the crew of the *Endeavour* at Botany Bay. Above, an engraving from 1802 showing the most unlikely sight of a kangaroo with more than one joey in its pouch.

from then on, but whatever the Aborigines' response, the white man was here to stay.

The *Endeavour* stayed a week. No naturalists before or since Solander and Banks have ever collected in such a short time so many new specimens of plant, bird and animal life. Meanwhile, the sailors ate their fill of seafoods, causing Cook to name the place Stingray Harbour. He later changed it to Botany Bay because of Solander and Banks' discoveries.

Sailing north, Cook sighted and named (but did not enter) Port Jackson, Sydney's great harbour. On Aug. 22, at Possession Island off the tip of Cape York he hoisted the British colours and claimed the whole of the eastern continent under "the name of New South Wales" for George III.

Reflecting during his homeward journey upon the state of the Australian Aborigine, he took a far more enlightened and sanguine view than had any of his European predecessors. He wrote the classic description of the "noble savage":

*...in reality they are far more happier than we Europeans; being wholly unacquainted with not only the superfluous but the necessary Conveniences so much sought after in Europe... the Earth and sea of their own accord furnishes them with all things necessary for life...*

Upon reaching London in 1771, Cook reported to the Admiralty that he had found the east coast of New Holland, but not the Great South Land—if indeed such a place existed. The Lords of the Admiralty were not convinced and sent him out again.

During his voyage of 1772 to 1775, he finally destroyed the historical myth of the Great South Land by using the westerlies to circumnavigate the Antarctic continent. He then used the trade winds to sweep the Pacific Ocean and to prove it predominantly landless. Thus he had shown that the unknown southland did not exist and that the *known* southland of New Holland was a place which could better excite the imagination than the greed of those who observed it.

Cook's third voyage, of 1776 to 1779, was of less significance to Australia. It ended with his death in the islands which he had discovered, Hawaii. Having secured some of the most important geographic and scientific information in history, as well as revolutionizing sea journeys by the use of longitudinal calculation and an anti-scurvy diet, this self-educated genius of navigation exhibited his fatal hubris. Certain that no Polynesian would lay a hand upon him, he turned his back on a group of angry natives. Attacked from behind, he was felled by clubs and spears.

# COLONIZATION AND EXPLORATION

*All my young Dookies and Duchesses,*
*Take warning from what I've to say,*
*Mind all is your own that you touchesses,*
*Or you'll find us in Botany Bay.*
— Folk Song

A dumping ground for rebels, poachers, prostitutes and murderers. A cage for felons policed by worse felons in uniform. A prisoner's island, its outlying cells founded by warders, whalers, escapees and anxious politicians. The auguries for Australia's future were not those of the Promised Land. Yet, from the little huddle of "iron gang" convicts and redcoats who in 1788 planted the cross and gallows of Europe's harsh order on this time-forgotten coast, a society of sorts took root.

With the loss of Maryland and Georgia in the American War of Independence, England was forced to find another place of exile for her convicts. They were temporarily stuffed into rotting river hulks around London, but these sinks of disease, depravity and escape soon became a source of public outcry. In desperation, the government took up Sir Joseph Banks' suggestion that Botany Bay in New Holland should house what poet Les Murray has called "England's buried Gulag."

### The First Fleet

In May 1787, the 11 small ships of "the first fleet" under Captain (later Governor) Arthur Phillip sailed from Portsmouth. Eight months later, the 1,000 passengers— three-quarters of them convicts—arrived at Botany Bay. A quick survey showed two things: Cook's description of the waterless place had been far too generous; and two ships of Comte de la Perouse were also there, shopping for a new continent on behalf of Louis XVI of France.

Phillip hurriedly sailed 20 kilometres (12 miles) up the coast to Port Jackson and (after a few toasts and a fusillade) raised the flag for George III on Jan. 26, 1788. Officers, marines, transportees, sheep, goats and cattle were disgorged by these latter-day

Left, celebrated Aborigine Bungaree accompanied Matthew Flinders on his voyages around Australia and drew attention for his ability to mimic officers. Right and preceding pages, natives still don similar uniforms.

Noah's arks into a sheltered cove now overlooked by the Sydney Opera House.

The surgeon-general to the fleet raptured that Port Jackson was "the finest and most extensive harbour in the Universe." It is said that even the convicts, upon sighting its fine blue bays and glistening sandstone headlands, raised a cheer of joy. It is also noted that two Aborigines shouted "Warra Warra Warra!"—Go Away!—but no one heeded them.

Thus the colony stumbled to life. And a hard one it was at first. Marooned halfway

around the world, far from God, King and Country, these first New South Welshmen found that their seed-wheat, which had been damaged at sea, failed to germinate in the sandy soil. Their cattle went bush, and the sheep fell foul of convicts, Aborigines and dingoes.

After 30 months of isolation and famine, locked in by the natural prison of this alien Australian bush, the settlement was down to half-rations. When a ship finally appeared, to their despair, it was not carrying supplies but 222 elderly and ill female convicts. Fortunately, the supply ships of the Second Fleet were close behind.

Sydney (after Viscount Sydney, secretary of the Home Department which supervised colonial affairs) was simply expropriated from the local Aborigines. No treaty, no beads, no thanks. Thereafter Phillip, naively overlooking his own status as a gate-crasher, strove to foster friendly and fair relations between his tribe and the blacks. For his pains he was speared in the shoulder at Manly Cove. Indeed, an abyss of incomprehension separated the two races.

The tents at Sydney Cove were soon replaced by brick and timber huts. Phillip attempted to lay out a town upon orderly lines, but it was not in the nature of its inhabitants to obey unenforced laws. Short cuts soon became streets, and the convenient jigsaw jumble that resulted can still be seen today as the ground plan of Sydney's high-rise pile-up.

Sydney Town expanded west toward the fertile farming lands of Parramatta, but was still hemmed in by the impenetrable escarpment of the Blue Mountains. Explorers fanned out by land and sea to open new pastures and farms, and to found even more isolated and savage prisons, such as Norfolk Island for second offenders. Norfolk had originally figured in English strategy as a potential source of flax, hemp and masts for its Pacific naval and trade fleets. The plan failed, and the island's true "success" was as a hell-hole of sadism.

New South Wales was still costing London dearly (£1 million in the first 12 years), but it was turning a profit for its local land-owners and the officers of the NSW Corps, other-

wise known as "The Rum Corps." The Corps stood up against the extortionate demands of trading vessel masters, while at the same time developing its own monopolies. The colony had become such a vat of drunkenness and the demand for Bengal rum, which the Corps controlled, so great that rum almost became the currency of the colony.

## 'Hell on Earth'

Governor Bligh (of *Bounty* fame) was despatched to clean up their act, and to encourage free settlers to come to Sydney. However, the Rum Corps, at the bidding of farmer and officer John MacArthur, pulled the second of the famous mutinies in Bligh's career, and in 1808 deposed him.

New South Wales and its satellite penal settlements for the doubly-damned at Moreton Bay (now Brisbane), Norfolk Island and Van Diemansland (Tasmania) entered the 19th Century with a reputation of "hell on earth," a reputation the English had intended and had hoped would function as a deterrent at home.

Stealers of buckles or loaves of bread, Irish rebels, girls on the avenue and Tolpuddle Martyrs were thrown together in Australia, when the noose would often have been more merciful. In attempting to escape, some became the interior's first explorers. Pathetically, they fled into the bush, some believing that China lay beyond the Blue Mountains or that a colony of free whites dwelt inland. The only sure way of escape from the pathological violence on Norfolk Island was to commit murder in the hope of being hung.

The picture was one of cruelty, corruption, floggings and greed. Yet these excesses were also tempered by the high-mindedness and reforms of Governor Lachlan Macquarie (1810-1821), the hopes of some emancipists (freed convicts) that morality and dignity *could* prevail, and by a growing prosperity through trade. Macquarie, a paternalistic autocrat, stifled the Rum Corps monopoly on the import of spirit, established the colony's own currency (1813) and first bank (1817), and encouraged the first crossing of the Blue Mountains (1813). His program of public works construction and town planning (265 projects in 11 years) owes much to Francis Greenway, an emancipist sent to Sydney as a forger, who became the young colony's leading architect.

Transportation to Australia's various penal settlements had ceased by 1868. By then some 160,000 convicts had arrived; only

25,000 of those were women, a distortion which left its stamp in the harsh, male-dominated "frontier" society for decades to come.

## Domestic Exploration

A continent of 7,700,000 square km (2,960,000 sq mi), much of it searing desert or dense scrub, is not explored quickly or easily. The revelation of Australia's interior progressed in fits and starts.

Prior to the crossing of the Blue Mountains in 1813, most significant exploration took place by sea. Bass and Flinders guessed correctly at the separation of Tasmania from the mainland. The French ships of Baudin in 1802, and later Dumont D'Urville in 1826, land, and the southern and northern coasts had been substantially explored. In 1860 the continent was first crossed from south to north (by Burke and Wills), but huge tracts of Western Australia remained untouched and unclaimed by settlers. It was not until the 1930s that the surveying of Australia was completed.

Early explorers believed that the westward-flowing rivers of the NSW interior led towards a vast inland sea. In 1830 Charles Sturt and his party set out on the Murrumbidgee River, following its current into the Lachlan and Murray rivers, finally reaching Lake Alexandrina near the South Australia coast. After a journey of more than 1,000 km (620 miles) they were within sight of the sea, but were unable to reach it.

scared the colonial authorities into establishing settlements in Tasmania and Western Australia respectively. Once the Great Dividing Range had been penetrated in 1813, the drive for new lands, minerals and the glory of being "first there"—wherever it may be—lured men on.

By 1836 the vast river systems of the southeastern continent had been charted. Tasmania had been explored, and the genocide of its natives had begun. A decade later most of New South Wales, half of Queens-

Left, the convicts who embarked for Botany Bay were a wretched lot, as is extravagantly illustrated in this 1792 engraving. Above, the founding of Port Jackson.

Instead, they had to row back against the current toward their starting point. Their 47-day row, on meagre rations and against flood tides, left Sturt temporarily blind, but is one of the most heroic journeys in Australian exploration. The myth of the inland sea had been dispelled.

### Leichhardt's Vanishing Act

In 1842, a 29-year-old Prussian draft dodger landed in Sydney. His name was Ludwig Leichhardt. He did not have good qualifications for an aspiring explorer; he could neither shoot nor see very well, and he also had a bad sense of direction. He did, however, know how to spot benefactors.

By 1844, he had found sufficient backers for an ambitious northwesterly thrust across Queensland and into the Northern Territory. His ambition was to open up the land from Brisbane to Port Essington (Darwin), a distance of 4,800 km (3,000 miles). With 10 companions and Aboriginal guides, plus a bullock team, he ran into innumerable difficulties, lost his provisions, and saw three of his men speared (one fatally) by natives.

Fourteen months after their departure, and long after being given up for dead, Leichhardt and his party staggered into Port Essington. Returning by sea to Sydney these "men from the grave" were feted as national heroes; Leichhardt even received a pardon from the Prussian government for his military "desertion."

In April 1848, he set out again, this time on a proposed transcontinental trek from Roma in southern Queensland to the Indian Ocean. His party of seven men and 77 beasts was never seen again, but their fate was to become one of the great mysteries of the Australian bush. The first search parties could only report that the missing men had probably been speared by Aborigines in Western Queensland. But searchers continued to go out for years, spurred on by finds of skeletons, relics, pack horses and rumour. Stories of a wild white man living among Queensland aboriginals in the 1860s suggest that one member, Adolf Classen, survived for some years.

Between 1852 and 1938, nine major searches were conducted for survivors, and then evidence, of Leichhardt's party. These searches themselves were often occasions of great courage, new discoveries—and further deaths. For all these efforts, the bush and the desert have never relinquished the tale of Leichhardt's fate.

### Heroes and Villains

Aborigines played a major part in the European penetration of Australia, sometimes assisting and sometimes resisting it. Various stories of loyalty and treachery have been recorded.

In 1848, Edmund Kennedy's party was exploring the interior of Cape York Peninsula. Difficulties with supply, hostile natives and rugged terrain forced him to despatch his companions to the coast, while he pushed on with his guide Jacky Jacky. Kennedy was speared by local natives, and died in Jacky's arms. The latter was also wounded, but struggled through the jungle to the Cape and informed the waiting schooner of the whereabouts of the other survivors who were stranded on the coast.

Edward John Eyre made an extraordinary journey in 1840, on foot, east to west along the coast of the Great Australian Bight. He began with an assistant, John Baxter, and three Aborigines. Four and a half months and 2,000 km (1,250 miles) later, after an appalling journey mostly through desert, he and one Aborigine, Wylie, walked into Albany on King George Sound. Baxter had been murdered by the other two, who had then run away.

There are many such explorers' tales of courage and folly, some still carved as messages on tree trunks, or buried beside dried-up billabongs. Others are just blood on the sand of the Simpson and Gibson deserts.

In August 1860, Robert O'Hara Burke and W. J. Wills departed Melbourne with a well-equipped team and a camel train (especially imported from Afghanistan for the journey). Their intention was to be the first party to cross the continent from coast to coast.

Burke was brash, inexperienced, supremely confident and a glory-seeker. Too impatient to wait for the supply camels to keep up, he took Wills, Grey and King with him, and from Innamincka on Cooper's Creek, he forged ahead in 60°C (140°F) heat. They reached the Gulf of Carpentaria in February 1861 and immediately began retracing their footsteps. Grey died on the way. The three emaciated survivors finally reached their earlier camp at Innamincka where they had left a companion, Brahe. But Brahe, who had waited four months for them, had departed only seven hours earlier. Burke and Wills died soon after in the implacable Stony Desert. Only King, cared for by Aborigines, survived to tell the story.

Lasseter's Reef is another of the lodestone legends of Australia. Like the stories of Leichhardt and the bushranger Ned Kelly, it has entered the country's mythology, art and literature.

Harry Lasseter claimed that, in 1900, while travelling alone from Alice Springs to Carnarvon on the west coast, he discovered a reef of gold, one metre deep and 16 kilometres (10 miles) long. Few believed him, and the task of relocating the vein seemed too difficult in any case.

During the Depression, however, he again publicized his claims in Sydney. A search party was formed, and in 1930 it set out for the trove with Lasseter as guide. After months of fruitless searching, the scheme was abandoned and Lasseter was left with two camels to continue his search for the mythical gold. He was never seen alive again, but his diary was found, and, some claim, his body. The diary tells of how he

pegged the gold only to have his camels bolt, leaving him to wander, mad, and die in the Petermann Ranges on the edge of the Gibson Desert.

The controversy about his find, his death and his diaries lived on, and expeditions continued until as recently as 1970 to search for Lasseter's Reef. As with Leichhardt, the desert would give up neither its dead nor his story.

Exploration in Australia will probably never end. While the great trails have been blazed, the other personal quests will always remain.

In 1977, a young city woman, Robyn Davidson, made a solo camel journey from Alice Springs to the Indian Ocean, across 2,700 km (about 1,700 miles) of desert and scrub. Her book *Tracks* touches upon the "spirit of place" which a traveller in Australia may come to feel. It is a reminder that, to the Aborigines, the whole continent and all its life forms are a vast mythological blueprint of both their spiritual and physical survival.

In 1973 Attila Kiraly drove his Volkswagen beetle a distance of 5,000 km (3,100 miles) from the Indian to the Pacific Ocean, following the Tropic of Capricorn. He became the first person to cross both the Gibson and Simpson deserts alone. When he reached New South Wales, a policeman—perhaps a descendant of the Rum Corps—gave him traffic tickets for his "defective" vehicle.

**Above, a view of Sydney Cove in 1792 shows the clearing of a sizeable area of land and a number of buildings, including a shipyard, constructed by Governor Hunter.**

# V. £400 REWARD R.

Colonial Secretary's Office,
Melbourne, 18th December, 1854.

Whereas Two Persons of the Names of

# Lawlor & Black,
## LATE OF BALLAARAT,

Did on or about the 13th day of November last, at that place, use certain
**TREASONABLE AND SEDITIOUS LANGUAGE,**
And incite Men to take up Arms, with a view to make war against
Our Sovereign Lady the QUEEN :

# NOTICE IS HEREBY GIVEN

That a Reward of £200 will be paid to any person or persons giving such
information as may lead to the Apprehension of either of the abovenamed
parties.

## DESCRIPTIONS.

LAWLOR.—Height 5 ft. 11 in., age 35, hair dark brown, whiskers dark brown and shaved under the chin, no
    moustache, long face, rather good looking, and is a well made man.
BLACK.—Height over 6 feet, straight figure, slight build, bright red hair worn in general rather long and
    brushed backwards, red and large whiskers, meeting under the chin, blue eyes, large thin nose, ruddy
    complexion, and rather small mouth.

*By His Excellency's Command,*

## WILLIAM C. HAINES.

BY AUTHORITY: JOHN FERRES, GOVERNMENT PRINTER, MELBOURNE.

# GOLD RUSHES AND BUSHRANGERS

*The law locks up the man or woman*
*Who steals the goose from off the common,*
*But leaves the greater villain loose*
*Who steals the common from the goose.*

              —18th Century ballad

While explorers disappeared for months or forever into the great ochre interior of Australia, the settlers they left behind continued to work—and plunder—their way towards a better society.

The first half of the 19th Century saw a clear change in European settlement. The transportation of convicts was phased out between 1840 and 1868. By 1860, the continent had been divided into five separate colonies, with each exhibiting more loyalty to Mother London, at times, than to its neighbouring siblings.

A major force within the colonies was the "squatocracy," the rich officers and free settlers who had followed the explorers into the fertile hinterlands. They had simply laid claim to or "squatted" upon enormous tracts of land, often 20,000 acres (over 8,000 hectares) and more. Like the merino sheep they brought with them, the squatters both lived off and *were* "the fat of the land."

There were social tensions between squatters and the new small farmers ("free selectors"), between the rural squatocracy and the urban bourgeoisie, and between "the Currency lads" (the Australian-born) and the immigrants. The tension between black and white also continued, with guns, poison and expropriation of lands achieving their sad ends. Yet for all this, the continent and its new culture still seemed to be waiting for another awakening.

### The Discovery of Gold

The awakening came in 1851. Edward Hargraves, an Australian "49er," returned from the California gold rush. He was certain, given the geological similarities he had observed, that gold *must* also exist in New South Wales. (Unbeknown to him, gold had been found 10 years earlier by a Rev. W. B. Clarke, but news of the discovery had been suppressed. Upon seeing the gold, the governor, Sir George Gipps, had

Left, a reward poster for the capture of Peter Lalor and George Black, leaders of the Eureka rebellion. Right, poet Banjo Paterson helped created the legends of bushrangers.

said: "Put it away, Mr Clarke, or we shall all have our throats cut!")

Having been roundly mocked in Sydney town when he stated his intention of finding gold, Hargraves set out for the tributaries of the Macquarie River near Bathurst, 170 km (106 miles) west of Sydney. Once there, he dug a panful of earth, washed it and announced to his incredulous companion:

"Here it is. This is a memorable day in the history of New South Wales. I shall be a baronet. You will be knighted, and my old horse will be stuffed, put into a glass

case, and sent to the British Museum!"

The announcement on May 15, 1851, of "Gold Discovered!" sent shock waves through the Australian colonies. The rush of prospectors to Bathurst was so great that the economy and the population of Victoria went into an immediate nosedive. Melbourne employers rapidly offered a £200 reward for the discovery of gold near *their* city.

By July the prize had been claimed, and before the end of the year incredibly rich fields were in production at Ballarat, Bendigo and Castlemaine. For the businessmen of the city, the finds were a mixed blessing. While the prices of flour, blankets, bread, shovels and mining gear doubled and tripled, there was often no one to sell them. Melbourne and Geelong were almost emptied of men.

### 'The Roaring Days'

The scene in the goldfields was one of frantic activity where teams of four or six men worked a claim, digging, shovelling, washing and cradling from dawn to dusk. In a lunar landscape of shafts, mullock heaps, shanties, tents and sly-grog shops, they laboured for returns which ranged from nothing to nuggets such as the "Welcome Stranger" of over 78,000 grams (2,750 ounces) gross.

For all the chaos of the diggings there was also considerable order, honesty, discipline

the continent during the next two decades, and then sporadically for the rest of the century. The last great find was the Kalgoorlie-Coolgardie field in Western Australia in 1892–1893.

It was not only the shop assistants of Sydney and the sailors of Port Phillip whose imaginations were fired with gold fever. The rest of the world, on hearing tales of giant nuggets and creeks paved with gold, set sail. In 1852, 95,000 new arrivals flooded into New South Wales and Victoria. By 1860 the population had passed 1 million—a growth of over 600,000 in a decade.

### Eureka Stockade

To an Australian, the word "Eureka"

and political solidarity between the diggers, contrasting with the lynch law of the California fields. But once the bright-shirted, bearded and booted miners returned to town, they let it rip. Often blowing hundreds of pounds in a day, they regaled the city folk with wild tales and champagne, lit their cigars with "fivers" (£5 notes) and careened around the streets on horseback or in cabs.

These were the "Roaring Days." At a Melbourne theatre, reported one eyewitness, the actors "were obliged to appear before the footlights to bear a pelting shower of nuggets—a substitute for bouquets—many over half an ounce, and several of which fell short of the mark into the orchestra."

Gold rushes flared like bushfire around

does not evoke images of Aristotle finding a method of detecting the amount of alloy in the crown of the king of Syracuse. Instead, it is coupled with the word "Stockade" and signifies armed insurrection against oppressive authority, and the first stirrings of an independent, republican consciousness.

At Ballarat, near Melbourne, the early gold diggers smarted under the imposition, whether they struck gold or not, of a £1 per month licence fee. Raids by thuggish police (often ex-cons from Tasmania, known as "Vandemonians") who enforced the licence fee and collected half the fine on every defaulter added to their rancour.

In October 1854, a miner was kicked to death by a local publican, who (despite strong evidence against him) was cleared of the crime. Mass meetings attended by up to 5,000 miners railed against these injustices. The men demanded universal franchise and the abolition of licence fees. They formed the Ballarat Reform League and on Nov. 29 made a bonfire of their mining licences.

The Lieutenant-Governor of Victoria, Sir Charles Hotham, sent in the "traps" (policemen) and troopers. Five hundred diggers built a stockade, swore to "fight to defend our rights and liberties," and hoisted the blue-and-white flag with the stars of the Southern Cross. No Union Jack for them.

In the early hours of Dec. 3, 1854, a force of 300 infantry, cavalry men and mounted police savagely attached the sleeping stockade, whose defenders by that time had

colonialism and bourgeois authority. As Mark Twain commented, Eureka was "the finest thing in Australian history . . . another instance of a victory won by a lost battle."

Paradoxically, the monument erected in Ballarat in 1923 to mark the site of the rebellion takes a more ambivalent stance:

*To the honoured memory of the heroic pioneers who fought and fell, on this sacred spot, in the cause of liberty, and the soldiers who fell at Duty's call.*

### Bushrangers and Rebels

Bushranging—the artful dodge of relieving travellers of their jewels, cash and other encumbrances—had been practised on the lonely bush roads of the colonies since the

dwindled to 150. Within 15 minutes it was all over. Six soldiers and 24 miners were dead. The rebel leader, Peter Lalor, had escaped, but 13 others were charged with high treason.

Eventually all charges were dropped, an amnesty was proclaimed for Lalor and the other leaders, and the licence fee was abolished. While the incident is replete with tragedy and some farce, the symbol of Eureka Stockade—and its flag—have continued to evoke the ideals of revolt against

*Left, gold washing at Fitzroy Bar, New South Wales. Above, the monthly licence imposed on gold prospectors not surprisingly prompted them to evade the collectors.*

1790s, usually by "bolters," runaway convicts. By 1820 it had become so prevalent that its practitioners increasingly found themselves with a price on their heads and then a noose.

From the beginning, bushrangers were often sheltered by the rural poor, many of whom were Irish immigrants or descendants of political transportees. They harboured strong Republican sentiments, and saw some of the outlaws as rebels against the same English, protestant landlords and authorities who had persecuted them in the old country.

From 1827 to 1830, "Bold Jack Donahue" harassed settlers on the Windsor Road west of Sydney. He was immortalized in a ballad which became so popular that the singing of it in public houses was banned.

These colonial highwaymen often had names as colourful as their reputations. "Yankee Jack" Ellis, Black Caesar, Captain Thunderbolt, Captain Moonlight, the pathological "Mad Dan" Morgan, the Jewboy Gang and "Gentleman Matt" Cash were among the many who rode out from behind a rock outcrop or a stand of gum trees and bailed up the Cobb & Co. stagecoach, the gold escort or the lone traveller.

### Bushranger Boom

If the takeoff point for the growth of Australia's population, its economy, and ultimately its sense of nationhood came with the gold rush, it also created a new

of three, working the Sydney-to-Melbourne road, rounded up 60 travellers at once. Then came the prize for which they were waiting—the armed mail coach. While one bushranger covered the 60 captives, Hall and Gilbert shot the police guard and robbed the coach. Several of the captives came out of the bush, not to assist the police, but to watch the shoot-out.

### The Kelly Gang

Ned Kelly was born in 1854 and grew up among impoverished Irish farm-families near Benalla, northern Victoria. He first ran foul of the law in 1877 when he shot a constable in the wrist. Teaming up with his brother Dan and two friends, Joe Byrne and

boom in bushranging. Many an "old lag" (an ex-convict) or an escaped Vandemonian, as well as poor settlers, saw quickly that gold need not necessarily be dug from the ground. The proceeds of a stick-up could be good, and the work a lot cleaner than digging. One Victorian gang in 1853 relieved the gold escort of 70,000 grams (over 2,400 oz) and £700 in cash. Three gang members were also sent to the gallows.

In NSW of the 1860s, the most famous of the "Wild Colonial Boys" were the bushrangers Ben Hall, Frank Gardiner and John Gilbert. Well-armed and superbly mounted—often on a squatter's best, but stolen, racehorse—they pulled off audacious raids. In November 1864, Hall's gang

Steve Hart, he fled to the bush and turned outlaw. The following year in a shoot-out at Stringybark Creek, Ned killed three of a party of four police who were hunting him. From then on, the Kellys became part of Victorian, and Australian, folklore. Society became divided in its attitude to the outlaws; the upper classes and bourgeoisie saw Ned as a callous, bloodthirsty ruffian while the working classes in both town and country turned him into a hero.

Ned saw himself as a latter-day Robin

Bushrangers meet their end. Left, Ben Hall was hit 27 times in the police ambush of May 6th, 1865 in New South Wales. Right, the death mask of Ned Kelly.

42

Hood, a police-baiter and a defender of the free against the oppressions of English overlords. His escapades were always daring and dramatic. Instead of robbing coaches, his gang bailed-up whole towns, usually cutting the telegraph and robbing the bank before escaping.

The gang hid out in the Wombat Ranges in 1879, but in June 1880, on hearing that they had been betrayed and that a trainload of police was on the way to arrest them, they came out to fight. Having executed their suspected betrayer (an old friend), they captured the town of Glenrowan, Victoria; held all the townsfolk prisoner in the pub; and ripped up the tracks upon which the police train was to arrive.

One captive, however, convinced the

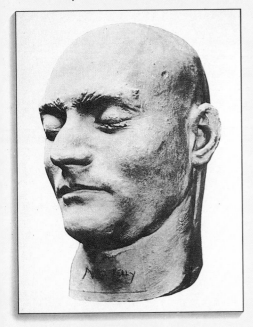

sometimes compassionate Ned to let him go. He immediately fled and warned the approaching train. A furious shoot-out erupted between the Kellys inside the Glenrowan Hotel and the traps outside and went on until dawn. The wounded Ned donned his suit of homemade armour and attempted to escape. Instead, he stumbled into the police who at first thought they were seeing a ghostly apparition. Ned was cut down but not killed. The police torched the hotel and the other three members of the Kelly Gang died within it, rather than surrender. Four months later in Melbourne, after one of the most celebrated trials in Australian history, Ned, still only 26, was sentenced.

The judge, Sir Redmond Barry, a respect-able, prosperous and free immigrant, represented the pole opposite to Ned and his impoverished, rebellious ilk. "Edward Kelly," intoned Barry, "I hereby sentence you to death by hanging. May the Lord have mercy on your soul." Ned, who was never one to miss his cue, replied in a clear, level voice: "Yes. I will meet you there (in death)." Kelly was hung on Nov. 11, 1880. Redmond Barry died a fortnight later of lung congestion.

### The Chinese Influx

"Without evil there can be no history," writes Australian historian Manning Clark. If one benefit of the gold rushes was to push Australia towards a population of 2 million by 1880, and to bring about parliamentary elections through manhood suffrage and secret ballots, then one adverse effect was the entrenchment of the racism which had attended the country's birth.

The vast majority of diggers were British; but of the foreigners the Chinese were the most numerous. In the five years from 1854, 40,000 Chinese flocked to the Victorian fields. In the 1870s, 20,000 of them turned the Palmer River diggings in Queensland into an almost exclusively Chinese province.

The Chinese did not come to settle in Australia (or *Hsing Chin Shan*, "New Gold Mountain," as they knew it), but to make quick fortunes. Nor did they bring their wives, for they hoped to return after a short time. They lived in their own communities and were usually diligent labourers. They sometimes wasted precious water, however, and this, along with the resentment of "Chinaman's luck," prompted malevolent attitudes toward them, and sometimes physical assault.

After riots at Bendigo in the 1850s and Lambing Flat, NSW, in 1861, the colonial governments began to restrict Chinese entry. By 1887, Asiatic immigration had been stifled. Australia inaugurated "the White Australia Policy" along with federation and nationhood, in 1901. The Immigration Act required that a dictation test in *any* European language (and one so chosen that the applicant was bound to fail) be given to all non-European arrivals.

Asians no longer applied and Australia's Chinese population fell from 50,000 in 1888 to 11,000 in 1933. It was not until 1966 that there was any genuine reversal of this race-based exclusion. In the face of such racism, it is perhaps comforting to know that there had even been one Chinese Bushranger, San Poo.

# FEDERATION AND THE WORLD WARS

The Australasian will be a square-headed, masterful man... His teeth will be bad and his lung good. He will suffer from liver disease, and become prematurely bald... His religion will be a form of Presbyterianism; his national policy a democracy tempered by the rate of exchange.
— *Marcus Clarke*, 1877

In September 1900, Queen Victoria regally proclaimed that on Jan. 1, 1901, not only a new century, but also a new nation, would be born. The table at which she signed this proclamation was then shipped from London to Sydney where, in Centennial Park on New Year's Day, the "indissoluble Federal Commonwealth" of Australia was inaugurated by the first Governor-General, Lord Hopetoun.

Nationhood and federation for the six Australian colonies was no revolt against the old gods, queens and country of a distant culture. It was more the dutiful coming-out of an offspring who was appropriately "young, white, happy and wholesome." It was also nervous. It had taken the adolescent since 1850 to decide whether coming out from behind Mother England's skirt was a good idea, what with the Russians and the increasingly strong Japanese prowling the Pacific.

Not wishing to step too far out, Australia's constitution was tame. The Queen remained head of state, retaining the power over all foreign affairs; her direct representative in Australia was the Governor-General. British parliamentary legislation could supercede any laws passed by the Commonwealth, and legal appeals ultimately were settled by the Privy Council in London. Few Australians objected to this readjustment of colonial relations, for each of the six colonies felt more at ease in its dealings with the motherland than with the other colonies.

For her part Mother England wasn't going to let the new nation escape the interests of imperialism. She expected, and got, continuing support from Australia in her military involvements, and ample returns on her substantial investments here.

*Left, two world wars helped forge Australia's sense of nationhood though at a tragically high cost in lives. Right, the 1913 "kangaroo" series, first issue of Commonwealth stamps.*

One of the first events to fray the imperial spell was the execution by the British Army in 1902 of two Australian Boer War soldiers, "Breaker" Morant and Lieutenant Handcock. At that time Morant represented the epitome of Australian manhood, the bushman. According to historian Russell Ward, he was "a legendary figure in outback Queensland and New South Wales "—horseman, musician, gambler, drinker, and "male chauvinist pig of the worst sort."

Morant and Handcock were court-nartialled and shot for having murdered

Boer prisoners. Australians felt Morant had been selected as the scapegoat for the crimes of the whole British Army and Lord Kitchener, *because* he was an outstandingly "typical" Australian. He and Handcock joined the ranks of Australian underdog folk heroes.

### Politics and War

Australia's first prime minister was Edmund Barton, a member of the Liberal Protectionist Party. His opponents in Parliament were the Conservative Free Traders and the Labor Party. (The three parties were on an equal footing until 1910 when Labor achieved an absolute majority in the House of Representatives.) The names of the parties embodied the various political factions and philosophies of the time—protectionists from Victoria versus New South Wales' free traders versus the labor movement. However, all three parties agreed that Australia was to be a white, European-styled, liberal democracy, whose citizens were to be protected by trade tariffs and social service legislation.

The nation needed a capital. Sydney and Melbourne each wished it in their own state, and being longstanding rivals, neither would permit it in the other's. After considerable backbiting, a separate Australian Capital Territory was established 320 kilometres (200 miles) from Sydney on the beautiful Monaro Tablelands. Some suggested nam-

was intended to relieve Turkish pressure on Russia's troops by forcing an entrance to the Black Sea. He wished to take the Dardanelles, and ordered the waiting Australian, New Zealand, French, British, Indian and Gurkha divisions to attack from the sea.

## Baptism of a Nation

The Turks, who had been warned of these intentions, were entrenched in fortified positions along the ridges of Gallipoli Peninsula. Their commanders, Mustafa Kemal and German general Liman von Sanders were able to safely direct their fire down upon the exposed beaches below.

From April 25, 1915, when they landed, until December 20 when they withdrew, the

ing the capital Shakespeare, hardly an appropriate choice for the anti-intellectual, slang-tongued collection of cultural cringers some Australians can be. In 1913 the Aboriginal word, "Canberra," was chosen instead.

When Britain declared war on Germany on Aug. 4, 1914, Australia, as a member of the British Empire, was automatically at war, too. The response to the call to arms by both Labor and Liberal parties was immediate. By the end of October the First Australian Infantry Force of 20,000 volunteers had been trained and despatched to Europe via Egypt.

While the troops continued to train in Egypt, Winston Churchill (then First Lord of the Admiralty) conceived a plan which

British forces were pinned to the near-vertical cliffs and narrow coves. There was horrendous carnage and epic heroism upon the ridges and beaches of Anzac Cove, Cape Hellas, Lone Pine and Suvla Bay—names which remain on countless Australian war memorials.

The defeat at Gallipoli gave Australia and New Zealand the legend of the ANZAC. Thereafter, the two countries would remember the troops of the Australian and New Zealand Army Corps in terms such as those used by Poet Laureate John Masefield: "They were ... the finest body of young men ever brought together in modern times. For physical beauty and nobility of bearing they surpassed any men I have ever seen; they walked and looked like the kings in old poems."

On the British side there were 78,000 wounded and 33,500 deaths. Of the dead, 8,587 were "Anzacs." Australians often overlook the fact that almost as many French died there, and that *twice* as many English, Indians and Nepalese died; perhaps it is because those nations already had their own creation-destruction myths and Australia did not. Out of this baptism by fire, mud, shrapnel and gallantry arose Australia's first coherent sense of nationhood and identity.

### The Western Front

The Australian "Diggers" were deployed in France, on the Western Front, from April

trade war." But at Australia's helm was a feisty and dogged little man who was loved and loathed with equal passion: William Morris ("Billy") Hughes, the "Little Digger."

In 1916 Hughes had pledged a supply of 16,500 Australian troops per month. Such a number could only be raised by conscription. The public outcry at the proposed legislation was bitter. Hughes' own Labor Party was firmly opposed to conscription. The proposal was defeated narrowly at a referendum, and Hughes was expelled from his party.

He formed a National coalition government and held a second referendum in December 1917. Again, he was defeated. Hughes himself bounced back, and deman-

1916. In the grizzly attacks through mud, mustard gas and frozen winters, their losses were again appalling—23,000 dead in nine weeks in the First Battle of the Somme, 38,000 at Ypres, 10,000 at Bullecourt. These places along with others like Pozieres, Villers Bretonneux and the Hindenburg Line saw a generation decimated. If nationhood was being born, the nation itself was being cut down.

Many Australians were now openly expressing doubt at the sense of supporting Britain in what they saw as her own "sordid

**Left, a civic parade for Lord Hopetoun for the opening of Federal Parliament in May, 1901. Right, a watercolour vision of Canberra.**

ded a seat at the Versailles Peace Conference where, with characteristic showmanship and acerbity, he defended what most Australians then considered to be their national interests.

When U.S. President Woodrow Wilson objected to the "Little Digger's" noisy delays, Hughes replied crushingly, "Mr. President, I speak for 60,000 dead. How many do you speak for?" He fought, though not alone, to prevent a Japanese move to insert in the preamble of the League of Nations covenant a declaration of racial equality.

Billy Hughes returned home a hero. The nation needed one; of the 330,000 troops who had fought, 226,000 (68½ per cent) were casualties, a greater percentage by far than for any other country among the Allies.

## The Depression

Between 1929 and 1933 every government in Australia, both state and federal, was thrown out of office by an electorate voting on the principle of "give the other mob a go—they couldn't be worse."

Nor could they do any better, for the Great Depression had arrived. Thirty percent of the country's breadwinners were on "Susso" (sustenance benefits). Wearing war surplus greatcoats which the government had dyed black before distributing free, hundreds of them were tramping the outback roads as "swagmen" looking for rural work.

Australia's economy was based heavily upon the export of wheat and wool, and upon continued borrowings from Britain. When world prices for primary products slumped by 50 percent, and when Britain withdrew £30 million from the Australian economy, the result was traumatic, especially to those at the lower end of the social scale.

Sir Otto Niemeyer of the Bank of England was despatched to scold Australians for living at an unsustainably high standard, to advise wage cuts and retrenchments, and to make sure that the interest was still paid on his loans. Many Australians saw him as an itinerant British bailiff.

However, when New South Wales Labor Premier Jack Lang depicted Niemeyer as a Shylock and attempted to cut the interest repayments to England on his state loans, neither the establishment nor the electorate could go along with the revolt; Lang was dismissed in 1932 by the Governor, and then by the voters.

Australia was in a slump; even sport was having its ups and downs. The 1932/33 England-Australia cricket Test Series was marred by a controversial and dangerous style·of bowling—known as "bodyline." So great was the local ire at this English innovation that friendly relations between the two countries were, for a time, severely strained.

On the racetrack, it was a brighter story. Australia's greatest galloper, Phar Lap, a horse that was actually born in New Zealand, was winning the hearts and minds of thousands of punters. Having won every race in Australia, including the 1930 Melbourne Cup, the "Red Terror" was sent to California where, shortly after winning the

world's richest horse race, he died. Australians have always suspected it was Yankee skullduggery. Phar Lap now "lives" on in three different museums: his skeleton is in New Zealand; his stuffed hide is in Melbourne; and his treasured, huge heart is in the Canberra Institute of Anatomy. As journalist Les Carlyon wrote: "It says something about Australia that the strongest strands in our folklore concern a military failure (Gallipoli), an outlaw (Ned Kelly) and a racehorse."

## World War Two

When England and Germany again went to war in September 1939, Australia once more automatically entered the conflict. A Second Australian Infantry Force was raised and despatched to the Middle East.

In 1939 Australia's prime minister, and leader of the United Australia Party, was Robert Gordon Menzies, a clever, witty barrister and a deeply conservative Anglophile. He had earned the nickname of "Pig-Iron Bob" by selling pig-iron to the rearming Japanese, of whom Australia had become increasingly nervous. Japan was now threatening Southeast Asia and had marked Australia for invasion.

While Australian air, land and sea forces fought in Britain, the Mediterranean, North Africa, Greece and the Middle East, Japan began to move south, first into French Indochina. Australian forces were sent to Malaya, the Dutch East Indies, Darwin and Rabaul (New Britain) to try to stem the Japanese tide.

In Canberra, "Pig Iron Bob" was being reviled for his Chamberlain-like, pre-war appeasement of the Axis powers. His oratory and wit could save neither him nor his party, and by October 1941, a Labor Government under John Curtin was in power. (Menzies later made a triumphant comeback and went on to serve as prime minister from 1949 to 1966.)

## A Nation Comes of Age

The Japanese attack on Pearl Harbor confirmed Australia's great fear: to be isolated and white in an Asia at war. When Singapore fell on Feb. 15, 1942, 15,000 of the 130,000 captured troops were Australian. The country was faced with the fact that a distant and beleaguered Britain could be of no assistance against an imminent Japanese invasion. Curtin had already announced, "Without inhibitions of any kind, I make it quite clear that Australia looks to America, free of any pangs as to our traditional links or kinship with the United Kingdom."

Japanese planes bombed Darwin and Broome on Februray 19. The Australian war cabinet then outraged Winston Churchill by diverting the 7th Australian Division from the defence of British Burma to the New Guinea and Pacific theatres.

If it is true that the Australian nation was born at Gallipoli, it is no less true that with the fall of Singapore it finally came of age.

The tide began to turn against Japan in May 1942 when a combined American-Australian fleet checked a Japanese force at the Battle of the Coral Sea. The American victory at Midway in June assured Allied

Papuan resistance (sometimes known as the Fuzzy Wuzzy Angels). In September the Japanese were only 52 km (32 miles) from Port Moresby, but by November they had been pushed back to beachhead positions on the northeast coast. As the threat of invasion receded so another Australian archetype— the Jungle Soldier—joined the Bushman, the Digger and the Lifesaver.

### The Tide Turns

By the end of 1942 the tide had also turned in Europe. The Australian 9th Division had helped eliminate the Germans and Italians from North Africa at the decisive Battle of El Alamein. The Russian armies routed the Germans at Stalingrad. The Axis

control of the Pacific, but on New Guinea, Japanese foot soldiers were closing in on Australia's main base at Port Moresby. Then, in August, a scratch force of Australians stopped the Japanese in a week of savage, hand-to-hand jungle fighting.

The Japanese continued to advance along a sodden, malarial mountain track which crossed New Guinea's Owen Stanley Ranges. This was the Kokoda Trail, scene of months of bloody guerrilla combat by the Australian 25th Brigade supported by the

Above, for eight months in 1915 Allied forces were pinned down at Gallipoli. The ANZAC sacrifice, stamped on memorials in Australia (and New Zealand), has not been forgotten.

powers were on the defensive.

Of the 1 million Australian servicemen and women who had enlisted, almost 10,000 died in Europe and more than 17,000 in the Pacific. Of those taken prisoner by the Japanese 8,000 did not survive the terrible privations and humiliations to which they were subjected.

Victory came too late for John Curtin who died in office in May 1945. At 9 a.m. on Saturday, August 15, Prime Minister Ben Chifley announced that the war had ended. All of Australia exploded in celebration. In Melbourne, over 200,000 people attended a thanksgiving service at the Shrine of Remembrance. Yet another of wars "to end all wars" was over.

51

# PIX

Vol. 18, No. 11     September 14, 1946

Registered at G.P.O., Sydney, for transmission by post as a newspaper

CHIPS RAFFERTY IN
"THE OVERLANDERS"
(Pages 16-19)

# THE MODERN ERA

Australian history since the Second World War has been an up-and-down saga. For a small and fairly provincial country, of which it's sometimes said "nothing ever happens," there has been an amazing succession of booms, recessions, droughts, political crises, wars, culture shock and social change— coupled with a snail's pace advance towards a better society, an advance which people still call, though with a certain scepticism, "progress."

Australians today enjoy a higher standard of living, a more cosmopolitan society, and a freer choice of lifestyles than ever before; but it's been at the price of unprecedentedly high unemployment, a growing gulf between the rich and the poor, and real social problems which manifest themselves in, among other things, crime, pollution and violence in the streets.

The 1940s were certainly the most dangerous and harrowing years in Australia's recent history. The war against Japan brought home to Australians just how vulnerable they were. The war also shook up Australian society internally; many women served in the armed forces, or worked in factories and office jobs which had previously been reserved for men, and were reluctant to go back to the old inequality between the sexes. The dramatic drive of Australian women for a changed position in the world, climaxing in the "women's lib" movement of the 1970s, began at that time. Ex-servicemen didn't want to go back to the old order either. A year after the war ended they helped vote an activist Labor government, led by Ben Chifley, back into power and supported an expanded social welfare programme, the setting up of a government airline (TAA), government initiatives in housing and education, and projects such as the Snowy Mountains Scheme and the Australian National University.

## The Immigrants

The most radical change, however, occurred in immigration. With its new-found vulnerability, Australia realised it had to increase its population rapidly if it were to

defend itself against the sort of attack which had threatened in World War Two. Labor's immigration minister, Arthur Calwell, embarked upon one of the most spectacular migration programmes of the 20th Century. Half of the assisted migrants were to be British, but the other half could come from anywhere—as long as they were white. More than 2 million migrants arrived, between 1945 and 1965, and the nation's population rose from 7½ million to 11 million. Today a quarter of the population are migrants or the children of migrants.

The nation still clung to its White Australia policy and Calwell himself was a racist; when ordering the deportation of an illegal Chinese immigrant named Wong he wisecracked: "Two Wongs don't make a white." The policy was modified slowly in later years until it was formally abolished in the 1970s, though quotas on Asian immigration have remained. At the present time one third of all immigrants into the country are Asian.

The effect of this migration was far-reaching. Australia had been a conformist, predominantly Anglo-Saxon country in which 90 percent of the people had a British background. Suddenly it was confronted with a massive influx of Italians, Greeks, Germans, Dutch and Yugoslavs who could hardly speak English and who set up their own communities, shops and newspapers, invaded the work force and schools, and very soon shattered the complacent, sterile mould of Aussie life. It all happened with surprisingly little friction but with great hardship on the part of the migrants.

They were the work force for much of the intense development of the 1950s and 1960s, providing hard manual labour in steelworks, mines, factories and on the roads, as well as on major national projects such as the Snowy Mountains Scheme. (In the mid Sixties, for example, nearly half the workers in the port Kembla steelworks in New South Wales were migrants.)

At the same time, they began slowly transforming the social customs of the new country. The introduction of delicatessens, European food, soccer, open-air cafes, the Sunday stroll, and a hectic sort of cosmopolitanism, which was hardly imaginable before, was important, but the new migrants were also responsible for opening the old order up to new ideas, customs and ways of looking at things, and for providing options. Australia

Preceding pages, Whyalla Steel Mill, South Australia. Left, Chips Rafferty, an actor who became the archetypal Aussie and one of the pillars of the fledgling film industry.

began to develop a plurality of ethics instead of the old, heroic, single-culture code of the pre-war years. The cultural mix which is so apparent in Australia today is very much the creation of the people who began arriving by shiploads after World War Two.

In the years immediately after the war, Australia was a dour, conformist, strikingly rigid society, one which had grown up in comparative isolation from both Europe and America and was old-fashioned and illiberal. It was dominated by men still, despite the challenge, after the war ended, from women; male rituals like sport, drinking and brawling predominated, homosexuals were persecuted as "poofters," and anyone who had a beard or long hair was dubbed a "weirdo." Male rituals such as mateship

*ikeys* . . . and, sometimes, by the official label of "New Australians." Yet, by the time the 1940s ended, it was clear Australia was beginning to emerge from its geographic and cultural isolation and a new sort of ambience was developing.

## The Boring Fifties

The next decade has also been referred to as the "Boring Fifties" and the reason for this is primarily political. In 1947 the Labor prime minister, Chifley, set out to nationalise the banks; the legislation was ruled unconstitutional by the High Court and a revived conservative party, renamed the Liberal Party and led by Robert Gordon Menzies, was able to attack the Labor Party

were extolled while women were expected to stay at home and look after the kids. It seemed, visually and ethically, a very working-class society, a land of boots, gladstone bags and felt hats where most people called each other "mate" or "sport" or, occasionally, "the missus."

The churches, especially the Roman Catholic church, dominated morals; divorce, unlike abortions, was legal, but it was condemned and hard to get. The nation was burdened with a suffocating puritanism which Australians labelled "wowserism."

The language of the people was stamped with the prejudices of the time. The waves of migrants didn't escape: they were called *reffos* (refugees), *Balts*, *wogs*, *dagos*, *ities*,

for being "socialist" and unduly influenced by Communists.

In the 1949 election Menzies promised to end petrol rationing and to mount a full-scale offensive against the Communist Party; he won comfortably and proceeded to live up to both promises. His attempt to outlaw the Communist Party, however, was narrowly defeated at a referendum, and when rising unemployment threatened to turn the Liberals out of office at a subsequent election, Menzies decided to plump for safe, middle-

Right, prime minister Chifley introduces the first Australian-manufactured car in 1948. Left, Parliament House in the city of Canberra chosen as the federal capital in 1913.

54

of-the-road policies which would disturb neither extreme of the electrorate and the nation settled down to what has been called "The Big Sleep."

Development, an unexciting theme if ever there was one, became the national slogan; there were big posters everywhere stressing peace, prosperity and progress and even the arrival of rock 'n' roll from the United States didn't seem to disturb the social equanimity. There were a few rebel groups, such as the *bodgies* (male) and *widgies* (female), who did such revolutionary things as wearing drape suits and tight sweaters and listening to bop, but it was hardly more than a milk-bar menace. Another nonconformist group was the Sydney "push," a group of freethinkers and libertarians who gathered

shops flourished alongside sly-grog joints, where liquor could be bought after hours.

The decade is notable for other events. The Labor Party split apart in 1955 and effectively kept itself out of power for another 17 years. Every year hundreds of thousands of young Australians left on their equivalent of the Grand Tour of London and Europe, seeking excitement and the sort of mind-broadening which, despite the immigration programme, was unavailable at home. They could hardly be blamed.

The district of Earls Court in London became an Aussie ghetto; Rolf Harris, the entertainer, started on his climb to fame by singing *Tie Me Kangaroo Down, Sport* at the Down Under Club. The nation's best artists, too, lured by other countries, turned them-

at pubs and coffee inns and scorned the grey-flannel-suited businessmen who surrounded them. They wrote poetry and bawdy songs and, though mainly a male group, produced two remarkable women— Germaine Greer, author of *The Female Eunuch*, and Lillian Roxon, author of the first *Rock Encyclopedia.*

The newsreels of the time, looked at now, are embarrassingly nationalistic, racist and sexist. It was a time of dreadful puritanism and conformity. The pubs closed at 6 p.m. sharp each weekday, producing the infamous "six o'clock swill" during which time men crammed into bars and guzzled as much as they could before closing time. Off-course betting was illegal so SP (starting price)

selves into expatriates. At the time it seemed that nothing was happenning back in Aussie at all.

## The Affluent Sixties

Australia had begun turning itself from a nation of primary industry (sheep, wheat, cattle) to one of secondary industry. There was an enormous expansion and diversification of manufacturing; between 1940 and 1960 the number of factories doubled and the value of manufactured goods tripled. consumer goods such as refrigerators, washing machines, vacuum cleaners and cars became available to the great mass of the population for the first time. Exports increased and new home industries started up, spurred on by migrant labour and the increase in the size of the local market.

By the mid 1960s, Australia was experiencing a period of unprecedented prosperity and its citizens were enjoying, after Americans, the highest standard of living in the world. Australians could even claim to have occupied the No. 1 position due to the fact that this new-found affluence was more evenly spread throughout the population than was the case in the United States. They were also living in the most urbanized nation in the world, with three-quarters of the population living in cities and more than half in the main cities of the eastern seaboard.

Shortly after World War Two, General

in hand with a spectacular increase in tertiary and service industries and the white-collar work force which predominated in them. In the early 1960s the number of white-collar workers exceeded, for the first time, the number of blue-collar workers and then streaked ahead. Most of the former regarded themselves as middle class; they typically lived in comfortable suburban homes, owned a car and a TV set, had a chequing account, and voted Liberal. Australia, which had been regarded for so long as a working man's country, "the last stronghold of egalitarian democracy," as American historian Hartley Grattan put it, had, almost unnoticed, transformed itself into one of the most middle-class nations in the world.

Motors set up Australia's first car manufacturing plant and began producing the Holden, which in its various forms (car, station wagon, utility) became the clear market leader. Ford followed suit and released the Falcon, but the "Holdy" was preeminent.

Its success is a symbol of the decade; it combined American finance, European migrant labour and an affluent Australian consumer market. The subsequent eclipse of General Motors in the 1980s by Ford and the Japanese car makers is a sign of more recent times which have seen the decline of manufacturing, a rise in unemployment and competition from the new technology.

The most dramatic change, however, was social. Manufacturing expansion went hand

Politically this showed up in almost a quarter of a century of unbroken conservative rule. Socially the old Aussie ideals of mateship and equality were eroded by the new ethic of success and competition. The trade unions declined in power and militancy while the rest of the nation seemed to go on a prolonged shopping spree down Parramatta Road in Sydney and St. Kilda Road in Melbourne. House prices soared, the boom climbed higher still, and the nation's catch-cry might well have been the Beatle's lyric

Above, (Canberra 1975), Whitlam listens to an edict from the secretary to Governor John Kerr dismissing his government. Right, Sydney Stock Exchange.

56

"Nothing's going to change my world."

As the decade drew to a close there was a speculative and symbolic mineral resources boom which, before it died, assumed dizzying proportions on the stock exchanges.

Donald Horne, writing of Australia, called it *The Lucky Country*. Another writer, Ian Moffitt, disillusionedly called it *The U-Jack Society*. The Australian social ideal of communality was changing and with it, apparently, the Australian character.

## The Turbulent Seventies

Cracks were beginning to appear in the bland surface of Australian contentment. Australia became involved in the Vietnam war and sent conscripts who had been ployed.

While Menzies had been succeeded by less able Liberal leaders such as Holt, Gorton and McMahon, a revivified Labor Party was arguing for new policies on a grand scale and was being led by its most inspiring politician for years, Gough Whitlam. When, in 1972, the Labor Party finally won office, under the slogan of *It's Time*, it seemed to many people that a clean break with the past had occurred and a new, progressive era was about to begin.

This wasn't the case. Whitlam was a reformer who moved quickly to abolish conscription, end Australia's involvement in Vietnam, recognize China and begin the long task of reconstructing the social welfare system. But he didn't reckon on the strength

chosen by lottery off to their death. A tour by the Springbok (South African) Rugby Union team sparked off nationwide demonstrations supported by the trade union movement and its leader, Bob Hawke—later to become prime minister.

As the Sixties gave way to the Seventies the nation moved, imperceptibly at first, into an era of crisis. Student power, the women's movement, black power and the sexual liberation groups, the characteristic neo-political movements of the decade, began challenging the conservative consensus. It was estimated that 10 percent of Australians were living in chronic poverty; they included many aborigines, single parents, the sick and handicapped, and the unem-

of the conservative resistance and the weighting of key institutions (the High Court, the electoral system, and the Monarchy) against Labor. He managed to win another election in 1974 but the economy, exhibiting the unfamiliar twin symptoms of high inflation and high unemployment was already moving into recession and the government was beset by a series of scandals, including an attempt to borrow 4,000 million petrodollars through a questionable intermediary. Labor tried to gain control of the conservative Senate but failed.

In 1975 the Liberal-National Country Party opposition, led by Malcolm Fraser, used the Senate to refuse the government the money it needed to carry on; Whitlam refused to resign; and the nation was thrust into the gravest political and constitutional crisis of its history. It was resolved in a manner which may divide Australians for generations: the Governor-General, Sir John Kerr, in an act which many people regard as illegal, dismissed Whitlam as Prime Minister and made Fraser head of a caretaker government. Fraser won the following election, consolidated his power and swore he would take politics off the front page.

For much of the following seven-year period he succeeded. Australians' seemed sick of political turmoil and unready for further reforms. Fraser presided over a clearly reactionary government which set its face against many of the Whitlam govern-

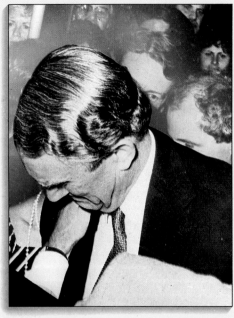

ment's initiatives, dismantled the national health scheme and followed closely the initiatives of the United States in foreign policy.

### The Anxious Eighties

Once again, Australia was changing. The economy slid deeper and deeper into recession. Unemployment continued to grow, heightened by the structural inflexibility of large sectors of industry and the introduction of new computer technology.

The conservation movement took over where some of the other militant movements had left off. There was a sense of fragmentation and growing unease as the extremes of

Australian society—the wealthy and the poor, those with jobs and those without, the safely old and the insecure young—drew further and further apart. The affluent, burgeoning middle class began to split up, as disaffected groups began to seek their identity away from the workplace and in alternative lifestyles, from hipple to surfie to gay to punk.

As the recession grew worse and the new technology took over, the white-collar workplace grew to look more and more like the blue-collar workplace, and white-collar unions became increasingly militant; being middle class didn't make anybody invulnerable anymore.

This was the background to the election, in 1983, of the Labor government led by Bob Hawke. Although the Labor victory of 1983 surprised many people, there had been precursors; Labor had already won power in New South Wales, Victoria and South Australia, and during the election campaign it also won in Western Australia.

The Australian electorate, far from setting down into the sloth characteristic of the 1960s, has become increasingly volatile and impatient with governments which seem able to provide solutions to the economic crisis. It may, eventually, turn against Labor as swiftly as it turned against the Liberals.

Hawke's enormous personal popularity has helped his party. He is a very "Australian" figure, able to appeal right across the broad spectrum of local majorities and minorities without seeming insincere; he gave up the grog for the sake of the Prime Ministership, and won it. But beyond Hawke's personality lie some formidable questions for Australians and their nation: Will Labor be able to solve the economic crisis, or are such international problems now beyond the scope of leaders? Will unemployment rise above 10 percent to even higher levels? Is Australia ready to tackle the grave structural problems posed by computer technology and is it ready to share both work and unemployment between men and women, young and old, skilled and unskilled, black and white, migrant and native-born, full-time and part-time? Can Australian society stand the strain of huge numbers of young people being out of work with the consequent rise in social distress and violence?

Left, Fraser sheds a tear after his 1983 electoral defeat. Right, politician Bob Hawke at a rally during his 1983 campaign for the prime ministership.

Bob Hawke. Bringing Australia Together.

'DO THE RIGHT THING'

STOP FRASER SAVE JOBS

Bob Hawke. Bringing Australia Together.

SA Fr

Bob Hawl

# PEOPLE

Once the last outpost of British Empire, Australia is now a melting pot at the bottom of Asia. Its people are cosmopolitan, vibrant, multi-coloured and increasingly aware of their regional priorities. In a world growing ever smaller, there is no place for division by race, colour or creed.

The caricature Australian has, until recently, been seen abroad in much the same light as the caricature South African—the bumbling "van der Moewe," preaching racism and carrying a big stick. But things have changed, if not entirely. No longer does Australia have ministers of state opposing Asian immigration with phrases like "two Wongs don't make a white." No longer do Australians sing "God Save the Queen" before the movie starts, wear tweed suits and eat roast duck on Christmas Day despite the heat wave.

The people are becoming truly independent. And with it there is a definite—and hopefully temporary—streak of neo-nationalistic jingoism. Call it aggressive "ockerism."

On the world stage, suddenly it's okay to be Australian. A syndrome known within the country as "flavor of the month" has arisen with the development of the Australian communications industry. Films, books, theatre and press have all helped shape a vision of Australia that is almost true.

But never ask an Australian about his country. Scratch an Aussie and you've got a patriot. He'll lie if he has to and exaggerate beyond belief. An Aussie can say that about another Aussie. If the traveller wished to make similar observations, he would be well advised to bring boxing gloves, a sense of humour and a return ticket.

66

# THE URBAN AUSSIE

In this huge land of paradox most Australians huddle in cities, their lives bordered by rows of hedge and backyard paling fences.

Europeans on the wrong side of the world, they are in awe, and perhaps still scared, of their harsh environment. As Malcolm Muggeridge once observed, they cling to the coastline as though their stay were destined to be so temporary as to render purposeless further exploration.

With the exception of Canberra, all the major cities of Australia are coastal, and their combined population represents more than 70 per cent of the national total. Make no mistake, despite wide-brimmed hats, Bryan Brown and dreams of Marlboro Man machismo, Aussies are distinctly urban animals.

This has been the case since the first white settlement of Australia, and yet a curious malaise—a national identity crisis, perhaps—has until quite recently sent the Australian scurrying for the banjo and the fly swatter every time the question of national identity arose. There seems to have been a need to identify with the lore of the bushman, the mystique of the wide brown land, while at the same time donning three-piece European suits for downtown meetings with Asian merchant bankers.

## The Myth Perpetuated

The myth of the sun-tanned stockman presiding over the emptiness (both physical and cultural) has been perpetuated in literature and cinema. It is particularly interesting to note that in the renaissance of the Australian film industry—a 1970s development which has touched the popular and the high culture—the biggest moneyspinners have been the films which enlarged and perpetuated the Aussie myth. Movies like *Gallipoli, The Man From Snowy River* and *Phar Lap* have been box-office dynamite, while those which have dealt with contemporary, urban characterisations—*Heatwave, The Year of Living Dangerously, The Last Wave*—have fared less well. Celluloid heroes (the aforementioned Bryan Brown, Mel Gibson, Jack Thompson) are lean-jawed, squint-eyed monuments to Outback

Left, the surfer is a reminder that as the majority of city dwellers live on the coast, so city life can mean beach life.

living, regardless of the urbane nature of the roles they play. In short, Aussies like to think they are one with the bush.

Nothing could be further from the truth. At least 70 per cent of Australians live lives not very dissimilar from those of their counterparts in New York, London, Milan, Phoenix, Toronto, Paris or any other temperate zone city of the Western world. They work all week in factories and offices and suffer the pressures of high-density urban living. At the weekend they relax by driving their cars to places as removed from their work as time and distance will allow. They have an inborn desire to escape from the constraints of the city, but don't misunderstand: they are city folk through and through.

Australia is the least densely populated country on earth and the most highly urbanised. Its citizens are moths drawn to the bright lights.

Since a modicum of world recognition in the areas of sport, art and geopolitics made Australia "flavor of the week" a couple of years ago (and at the time of writing there is no sign of this abating, even though it is inevitable that it will), barely a month goes by without a team from this magazine or that television network descending upon Australia to reveal to the world the essential *je ne sais quoi* of being Australian. These journalists, photographers, documentary filmmakers and others go about this task in much the same way Australia's own media people go about preparing material on, say, "the new Israel." That is to say, they check into a Hyatt or a Hilton and have all available literature sent up to the room with a couple of cold beers.

Later, armed with their conclusions but lacking evidence, they will repair to the nearest available source. For example, if the reporter has decided that the key to the new Australia is that its people have finally come to terms with the old Australia, he or she will go to Ayers Rock and film the sunrise while the plaintive wail of the didgeridoo frames the Final Assessment, which might be: "Australians, riding the crest of a new wave of prosperity, national pride and achievement, are starting to look to the vast heart and soul of their country in search of their own identity." *Aaahoooo!* Hear the dingo howl.

So much has been written, filmed and

spoken, yet so little of it comes close to the realities of being Australian, principally because the world-at-large has been fed a lie for so long. Australia is not, and has never been, a rural country. Aussies have never ridden on the sheep's back, despite the fact that they have more land than they, or even the agencies of the United States government, will ever know what to do with.

## Towards a National Identity

The average Australian has always been the urban Australian, however insular he may have been in his urbanity.

What *has* changed significantly in the past decade is the way in which the urban Aussie sees the world, and his part in it. In the 1950s

southside. There was considerable flag-waving when they won sporting events or helped out in foreign wars, but the Australian identity—the reality of it—didn't surface until the rise and fall of Gough Whitlam. Here they had a leader who, for all his faults, was a dogmatic, aggressive and cultured urban Australian. Regardless of its political imputations, his dismissal in 1975 by the Queen's representative signalled an end to Australia's cultural identification with its mentor.

Of course, the process had started long before then. Instead of just looking to Britain, Australia had begun looking to America, and not just for military might. As sociologist and author Craig McGregor has noted, so bereft of original ideas were

and even into the 1960s it was *de rigeuer* for go-ahead young Australians to take the "Grand Tour," which meant anything from a year to three years discovering real life in the Olde Countrye (read England). Despite 50 years of self-government, Australians were unashamedly colonial in outlook and sentiment, and their leaders encouraged them to be so. The post-war conservative leader Sir Robert Menzie was the last great Anglophile. On the other side of the political spectrum, Labor's Arthur Calwell saw the protection of the Crown as a hedge against his obsessive fear of "the Asian hordes."

Until the end of the Sixties, Australians were isolationist, racist and basically stupid in their approach to living on Asia's affluent

Australians that in the early sixties, when the surfing cult arrived from California, its Australian followers topped their aloha shirts with British duffle coats! Hula hoops, The Beatles, the stomp, pointed shoes...as long as it came from the Northern Hemisphere it was okay.

So it was against this background that urban Australians began to question the conventional wisdom about their country. Not knowingly, no doubt, but in small ways they began to see themselves as part of the

**Above, four urbane urbanites at the Melbourne Cup. Right, all on the streets of Sydney, the Hare Krishna devotees offer a stark contrast to the conventional look of the woman.**

world, not as the inhabitants of its last outpost. And although Aussies still tread warily in certain ways, in the 1980s they tend to do it in jackboots.

There is an old joke (yes, Aussies do tell jokes against themselves) which has it that a well-balanced Australian has a chip on both shoulders. Like most jokes, there is an element of truth in it. Urban Aussies protect their inferiority complexes behind shields of "ocker" bravado. The Aussie knows he's as good as the next bloke; so increasingly the educated classes (and there is still a class system, still rigid in funny ways) use the vernacular. Australia's current prime minister speaks in what used to be described as "broad Australian." So do newscasters and all kinds of public figures. There is pride

aspects of Australian urban life, and in its wake the perception of the urban Aussie is becoming the reality. Life imitates art. Even among trendy, left-of-centre city types it is now okay to drink cans of beer at the cricket match, tell racist and sexist jokes but not mean them, and exalt male friendship to an almost weird level. Aussies have found their own stereotype and are not only learning to live with it; they are embracing it.

The Aussies' saviour in some ways—and the man himself believes in all ways—is their prime minister, Bob Hawke. Just when Aussies were beginning to believe that to "feel like a Tooheys" (a slogan from a beer commercial) was a national obligation, enter centre stage a man who is as Australian as a kangaroo steak and yet as worldly as some-

rather than stigma attached to the unique way in which Aussies speak.

## Ockerdom

This "ocker" syndrome deserves more than passing reference. Once a term of derision (although its origin is uncertain), "ocker" has come to be a synonym for patriot. In a world growing ever smaller, urban Australians and their advertising agencies cling to the idea of the Australian who is obsessed with sport, winning, beer and his mates. Note the "his." Ockerinas are still seen but not heard, at least according to legend.

The cult of ockerdom has permeated most

one from the real world; a man who as a student held a world beer-drinking record and yet gave up the booze to pursue ambition; a man who is good at sport *and* economics, who cuts the throats of his political opponents and cries in public, who swears like a trooper and constructs the longest sentences recorded in the English language.

Hawke is the quintessential ocker, but he is also the urban Australian of the 1980s. He is a man at ease in any company, brash, forceful, given to flights of weirdness and totally compassionate when it is least expected. He is the bridge between ockerdom and the reality of Eighties' Ozman.

For urban Aussie, read Bob Hawke.

# BUSHMEN'S LORE

The year after the drought of the century broke, the season's wheat crop on the eastern side of the continent emerged from the flood waters and then promptly caught on fire. It is that sort of regular happening that gives rural Australians their unique view of the world. It also sends them in droves to the public bars of Outback hotels to consume an abstemious glass or nine of Bundaberg overproof rum.

It also gives rural Australians a very peculiar sense of humour indeed, perhaps best described as the joy-through-disaster sense of comedy. The phrase, "You wouldn't be dead for quids," is frequently heard.

Rural Australia, sometimes referred to as West of the Divide, Back of Beyond or The Mulga, is in some respects a great Antipodean myth. But despite the fact that most of the country's people get up every morning to spend another urbanised day canning asparagus or telling their peers that they haven't filled form 13B out in the correct sequence (and it should be in triplicate, anyway), most of them have this bizarre belief that they really belong on the Wallaby Track, with their swags over their shoulders and their faithful blue-heeler cattle dog scuffing along in the dust beside them.

Paradoxically, while urban Australians themselves dream of taking to the Wallaby, they express absolute horror if anyone looks like actually doing so. For a visitor to express a desire to abandon the delights of, say, Sydney Harbour and go to perhaps Bourke or even Kalgoorlie, simply to see what it is like, is regarded as something akin to madness. The attitude is that the traveller will get "bugger all" (nothing) to eat (all Australians by and large speak this way despite class differences); that he or she will get "crook in the guts" (ill); that any form of transport will invariably break down; that the one pub in the town will have no bathrooms apart from the "dunny" (toilet) out the back; and that there will be plagues of both "mozzies" (mosquitoes) and blowflies. The pub in question will be infested with drunken shearer's cooks, universal "speilers" (tellers of tall tales), "bots" (beef

Left, farmers from the state of Victoria and, right; "outback kids"—the youngest members of the Ward family, Central Western Australia.

thiefs) and mad dogs.

Sometimes the informants are right on all counts. But more often they are wrong. Distinguished author Donald Horne retraced his journeys of younger days around parts of Australia's inland and found that what he was searching for, "the sincere crumminess" of the country's inland towns and hamlets, was (to his alarm) in danger of extinction. Not only was the beer always cold; quite a lot of the pubs were air-conditioned.

The bizarre love of the Outback tradition on the one hand and the distaste for it on the

other can be traced back to turn-of-the-20th-Century author and poet Henry Lawson, one of Australia's literary folk heroes.

After a wretched childhood on the western New South Wales goldfields, Lawson kept returning to the bush to reinforce his dislike of it. He hated the dreary grey-green of the eucalyptus, the monotony and hopelessness (his word) of the countryside whether it was "in the wet" or "in the dry," the terrible heat on the track to Hungerford, the "bloody flies," the thieving publicans, the bosses, the squatters and the police. He did, however, like the bush battlers, the staunch early unionists and the great outback tradition of mateship.

But in his poems, Lawson also put the fear

of god into city people about living "out there." One example should suffice. It is a slice of a poem called *Past Carin'*:

*Now up and down the siding brown*
*The great black crows are flyin'*
*And down below the spur, I know,*
*Another milker's dyin';*
*The crops have withered from the ground*
*The tank's clay bed is glarin'*
*But from my heart no tear nor sound*
*For I have got past carin'. . . .*

As Lawson's best writing was done either before or around the turn of the century (*Past Carin'* was written in 1899) when pioneer families were indeed living basic and often brutal lives in slab huts with no water,

when the Afghan camel teams were in many cases the only contact people in the interior and the Top End (Northern Territory) had with the outside world for months on end, the bush people themselves felt Lawson was speaking for them.

### Tales of Dad and Dave

Although Lawson died drunk and destitute in 1922, his attitudes have permeated the urban nation's thinking, despite the fact that a really genuine swagman (tramp) or whaler, as these wanderers were once known, has not been seen on the Wallaby Track for many years now. Although air transport, air conditioning and refrigeration

have long since replaced the bullock dray, most Australians want to believe that the Outback is stuck in this time warp.

If it is not a Lawson time warp, mind you, it is a Steele Rudd time warp. Rudd, a contemporary of Lawson, wrote a series known as *On Our Selection*. It featured Dad, Dave, Mum and Ethel. It was the Australian version of *Lil' Abner*, except that Dad had a bloody sight more sense than Abner's Pa, and Mum didn't smoke a pipe.

These bush people belong to the country's past, but there still remains a lot of flavour in the inland. One has never struck a publican in a city hotel who slams his false teeth on the bar before he offers you out for a fight.

On the human side, there's a certain helpfulness in the bush which is not immediately apparent to the visitor, plus more than a little bush mischief on the side. Any enquiry for directions, for instance, can be met with a slow "buggered-if-I-know" reply, followed almost instantaneously with an exceedingly complicated series of directions. Australians don't deliberately misdirect visitors, for in the Outback, misdirection can mean death by bushfires or thirst.

The Outback Australian is also a great yarner (storyteller). But the tales are not of the Texan variety. The stories told have everything to do with disaster and nothing whatsoever to do with success. Prominent themes are the idiocy of working dogs, the stupidity of sheep, the cunning of the blow-fly swarms and the fact that any anti-hero of any story didn't quite make it. "And then, stone me, buggered if I know how he did it, but after he'd got the mob of sheep across and saved the boss' daughter from the flood, the silly bugger fell off his horse and broke his neck. Goes to show, don't it?" All this is delivered in a flat monotone.

It is indeed another world outside of the cities. And these days, one doesn't have to pack a swag to find it. It is not a matter of tracking to the dead heart, where the only establishment within 500 miles is a lone pub with warm beer and a desolate emu stamping around a chicken wire cage. It can be found in any small district town which supplies a broad rural area, in any state where the architecture is at least semi-colonial and where the inhabitants still fervently believe that they come straight out of the pages of Henry Lawson's short stories and poems.

There still remains a lot of "rural flavour" in the inland. The young girl, left, is from New South Wales. The ranchhand, right, is from Cordillo Downs, South Australia.

# THE NEW AUSTRALIANS

For many, the dream is over. Australia, land of opportunity, is closing its portals. Only people with very specific circumstances in their lives may immigrate Down Under these days. By rearranging its policies, the government has thoroughly altered Australian immigration in the 1980s.

The change took effect in April 1982, when the "points system"—whereby the applicant's occupation, age, education, economic prospects and other qualities are assessed—was restructured to favour people with relatives already living in Australia. In encouraging extended families to reunite, the government requires a guarantee of sponsorship from those relatives in Australia, thereby reducing pressure on the country's social services. The result is that fewer "unattached" immigrants are accepted largely for their job skills, with more people coming from Asian countries in particular.

The reason for the latter situation is that immigrants from some of the traditional "source" countries—Britian, Greece, Italy, and (to a degree) Germany and the Netherlands—have been balanced out by Asians, who are taking advantage of the impartial immigration laws which have replaced the racist "White Australia" policies of the past. Accordingly, Asians (who now comprise roughly one-quarter of all new arrivals and are expected to total about 3.4 percent of the Australian population by 1986) have more relatives ready and willing to come over than do the longer-settled immigrants from Southern Europe. Also, a greater emphasis is being placed now on refugees than in the past, with about 20,000 expected in fiscal year 1983-84, many of them from Asian countries.

## The Migrant Reduction

Approximately two-thirds of the 80,000 to 90,000 immigrants in 1983-84 will come either under the refugee or family migration plan. Only about 2,500 will be admitted because their jobs are in demand. This contrasts to 19,000 people who arrived under the "jobs in demand" category during the previous fiscal year.

However, immigration numbers are not

Left, girls at the Greek National Day Festival, Sydney. The Greeks make up one of the largest immigrant groups in the country.

declining across the board. There was a drop-off in settler arrivals during the mid-1970s, but it picked up to 110,000 in botn 1980-81 and 1981-82, which was a total comparable to all but the best of the last 25 years. The difference, then, is not in how many people qualify, but in how they qualify.

"We are one of the last countries for immigrants," states Tom Stratton of the Department of Immigration and Ethnic Affairs. "Who else wants people?"

One of the world's few other places that still wants immigrants (for obvious reasons) is South Africa. Conversely, in financial year 1982-83, some 3.3 percent of all immigrants to Australia "escaped" from South Africa, placing it sixth among top suppliers that year of immigrants Down Under. (The first five countries, in order, were the United Kingdom, New Zealand, Germany, Malaysia and Thailand, with Hong Kong ranking seventh.)

Geoff Stewart, a 30-year-old insurance broker, is a South African who arrived on Sept. 4, 1983. A highly motivated and well-organised individual, Stewart managed to be accepted despite the facts that he has no relatives in Australia, he isn't a refugee, and he is neither famous nor rich.

After an immigration consul interviewed him in Durban, the official said it would take four to six weeks for a decision. Stewart had heard that the embassy in Pretoria received a regularly revised list of occupations in demand from Australian authorities. When he applied, insurance brokers were in minor demand. To make sure it stayed that way, Stewart telephoned Pretoria about 10 days after his interview, and managed to coerce officers there into verbal confirmation of his acceptance.

Not content, however, with this promise, Stewart flew to Pretoria for written confirmation, rather than waiting for it to arrive by post. "In South Africa, they said you can't get into Australia these days," he said. "That's absolute rubbish. If you try hard and present a good curriculum vitae, you can make it."

Nevertheless, Stewart was fortunate to have one of the few skills in demand nowadays. At time of writing, the latest "demand" schedule listed no jobs whatsoever in major demand and only 18 in minor demand throughout the nation. Those few skills were mostly either highly specialized or idiosyncratic, such as pastry cook, upholsterer, precision instrument maker, engraver and patternmaker. Although there were some positions available in computing, accounting, teaching, insurance and the restaurant business, many of these jobs were to be had only in certain regions, and few existed in the most populous state, New South Wales.

### The Family Connection

The new wave is one of refugees and people reuniting with family members. John Lam arrived in 1979 under both programs. When he was 16, his parents journeyed to Cambodia from their home in South Vietnam, taking their two youngest sons with them. John never saw any of them again. But he had an older brother, a sister, and an aunt and uncle who had come to Australia in 1978. He and yet another brother soon followed.

For his first two months, John stayed in a migrant hostel, receiving $36 per week in benefits, plus food and some clothing. After that, he moved in with his aunt and uncle, started working in a kitchen, then eventually became a barman. He now speaks good, if not fluent, English, owns a house with his two brothers and sister, and has become an Australian citizen. For three years now, he and his siblings have been trying to sponsor the immigration of a 29-year-old sister, her husband and two children from South Vietnam. They're still hopeful, and it's looking better now.

Both Geoff Stewart and John Lam have nothing but praise for Australia. This enthusiasm, or in some cases politeness, seems to be a hallmark of new arrivals to the country. Often, though, immigrants are willing to admit that they miss their home countries, and that the trauma of relocation is not easily overcome.

"The first two weeks, I was sick, totally homesick," William Ho of Hong Kong recalled, "because the country was new and I had no friends here and all my customers were new, so I had to start all over again." Ho arrived in 1981 under the Employer Nomination Scheme. He had worked in Singapore for eight years as a restaurant manager, renewing his work visa annually. He became interested in Australia through a friend, a chef, who was immigrating. The friend knew that the owner of one of Australia's best Chinese restaurants was looking for a manager. Ho contacted the owner by mail and an employer sponsorship was arranged. The entire process took about five months. Nowadays, employer nomination is still in operation, but is being de-emphasized by the government.

After his initial "culture shock," Ho adapted and began to find bright spots in his changed life. He's happy with the standard and the cost of living in Australia compared to Hong Kong, and the less crowded conditions. "Also, Hong Kong is not a country, so no one protects you. When you're old, you may be poor, and there will be no help from the government. There's no future."

Still, Ho is not over his homesickness. He thinks Hong Kong is the best place in the world to eat and to shop. Although the overcrowding bothers him, the compactness of the area makes it easy to get goods and services in short order, especially compared to the sprawl of Australia.

Ho rents a flat in a middle-class suburb with his Singaporean wife and their infant child. Like John Lam, many of Ho's friends are Asian. Both Lam and Ho appreciate this strong sense of community. It exists outside Sydney as well. Melbourne, Brisbane and other cities boast suburbs with distinctly Chinese, Lebanese, Greek or Italian atmospheres. Even some country towns follow this pattern. For example, several wine grape-bearing valleys of South Australia, settled by Silesians in the 1840s, are still Teutonic in architecture, art and community festivals.

In recent years, the government has made attempts to identify "growing areas." Migrants have been encouraged to settle in these places by awarding them extra points on the question-and-answer application form. However, the Immigration Department's Stratton admits that this plan has not lived up to expectations, partially because the designated areas keep changing from state to state and partially because decentralisation is not easily accomplished when many people are rejoining families already living in major cities.

Thus most immigrants continue to come to the big towns, not only for jobs but to be with their relatives and friends. The day of the "wanderer" who comes for a visit, travels around a bit and decides to remain, is on the wane. That's the way a good many New Zealanders have settled in Australia, and it's still the only country from which visitors are not required by Australian authorities to have a visa. But by far the largest number of immigrants always has come from England (28.7 percent in fiscal year 1982-83, compared to 8.4 percent from the second-ranking New Zealand).

## The Working Holiday

Celia Smith, a 31-year-old English nurse, came to Australia under circumstances that were typical just three years ago. She had a "working holiday" visa which was good for one year. She bought an old car and drove about the country for six months, camping along the way. She said the prospect of travel and the new possibilities that were opened up by living on the other side of the world were what brought her to Australia.

Technical and academic qualifications from England are readily recognised in Oz, and Celia had no trouble finding work in a hospital's emergency unit. Before her visa expired, she applied for permanent residency and received confirmation after about

the outdoors lifestyle of beaches and barbeques, the friendliness of the people (especially in the rural north and west), and the accessibility to places not easily reached from Europe as advantages that keep Australia intriguing for her. Also, the size: "Australia is a continent, it's the whole of Europe, and that's hard to realise—you don't really believe it until you drive for a day and don't see anything except a dead kangaroo or a rabbit."

She realises, too, that she was lucky to have come to Australia before the immigration policies were revised in 1982. Among the many changes were ones to the working holiday program, which affects young people from Britain, Canada, Japan and the Netherlands, because those countries have

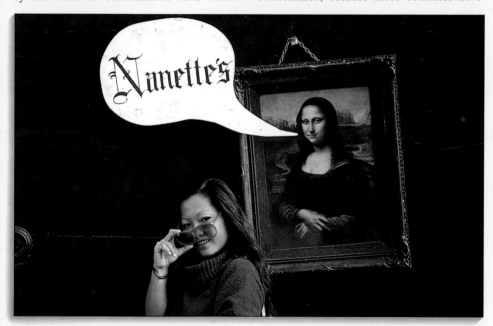

nine months. As is the case with many English and American citizens, Celia is not planning to apply for Australian citizenship. Even without it, though, she can leave Australia with no change in her permanent resident status, so long as she re-enters the country within three years.

Having learned to cope, however grudgingly, with the mosquitoes and flies that thrive in this warm climate, Celia also is finding that the pangs of friends and family back home are lessening with the passage of time. She cites the country's rugged beauty,

The attitude to Asian immigration implicit in the famous statement: "Two Wongs don't make a white," no longer exists.

reciprocal programs for Australians. It's now virtually impossible for a young visitor to change his or her status from a working holidayer to a permanent resident, as Celia and many others once did.

### The Business Migration Program

But despite the changes in law, there still are ways for the non-refugee who is not joining family members to move to Australia. One way is to have $250,000 or more, the ability and intent to set up a business, and a demonstrably good character. About 2,000 people and their families are expected under this Business Migration Program in 1983-84.

This category used to mean people could virtually buy their way in. But Stewart West, Minister of Immigration and Ethnic Affairs under the current Labor Party government, has redrawn the rules to stress business experience and the viability in Australia of the applicant's business plan.

Early in 1983, West declared: "Previous policy made it easy for people with nothing more than money to be accepted in this category. I have removed a concession that allowed wealthy people to migrate who did not intend to set up a business." To help insure this good intention, the prospective business migrant is required to visit Australia before submitting an application.

In the points system, business migrants score 25 just for being in that category—

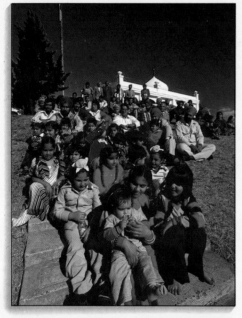

which is a long way toward the 60-point minimum (out of a possible 100) required to be accepted as a permanent resident. In fact, the only category that scores higher than business migrants is for applicants who have a full sponsorship by an Australian citizen (good for 28 points, or 25 if it's by a non-citizen). Full sponsorship, however, means that someone Down Under agrees to provide the immigrant with housing, food and other necessities for up to 12 months.

## Adding Up the Points

Another way to get in is to be well-off and old. People who have reached Australian retirement age (65 for males, 60 for females), and who have enough capital to set up a home and take care of themselves, have a good chance of being accepted as permanent residents.

To those who haven't attained those years yet, eight points are given under the regular system for being aged 25 to 35 inclusive, and less points for everyone else. Education counts, too—from eight points for a university degree to three for "some education." An outstanding employment record garners 10 more points; documented history of employment, a record of achievement and references are of value in this section.

Persons with reputations in the arts or sports, or whose other achievements are deemed valuable to Australia, may be welcomed into the country.

When all the points have been added up, yet another analysis, called a general assessment, is made. This is based on an interview and printed information that the applicant already has supplied. The selection officer assesses the applicant's ability to cope with immigration, his or her capacity to adapt to Australian society, and the degree of support from the prospective immigrant's family. In short, it's more of an attitudinal or even psychological analysis than that of the points system.

Obviously, the many elements of the selection process can be, and are, adjusted and interpreted to best suit the government's current immigration priorities. And while this system can have an indirect effect on how new arrivals might cope with a strange country, it's of no help once the entry visa is imprinted on the passport. That sort of aid is left to resettlement programs, to clubs and, most important, to society. In the latter case there's still room for improvement.

## Southern Europeans

The wave of Southern European migrants in the 1960s has abated, but the approximately 275,000 Greeks and Italians who arrived in Australia during that decade have placed their stamp on the cities of the nation. In Melbourne, often touted as having one of the largest Greek populations among all cities of the world, the trade and service industries abound with owner/managers who are industrious to the point of exhaustion. The same can be said of Perth, Adelaide, Brisbane and Sydney. Many of these entrepreneurs at the corner restaurant, shop or take-away food bar are from Southern Europe.

In fact, Greeks, Italians and Lebanese have become famous in Australia for their application to duty. This trait has elicited mixed reactions: admiration from many but envy and spite from some of the traditionally relaxed Australian natives. In the case of Southern Europeans and Asians, the usual language difficulties for most immigrants are compounded by skin tone. Even among the upper middle class, racist "jokes" and slurs are not uncommon, and this is a major reason why some people who have been Australian citizens for years still feel like outsiders.

As a result, they cluster, for relief from disapproval as well as for the companionship of cultural peers and a common language. Being "newcomers" of, say, only half a lifetime's standing, many immigrants are reluctant to condemn long-term Australians

other families from Kalymnos. Her father had arrived two years earlier, in response to the then-prevalent belief that Australia was the land of opportunity. Kathy's father wrote home to say that it wasn't as good as the people on Kalymnos thought.

Kathy's mother was adamant, though. With no assistance from the Australian government, she took her children from their home to live in the rented Sydney house, which they shared for a year and a half. Kathy remembers it as a time of strife and alienation. But her family was lucky. Both parents found work and were able to buy a house about 20 months after they were reunited. Of about 10 other Greek families they knew, the Papases were the only ones to progress so rapidly.

for these unsophisticated attitudes. There are some, though, who are willing to criticize for the record.

### A Greek Profile

Kathy Gianikouris (née Papas) is one. Born on the island of Kalymnos in Greece, she immigrated with her family in 1955. The eldest of four children, Kathy was only eight when they left the island to share a four-bedroom rented house in Sydney with three

Left, the Woolgoolga Sikh community, New South Wales, is a reminder of Australia's ethnic diversity. Above, ethnic eating: the Salona Greek restaurant, Melbourne.

Nevertheless, her parents never did adjust to the change. "Language was a problem," Kathy recalls. "We were treated as though we were nothing. We felt like refugees. Every minute, my parents regretted that they had left home to come out here." In 1970, Kathy's parents finally moved back to Greece, although she claims they haven't left Australia for good.

Kathy's parents left Australia because they missed the hospitality, the lack of fear and tension, the closeness to nature, and the blurred lines between work and leisure that characterise Greek island life. In order to at least partially retain that feeling, Kathy and her husband Manuel socialise almost entirely with other Greek-Australians.

Manuel was a committee member of the Kalymnian Brotherhood for three years, during which time he helped to organize picnics, dances and other social events which the couple still attend regularly. For Kathy, each such gathering is a welcome break from 20 years of seven-day-a-week labour. She and Manuel work in a corner grocery store that they owned until selling out six years ago. From 7 am to 9 pm they run this small business, prompting Kathy to comment: "This is why a lot of Greeks don't like Australia—because they've never seen it."

The Gianikourises own a home in a heavily Greek-populated eastern suburb of Sydney. Their three children attend public schools, but Kathy has followed her mother's example by sending her children to

a special Greek language school for two days a week after regular classes. (Manuel, who immigrated later in life than Kathy, has only about 50 percent competency in English.) Despite the fact that the couple's children were born in Australia, they occasionally return from school with stories of ridicule by classmates because they are "foreigners."

It would be hard to find two more opposed attitudes about being an immigrant to Australia than those of Kathy Gianikouris and Teresa Cupri. And yet Teresa, who claims to love everything about Australia, can think of one thing she doesn't like: the name-calling. Teresa immigrated from Italy with her family as a teenager in 1970. Recounting those days, she can remember a

few other things that weren't so wonderful, either.

It took her family two years to receive permission to migrate from Naples. When it finally was granted, the family had to be divided because there weren't enough places allotted for all 10 members. The eldest children, including Teresa, went with their father, and the others followed with their mother about six months later.

They stayed in a barracks-like hostel that was cold and damp, although Teresa remembers that the food was adequate. Passage and accommodation were government-assisted; the entire family paid $50.

Teresa went to work in a factory three days after their arrival. Poor conditions and low pay led her to seek another job, which she found in a nursing home. She stayed there for five years, learned English, and has been working steadily ever since.

With her husband Johnny, Teresa now owns a popular Italian restaurant. The couple met in Australia. Johnny originally left Italy to work in Germany, but under the sponsorship of a brother, he then migrated to Australia. The adult members of Teresa's family own homes and several of her siblings also have their own businesses. For her and hers, hard work has produced the promised comforts, despite their impoverished beginnings and total lack of English on arrival.

Since she and Johnny often work 14-hour days, they have little time for clubs or other organisations. With a wide range of nationalities as clientele, they do not spend a great deal of time among fellow immigrants from Italy. Teresa believes this puts the couple in a minority of perhaps one-third of Italian immigrants who don't circulate primarily among fellow countrymen.

The Australian government has estimated that 1 million "New Australians" cannot speak English. That's a sizeable sum in a country with a population of about 15 million, and certainly the overriding reason for the solidity of ethnic groups here.

As an urban country, with the bulk of its population collected in a few cities on the eastern seaboard, the proximity of different cultures to one another should breed acceptance, if not appreciation. There's still plenty of room for expansion, too. And as people from around the globe continue to bring their skills, visions and cultures into the life of this continent, it continues to increase in understanding and potential.

Australians leading new lives in a new land. Left, Gerda, a German immigrant. Right, mother and daughter by the sea.

# THE ABORIGINE TODAY

The arrival of European settlers in Australia in the late 18th Century changed the Aboriginal lifestyle in a way which had a devastating effect. As the early colonial settlements expanded, taking the most fertile areas of land, the nomadic way of traditional Aboriginal life was disrupted. Forceful measures were taken by white settlers in their quest for development. Tribes, clans and families were dispersed simultaneously with the taking of land.

By the beginning of the 20th Century many of the tribal languages had been lost and the estimated population of 300,000 Aboriginal people at the time of the arrival of European settlers had been reduced to about 60,000.

Early efforts by governments and churches to help Aboriginal people saw the implementation of protectionist policies, with the establishment of missions and reserves, prohibition of alcohol and regulation of much of their social life. When these failed to redress the decline in the conditions of Aboriginal people, assimilationist policies—aimed at helping Aboriginal people adopt a European way of life—were implemented.

Increased expenditure by governments on health and housing services was beginning to produce results in terms of reducing the population decline. However, opposition arose among Aboriginal and other Australian people against these measures which removed the right of Aboriginal people to decide their own futures. Australian governments then formulated policies which encouraged greater participation by Aboriginal people. Laws were changed which entitled Aborigines to the same rights and social security benefits as other Australians.

### Redressing the Injustices

There also emerged greater recognition of Aboriginal culture and of the right of Aboriginal people to practise their lifestyle.

The Aboriginal population today numbers about 160,000 with many located in the northern parts of Australia or in the rural centres. However, about two-thirds now live in the cities and have adopted a suburban lifestyle. The socio-economic conditions of almost all of them remain poor and Aboriginal people are the single most disadvantaged group in Australia. Recent attempts to assist them to regain control over their own lives have become complex, confused, emotional and political.

Aboriginal people see self-development as encompassing a variety of issues ranging from land rights to improved housing, health, education, employment and cultural expression.

At a national referendum in 1967, the Australian people gave the Commonwealth the responsibility for Aboriginal affairs. Although the various state and territory governments provide services and programs to Aboriginal people, the major thrust has been developed at a national level. The federal government's policies are based on the premise of self-management and self-determination. Strategies and the necessary administrative machinery to implement them were developed only after considerable consultation with Aboriginal people.

During the 1970s many Aboriginal organisations were established by governments and by Aboriginal people themselves. The National Aboriginal Conference (NAC)—a

Aborigines are trying to preserve their identity; left, the Corroboree is still performed. Right, one of the Gagadju tribe, traditional owners of an area in the Kakadu National Park.

body of 36 selected Aborigines which represents Aboriginal opinion and provides advice to the federal government on Aboriginal matters—was created in 1976. The NAC provides a forum for Aboriginal opinion at a national, regional, and local level on a wide range of issues.

A major task of the NAC is the proposed implementation of a *makarrata* or treaty, a concept which has been discussed with Aboriginal groups throughout Australia. If adopted it would include such advances as recognition of Aboriginal prior ownership of Australia, cash compensation for dispossession of land, Aboriginal electoral representation in governments, and protection for Aboriginal culture and sacred artefacts.

Members of the NAC have also taken the accommodation network.

While the NAC and AHL provide important contributions at the political, social and welfare levels, there is still an urgent need for Aboriginal people to develop their economic base. In 1974 the federal government created the Aboriginal Loans Commission and the Aboriginal Land Fund Commission, two Commonwealth statutory authorities which provided funds for housing, business enterprises and land acquisition. In 1980 these two organisations were superceded by the Aboriginal Development Commission (ADC), a federal statutory authority, which was seen by many as the most significant initiative in Aboriginal advancement.

Through the ADC, Aboriginal people have the means to help recreate their en-

case for Aboriginal advancement to the international forum through the United Nations and the World Council of Indigenous Peoples.

### A Sound Economic Base

Aboriginal advancement programs also require appropriate support services. For example, federal government initiatives in Aboriginal education and employment programs, usually implemented in the larger cities, often mean that Aboriginal people must travel away from their communities. Aboriginal Hostels Limited (AHL)—a public company with Aboriginal directors and senior executives—helps provide a national

vironment and to achieve self-management and thus self-sufficiency. The ADC has a single practical purpose—to advance the economic well-being of Aborigines and Torres Strait Islanders by acquiring land for Aboriginal communities and groups, lending and granting money to Aboriginal people and organisations for housing and for business ventures.

By acquiring land for Aboriginal groups the ADC can help meet the spiritual as well as the economic needs of Aborigines. Land,

Above, early engraving of a Corroboree. Right, well-intentioned whites attempted to break the tribal ways of Aborigines with religion and European dress and culture.

to Aboriginal people, is part of their being. The spirit of the people is derived from the land or, more specifically, from the sacred sites of the Dreamtime.

But adequate housing for Aborigines in Australia is perhaps the most urgent need. Most Aboriginal people do not have the financial resources or access to conventional lending institutions such as building societies, banks or private housing schemes. Many are trapped in a depressing cycle of poverty with low incomes limiting their housing markets, which in turn jeopardises their physical and mental health, their education potential and their subsequent employment opportunities.

Because of the diverse housing needs of the many Aboriginal groups, the ADC's

designed to provide an economic base for Aboriginal communities and individuals. These include Aboriginal-run artefact shops at Ayers Rock; abalone and mutton bird harvesting collectives; and the running of pastoral properties in the north of Australia.

Aboriginals have had a long-standing link with the pastoral industry, working as stockmen and rousabouts on white-run cattle properties in outback Australia. But with the purchase by the ADC of a large pastoral property in Queensland's remote Gulf of Carpentaria, Aboriginal people became the owners of a property—no longer to work for the white man, but to work their own land and cattle. The 4,000-square-kilometre (1,540-square-mile) Delta Downs station is worth several million dollars and carries

housing policy has focused on providing accommodation which will enable Aboriginals to have an acceptable standard of health and social well-being within the lifestyle of their choice. This may take the form of conventional homes in suburbia, larger community-style centres in other areas, or simple shelters for tribal communities.

For Aboriginal people to participate in the mainstream of Australian life if they so desire, they need to be on a similar economic footing to other Australians. Many remote communities have little or no income and are dependent on government welfare assistance.

Through the ADC, the Australian government has implemented enterprise programs

20,000 prime cattle. While the Aboriginal owners are having to learn such skills as management and accounting, early estimates indicate the venture will soon become a viable enterprise, with the potential to tap into the valuable overseas live-meat export markets in which Australia plays a major role.

### Health Problems

Aboriginal health is far worse than the general Australian health standard. Major health problems facing Aborigines in Australia today include trachome, tuberculosis, leprosy, infant mortality, alcoholism and respiratory infections.

Governments have attempted to combat the causes of low Aboriginal health standards by providing improved housing, water supplies, sewage, nutrition and alcohol rehabilitation programs. In recent years the federal government and state and territory health authorities have developed a number of strategies to increase Aboriginal involvement in health-care programs.

### The Cutting Edge

The support and expansion of Aborigine-controlled medical and dental services is seen as offering a solution to many of the problems, with the organisation employing professional staff along with ancilliary Aboriginal staff and executives. These organisations

iginal people, have helped significantly reduce the extent of sentences on Aborigines. Aboriginal legal services also play an active role in fostering improved Aboriginal/police liaison and in developing better community relationships.

### Education and Job Training

An important proposal being considered by the federal government is the recognition and introduction of Aboriginal customary or tribal law within the Australian legal system. Aspects such as the recognition of tribal marriages, custody of Aboriginal children, tribal sentences and punishment, as well as problems of evidence and procedure, are currently being examined by the Australia

are managed on a community or regional basis, but affiliated under an umbrella body—the National Aboriginal and Islander Health Organisation.

The legal system and its application has been described as the cutting edge of contact between black and white communites in Australia. Gross injustice to Aborigines, or the dangers of injustice to others of allowing too many exceptions for Aborigines, are issues which evoke academic debate.

The real fact is, however, that the numbers of Aboriginal people imprisoned is far greater than the national average. Aborigine-controlled legal services, which have been established by the federal government to cater for the legal needs of Abor-

Law Reform Commission.

The federal government's strategy on education for Aboriginals is developed by the Department of Education with advice from the National Aboriginal Education Committee—an 18-member organisation of Aboriginal educators. Special programs to boost Aboriginal education levels include the Aboriginal Secondary Grants Scheme, Aboriginal Study Grants Scheme and the Aboriginal Overseas Study Awards schemes, all of which provide funds to Abor-

Above, an "embassy" is set up outside Parliament House in Canberra. Right, more protest; housing, education, work, health and land rights are all Aboriginal issues.

iginal and Torres Strait Islander students. Aboriginal people and teachers are also urging that increased efforts be made to train more Aboriginal teachers.

Efforts are also being made to have Aboriginal studies placed on the curricula of Australian schools, to include the study of Aboriginal languages in certain schools, and to place responsibility for distributing funds for Aboriginal education under the direction of Aboriginal people.

Aboriginals have a higher unemployment rate and fewer jobs skills than other Australians. Lack of education, employer discrimination and the recent contracted state of the economy contribute to this situation.

The federal government has initiated a National Employment Strategy for Abor-

iginals (NESA) which is aimed at helping Aboriginals obtain employment and training opportunities.

## Victims of Circumstance

While today's Aborigines may be the victims of history and social circumstance, often the pawns in white man's ideology and politics, they still embrace their culture.

Despite the intrusion of Western culture, which has modified the culture of many urban Aboriginal people, tribal Aboriginal people see traditional lifestyles as being a bulwark to protect and strengthen their lifestyle, their heritage and their future.

The recognition and expression of that culture is reflected in many ways, varying from region to region, group to group, and individual to individual. Traditional artists in central and northern Australia conduct their skills in much the same way as their forefathers did—decorating weapons, tools and totems with the traditional colours of their region. Tribal dancers in these areas stir clouds of red earth as their dancing, music and chanting expresses a culture of the Dreaming of 40,000 years.

By contrast, contemporary plays, music and dances, written and performed by today's urban Aboriginals, often portray a fusion of cultures—that of the tribal past, rich with tradition and pride, and that of today, often reflecting despair.

If the tragedy of the black-white culture clash in Australia can best be illustrated in one anecdote, the story of Albert Namatjira states the case. Under tutoring, Namatjira became the first Aboriginal painter to interpret the rugged landscapes of his tribal country in Western traditional watercolour paintings. In his own style, Namatjira captured the MacDonnell Ranges and their beautiful interplay with the brilliant central Australian light in compelling fashion.

While his work received international acclaim, Namatjira could not handle the huge cultural differences between black and white society. He had official citizenship and the accompanying right to drink bestowed upon him at a time when Aborigines were not normally afforded these privileges. His patrons invested him with the trappings of the white world but refused to recognise his tribal obligations. While his money was shared among his kin, Namatjira went from alcoholism to jail in a decline that saw this gentle man of dignity and skill die prematurely, a disillusioned fringe dweller.

Some Aboriginals, however, have made the step into white society on their own terms. Neville Bonner became a senator in federal Parliament; pastor Sir Doug Nichols was knighted by the Queen of England and in 1976 appointed governor of South Australia; Evonne Goolagong won international tennis acclaim; and Kath Walker is one of Australia's greatest poets. There are Aboriginal sports stars, actors, ballerinas and university graduates. But on the whole, they are the exception.

In the main, Aborigines remain a disadvantaged minority, often treated like strangers in their own country. White attitudes, particularly at the vital schools level, are changing. Hopefully, the process will be speedy enough to save what is left of a unique culture.

# PLACES

Australia is the largest island, continent if you will, almost as big as the mainland United States and just as varied in climate, topography and inhabitants.

It goes without saying, therefore, that no temporary visitor will see the country from side to side, end to end. Very few Australians, in fact, have that privilege in their lifetimes. But we determined not to allow the vastness of our subject be a deterrent to comprehensive viewing. It's true, you can't see Australia in a week, month or even three months. But you can see representative slabs of it.

Our routes—our Grand Tour system—is based on the assumption that you will land in one of the capital cities and venture forth from there. If you are going directly to Upper Grong Grong, then we have failed you. However, our Grand Tour traces well-defined major routes between the big cities of Australia, offering diversions and detours along the way. First we examine the cities, then we explain what you can see as you leave them, en route for other places.

It is not a perfect system, but it may be used in whole or in part. It is important, however, that the traveller disabuse himself of the idea of seeing it all at once. In the centre there is vast nothingness. Few Americans would contemplate a leisurely New York-Los Angeles road trip in less than a week. Sydney to Perth is longer and the roads are much worse. Consult your map and have fun. If you don't, you won't.

*The Grand Tour comprises ten journeys, all numbered in the map, left. Some tours (Sydney-Adelaide is one example) involve two different routes. Between pages 145 and 265 chapter headings refer to starting and finishing points only; footnotes at the bottom right-hand corner refer again to tour numbers.*

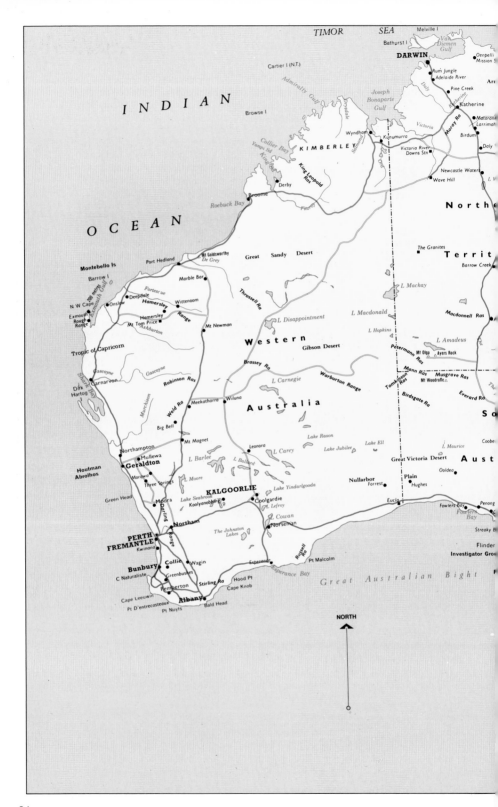

TIMOR SEA

INDIAN

OCEAN

NORTH

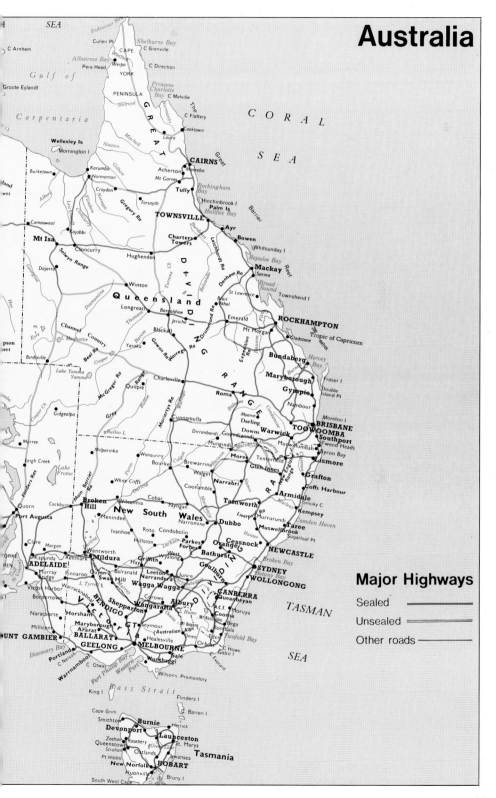

# Australia

**Major Highways**

Sealed ————————

Unsealed ════════

Other roads ————————

# SYDNEY: BEST ADDRESS ON EARTH?

Let's not be coy about it. Kangaroos and didgeridoos aside, Sydney, for many people, *is* Australia. After all, one quarter of the population of Australia lives here, and most people arriving from elsewhere land here.

And in the 1980s Australia, a.k.a. Sydney, has been discovered by the makers, shakers, bon vivants and flavor-of-the-month-ers. According to one theory, the well-kept secret that Sydney is a great place to *live*, is about to be blown by an influx of jet laggards who will treat it as just another place to *visit*.

We shall have to wait for history to prove or disprove this "fear of flying people." Meanwhile, Sydney goes on, increasingly singing its own praises. One trendy local magazine has as its motto, "Sydney, best address on earth." The modest may wince, as may the secretive types, but really they don't disagree.

This new-found pride is not so much born of Ocker braggadocio, or defensive provincialism, as of home-grown appreciation. There may be other cities with better sunshine and harbours, looser manner, prettier people and easier solitudes; but Sydneysiders haven't heard of them—especially all rolled into one.

So much for the secret. It's *out*, and you're flying in. With a bit of luck you'll circle a coastline of blue brilliance and lace surf, a glass-and-girders downtown and then, seemingly, a zillion acres of red-roofed suburban sprawl. The anonymity of the suburbs is on your side. Sydney's not jealous of itself, and you are as entitled to feel at home as anyone who's lived all his or her life here. (The fact is, a quarter of Sydney's population wasn't even born in Australia. So you're all right, Jack.)

### National Nativity

It was the birthplace of Australia. A vast harbour hemmed by low hills and sandstone headlands, and a freshwater stream feeding into it. Captain Phillip camped beside that flow, the Tank Stream, and pitched tents which became slab huts and then brick cottages,

sandstone and timber edifices, office blocks and, finally, a jumble of high-rises. Since 1778, Sydney has grown from 1,000 to 3,500,000 people. Its beauty now glitters alongside the customary scars and bars of any Western city: smog, unemployment, corruption, the usual.

The city has now spread to a great infra-red blot on the Landsat photographs, an irregular half-circle bounded on its eastern diameter by a 60-kilometre (37-mile) necklace of beaches and inlets. To the west, its satellite towns advance 75 kilometres (47 miles) across the once-rural plains to the base of the Blue Mountains. The coal and steel cities of Newcastle to the north and Wollongong to the south, as well as Katoomba in the mountains, are being drawn into the web of the vast urban sprawl.

Perhaps Sydney is already too big. Certainly the Australian dream of a house and land for every family has contributed to its girth. Over 60 percent of New South Wales' population is located here, as is most of the state's manufacturing, commerce, banking and shipping. This great critical mass of

human settlement perches on the coast, with all of empty Australia at its back.

At times it seems as though the city—for all its beaches, bushland and waterways—is in chrome-plated, chlorinated retreat from the unpredictable vagaries and viciousness of the Australian bush surrounding it. The absoluteness of the contrast is encapsuled in the Australian term "Sydney or the bush," meaning all or nothing.

Sydney's "all" in recent years has become a creative melting pot out of which the renaissance in Australian film has emerged. It shares with Australia's other capitals an irrepressible rock music circuit (from corner pubs to sports arenas), as well as wide exposure to the more sedate performing arts. Finally emerging from its cultural cringe under the Anglo-American marquee, Sydney has recently been mooted as the Paris of the Pacific, a claim which may be a little premature. To the rural people of the state it is often referred to simply as "The Big Smoke."

It doesn't take much to survive in Sydney (other than money: it's *not* a cheap city).

The weather is temperate with a February summer average of 21.4°C (72.1°F) and a July winter average of 12.6°C (54.1°F). Averages aside, there are also stifling summer heat waves and wretchedly cold, wet winter's days, but no snow or ice. Rainfall is around 1,200 mm (50 inches) per year, with April to June the wettest months.

The people too are fairly temperate. The original Anglo-Celtic genetic monopoly has been diluted since World War II by heavy immigration from southern and northern Europe and, more recently, from Southeast Asia and the Pacific. The result is an increasingly cosmopolitan hybrid, with the casual egalitarianism of the convict streak getting a lift from a change of diet (away from those soggy English vegetables), music and better-tailored shirts.

There are a thousand things to do in Sydney, from koala sanctuaries and lion parks to water taxis on the harbour and scenic flights to Palm Beach. Jazz clubs, workers' pubs, horse racing, drag racing, opera, surf carnivals . . . the smorgasbord is yours. Six months may not be enough for some. For others, a day may offer a fair taste. Let's pick a day, say Sunday, and fill it with Sydney.

Left, early morning surfer.

## The Beach at Bondi

**Bondi Beach** (that's *Bon-die*, not *Bondy*—he's a yachtman) is as famous a place as any from which to start. It's a $4 taxi ride from the city or $1 on the bus. You emerge from a red-brick thicket of apartments and funny "eccents" (there are more New Zealanders in Bondi than in many towns across the Tasman Sea) and ah! there it is: Bondi! A half-mile crescent of sea, sand and exertions.

It's no passive sea-dream of a place. As the closest surfing beach to town, and as a decompression chamber for the populous eastern suburbs, Bondi conducts a bizarre orchestra of morning players.

The first to surface, either from snores or all-night beer-and-bong sessions, are the board riders. In its time, Bondi has thrown up many world-class surfers, such as Cheyne Horan, and with a bit of luck you'll see a pack of hotfoots shredding their way across the waves.

Lumbering up and down the south-end pool are the "Icebergs," ancient walnut-skinned human walruses who were probably hot surfers back in *their* day. Seemingly impervious to cold, they swim year-round.

A few yards from them, but definitely pervious to the environment—meteorological and human—there is usually a score of near-naked, sun bathing women. Lovely scenery.

Resolutely thundering past these morning glories come the joggers, then the strollers, then the metal-detectors. There's *tai chi* on the lawns, hangovers on the promenade. In all, a great place for physical jerks. Bring your swimsuit and brave it.

Bondi Beach and **Bondi Junction** have numerous coffee shops, snack bars, fruit vendors and Jewish delicatessens where you may complete your morning constitutional with a breakfast of your choice. After that, a cab back to town, to the **Opera House.**

### Operatic Overture

It sits on **Bennelong Point**, this great crystal of a building, so audacious in its white, billowing sails that it threatens to set itself adrift and to sail majestically up the harbour.

ydney
Harbour
Bridge.

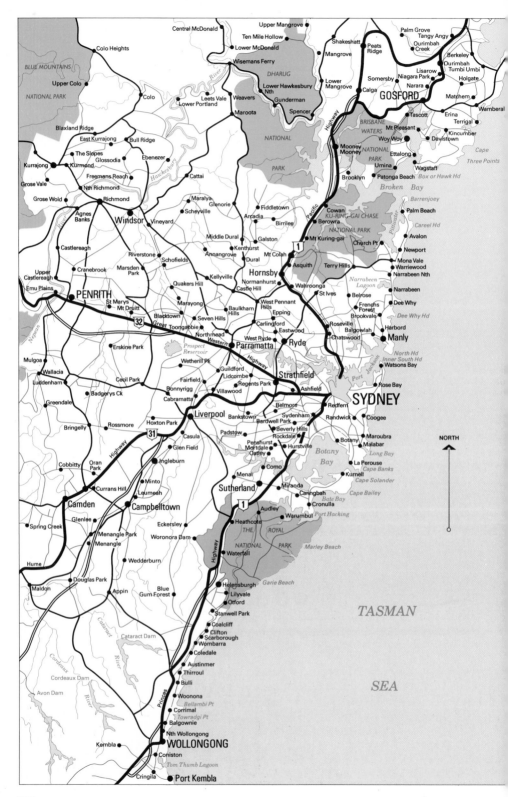

Its history is as eccentric and as passionate as its presence. From sketch plans which won the 1957 competition for its design, the state government estimated that the Opera House would cost $7 million and be five years in construction. Sixteen years and $102 million later, Queen Elizabeth II opened it in 1973. By then, heads had rolled, governments had almost toppled and its architect, Danish-born Jørn Utzon had departed the project and the country. At the time of writing he had never seen the completed version of his masterpiece, a building often hailed as one of the architectural hallmarks of the 20th Century.

The *Opera* House—the term is a misnomer, because the building houses theatres, restaurants, a cinema and more—embodies some impressive statistics. Its great shell roofs soar to 67 meters (220 feet); they are covered by more than 1 million Swedish ceramic tiles, weigh a total of 158,000 tons and are held together (and up) by 350 kilometres (217 miles) of tensioned cables. Over 6,200 square meters (67,000 square feet) of tinted French glass enclose its Space Gothic cathedral interiors. Sydney is *very* proud of this particular white elephant.

You may wander around the Opera House at will. Guided tours through the Opera Theatre and the Concert Hall can be joined between 9 a.m. and 4 p.m. for $2. The sunlit corners, the fanning spandrels and mullions, the panoramas of the harbour, the gourmet seagulls mounting snack attacks at the outdoor cafe... there's plenty to see.

By now you've probably realised that you need two things to meet Sydney on its own terms—good walking shoes and lunch. If you tug your bootlaces and belt a little tighter and head off west from the Opera House, you walk around Sydney Cove to the **Circular Quay** ferry wharves. Here a cosmopolitan blend of winos, office workers, buskers, graffitists and sightseers ambles in what is hopefully the noonday sun. You can grab a quick bite here or continue around to George Street and the Rocks.

### Historic Strolls

**The Rocks** really is the place where Australia (that is *European* Australia)

began. Upon its rocky ridge, the colony of New South Wales took root, and successive waves of convicts, builders, merchants, sailors, press-gangs, demolishers, plague victims and developers have left their marks.

The roistering brothels, razor gangs, shanghaiing cells and whipping posts are long gone. Nowadays the great bond-stores and warehouses are full of a different booty—Australiana, opals, art galleries and eateries. But down the freshly painted dogleg alleys like Suez Canal (formerly Sewer's Canal) you can still almost see the masts of windjammers and feel the steel, smell the fear of the Rum Corps and the press gangs.

If your imagination isn't that lurid, wander over to **The Rocks Visitors Centre** (104 George St.) and catch their 10-minute documentary which nutshells the area's history from Governor Phillip to the new Redevelopment Authority.

By now you'll feel like you're on starvation rations. There's a good buffet lunch in the **Argyle Tavern**; and there are any number of cafes, restaurants and sandwich bars on George Street. A pub counter lunch at around $3 is an ample, unpretentious feed, and a chance to meet the native in his cups.

Digest your lunch and history, too, with a one-hour Rocks walking tour. It leaves the Argyle Centre four times daily for $2.50. You'll see Sydney's oldest cottage and its shortest street, bond-stores, barracks, cells and sandstone pubs. The approaches to the Harbour Bridge bisect the Rocks. On its western side, the social character changes: there are the elegant Georgian homes of the gentry, the **Garrison Church** with its village green, row houses, Captain/Governor **Bligh's House** and a few quiet watering holes.

The still-gallant **Hero of Waterloo Pub** (1844) and the lovely old brick-and-tile **Palisades Hotel** are both good for a beer. (If you've lasted this long, there's an excellent restaurant in the Palisades.) They are also suitable places to reflect upon how far the place has come since Lord Sydney, the British Home Secretary (1784-1789), suggested establishing here a penal colony to replace those lost in the American War of Independence. Spare a thought for the city motto, "I Take But I Surrender," a homily which promises to be awkward in the light of recent Aboriginal land

Strand Arcade.

claims that have been made over Sydney bush land.

## Ratbags on Soapboxes

Sunday afternoon in **The Domain** (a short taxi-ride from the Rocks) is a bit of a lark. Here, a fine collection of ratbags, wowsers and idealists climb onto soapboxes and harangue you on everything from politics to the shape of the planet.

The Domain and the Botanic Gardens (again, bisected by a highway) form a 170-acre oasis of lawn, giant Moreton Bat fig trees and exotic flora, perfect for strolling or snoozing. The parks run right down to the harbour and provide a relief for large, picnicking Mediterranean families from the grass-less world found in the central business district.

Sydney's transnational skyline gleams (or glowers, depending upon your weather) over the Domain's greensward. To the east, the neo-classical sandstone of the Art Gallery of New South Wales presents an easier visage. Entry is free and the Gallery houses excellent collections of all periods of Australian art, from Aboriginal through colonial to contemporary masters.

If you walk back down to Circular Quay, to No.5 Wharf, soon enough there will be a ferry to **Taronga Park Zoo**. The zoo closes at 5 p.m. so you'll want to be on the 3.30 p.m. ferry at the latest. Now one ferry ride on **Sydney Harbour** is not enough, so this one's a taste of things to come.

Later you might chug (or rip, if you're on the hydrofoil) across to **Manly**; or catch a coffee cruise on the *Captain Cook*; or simply dawdle around on the **Balmain**, **Lavender Bay** or **Hunter's Hill** commuter ferries.

## A Cruise on the Harbour

The harbour shows Sydney at its best. It is the heart of its matter, the blue blood of its pulse; 57 sq km (22 sq miles) of sheltered water bounded by 240 km (148 miles) of meandering bays, coves and beaches stretch out around you. Gulls keep pace beside your ferry and a rainbow flotilla of yachts, skiffs, sailboards and runabouts tacks every which way about you. The expensive apartment blocks of **Kirribilli** (on the north-

arbourside
staurant,
Rocks."

ern shore) and **Elizabeth, Double and Rose bays** (on the city-side, the southern shore) reflect upon their own good fortune.

You glide out of Sydney Cove, past the Opera House, and are immediately confronted by the grim stones of **Pinchgut**, a tiny island fort upon which hapless 18th Century convicts were incarcerated on starvation rations. Across the water on Kirribilli Point the vice-regal elegance of **Admiralty House** holds court. Its stately colonnades, wrought-iron and white chimneys are home to the Queen's representative and head-of-state, the Governor General, whenever he's in town. (This is infrequently as he lives in Canberra.)

A glance backwards shows "The Old Coat-hanger," the **Harbour Bridge**, the largest arch bridge in the world, leap-frogging 134 metres (440 feet, at its highest point) between the Rocks and **Milson's Point**. Its main span is 503 metres (1,650 feet); it contains 52,000 tons of steel, and was completed in 1932. You may cross it by train, bus, car, bicycle or foot; but right now you're still on the ferry and approaching the zoo.

Taronga ('Aboriginal for "water view") Park occupies part of a peninsula at **Mosman Bay** and, surrounded as it is by virgin bush and the harbour, is one of the most beautiful zoo sites in the world. Among its collections of 5,000 mammals, birds, reptiles and fish are such uniquely Australian creatures as the emu, platypus, kangaroo, wombat, spiny anteater, dingo and kookaburra.

The zoo is clean and leafy, easy to get around (especially by the free road train) and generally does not contain too many distressing monuments to human inquisitiveness. It has an aquarium, a house for nocturnal animals, rainforest aviary, a seal show and a koala house. As with zoos anywhere, watching the kids watching the animals—especially the big cats—is half the fun.

They'll throw you out at closing time. After another 15-minute ride back to Circular Quay, your stomach should be growling again. Sydney has continents of ethnic restaurants, but since it *is* a city obsessed with sailing, diving, waterskiing and swimming, you should at least try the seafoods.

A $10 taxi ride out through the

Vaucluse House.

well-endowed Eastern Suburbs brings you to the harbour's southern headland and to **Watson's Bay**. There's a great pub here (for sinking ales to the sinking sun); a spectacular sandstone cliff called **The Gap** (Sydney's favourite suicide spot); and there's also **Doyle's Seafood Restaurant**.

### Spice and Vice

Doyle's is the most famous seafood place in town—in the *country* for that matter—and has been run by the same family for a century. When it first opened, elegant diners used to arrive by horse coach or sailing cutter. Today, take your choice of the reef: barramundi, whiting, bream, lobster, shrimp and oysters.

On the way back to the city, stop to look at **Vaucluse House**, a model of 19th Century elegance in trendy Vaucluse.

Now there's only one thing between you and your hotel—some night life. The obvious choice is **Kings Cross**, once described in an Australian encyclopedia as "an area of cosmopolitan eating houses, and of urban adventure from spice to vice." The Cross is a skin circus, an insomniac's delight of electric pointillism, a sleazy-glittery, stripping, ripping, night-tripping yarn of a place. Every doorway promises a different indulgence: sex and drugs and rock 'n' roll; coffee, porn or just a Lebanese roll.

You wade through the demimondaines and doormen, maybe catch some black dancing at the **Talofa Club**, some desperate rock at the **Manzil Room**, a drink at the **Texas Tavern** or your breath at the **Piccolo**. It could take all night.

Half a mile away on Oxford Street the world isn't quite so hetro-retro. It's new-wave gay: more small clubs, eating places and bars.

Such scenes, of course, may not be your choice. And choice is what Sydney's really about. On *Monday* you might take a bus-ride north to **Palm Beach**, a train ride south to the **Royal National Park**, or a rent-a-car to colonial **Winsdor** and **Richmond**. You might explore the working week in the Western Suburbs; or go rock-fishing at dawn, dancing at midnight, or . . . or . . .

You never know your luck in the Big Smoke.

Doyle's
seafood
restaurant.

# Melbourne: The Queen City

Legend has it that when a visitor arrives in Perth locals first ask where he is from; in Adelaide what church he belongs to; in Sydney how much money he makes; and in Brisbane simply if he'd like a beer. In Melbourne they're desperate to find out what your school was.

While the story may be apocryphal, the sentiments expressed are not without foundation. Melbourne has long enjoyed a reputation as the seat of Australia's Establishment and, as such, questions of background and connections still have their relevance in the corridors of power.

In the Queen City of the South (and this title has nothing to do with the sexual preference of her citizens), stockbrokers, lawyers, bankers and company directors are more often than not the product of one of the nine or 10 elite grammar schools and colleges. There are waiting lists to enter these schools with their proud aura of tradition and achievement. Think of old clock towers and quadrangles, distinctive school blazers, playing fields and cricket pitches—the legacy of the great schools of England—and you're beginning to get the picture.

Melbourne's image has been one of conservative lifestyles and refined tastes. While Sydney still has a sense of the rough diamond about it, Melbourne is seen to be more like a cultured pearl: lots of character and class but not much sparkle. It's a nice analogy, perhaps, but the image of Melbourne being dull is not always consistent with the truth.

## A Conservative City of Style

Melbourne is a city long known for its fashion and theatre, its art galleries, restaurants and shops, its public gardens and fountains, its wide, leafy streets and its architectural gems of yesteryear. It has been this way since the latter half of the 19th Century when gold became the cornerstone of its prosperity.

However, a persona based on conservatism and a penchant for tradition elicits some contradictory responses. In the 1950s, evangelist Billy Graham dubbed Melbourne "the most moral city in the world." (Little did he know, but more of that later.) And in the Sixties actress Ava Gardner—in Melbourne working on the film *On The Beach*—was quoted as saying that it was the perfect place to make a film about the end of the world. (Recently a Sydney journalist has claimed that he, in fact, invented the quote to add fire to the long-standing rivalry between Sydney and Melbourne.)

The evidence of history, and indeed the current climate, demonstrate that the capital of the State of Victoria is far from being the dowager she is painted. The facts would liken her more to a spirited woman who periodically kicks up her skirts and enjoys life to the full. But let's go back. Perhaps the genesis of Melbourne's reputation had to do with its beginning.

### Free Men From the Start

Unlike Sydney, Melbourne was not founded as a penal colony. Instead of a core of recalcitrant convicts and their keepers, Melbourne's early settlers were free men intent on building a new

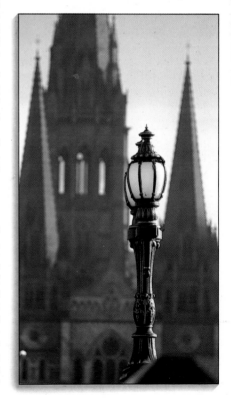

*Left, aerial view of Melbourne. Right, Melbourne Cathedral.*

and prosperous life for themselves. In June 1835, John Batman, a land speculator from Tasmania, sailed the 30-ton schooner *Rebecca* deep into Port Phillip Bay, rowed up a broad river with members of his syndicate, and declared: "This will be the place for a village."

With a payment of goods including blankets, mirrors and axes, he persuaded the local Aborigines to "sell" him 600,000 acres of prime land and drew up a document to legalise the purchase. This was later discounted as a farce by the British government who accused Batman of trespassing on Crown Land. Over the decades, and especially in more recent times, Batman's precedent of chicanery has not gone unheeded by other land speculators, whose interest in the development of Melbourne could hardly be called altruistic.

A year later the settlement beside the Yarra River was officially named Melbourne in honour of Lord Melbourne, Prime Minister of England. The first land sales took place soon after. Small properties at the centre of the settlement sold for £150. Two years later the same properties were changing hands for £10,000, a good indication of Batman's keen sense for speculative real estate.

Thus it was not enforced labour and the clank of chains and shackles that nurtured the youthful Melbourne, but the vision and industry of resourceful pioneers, and later merchant princes, that ensured Melbourne would prosper and grow into a grand city.

If it was these auspicious beginnings that laid the foundation for Melbourne's Establishment and the city's ongoing role as the financial centre of Australia, it was the discovery of gold at nearby Ballarat in 1851 that was responsible for the sudden growth in people and prosperity which determined its character. The fabulous finds, just 115 kilometres (71 miles) from Melbourne, drew thousands of fortune seekers from Europe, America and China. Gold fever swept the country: it was the greatest gold-rush the world had ever seen.

But in time the alluvial gold ran out. Once the big company mines had been established, thousands of diggers left the goldfields and made Melbourne their home. The population more than

Left, Malcolm Fraser is one of the city's best-known citizens.

quadrupled in 10 years and the gold revenue supplied the capital to pay for the new development in a rapidly expanding city determined to grow with a grand style.

When American novelist Mark Twain visited Melbourne on a lecture tour in 1895 he was entranced by what he saw: *It is a stately city architecturally as well as in magnitude. It has an elaborate system of cable-car service; it has museums, and colleges, and schools, and public gardens, and electricity, and gas, and libraries, and theatres, and mining centres and wool centres, and centres of the arts and sciences, and boards of trade, and ships, and railroads, and a harbor, and social clubs, and journalistic clubs and racing clubs, and a squatter club sumptuously housed and appointed, and as many churches and banks as can make a living. In a word, it is equipped with everything that goes to make the modern great city.*

## A Cosmopolitan Centre

One hundred years later the Melbourne of the 1980s is no longer the largest city in the country but it is the fastest growing, and with a sizable migrant population from Europe and Asia, it is cosmopolitan and colourful.

Melbourne is not one of those spectacular, assertive cities that confronts the visitor with its visual impact or its energy. It is not a New York or a Hong Kong or a Rome. It is not even a Sydney, whose spectacular harbour setting is quite overwhelming. Rather, it insinuates itself into your subconscious, and visitors invariably find it an agreeable place with a magnetic attraction distinctly its own.

Melbourne nestles comfortably on the banks of the **Yarra River** close to where it enters Port Phillip Bay. It is a city of almost 3 million people, most of them living in the suburban sprawl that fans out from the bay towards the Dandenong Hills. The old inner city suburbs include many of the original 19th Century two-storey terrace houses with their distinctive and decorative cast-iron balconies.

Melbourne's **Toorak** is Australia's finest and richest suburb—an enclave of mansions set in imposing gardens bordered by streets lined with large

The Yarra River.

European trees. It is an elite suburb where, according to one wit, they even gift-wrap their rubbish.

Some Melburnians like to live closer to the bush and commute to the city. In the **Eltham** area, some 30 kilometres (19 miles) out of town on the upper reaches of the Yarra River, these people have built homes using natural materials and design influences of the old squatter homesteads. Mud-brick walls and slate floors, heavy wood and beams, wide all-round verandahs to ward off the sun and large landscaped gardens of gum trees and native plants have created some of the most attractive and uniquely Australian homes in the country.

Back in town the ornate old bridges that span the Yarra, and the precisely coordinated movements of the rowing eights which train in the shadow of the skyscrapers, lend a special graciousness to a city that has all the architectural dynamics of a modern capital, but still retains those vestiges of the past that remind one of its heritage.

Melbourne is laid out on a convenient grid system that makes it easy to find your way around. In Collins Street and Bourke Street, amongst the soaring office towers of glass and steel, you can find some fine examples of late 19th Century and early 20th Century buildings. The banking chamber of the CBA (Commonwealth Banking Association) bank at 335 Collins St. is a masterpiece of baroque imagination. Other nearby buildings not to be missed are the gothic-styled ANZ (Australia-New Zealand) Bank, the **Rialto Building**, and **St. Paul's Cathedral** on the corner of Swanston and Flinders streets. At the other end of town on Spring Street, the stately **Windsor Hotel**, which has been restored to its 19th-Century opulence, is worth a good look, as are the **Princess Theatre** and the **Victorian Houses of Parliament**, which have guided tours.

Melbourne is the only city in Australia that still has trams, both the old kind and the very modern. A tram ride down St. Kilda Road is mandatory for the visitor who really wants to get the feel of the town. If your timing is good you may ride in one of the 12 old trams which have been completely decorated by some of the city's best known artists. Riding inside a mobile canvas is a novel arts experiment.

Melbourne has 1,700 acres of landscaped parks and gardens that surround the city proper and encroach on its boundaries. These havens are one of the great joys of Melbourne. The **Treasury Gardens**, with avenues of giant trees, extensive lawns and rock pools, almost reach into the central city at the top end of Collins Street. At lunchtime on warm days the lawns are dotted with sunbaking office workers while sweat-glistening joggers stride its paths.

During summer these gardens are also the main site of FEIP ("Free Entertainment in the Parks"), an imaginative and varied programme produced by the Melbourne City Council.

The **Fitzroy Gardens** are an extension of the Treasury Gardens, and the location of **Captain Cook's Cottage**, the home of the great mariner who put Australia on the map. It was brought to Melbourne piece by piece from its original site in Yorkshire.

But Melbourne's supreme park, and surely one of the finest in the world, is the **Royal Botanic Gardens**. Fifteen minutes by tram from downtown, these undulating gardens beside the Yarra River offer a tranquil breathing space where visitors can get lost in fern grottoes and cactus gardens, watch black swans cruise regally over the lake as they picnic on its banks, or explore its 88 acres of green lawns and thousands of native and exotic plants. On weekends you'll find a great potpourri of Melburnians doing their thing in the Botanic Gardens. Greek families with mountains of food and bazouki music, promenading lovers, nature freaks, sunbakers, elderly couples reliving their youth, martial arts experts practising their movements, and kids allowing their adventurous spirits to run free.

A five-km (three-mile) course around the gardens is Melbourne's most popular and picturesque jogging track. On the nearby banks of the Yarra coin-in-the-slot gas barbecues attract crowds of leisure seekers, often after work, who cook chops, steaks and sausages, and wash it all down with beer.

Popular Bayside beaches close to the city are **St. Kilda**, **South Melbourne**, **Middle Park** and **Albert Park**. While strip shows are popular at several of Melbourne's R-rated movie houses and some suburban hotels, you will find a good deal more flesh exposed on a hot day at these latter two beaches each of which is a well-known rendezvous for

local trendies.

## Shopping in the Melting Pot

The beaches of Melbourne are great communal melting pots but no more so than several key shopping streets in near-city suburbs, each with its own personality and energy. Lygon Street in **Carlton**, just 10 minutes by tram from the city centre, is sometimes known as Little Italy. It was this area that the waves of post-World-War-II Italian migrants adopted as their own. Today a lively community of Italians, professional people, actors and entertainers, and students from adjacent **Melbourne University** give it a vibe all its own. Espresso coffee bars, bistros, trattorias, noisy pubs and pool rooms contribute to a lively atmosphere.

Toorak Road, which is also serviced by trams, runs through the suburbs of **South Yarra** and Toorak. Here affluence is the common denominator. Fashionable boutiques, bookshops, restaurants and beauty salons beckon to rich young mums and well-heeled secretaries. Shiny European sports cars and the occasional Rolls Royce cruise with panache. If you're into image, Toorak Road is where it pays to be seen.

At its South Yarra end, Toorak Road is bisected by Chapel Street, The Kings Road of Melbourne. A bustling shopping street that accommodates everything from the avant-garde to the mundane, it's a real resource centre for the many ethnic communities (particularly Greeks) and flat dwellers living in the **Prahran** area. It also gives access to Prahran Market, one of Melbourne's great Saturday morning experiences if you respond to exotic foods and equally interesting people. **The Jam Factory**, a complex of classy shops and restaurants, deserves special mention; so does Greville Street, a small funky street of antique bookshops and fashions of the new wave and second-hand variety. Prahran High Street runs off Chapel Street. If you travel east you will venture into a wonderful world of antique shops and markets that bulge with all kinds of treasures.

For a wander down a tawdry street of surprises, try Brunswick Street in **Fitzroy**, adjacent to the city and north. Wine bars, ethnic cuisines, artists' cafes of the type popular in the Fifties and

Left, Young and Jackson pub painting. Right, window fashion.

Sixties, clothing from the same periods, lesbians and confused looking characters who look like they escaped from a Camus novel ... it can be a most revealing excursion.

Some will tell you that Sundays in Melbourne are dull. Not true. They are the ones who've watched "World of Sport" on television for years and let Sunday pass them by. Ackland Street, **St. Kilda**, is a busy Sunday shopping centre the Jewish community have made their own. It is famous for its cafes and cake shops: the palate-pleasing influences of Vienna and Warsaw, Budapest, Prague and Tel Aviv are everywhere. Men in hats stand in little groups on the footpath and debate with restrained passion. Families crowd into the cafes and plump women amble home with boxes of creamy delights. Go there for brunch but don't expect to hear a lot of English spoken.

Once you've eaten, walk towards the beach, past adult bookshops and **Lura Park**'s clattering roller coaster and onto the **Upper Esplanade** to the Sunday arts-and-crafts market. Here stall holders will offer you all manner of jewellery, leatherware, paintings, ceramic and glass work.

Melbourne likes its Sunday markets. The biggest is **Victoria Market** in West Melbourne, right on the edge of the city proper. On Tuesday, Friday and Saturday mornings it is essentially a food market—a sprawling collection of fruit and vegetable stalls that seem to go on forever. But on Sundays the food is replaced by purveyors of every imaginable item and shopping becomes even more of an adventure. For a flea market of decidedly bohemian bent, don't miss the one at **Camberwell Junction**.

About 50 km (31 miles) east of Melbourne, the **Dandenong Ranges**—sometimes known as the "Blue Dandenongs"—lift their seductive skirts of fern gullies and art galleries to attract the attention of Melbourne residents and visitors alike. Small towns like Belgrave and Olinda are lovely destinations for day trips, and attractions like the **William Ricketts Sanctuary** (where Aboriginal spirit figures have been carved from wood in a forest setting by an elderly white sculptor) and **Puffing Billy** (a narrow-gauge steam railroad which plies a track from Belgrave to Menzies Creek) are worthwhile stops. From the

urke
eet Tram.

restaurant and television towers atop **Mount Dandenong**, 633 meters (2,077 feet), there is a glorious view across Melbourne.

## Footy Fever and The Cup

In winter a strange malaise infects the people of Melbourne. They call it "footy fever." Football Australian-style was invented in Melbourne way back in 1858. It has been an obsession ever since. It invades the very soul of the city, infiltrates every bar conversation. It was once suggested that Melbourne has no summer, only a period of hibernation between football seasons. Don't fight it. Give in and join the very vocal crowds at a Victorian Football League Saturday match at the **MCG Stadium**. It's a fast, violent, skillful, spectacular and unique style of football.

The game is mainly played in the southern states. In Melbourne, the spiritual home of Australian football, the Grand Final match to decide the premier team of the year is played at the MCG before 100,000 screaming, beer-drinking fans.

The only day of the year to rival football's Grand Final day is the first Tuesday in November when the famous Melbourne Cup horse race is held. It is a remarkable event—not only because it is a handicap race which has been won by colts and seven-year-olds alike, not only because it is one of the great social occasions of the year, but especially because of the way it brings a whole nation to a standstill.

At 2.40 p.m. on this traditional Tuesday, Australia waits with bated breath. Office girls produce transistor radios from their filing cabinets, schoolboys surreptitiously palm earplugs into place, and motorists pull over to the kerbside where pedestrians crowd around and listen to the car radios. In Canberra politicians take a break from their heady debating and on the docks the wharfies down their baling hooks. In Victoria the whole state takes an official holiday!

Almost everyone has a bet on The Cup. It's estimated that over $30 million is wagered on the race. Its fate is decided in three minutes as the horses strain around the 3,200-metre course at **Flemington Racetrack**. But the Melbourne Cup is more than just a horse

Port Philip Bay

race. It is also the year's biggest social carnival and draws more than 30,000 visitors from overseas and interstate. Special trains and planes are scheduled to cope with the influx and cruise ships make Melbourne their destination.

The Melbourne Cup has always been ritual. Privileged people reserve favoured positions in the Members' Car Park where they enjoy the traditional chicken and champagne picnic luncheon from the boots of their cars.

The bonhomie lasts all day and rolls across Flemington in a way that transcends the usual social barriers.

### Festivals and Fun

The other big annual event for Melburnians is Moomba, a 30-year-old festival in the Mardi Gras spirit held during the first two weeks in March. Moomba is an Aboriginal word which means "let's get together and have fun." Over 200 planned activities and events keep the energy level high. The world's best waterskiers slice up the normally benign Yarra River; a showboat offers free cabaret and jazz. There's a multi-cultural wine and food festival, dancing in the streets and, at the **Alexandra Gardens** beside the Yarra, there are carnival games, rides for thrill seekers and music to cater to every taste. It all culminates in a grand procession of floats through the city.

Melbourne pubs are legion. Many of them have good, reasonably priced bistros and, of course, offer the internationally acclaimed Foster's Lager.

Many pubs are also venues for innovative live rock music—Men at Work, Little River Band and Air Supply all cut their teeth on the Melbourne pub circuit before topping the charts. Check out The Grain Store, The Prospect Hill, The Venue, The Club, Central Club Hotel, Council Club Hotel and Billboard.

If you are a mover and a shaker, the city's top discos are worth a visit too— The Melbourne Underground is a celebrity rendezvous, Inflation caters to the outrageous, Madison's is for upmarket over-25s, and Sheik's and Chaser's are for young narcissistics.

The curious and energetic will find Melbourne a city for all seasons—a bit like its bizarre weather which can offer a taste of all four seasons in one day.

e
ndenongs.

# BRISBANE: A COUNTRY SPIRIT

Australia's third largest city spreads its million inhabitants so effectively over a series of low hills that at times it's easy to forget Brisbane is really situated on a river.

If Brisbane were spread on a plain, the sheer size of its urban sprawl might deprive it of all character. But the intimacy offered by the hills gives a sizable city the feel of a large country town. For these reasons it does not have that "city-by-a-river" image of Hobart or Perth.

Brisbane's reluctant progress into the 20th Century is due in no small measure to the fact that it is still not quite a real city. Technically, it's a city—a city with the largest area (1,220 square kilometres; 471 sq miles) of any metropolis in the country—but in spirit Brisbane remains the world's biggest country town.

It has a country heart and traces of country morality. It is a rich city, but still raw, still suspicious of outsiders.

Conversely, it is as hospitable a place as you are likely to encounter. Brisbane is capital of a state assertive in its economic and developmental drive yet locked in a time-freeze of social and political conservatism. Joh Bjelke-Petersen, has been the premier of Queensland for so long that the city is often called "Johburg" and Bjelke-Petersen's tenure "Status Joh."

## Bay to Mountains

There is little sense of being within 10 minutes of a major city. Within half-an-hour at most, Brisbane folk can reach the varied beaches of **Moreton Bay**, downstream via the **Brisbane River**. It gives access to the bay itself and numerous unpopulated islands that make this vast quasi-inland sea a fishing and sailing paradise.

To the west, rainforest-cloaked mountains shelter the city and offer a bewildering choice of picnic spots, bush walks and wilderness area—all within 30 minutes of Brisbane's centre.

Almost half of Queensland's population lives within Brisbane's greater metropolitan area. Locals find it ironic that

ft, sunrise Brisbane.

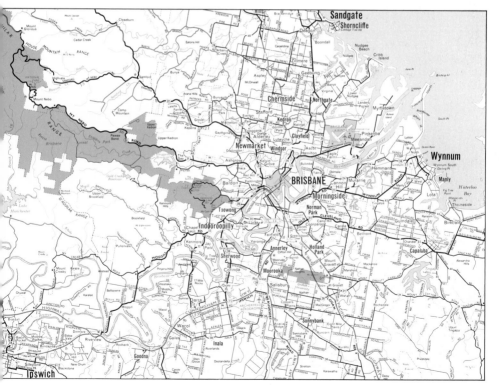

such an easy-going city should have emerged from such nightmarish beginnings as a barbarous penal settlement for "the worst class of offenders."

On July 22, 1824, Sir Thomas Brisbane (then Governor of New South Wales) was notified that approval had been granted to form a convict settlement "at the new river discovered by Mr. Oxley." (NSW Surveyor General John Oxley had, the previous year, named the river after Sir Thomas.) In September 1824, a detachment of the 40th Regiment and the first party of unfortunate convicts arrived from Sydney in the south.

Thus began 15 years of living hell for those convicts deemed troublesome enough to warrant a stint in Brisbane. Many died, victims of the tyrannies of the guards, disease and a justifiable indifference toward prolonging their wretched lives.

The actual penal settlement shifted location several times. Records indicate it was at its bloodthirsty worst when it moved to St. Helena Island in Moreton Bay. Here, with no escape save into the shark-infested waters, the prisoners left their own tragic mark on history in the form of scores of headstones.

While modern Brisbane displays just a few scars and reminders of those days, it is hardly fair to say the pace of progress has overhauled the city's history. For better or worse, the real impact of bricks and mortar development in southeast Queensland has been felt most in the resort locations of the Gold Coast and Surfers Paradise. Most Brisbane dwellers are not unhappy with that turn of events, preferring to lead their relaxed lives, moving between their wooden dwellings on stilts (to maximise the circulation of cooling air) and the pub or workplace, with the leisurely pace usually associated with country dwellers.

### Parks and Bridges

It is still a city of open space. The **Botanic Gardens** is but one of the many riverside parks, and sites like **King George Square** (adjacent to the imposing sandstone **City Hall**) are a restful spot for city workers at lunchtime and for shoppers.

The old residential area of **Spring Hill** defies Queensland's development-

The city, early evening.

120

mindedness with its maze of early homes. Since it was raised in 1889 the spire of nearby **St. Paul's Presbyterian Church** has been a Brisbane landmark. In the past 20 years newer office blocks have begun to dominate the city skyline, but Brisbane retains architectural characteristics that will always be associated with the Queensland capital. Lovers of architectural history acclaim the **Treasury Building** as the finest example of Italian Renaissance in the Southern Hemisphere. And there will always be the bridges. They span the river, forming a link with the city's centre. The **William Jolly Bridge** was the first built; named after the first mayor of Brisbane, it was opened in 1930. The **Story Bridge** is probably the most famous and photographed while the **Victoria** and **Captain Cook** bridges were completed later in 1970 and 1972 respectively.

In the midst of this mood of apparent rural somnolence it's almost surprising to find a campus as vital and thriving as that of the **University of Queensland**. When the university was founded in 1909 it was seen as a city-based institution. But by 1939 it had so outgrown its cramped confines that the decision was made to relocate to **St. Lucia**. Almost surrounded by the river as it arcs radically, the campus is an expanse of spacious parkland, fine sandstone buildings, sheltered walkways (called The Cloisters) and sculptures. With almost 20,000 students enrolled, it is the second largest university in Australia.

One building which has not changed its location since its foundation in 1865 is **Parliament House**. Twenty-four years of sporadic building saw the work to completion, much to the frustration of architect Charles Tiffin, who had won a nationwide contest with his design based on French Renaissance lines. It's here that Bjelke-Petersen, the most flamboyant and controversial premier in modern Australian politics, presides over a special brand of Queensland conservatism as decreed by his National Party. It's a style that confounds southerners but Queenslanders find it agreeable enough to keep voting for it.

### Subtropical Strolls

Brisbane's subtropical setting is something that cannot be ignored: it

dictates so much about the pace, taste and lifestyle of all the city's dwellers. From city business executives seen strolling out to lunch attired in their summer dress of short-sleeved business shirt, shorts and long socks, to a party of revellers out for a moonlight river cruise on a warm summer's night, Brisbane is a city delightfully in the grip of its climate. In spring, the air in the city's 50 square km (19 sq miles) of parks, gardens and recreation areas is fragrant with the scent of subtropical flora. In addition to the Botanic Gardens, there is **New Farm Park**, with its plethora of jacarandas, rose bushes and poinciana trees. Just eight km (five miles) from the city centre is **Mt. Coot-tha Botanic Gardens**: spread over 141 acres (57 hectares) at the base of a mountain, the reserve is a haven of ponds and parkland where thousands of plant species thrive.

For regular visitors, Brisbane will always confuse by its contrasts. While progress-conscious city fathers point to the glass and steel might of the new tower blocks, artists can be seen capturing in oils the 1889 splendour of one of the city's oldest pubs, the **Breakfast Creek Hotel**.

Beneath the city's streets operates a metro underground rail system. And it comes as another surprise to learn that Brisbane was the first capital city in Australia to develop such a system, more than 60 years ago. Dwellers of other Australian capitals (and not a few overseas visitors) were amazed when Brisbane won permission to stage the 1982 Commonwealth Games. That the Games were held in an era fraught with the involvement of politics and cynicism in sport, but still managed to be conducted without a major hitch, was ample testimony to the organising skills and hospitality of Brisbane's people and administrators.

While southerners regularly drop in to holiday, observe and often poke fun at the seemingly endless eccentricities of this large country town, Brisbane folk claim criticism is something best left to those who actually live there. Yes, they'll freely admit shops close when you need them most and bureaucratic interference still runs high. They'll even agree dress restrictions for bars and clubs are a bit hard to follow, and perhaps those vast expanses of wooden

Cultural Centre.

suburbia could do with a coat of paint. But who cares? In this domain where the "hot sun has me in its will," the mañana spirit is alive and dozing on almost every rickety verandah.

It was Brisbane's own realisation that, after decades of chopping, poisoning and generally ridding the suburbs of all their trees, these strange green objects were not necessarily guilty of anything other than providing shade, oxygen and occasionally blocking up the odd sewerage pipe. So, in the last few years trees have staged a minor revival in the once barren suburbs.

### Burgeoning Cafe Society

Another saner development has been the relaxing of laws that forbade restauranteurs and cafe owners to set up tables for sidewalk trade. Now Brisbane diners can take advantage of their cosmopolitan lifestyle and do what they enjoy most—consume fine tucker out in the comfort of their subtropical climate. As material proof to these minor revolutions, Brisbane's Commonwealth Games preparations included the conversion of half the length of the city's main street—Queen Street—into a pedestrian mall with trees and sidewalk cafes.

It's this image of a city casually, and often clumsily, coming to grips with the allure of sophistication that can make Brisbane a confounding or compelling proposition. It has an elusive mystique that is completely lost on some visitors, but can just as eaily persuade ambitious business executives, optimistic young families, highly rewarded sportsmen or jaded tycoons to pause, sample and stay.

The women are brown and charming, while the men—according to statistics—have the highest level of obesity in Australia. While brown and charming men take advantage of this imbalance, fat blokes take solace in the food: giant mud crabs, just-ripe avocadoes, mangoes, barramundi, coral trout, oysters and other tropical delights. It is food to be consumed leisurely on the unpainted verandah, to be washed down perhaps with several bottles of good white wine, while the sun sinks behind Mt. Glorious and parrots say raucous goodnights at the foot of the garden.

bathing
eauty.

# ADELAIDE: THE FESTIVAL CITY

Mark Twain was one of the first tourists to pronounce himself thoroughly captivated by Adelaide during his Australian visit in 1895.

He praised its orderly layout, graceful parklands, the distinctive bluestone architecture and wide, tree-lined streets. He further declared that "if the rest of Australia or any small part were half so beautiful it was a fortunate country."

What a pity there was no enterprising civic official around at the time to arrange for the author of *Tom Sawyer* to take a cruise on a Murray River paddle steamer and give Adelaide one of the greatest tourist plugs of all time. Perhaps the idea did crop up but was dismissed for its vulgarity. Adelaide has never been a city to indulge the reckless impulse.

Situated on the southern rim of continental Australia, roughly one-third of the way from Sydney to Perth, Adelaide is ideally placed to ignore the rest of the world—which it does quite happily.

Adelaide epitomises small "C" conservatism. Indeed, there is a certain implacable smugness about Adelaide people, who are quite convinced they occupy one of the last truly civilised corners of the world. By letting the world pass it by, Adelaide has avoided the worst excesses of social upheaval, pollution, urban blight, street crime and traffic jams.

For the visitor Adelaide is to be savoured slowly. It is possible to rock around the clock in Adelaide, if you know where to go, but it can be done easier and better elsewhere. To get the most out of Adelaide you should shift down a gear or two, move at a leisurely pace and meet it on its own terms, which isn't hard. Adelaide has a way of seducing visitors.

## Lopsided Elegance

The first impression one gets is the prettiness of the city. This isn't an accident of nature. Adelaide was laid out in a choice location according to the grand design of a British Army engineer named Colonel William Light, who founded the city in 1836. It sits on a coastal plain with the Gulf of St. Vincent on the west and the Adelaide Hills, part of the Mount Lofty Ranges, on the east.

From the air the original city resembles a lopsided figure eight, with residential North Adelaide on one side and the central business district on the other. The two halves are connected by King William Street, at 42 metres (138 feet) wide the broadest main street of any capital city in Australia.

North Adelaide is the location of some of the grandest homes in Australia. It was intended as an exclusive enclave for the transplanted English gentry, some of whom shipped out grand pianos to put in their colonial salons.

The central business district measures exactly one imperial square mile. It is surrounded by extensive parklands studded with majestic gum trees which act as a scenic buffer between the city centre and the suburbs. The parklands are big enough to accommodate several playing fields, riding paths, gardens and picnic sites for lunching office workers. This green belt means it is impossible to go in and out of the city without passing

eft, North
errace.
ight,
cclesiastical
onework.

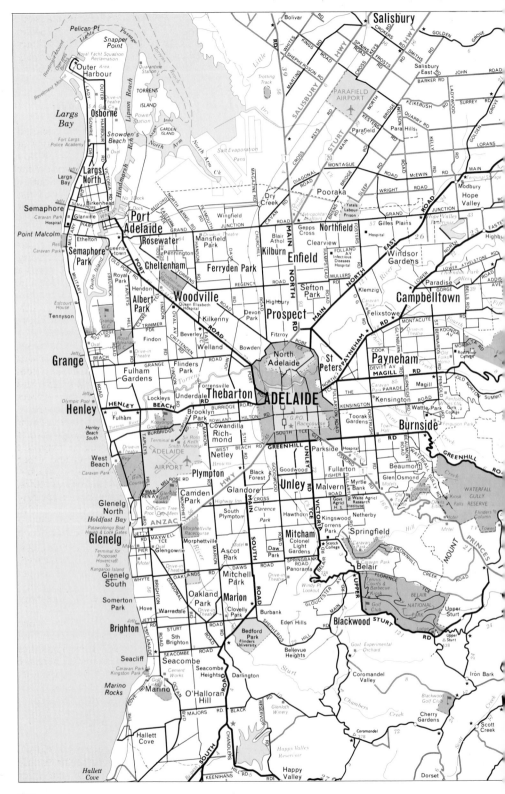

through restful greenery.

The main intersection in Adelaide is where North Terrace crosses King William Street. Every major attraction in the city is within a few minutes' walking distance of this intersection. The Festival Centre, Parliament House, the railway station with its unique marble hall used for the Cairo hotel scene in the film *Gallipoli* (and soon to be part of a casino complex), Rundle Mall, the art gallery, the museum and Ayers House are within easy reach.

## The Festival Centre

**The Festival Centre** boasts better acoustics than the Sydney Opera House. With its concert hall, playhouse, space theatre, outdoor amphitheatre, bistro and restaurant, it is home to the biggest arts festival in Australia—held every even-numbered year. The Centre overlooks the River Torrens which winds through the parklands. Visitors can choose to take a two-person pedal boat out on the river or ride in the launch *Popeye* with a guide to provide a running commentary.

Facing the Festival Centre from the other side of the Torrens is the most beautiful cricket ground in Australia, well worth a visit should you be there during the cricket season. Back on North Terrace, **Parliament House** is a monumental building, open to visitors. Just across the intersection, on the eastern side of King William Street is the governor's residence which, remarkably, is not open to visitors.

The eastern wing of North Terrace is easily the most impressive walk in the city centre. The **University of Adelaide** is here, and the art gallery and museum could have been transplanted from Oxford, ivy-covered walls, dreaming spires and all. The South Australian Museum houses the world's largest collection of Aboriginal artefacts, as well as an extensive Melanesian exhibit and a broad survey of regional natural history. The Art Gallery of South Australia has a renowned collection of 20,000 prints and drawings by hundreds of artists, many of them early European painters.

**Ayers House** can be found on this part of North Terrace. The home of Henry Ayers, who contrived to be premier of South Australia seven times (an Australian record), it is now a restaurant and living museum protected by the National Trust. An elegant bluestone mansion, it contains 40 rooms dating from 1846 to the 1870s. The hand-painted ceilings and ornate chandeliers of the dining-room and ballroom are particularly remarkable.

## 'Athens of the South'

**Rundle Mall** was the first enclosed shopping mall in Australia, an idea of former South Australian Premier Don Dunstan, who had a 1970s vision for Adelaide as "The Athens of the South."

It was Dunstan who originated the Festival Centre. He was also responsible for introducing some of the most progressive state laws in the Commonwealth of Australia, laws to protect consumers, to guarantee equal opportunity and freedom of information. Don was a bit of a shock to staid old Adelaide and remains a controversial figure to this day. The mall is his only legacy which *everyone* agrees was a wonderful idea.

A cobble-stoned shopper's paradise, Rundle Mall is dedicated to pedestrians who can mill about as they like, from shop to shop, enjoying restaurants and outdoor cafes or the buskers—street musicians, mimes and entertainers.

One of the joys of Adelaide is wandering down arrow-straight streets which temporarily surrender character to garages, car showrooms and office blocks, only to blossom out again farther on into a mini-village of cafes, antique shops, art galleries and clothing stores. If you're mobile you can drive along Unley Road or King William Street for a couple of kilometres, you'll pass several of these mini-villages clustered like leaves on the branch of a tree.

Adelaide has more restaurants per capita than any other Australian city, everything from the finest silver service to Lebanese take-aways. There is a United Nations of restaurants along Hindley Street, Adelaide's modest "hot spot." Squeezed next to the handful of strip clubs and singles joints there are Indian, Chinese, Italian, Japanese, Greek, Lebanese, Vietnamese, Russian, even Australian eateries.

## Hills and Beaches

Even though it is home to 950,000 people, Adelaide never seems to lose that country feeling. You can drive across the entire city in about half an hour; and you can be in beautiful countryside in very few minutes from any point within the city. Take any one of a dozen roads up into the **Adelaide Hills** and you can easily get lost in the leafy, winding laneways. The hills are littered with small commuter suburbs like **Blackwood**, **Aldgate** and **Crafers**, some of them strikingly pretty. There are pubs with hilltop views and restaurants like **Windy Point** where you can see the entire city laid out like a page from a fairy tale.

The pubs and restaurants of the Adelaide Hills make Adelaide just as pleasant to visit in the winter as in the summer. Indeed, there's a great deal of sense in the view that winter is the best time. The South Australian summers can scorch the hills a painful brown and there are weeks when temperatures hit an unbearable 40°C (104°F). In winter the hills are lush and green; there are plenty of conservation trails to walk with hotels at their end, where a roaring open fire and a soothing glass of port wait.

One of the Adelaide rituals is to take the **Glenelg** tram from the city centre. Glenelg is the city beach and the tram takes about 20 minutes to make the trip. While Glenelg has seen better times and is starting to look decidedly seedy, the beach is wide, white and wonderful. If it's a shade too crowded for your liking, all you have to do is stroll down a bit further; it goes for miles. Coming back, eat your fish and chips on the tram and wash the meal down with a bottle of locally produced Seaview champagne, the proletarian's picnic. The whole day would cost $20: fares, fish and chips, champagne and all.

If you prefer your fish and chips served a touch more elaborately, go to the **HMS Buffalo**, an exact replica of the ship which brought the first settlers from England to South Australia. You can dine in the main cabin off genuine pewter tableware and drink from pewter tankards. The Buffalo serves everything from calamari to crab, cray tails to whiting.

On the subject of South Australian seafood you should try the King George whiting, a fish exclusive to the cool waters of South Australia and known for its delicate, white meat. Gourmets prefer it to lobster (what the locals call cray); recently it has become more expensive, retailing at the market for $16 to $20 a kilogram.

Adelaide's **Central Market** is just out the back door of the Hilton Hotel and is easily one of the most colourful and comprehensive markets in Australia. A giant covered area packed with stalls, it sells cheap fruit, vegetables, cheeses, meats, spices and myriad esoteric imported foods. For $10 you can buy more than you can carry. Overseas visitors invariably find the market butchers an entertainment in their own right. They're all in the same row and each shop has a man out front, often in a blue-and-white-striped apron and with a voice like a cannon, auctioning off meat, cutting prices, offering deals on sides of lambs and meat trays piled with roasts and chops.

### For Oenophiles Only

Adelaide sits amidst one of the greatest wine regions in Australia. The Barossa Valley, to the north, is only half an hour's drive away. McLaren Vale, to the south, is about the same; Coonawarra, en route to Mount Gambier in the state's southeastern corner,

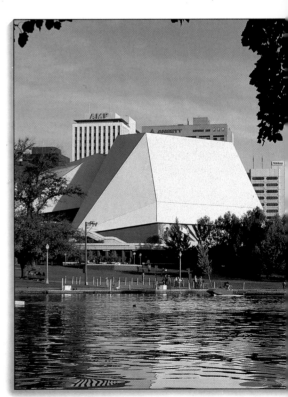

Festival Centre and Torrens River.

is about four hours' drive. Wine fanatics travel from Europe, Canada and the United States simply for the pleasure of drinking themselves silly.

**Coonawarra** is a fluke in the earth's crust, a strip of rich red soil about two kilometres wide and nine kilometres long, which produces premium Shiraz Cabernet grapes. Some say the rich red wines of Coonawarra rival the best reds of France and are only a fraction of the cost. While visiting Coonawarra, stay a night or two at the **Padthaway Homestead**, a rather exclusive and expensive guesthouse in the grand colonial style, but worth every penny.

The **Barossa Valley** holds its own wine festival, alternating every two years with the Festival of Arts. The easiest way to remember what is happening when is that the arts festival takes place on even-numbered years, the Barossa festival on odd-numbered years. The Barossa festival is a sprawling, boozy affair in which whole towns relinquish themselves to the grip of the grape. Main streets are closed to traffic in favour of parades, parties and picnics, all lubricated by rivers of cheap but excellent wine.

The winemakers of **McLaren Vale** have their own festival each November, called Bushing, which isn't quite as frenetic as the Barossa but manages to be just as hedonistic. McLaren Vale winemakers are often called "boutique" winemakers because they are small, independent operators and run their businesses from quaint, brick and timber rural properties.

Adelaide's coastal border is fringed by endless ribbons of white sandy beaches. If you're the sensual type, drive down Main South Road for about 20 kilometres (12½ miles) until you see the turnoff on the right to **Maslin's Beach**. (The turnoff to the left at that interseciton leads to McLaren Vale.) Maslin's is an official nude beach, one of the best in the state. It's a friendly, family-oriented beach, but be warned, the gulf waters are fed by the Southern Ocean and the water can be brisk.

After a morning of surf and sun, it's a short drive inland direct to McLaren Vale, where you can drop in at any of the 30 or so wineries, visit with the locals, taste the wines and buy a few bottles. They make everything from reds to sparkling whites, robust ports and even mead. You will also discover that most of these "boutique" winemakers suffer from an advanced case of character.

If you want a nourishing base for the booze, go to **The Barn** in McLaren Vale where the food is wholesome country fare, the bread is hot and fresh, and draft champagne, by the jug, is served straight from the tap.

Another spot worth visiting is the **Old Clarendon Winery** between McLaren Vale and Adelaide. It's an upmarket restaurant and winery complex with an art gallery displaying the work of local artists, especially David Dridan, one of South Australia's most celebrated painters. His work hangs in the National Gallery in Canberra; HRH The Duke of Edinburgh is known to own a couple of Dridan's works. The artist himself is a bit of a lad. If he's there when you visit, he can probably be persuaded to share a glass of wine or two and impart some of the unlikely stories behind his paintings. If the long and winding road is too much after a day of such unrestrained hedonism, don't worry: there are rooms and cabins available at pretty reasonable rates for overnighters and over-indulgers.

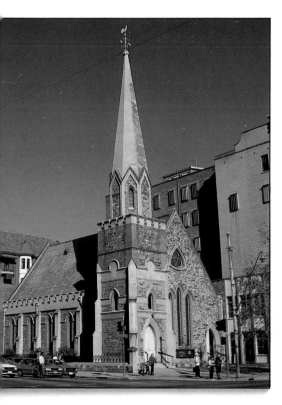

ulteney
treet.

# PERTH: THE WEST'S 'CITY OF LIGHT'

Set on the continent's west coast like a strategic counterweight to the heavily populated eastern cities, Perth is the new symbol of Australian confidence.

This pleasant city by the Swan River is the home base for international tycoons Robert Holmes Court and Alan Bond, two principals in the promotion of Australia as a vibrant, investment-worthy business community. Bond's drive in planning, coordinating and financing *Australia II's* successful America's Cup challenge, illustrated better than anything the assertiveness of the nation's "new frontier" city.

In 1983 government statisticians thought it likely that Perth's growing population had already outstripped that of Adelaide. With today's population hovering near the 1 million mark, the city has been the target not only for ambitious migrants from overseas, but also for eager settlers from the eastern states keen to make a new life in Western Australia. So much of the state's wealth is based upon mineral exploitation, that Perth has become like one giant assay office serving the needs of a miner's paradise.

Critics of Perth's new expansion are concerned that the city's social development caters too greatly to those involved in mining or technical professions. While there is an element of truth in this observation, Perth's defenders say the city's apparent affluence will guarantee that all good things come to those who strive: for Perth, perhaps more than any other Australian city, is an achiever's town.

## The French 'Threat'

Back in 1827, it wasn't a "go West, young man" spirit of fortune that motivated Captain James Stirling to explore the **Swan River** as a potential site for white settlement. He was sent by his British superiors because the London Colonial Office believed the French were contemplating settling the continent's western shores in response to the British presence in New South Wales.

Stirling's reports were so rapturous that in 1829 the first white settlers

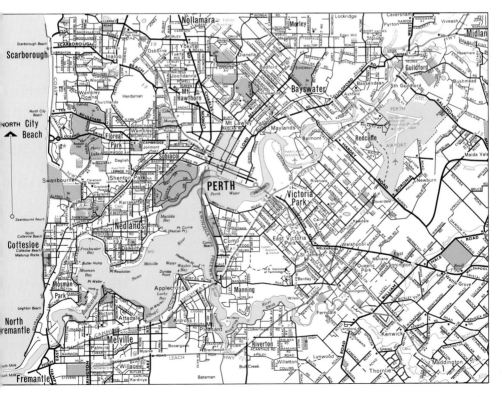

arrived to set up shop on a site Stirling had spotted 16 kilometres (10 miles) upstream from where the Swan emptied into the Indian Ocean. Amid the black swans that gave the river its name, a colony of some 300 residents developed. While the small township grew along modest lines, it was already proving a bonus for Captain Stirling. He was appointed first Lieutenant-Governor and later Governor. He was enterprising and popular and ended up being knighted for his services.

Inducing other colonists to head west, or persuading new settlers to choose Perth over the better-established colonies, was no easy matter in view of the outpost's isolation. By 1858, when the city council of Perth was founded, the population was barely 3,000. But gold fixed all that. When news of the great finds of the 1890s at fields to the east reached the outside world, Perth became the leaping-off point for the gold-rush. The population rocketed to 30,000 soon after the turn of the century and has been climbing steadily ever since.

Once the new arrivals got over the novelty of mineral wealth, they came to appreciate the area for many of the reasons today's inhabitants cherish the city.

Perth is blessed with an enviable climate. The vegetation is exotic and the natural setting conducive to attractive planning. The city's governing view is one over **Perth Water** where the Swan widens into a broad bay about a kilometre across. The river continues to widen as it nears the ocean; many people have taken advantage of the aquatic blessing by building attractive houses on the shoreline. Looking down this blue expanse with its many sailing and leisure craft, it's easy to see what sort of progression led Alan Bond halfway around the world to bring the America's Cup back to the **Royal Perth Yacht Club**.

Fringing the river mouth are some fine surfing beaches, completing the impression of a city basking in a kind climate and naturally provided with the amenities to make the most of it.

### Parks and Offices

The city centre is well-planned and gracious while provision has been made for plenty of open space in the suburbs.

View of Per from King's Garden.

More than 1,000 square kilometres (about 400 square miles) of parks, reserves and sports grounds point to the town planners' commitment to providing leisure room for Perth's burgeoning populace. On the edge of the city centre is **King's Park**, a 400-hectare (988-acre) reserve of botanic gardens and bushland that displays not only some of West Australia's natural flora but also plants from other lands with climates similar to that of Perth.

The mining boom of the past 20 years has seen many large multinational and West Australia-based companies build office blocks in Perth. Their erection has dramatically changed the city skyline causing older residents to complain that the city has lost its intimate country-town feel. But a town with the assertiveness of the W.A. Capital could hardly be expected to play anything but a front-line role in the fabric of the Australian urban lifestyle.

From the campuses of the **University of Western Australia** and **Murdoch University** came many people who were to shape the nation's history and help alter its social tone. Of late, the city's importance as a proving ground for all sorts of

endeavours has become evident. Prime Minister Bob Hawke, hard-headed politician and former State Premier Charles Court, mining magnate Lang Hancock, New York finance editor Max Newton, humorist Ron Saw and the former Speaker in the Australian Parliament, Sir Billy Snedden, have all, at different times, called Perth home.

Despite its reputation as a developer's town, Perth was the first capital to see a free university. It pioneered arts festivals and at one time seemed so isolated in its libertarian views it tried to persuade the rest of the state that a move to secede from Australia would be wise. The move went little farther, but to this day, whenever Perth feels the rest of the nation isn't in accord with W.A., the old secessionist slogans are usually trotted out.

Modern, well-designed structures like the 8,000-seat **Entertainment Centre** are the sorts of buildings one expects to find in a city with Perth's commitment to the good life. But perhaps even more pleasing is the discovery that many of the town's historic buildings have been retained and can be viewed by the visitor.

Perth's oldest building can be found

in **Stirling Gardens** next to the Supreme Court. The **Old Courthouse** looks pretty nondescript but its Doric columns against its modest structure indicate a lack of pretension that the city's modern architects have pursued. The court-house was built in 1837 which makes it considerably older than the jail (1856) where guilty parties were almost certain to be lodged. The jail with its fine stone doorway is now part of the **Western Australia Museum**; locals see a certain irony in the placement of a Henry Moore Reclining Figure sculpture on approximately the place where the gallows once stood.

Two sections of town with contrasting histories are **London Court** and **East Murray Street Precinct**. While London Court is a monument to mock Tudor kitsch and dates all the way back to 1937, East Murray is the genuine colonial item. The street appears on the original town plans of 1838. It now stands lined by early 20th-Century buildings and old public offices. A huge fig tree shades the street, offering a touch of gracious living to a precinct just a few blocks from the busy city centre.

Buildings that pre-date the gold-rush days are a rarity. For that reason **The Cloisters**, with its delightful Elizabethan style, is worthy of mention. It was established in 1858 as the first public school for boys. Its elaborate brickwork might have disappeared under the steamroller of development if public concern and a measure of conservation-ist interest on behalf of the Mount Newman mining group had not combined to save the building when the miner sought new office space. The old building was incorporated into the office block plan; developers even found a way to save the century-old fig tree that thrives in what were once schoolgrounds.

Still intact is the old **Town Hall**, and from the 1830s survives a mill—now converted to a museum—that once ground wheat from the colony's first harvest.

During the 1860s, convict labor was enlisted to complete **Government House**. Visitors remark on its similarity to the Tower of London with the notable exceptions that instead of grey stone the building is made of local brick, and that all occupants found their way into the Perth residence by choice.

Perth's increasing sophistication is not purely dependent on the state's material wealth, although it does help. Technical expertise arrives in droves to help develop new mining ventures or gas and oil bonanzas off the northwest coastline. Investment means capital for Perth and with it comes the sort of confidence and prosperity that makes the city a pacesetter.

### From Sports to Pavlova

An obvious area of the city's new push is sport. The *Australia II* victory is not the only recent W.A. sporting success saga. In the past decade the state has been the big achiever in Sheffield Shield cricket, providing play-ers like Dennis Lillee, Rod Marsh, Bruce Laird, Tom Hogan, Kim Hughes and Terry Alderman for national selec-tion. Australia's dominance in men's field hockey also stems from W.A. with Perth-based players, including team captain and federal politician Dr. Ric Charlesworth, dominating the Austra-lian team. The Perth Cup, run on New Year's Day at Ascot, is one of the country's premier thoroughbred events,

Left, London Court Tudor-style shopping arcade.

and international Test cricket matches are held at Perth's WACA ground.

The emergence of the city as a sporting force is no fluke. Some put the success down to the area's superb climate which offers sportsmen and women the facility to train without too much interruption. There is also an enlightened attitude to the provision of training facilities. It all adds up to make Perth a city that produces far more than its expected share of top athletes, with a strike rate that far outweighs its comparatively small population.

Some claim the city exudes an atmosphere conducive to physical endeavour. The air is certainly clean and on any fresh summer's day or night it is easy to see why Perth is worthy of its "City of Light" tag. Ironically, that title came about when Perth, discovering it was roughly below the flight path of John Glenn's inaugural world orbit, switched on its lights to show the astronaut that somebody was still at home.

In 1935 another historic precedent was set when globe-trotting Russian ballerina Anna Pavlova visited Perth. In the kitchen of the now-demolished Esplanade Hotel, chef Bert Sachse ex-pressed his love for the ballerina by creating a wondrous dessert based on egg whites, liberal amounts of sugar and a combination of fruit (including passion fruit) garnish. Sachse named his creation the *pavlova*; it has been tempting sweet-tooths ever since.

Any Perth-based corporate boss keen to woo an executive west would take his charge for the grand tour of **Dalkeith** and to the millionaires' row estates where fabulous houses offer views over the broad reaches of the Swan. He might also show his guest around the charms of residential **Claremont** with its delightful accesses to **Freshwater Bay** and its place in history as a staging point between Perth and Fremantle.

Compared to some Australian capitals, getting around Perth presents few problems. The city has the closest thing to a freeway system that exists in an Australian city and its urban transport systems are modern and very easy to understand.

Any opportunity to view Perth from the river should not be missed. Whether by private or public means, a river cruise offers a different and definitely the best view of the W.A. capital.

ndsurfing Perth.

# Canberra: The National Capital

During one of his many visits to Australia's national capital, the Duke of Edinburgh declared that Canberra was "a city without a soul." Admittedly this was many years ago, but the good citizens of Canberra are still miffed about this royal snub to their hometown. And indeed, they have a right to be. It is not a soul that Canberra lacks, although it would take a major metaphysician to locate the thing; it is more a sense of purpose.

Canberra, like many capital cities (and not only the modern ones like Brasilia; Asia is littered with ruined capitals which were built purely for the aggrandisement of the rulers of the time), is an artificial city. It was constructed not around any existing industrial, transport or rural settlement, but simply out of thin air.

The reason it was constructed at all was a result of colonial jealousy: in 1901, at the time of Australia's federation, there was intense rivalry (which still exists) between Sydney and Melbourne over which was really the chief city of Australia. After some wrangling, the founding fathers solved the problem through the compromise that the new capital had to be at an inconvenient distance from both. Thus a small and hitherto undistinguished valley in the southern tablelands of New South Wales was selected as the site, and the Aboriginal place name was adopted. There was only slight embarrassment when it was discovered that the word "canberra" actually means "a woman's breasts."

However, the news was all bad; the design competition for the new city was won by an American architect, Walter Burley-Griffin (after whom the lake which forms the city's centrepiece is named). Burley-Griffin was a radical for his time; he believed in careful planning, with everything in its place. Changing needs and financial strictures have caused his grand design to be modified over the years of construction (which is still going on), but it is fair to say that he would not have been too disappointed at the result. Canberra's soul might be hard to pin down, but almost all its residents agree that it is a beaut place to live.

## A Leafy Suburbia

Unfortunately for the tourist, it is not quite such an easy place to visit. For instance: a common complaint from tourists is that they can never find the centre of town. You frequently hear this complaint from those who are actually standing in it at the time. Canberra is simply not built as a commercial city, and it stubbornly refuses to look or act like one.

In fact, what it looks most like, apart from a spread of pleasantly wooded suburbs, is a kind of semi-dignified Disneyland. Visitors are impressed or bemused by the city's uncluttered, circular road system that often has a tendency to lead the unwary around in circles. Of equal wonder is the absence of external television antennas despoiling the urban skyscape, and the lack of front fences. In the name of aesthetics the city's planners have deemed that TV aerials and front garden fences are not compatible with Canberra's presentation. For similar reasons, new home buyers are supplied with a collection of

eft, Anzac arade with arliament ouse in the ackground.

young native trees and shrubs to promote Canberra's reputation as a leafy suburbia.

In contrast to the absence of planning in other Australian cities, the zeal with which the bureaucracy has monitored and moulded the city's character does impress. Canberra is a city of features: the **Parliament houses** (the old one falling down, the new one under construction); the **War Memorial-Museum** (oppressive from the outside but housing what experts consider the best collection of its kind in the world); the **National Library**, the **National Gallery** and the **High Court**; the Geneva-type spout in the lake, apparently designed to give Canberra's males a massive inferiority complex; the **Carillon** tower, a gift of the British government, which plays muzak-like selections to the residents at weekends; the **American War Memorial**, affectionately known to the locals as "Bugs Bunny" because from many angles the winged eagle which adorns its summit bears a striking resemblance to the cartoon character; and so on.

But in midst of all the architectual kitsch, Canberra retains considerable charm. It remains one of the few cities (as opposed to towns) in Australia where it is still possible, occasionally, to see kangaroos in the streets. For those who miss out on this spectacle the nearby **Tidbinbilla Nature Reserve** offers a range of Australian flora and fauna. Nature lovers should also visit the **Botanic Gardens**, which contain a huge range of Australian plants, by far the best of its kind in the country (and of course the universe). The surrounding bush is one of the great attractions of the place; indeed, it does not so much surround as encroach, overlapping suburbs in a way normal city dwellers may find alarming. To this, the residents reply smugly that Canberra has all the advantages of life in a leisurely country town, but very few of the usual accompanying disadvantages.

### A Free Show

This is now much truer than it used to be. In the last decade Canberra has absorbed an impressive range of restaurants of many nationalities, and a couple of international-class hotels to complement the range of comfortable

Left, Australia Telecommunications Tower. Right High Court and National Gallery.

accommodations available. Nightlife is still limited, although there are a few discos and nightclubs springing up, a couple of theatres and some very good music, ranging from classical to punk rock. And of course, for half the year, you can watch the Australian parliament in session, which on occasions is the best free show in town.

And Canberra, perhaps because it started out relatively isolated from civilisation, is an excellent jumping-off place for leisurely entertainment, particularly of the outdoors variety. There are easy day-trips to old mining and farming towns, such as **Captains Flat** and **Gundaroo**. A few hours' drive to the south are the **Snowy Mountains**, Australia's best ski resort in winter and the setting for spectacular bushwalking in summer. About the same distance east is the South Coast of New South Wales, with some of Australia's prettiest unspoilt beaches, both surf and still water. For those interested in rural life, there are a number of sheep stations around which accept visitors; and there is a bonus for astronomers, as Canberra is surrounded by optical and radio telescopes and a deep-space tracking station.

But for the ordinary tourist, Canberra is principally Australia's political capital, and visitors will probably be surprised at just how casual it appears. Politicians in town lead much the same life as normal people. Restaurants where they can frequently be caught during the session include **The Lobby**, **Charlie's**, **Peaches**, the **Shalimar**, and **E.J.'s**. A guide for anybody interested in celebrity spotting is available from Parliament House.

The best times to visit the city are *not* summer (when it is not only very hot, but also the bushfly capital of the world) or winter (when it's both cold and bleak). But in spring the place is fresh and green, and covered with blossom and wattle; in autumn the weather is balmy, and the deciduous trees are as beautiful as any city can possibly make them.

Canberra is still growing. It is pointless to try to give an up-to-date account of everything going on; best leave that to the city's excellent tourist bureau. It is a strange place, conceived by accident, built by bureaucrats, on the way from nowhere to nowhere.

ew from
ack
ountain.

# A TALE OF TWO DARWINS

Darwin is a city with two histories: pre-Tracy and post-Tracy. In four furious hours on Christmas Eve 1974, Cyclone Tracy swept in from the north and devastated the Northern Territory capital. With wind gusts as high as 280 kilometres (174 miles) an hour, the hurricane destroyed more than 5,000 homes. Fewer than 500 of the city's buildings were left intact. The dead and missing totalled 66 in what became the greatest natural disaster in the history of Australia.

With massive government and civil funding, the city was rebuilt in the knowledge that the character, style and ambience of the old Darwin was something that Tracy had blown away forever. Historical buildings and most of the old-style Darwin were gone for good, to be replaced by a modern, some say more commercialised, city.

Of the 45,000 residents evacuated in the nation's fastest-ever mass population shift, most have since returned. They have been joined by new residents involved in the rebuilding program or lured by opportunities a rebuilt Darwin might present. The city's population is now in excess of 55,000.

Ask the old residents what they think of the new Darwin and many will offer something less than complimentary. What remains of the easy-going town they once loved was buried by earth-moving equipment in the nearby Leanyer Swamp area. Darwin's low-profile skyline has been replaced by one dominated by taller business office and commercial blocks; its slow-paced personality has given way to a brisker, perhaps more frenetic pace. The emphasis is on progress but there is some debate between the old and the new just whether progress is a worthy pursuit.

Nothing epitomises Darwin's progressive zeal more than **Mindil Beach Casino**. Owned by the Federal Hotels group, the casino was seen as a perfect lure for the tourist dollar. But it has not yet fulfilled expectations. Only time will tell whether the project, given favoured treatment by the Northern Territory government, will remain a drag on the local economy or prove a boon.

Mindil Beach Casino.

## The 'Top End' Lifestyle

Ironically, it is Darwin's natural charm and the peculiarly "Top End" lifestyle that gives the city much of its appeal. The town is flanked by great expanses of white, sandy beaches and in the dry season—April to October or even later—the scene of sand, clear blue skies and tropical flora, including waving palms, makes Darwin not far short of paradise.

The city's harbour is magnificent. Six months of the year it becomes the playground of the area's boating populace. Every June, on nearby **Fannie Bay**, Darwin conducts its famous Beer Can Regatta. Thousands of beer cans are used to construct a fleet of imaginative craft. The city turns out to watch them race, wallow or flounder in the bay.

The event is in keeping with Darwin's reputation as the beer-drinking capital of the world. In this tropical, affluent city, it is claimed inhabitants drink more amber fluid per head of population than any other place in the world. The Darwin Stubby is reputedly the world's largest bottle of beer, containing 2.25 litres, and among their beer-drinking feats the locals count an annual rock-sitting contest in which teams of drinkers perch on surfside rocky outcrops with the winning prize going to those with the greatest powers of endurance.

The extrovert lifestyle is in keeping with the area's turbulent history. Darwin was the result of four failed attempts at settlement in the area. The port was discovered in 1839 by Captain J.C. Wickham of the *Beagle* who named the town after the ship's most famous past passenger, scientist Charles Darwin, who had been on the previous voyage. Darwin was established in 1869 and many of the city's prominent streets bear the name of members of the survey party.

The city's populace reflects the area's proximity to Asia: the racial mix provides a strong cosmopolitan flavour. That mix may have become more predominantly Asian had the Japanese advance in World War II not been stalled at New Guinea. The Japanese, however, left an indelible reminder of the threat by bombing the port and heightening the locals' fear that they would be the first to be overrun by the expected invasion.

Focal point of the city's defence was the **Old Navy Headquarters**. This simple stone building was built in 1884 as a police station and court house. It was used as the naval headquarters during the war and after being damaged by Cyclone Tracy was restored for use as the administrator's office. It and other historical buildings such as **Fannie Bay Jail** (1883) and **Brown's Mart**, built in 1885 and remaining as the oldest building in the city centre, contrast dramatically with Darwin's bold, new architecture.

When Tracy destroyed the city's town hall, a new home had to be found for the museum collection which had been housed in the old building. The rebuilding project included a multi-million dollar **Northern Territory Museum of Arts and Sciences**. Since its completion in 1981, its five display galleries have included some of the world's best collections of Aboriginal art and culture, and archaeological finds of the Pacific and Oceanic regions.

Darwin's tropical nature makes a visit to the 34-hectare (84-acre) **Botanical Gardens** an interesting diversion. As well as displaying hundreds of varieties of tropical and subtropical flora.

orthern
burbs.

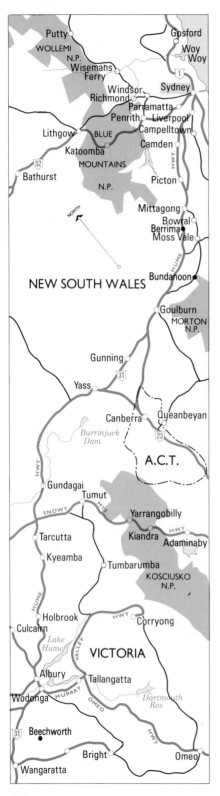

# SYDNEY-MELBOURNE: THE HUME HIGHWAY

Little more than a century ago, the road now known as the Hume Highway was haunted by notorious bands of bushrangers, by ragtag migrations of would-be gold miners, and by pertinacious pioneer agriculturalists en route to market with their earliest crops of wheat and grapes.

Today, only their ghosts continue the haunting. But the paths travelled by these 19th-Century Australians, the settlements they established, and the monuments they left behind make a trip down today's Hume Highway a journey of discovery into the nation's fascinating past.

The Hume may be the most-travelled major route on this island continent, directly connecting the two major cities of Sydney and Melbourne. Its 840 kilometres (525 miles) through rolling farm country can be traversed in 12 hours of solid driving by those in a hurry to get from one metropolis to the other. On the other hand, persons with more time to spare—those with two, three or even four days, plus a desire to occasionally get off the main route shared by long-distance lorries—can more fully appreciate the drive.

### Macarthur Country

Departing metropolitan Sydney, the older Hume Highway is more or less paralleled by the new six-lane South Western Freeway as far as Mittagong. The governments of New South Wales and Victoria states are optimistic that this freeway can be extended prior to the national bicentennial celebration in 1988. When that time comes, perhaps, the already-sleepy towns and villages lining the old route will become living antiques of a once-vivid past.

About 20 km (12½ miles) after leaving Greater Sydney at Liverpool, the freeway skirts **Campbelltown**, a rapidly growing satellite city built largely of red brick. The older downtown section of the town is of most interest: established in 1820, its handsome Georgian-style architecture is a reminder of past prosperity.

Campbelltown is best known today for the legend of Fisher's Ghost. In 1826, a settler named Fisher was murdered and his body thrown into a creek. A convict named Worrall took over Fisher's farm, claiming he had been left in charge when the owner returned suddenly to England. Three months passed, and suspicious neighbours lacked any proof that Fisher had been killed—until the dead man's ghost appeared to a farmer named Farley and directed him to the corpse. Worral was promptly arrested and brought to justice. An opera has been based on the legend, and every year in early November Campbelltown commemorates the legend with a Fisher's Ghost Festival.

Those who forego freeway travel and stay on the Hume Highway directly from Liverpool will approach the charming town of Camden via Leppington, where **Green's Motorcade Park** displays some 50 veteran and vintage cars and motorcycles; Catherine Field, where the $4 million Spanish-style entertainment complex known as **El Caballo Blanco** features Andalusian dancing stallions; and the 162-hectare (400-acre) **Gledswood Estate** with its 1810 winery and homestead restaurant offering "bush barbecues." At Narellan, the Camden-Campbelltown road joins the Hume Highway.

**Camden** has an extremely important place in Australian history, for it was here, in 1804, that John Macarthur was granted nearly 2,000 hectares (5,000 acres) to raise sheep. This was the beginning of the nation's great wool industry. Macarthur himself eventually expanded his holdings to about 12,000 hectares and carried out important experiments in the breeding of Merino sheep. Ironically, few sheep are seen in the district today, but the Camden-Campbelltown-Picton region is still known as Macarthur Country. **Camden Park Homestead** (1835), a short distance south of Camden, is owned by descendants of John Macarthur; it is open by appointment only. Today Camden (population 5,000) is the centre of a dairying region focused on the Nepean River Valley.

Sixteen kilometres (10 miles) southwest of Camden, beyond the Razorback Hills, tiny **Picton** also boasts numerous remnants of 19th-Century settlement. Upper Menangle Street is listed by the National Trust as "representing a typical country town street" of 100 years ago.

Picton is a fine base from which to explore the scenic surrounding region. To the southwest is the **Thirlmere Lakes National Park** and the **Rail Transport Museum**, featuring the oldest locomotive (1864) still to be found in Australia. (There are steam train rides on alternate Sundays.) To the east is the **Wilton Parachute Centre**, the largest sky-diving training centre in the country. To the south, on the Hume Highway, is **Tahmoor's Dollarium**, a collection of more than 2,000 dolls (open weekends and holidays), and the **Wirrimbirra Sanctuary**, a nature conservation centre near Bargo.

### The Southern Highlands

Mount Gibraltar, a denuded volcanic plug better known as The Gib Rock, rises above **Mittagong** and the surrounding terrain, marking the gateway to the Southern Highlands for Hume Highway travellers. Mittagong, home of Australia's first iron smelter (Fitz Roy Ironworks, 1848-1880), is one of several interesting towns in the district. Five km (three miles) farther, on the south slope of The Gib, is **Bowral**, a fashionable

tourist resort for Sydneysiders in the 1880s and today the site of a well-attended October Tulip Festival. The town offers access to the 24-hectare (60-acre) Mount Gibraltar Reserve, noted for its lyrebirds and koalas. **Moss Vale**, a 13-km (eight-mile) detour off Hume Highway toward Nowra (via the Highland Way), features the 1834 Throsby Park House. Nearby **Bundanoon**, a village of fewer than 1,000 residents, perches on the edge of the Illawarra Plateau overlooking the Shoalhaven River valley and, in the distance, the Pacific Ocean. Numerous bushwalks lead into 20,000—hectare (50,000-acre) **Morton National Park**, famed for its deep gorges, waterfalls and Glow Worm Glen.

But the gem of the Southern Highlands is **Berrima**, a small village preserved just as it was in the first half of the 19th Century. Straddling the Hume Highway about eight km (five miles) west of Bowral, all significant architecture in the village is protected by historic trusts. The township was established in 1831, but its growth stagnated three decades later when it was bypassed by the railway. Today,

Surveyor General Inn, Berrima.

many of its impressive old sandstone buildings have been converted to antique and craft galleries; most of those with historical artefacts are open from 10 a.m. to 4 p.m. daily. These include the Surveyor General Inn (1834), said to be the oldest continuously licensed pub in Australia (and still serving draught beer); the Court House (1838), now the Berrima School of Arts; the Gaol (1835), now a prison rehabilitation training centre; the Church of Holy Trinity (1847); and St. Francis Xavier's Roman Catholic Church (1849).

### Bushrangers and Bush Ballads

The big country town of **Goulburn**, population approaching 25,000, is located some 200 km (125 miles) southwest of Sydney, about midway between the Southern Highlands and the national capital of Canberra. Livestock, wool, wheat and potatoes provide the economic foundation for Goulburn, whose peaceful Georgian homes and two classical cathedrals belie its sobering 19th-Century history as a centre of police action against bushrangers who plagued the surrounding roads for decades.

Canine misdemeanour.

**Towrang Stockade**, 10 km (six miles) north, is sparse ruins today; outlaws like Ben Hall and Frank Gardiner gave this once-formidable penal settlement wide berth.

A short distance beyond Goulburn, the Federal Highway branches south for an hour's drive to Canberra. The Hume proceeds west, however, to **Yass**, itself once considered a potential site for the nation's capital. Iron hitching posts still stand outside some of the graceful commercial buildings on the town's main street. Hamilton Hume, the explorer after whom the Hume Highway is named, spent the last 40 years of his life in Yass; his Cooma Cottage is open for inspection, and his tombstone can be visited in the local cemetery.

When stagecoaches and bullock carts plied the Hume Highway, perhaps the most important item aboard was the tuckerbox—the lunch bucket, so to speak. It contained food and other provisions essential to the journey. Drivers often held their trusty dogs, among whose prime chores was to guard the tuckerbox, in more esteem than their own wives.

But the statue of the dog on the tuckerbox at **Five Mile Creek**, north of the town of Gundagai some 100 km (62 miles) from Yass, is not so much a tribute to the canine as to Australian folklore. Possibly the nation's most beloved bush ballad (after "Waltzing Matilda," of course) is "Nine Miles From Gundagai," whose lyrics reflect a horror story retold by a bullock driver:

*The dog shat in the tuckerbox*
*Nine miles from Gundagai!*

**Gundagai** town itself, where the Hume crosses the important Murrumbidgee River, has such a colourful name that several other songwriters have taken advantage and used it in their titles—"The Road to Gundagai," for example, or "when a Boy From Alabama Meets a Girl From Gundagai." The townsite still contains reminders of a devastating 1852 flashflood, the worst disaster of its kind in Australian history. Eighty-nine people in the community of 300 were drowned.

### The Snowy Mountains

It's a worthwhile detour to depart from the Hume Highway at Gundagai and head south on the Snowy Mountains Highway toward Kosciusko National Park. **Tumut**, 31 km (19 miles) from Gundagai, is a timber town best known for its autumn colours and its annual festival of the Falling Leaves in May. It is the northern gateway to the Snowy Mountains Irrigation and Hydro-electric Project, a 25-year, A\$800 million scheme to provide energy for Sydney, Melbourne and the rest of southeastern Australia while diverting water to irrigate vast dry stretches of the Riverina district west of the mountains. Completed in the mid Seventies, it comprises nearly 100 miles of tunnels and 16 dams on the Tumut, Murrumbidgee and Snowy rivers. Seven power stations generate 3.7 million kilowatts of electricity.

South of Tumut, the highway enters the national park and skirts the eastern shore of **Blowering Reservoir**, venue of numerous water-ski and speed boat records including the fastest (510 km, or 317 miles, per hour) and longest (1,673 km, or 1,040 miles) runs. The quaint township of **Talbingo** is near the Tumut 3 Power Station, largest in the Snowy Mountains Project with a generating capacity of 1.5 million kilowatts. Farth-

er on, the **Yarrangobilly Caves** have become one of the Snowy Mountains' leading attractions. About 60 caves have been discovered in a 2½-by-12 km (1½-by-7½-mile) limestone belt around the 300-metre (1,000-foot) deep Yarrangobilly River valley. Few caverns anywhere can rival the variety and beauty of their calcite formations. Four caves are open to the public for inspection, three of them by guided tour only.

The road climbs rapidly into **Kiandra**, 90 km (56 miles) from Tumut. Now a desolate road-junction village, it has two 19th-Century claims to fame: it was the site of Australia's highest goldfield (1,414 metres, or 4,639 feet) and the location of its first ski club. In fact, the 15,000 miners who lived in tents and shanties on these slopes in 1859 and 1860 were holding competitive ski races before the Swiss. They strapped fence palings—"butter pads"—to their boots to move around the surrounding countryside in the winter months. The Kiandra Snow-Shoe Club, established in 1878, numbered among its earliest members the poet Banjo Paterson. Banjo's famous ode, "The Man From Snowy River," was set in this general

An Aussie ski-scape.

region. (Kirk Douglas starred in a film version of the story in 1982.) The grave of Jack Riley, the horseman generally considered to be the man on whom the ballad was based, is in Corryong, just across the Snowy Mountains in Victoria state.

With 6,900 square km (2,664 miles) of territory, **Kosciusko National Park** is the largest protected area in the state of New South Wales. It contains Australia's highest peaks, topped by gentle **Mount Kosciusko** (*koz-ee-OSS-ko*), 2,230 metres (7,315 feet), and winter snowfields averaging 1,035 sq km (400 sq miles) in extent. Cross-country skiers, called *langlaufers*, find this treeless upland perfect for their sport, while keen downhill skiers can travel to six different resorts. With the exception of **Mount Selwyn** on the outskirts of Kiandra, all of these ski areas—as well as **Lake Eucumbene**, the largest reservoir created by the Snowy Mountains Project and a haven for trout fishermen in season—can be reached by continuing south from Kiandra on the Snowy Mountains Highway toward **Cooma**. (There is more direct access from Canberra via the Monaro Highway.) **Thred-**

bo and **Perisher Valley** are the most popular of the alpine resorts, Thredbo with a livelier European atmosphere and Perisher for family activities.

Travellers proceeding toward Melbourne should turn west at the Kiandra junction. The road climbs still higher to **Cabramurra**, a hydro-electric community that is the highest town (about 1,500 metres) in all of Australia. From this point, it's downhill 63 km (39 miles) to the park's western gateway at **Khancoban**. In the spring months of January through April, this road is a delightful pathway through fields of colourful wildflowers, forest stands of mountain ash and snow gum, a number of lovely blue lakes, and frequent herds of kangaroos and other native animals.

### Northeast Victoria

Just below Khancoban, the road crosses the headwaters of the Murray, Australia's greatest river, and wanders into **Corryong**. In addition to the Riley grave, this little town features a "Man From Snowy River" Folk Museum, whose collection includes mid 19th Century skis from Kiandra. A few miles

owering
eservoir in
e Snowy
ountains.

south is the village of **Nariel Creek**, where folk music festivals are held on an old Aboriginal corroboree ground on the New Year holidays and Victorian Labour Day weekend. Northwest of Corryong, with access from Cudgewa, is the **Burrowa Pine Mountain National Park**. The gently rolling countryside is left mainly for cattle grazing and some pine plantations.

**Tallangatta**, at the eastern tip of **Lake Hume**, is a new town, built in 1956 to replace the former community flooded by the damming of the Murray River and creation of the lake. Traces of the old township—lines of trees, streets, even some buildings—eerily reappear at times of low water. The lake, four times the size of Sydney Harbour, is now a playground for swimmers, water skiers, fishermen and bird watchers. It gradually widens as it arcs from Tallangatta toward Wodonga, 38 km (24 miles) west by highway.

**Wodonga** is the Victorian half of Australia's fastest growing inland metropolis. Its "big brother," **Albury**, across the Murray River in New South Wales, gives the twin cities a combined population of about 50,000. Hub of the Riverina district, which produces prodigious quantities of grain, fruit and livestock, Albury marks the site where explorers Hamilton Hume and William Hovell discovered the Murray in 1824 after trekking south from Sydney. Drage's Historical Aircraft Museum in Wodonga contains the nation's largest collection of biplanes.

### Ovens Valley Gold

The traveller can follow either of two routes from Wodonga to Wangaratta, the next major town to the southwest (66 km, or 41 miles) en route to Melbourne. All towns here have one thing in common—a history linked to gold. In 1853, when gold was discovered in the valley of the Ovens River, dozens of prosperous mining settlements sprang into life almost overnight. By 1870, most of them had folded as the precious mineral became harder to find. But some of the towns survive as vital reminders of a thrilling history.

Halfway to Wangaratta via the Hume Highway is **Chiltern**, established in the 1850s as Black Dog Creek. With its wide streets flanked by shops with Old Beechworth Victoria.

150

West facades, the town has provided a popular film set. Today its main claim to fame is "Lake View," the childhood home of novelist Henry Handel Richardson (*The Fortunes of Richard Mahony*). In the courtyard of the Old Grapevine Hotel is the world's largest grapevine, age (as of 1984) 117.

Sixteen km (10 miles) northwest of Chiltern is **Rutherglen**, centre of Australia's oldest wine-growing district and still the foremost producer of fortified ports, tokays, muscats, sherries and frontignacs. Maps to the 10 wineries in northeast Victoria are widely available in Rutherglen, Wodonga and Wangaratta. This region exported to England and France in the last century, but few vineyards survived an invasion of the *phylloxera* louse at the turn of the 20th Century. Those vintners who stubbornly persisted found the soil and climate ideal for sherries and dessert wines: they could ripen their grapes late in the season to a high sugar level.

Perhaps a more interesting route for history connoisseurs proceeds south from Wodonga. The entire township of **Yackandandah** has been classified by the National Trust. Miners who came from California and the Klondike in the 1860s helped give the town a lingering air of the American West. Today the town is the centre of Victoria's largest strawberry industry; Australia's only strawberry wine is produced at Allan's Flat Strawberry Farm, a short distance northeast on the road to Baranduda.

Nestled in the midst of rolling hill country is northeast Victoria's best preserved gold town, **Beechworth**. No fewer than 32 of its buildings have been classified by the National Trust, including the towered Post Office (1867) with its Victorian stone construction, Tanswell's Commercial Hotel (1873) with its handsome facade and wrought-iron veranda, and the Robert O'Hara Burke Memorial Museum (1856). This museum exhibits perhaps the finest provincial collection in Australia. Myriad relics and memorabilia of the gold rush era—when 3 million ounces of gold were garnered in just 14 years—are displayed along with other pioneer objects. There is even a life-sized recreation of Beechworth's former main street. During its heyday, the town had 61 hotels and a theatre which hosted international entertainment acts.

A long detour south from Beechworth takes the tireless traveller to a region of considerable natural beauty. **Myrtleford** is the thriving centre of a walnut, tobacco and hops-growing region; in February and March, the countryside is dotted by Mediterranean-style towers and drying racks for the latter two products. **Mount Buffalo National Park**, comprising a vast plateau at 1,370 metres (4,495 feet) elevation, is a huge snowfield in winter, a carpet of wildflowers in spring, and a popular spot for bushwalking in the summer and fall. **Bright**, a town of 5,000 famed for its fall colours, is a short distance farther. Oaks, maples and other hardwoods give the town a serene feeling which belies its violent gold-rush days, including the notorious 1857 Buckland riots when white prospectors brutally ousted Chinese miners from their claims.

### Kelly Country

All routes meet at **Wangaratta**, a skillfully planned agricultural centre of some 16,000 on the Ovens River. Today it is noted for its woollen mills; two interesting 19th-Century churches; and the Byrne House, a fine art gallery which displays indigenous Australian talent.

This is the heart of "Kelly Country," stomping grounds of the legendary Ned Kelly, Australia's most infamous bushranger. In the span of three short years, from 1878 to 1880, the exploits of the larcenous, murderous Kelly and his gang captured the passions of Australians. His superb horsemanship and his fantastic suit of armour, fashioned by hand from the mouldboard of a ploughshare, helped create his charismatic image. (Pity his poor horse: the armour, including the helmet, weighed 44 kilograms, or 97 pounds!)

Kelly's legend has been immortalized in poems, plays, paintings, even a movie starring Mick Jagger. Why should a man of obvious criminal ilk be so glorified? "When I am cool and logical," writes one of Kelly's biographers, Nancy Keesing, in *The Kelly Gang* (Summit, 1975), "I know Ned Kelly was a thief, a liar, and a killer. But my Australian blood also knows that Kelly is an emanation of our shared cruel, gallant and paradoxical country—hero and devil in one."

The site of Kelly's last stand was the Glenrowan Inn, 16 km (10 miles) southwest of Wangaratta. Kelly's comrades were killed in a shootout with police as the inn burned to the ground, and Ned himself was brought to trial in Melbourne, where he was hanged in November 1880. Today, travellers on the Hume Highway through **Glenrowan** cannot miss the tourist kitsch, try as they might. An armed, larger-than-life technicolour Ned Kelly looms over a block of tacky shops pushing Kelly masks, Kelly T-shirts, Kelly books, Kelly records, Kelly Postcards, Kelly ashtrays, Kelly keychains, Kelly mugs and other Kelly whatnots. Next door, the shootout is reenacted several times daily by men who might know better were it not their way to make a living.

More reminders of the Kelly days are on display in two museums in **Benalla**, which calls itself the "Rose City" after the thousands of bushes which bloom from October to April. These add colour to the unusual **Benalla Art Gallery** overlooking the Broken River. From Benalla, the Hume Highway proceeds 131 km (81 miles) southwest to Melbourne via the rich agricultural country around **Euroa**, **Seymour** and **Kilmore**.

A more interesting if longer last leg of the route to Melbourne traverses the Lake Eildon district via the Midland and Maroondah highways. **Mansfield**, at the junction of the two highways, is an important grazing and timber centre and the gateway to **Mount Buller** (1,808 metres or 5,932 feet), Victoria's largest ski resort. It lies just three kilometres from **Lake Eildon**, a 130-sq-km (50-sq-mile) body of water formed from the damming of five rivers to irrigate thousands of square miles of farmland in central Victoria. Today the lake is a year-round paradise for fishermen angling for brown and rainbow trout, perch and Murray cod.

Only 61 km (38 miles) from Melbourne is **Healesville**, best known for its **Sir Colin McKenzie Wildlife Sanctuary**. This world-renowned open-air zoo, established in 1934 to study and breed native fauna, is Victoria's No. 1 tourist attraction. Indeed, the sanctuary has played a key role in replenishing Australia's depleted koala population, and in successfully breeding platypuses in captivity. It is perhaps the best place in Australia to mingle with kangaroos and emus, woo the lazy wombat, or squawk at the raucous kookaburra.

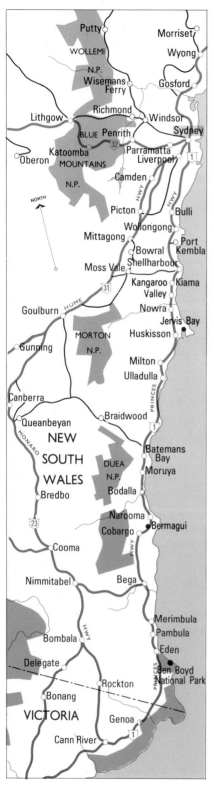

Putty
Morriset
WOLLEMI
Wyong
N.P.
Wisemans
Ferry
Gosford
Richmond
Lithgow
Windsor
Penrith
Sydney
BLUE
32
Katoomba
Parramatta
Oberon
MOUNTAINS
Liverpool
1
N.P.
Camden
NORTH
Picton
Bulli
Wollongong
Mittagong
Port
Bowral
Kembla
Shellharbour
Moss Vale
Kangaroo
Kiama
Valley
31
Goulburn
HUME
Nowra
Jervis Bay
MORTON
Huskisson
Gunning
N.P.
Milton
Ulladulla
Canberra
PRINCES
Queanbeyan
Braidwood
MONARO
NEW
1
SOUTH
Batemans
DUEA
Bay
WALES
N.P.
Moruya
Bredbo
Bodalla
23
Narooma
Cooma
Cobargo
Bermagui
Nimmitabel
Bega
Merimbula
Bombala
Pambula
HWY
Eden
Delegate
Ben Boyd
Rockton
National Park
PRINCES
Bonang
VICTORIA
Genoa
1
Cann River

Eden
1
Mallacoota
Inlet
CROAJINGOLONG
Genoa
Rockton
N.P.
Alfred
National Park
HWY
Cann
River
Lind National Park
Snowy River
National Park
PRINCES
Orbost
Buchan
INSET
Lakes
Entrance
WILSONS
PROMONTORY
Foster
N.P.
Bruthen
Bairnsdale
Gippsland Lakes
Coastal Park
VICTORIA
1
Stratford
Sale
NORTH
Port
A.M.H
Albert
Yarram
Walhalla
Traralgon
HWY
Morwell
Port Welshpool
SEE INSET
Moe
Foster
Warragul
GIPPSLAND
Leongatha
Korumburra
PRINCES
Warburton
Wonthaggi
Healesville
SOUTH
Dandenong
Frankston
Phillip Island
Melbourne
Cowes
Western Port
Port Phillip
Werribee
Queenscliffe

# SYDNEY-MELBOURNE: PRINCES HIGHWAY

There's a second major Sydney-to-Melbourne route that should be considered by travellers with at least two days to make the journey. The Princes Highway—a key link in the round-the-continent system known as "Australia One"—roughly parallels the Pacific coast for most of its 1,080-kilometre (670-mile) length. En route, it passes through a wildly diverse land of fishing ports and resort towns, steel mills and cheese factories, primal forest and coal country. It is only a short detour away from a windswept peninsular national park and an island whose best-known denizens are fairy penguins.

Departing the Sydney metropolis, the Princes Highway skirts the rim of the Illawarra Plateau until descending suddenly and spectacularly through Bulli Pass to **Wollongong**, a major industrial city in an impressive natural setting. Some may argue that the smokestacks of the nation's largest steel works provide an unsightly backdrop to the otherwise pristine scene of surf and sandstone cliffs, but the heavy industry is bread-and-butter for 10 per cent of Wollongong's population of 200,000.

That population is spread along 48 km (30 miles) of coastline from **Starwell Park** in the north to **Shellharbour** in the south. Most people are concentrated in the central Wollongong and **Port Kembla** townships, where the steel works, a copper smelter with a 198-metre (650-foot) chimney, engineering plants and an artificial harbour are located. The rich Bulli coal deposits at the northern end of the city produce some 8 million tonnes of coal annually.

Wollongong was established in 1816, and was originally dependent upon lumbering, grazing and dairy farming. That tie to the land is still evident in the botanic gardens of the University of Wollongong, a 19-hectare (47-acre) showcase of native and imported flora.

On the west side of Wollongong, clinging to the steep sides of the Illawarra Plateau, the hamlet of **Mount Kembla** is mired in a three-generation-old memory of Australia's worst mining disaster. In 1902, an explosion deep within a coal mine split the side of the mountain and buried 95 men inside. A marble monument on the grounds of the Soldiers and Miners Memorial Church, and a collection of old wooden miners' houses from the late 19th Century, are mute testimony.

## The Kiama Coast And Kangaroo Valley

Back in 1797, when Australia was a fledgling penal colony, explorer George Bass anchored his boat in tiny Kiama Bay and remarked on a "tremendous noise" emanating from a rocky headland. Today, the Blowhole is the most popular attraction of the fishing and market town of **Kiama**. When seas are sufficiently high to force water geyserlike through a rock fissure, the spout can reach 60 metres (197 feet) in height! Coloured lights play upon the spray at night.

South a short distance, some 20 km (12 miles) west of **Berry** ("The Town of Trees"), is **Kangaroo Valley**, a lovely and historic township set in an isolated vale among heavily forested slopes. Established in 1829, it is today a favourite haunt of picnickers, bushwalkers and spring wildflower lovers. The Pioneer Farm Museum contains a reconstructed 1880s dairy farm, an early settler's hut and pioneering farm equipment. Kangaroo Valley is the gateway to magnificent **Morton National Park**, which encompasses much of the Shoalhaven escarpment.

**Nowra** (population about 15,000) is the hub of the Shoalhaven district, 162 km (101 miles) south of Sydney. A regional farming centre and increasingly popular focus of tourism, this riverbank city is about 13 km (eight miles) from the mouth of the Shoalhaven River. Regional attractions include the *HMAS Albatross*, Australia's only naval air training station; Greenwell Point, where fresh oysters can be purchased direct from local growers at the wharf; and the Nowra Raceways, three separate modern tracks for gallops, trots and greyhounds. The gallops track is known as Archer Raceway after the home-bred winner of the first two Melbourne Cups (1861 and 1862) ever held. Archer's stall is still maintained as a veritable shrine at Terara House, a couple of kilometres east of downtown.

**Jervis Bay** once rivalled Sydney Harbour (Port Jackson) in importance as a colonial Australian port. Surrounded on all sides but the southeast by 50 km (31 miles) of headlands and beaches, it figures prominently in the nation's past, present and future. Captain James Cook sighted and named the bay in 1770; in the 19th Century, it was a centre of shipbuilding and a port for shipping timber, wool and wheat to Sydney. In 1915, 7,200 hectares (about 17,800 acres) of the bay's southern headland was annexed to the Australian Capital Territory under an act which stipulated that the national capital must have access to the sea. This A.C.T. territory is now the home of the Royal Australian Naval College *HMAS Creswell*, plus the expansive Jervis Bay Nature Reserve and National Botanic Gardens Annex. Proposals for future development of the bay include a large port with direct rail link to Canberra and/or a nuclear power station.

**Ulladulla** is a rapidly growing beach resort and fishing port which supplies a large percentage of Sydney's fresh fish daily. The importance of its fleet can be credited to Italian immigrants who in the 1930s created the town's artificial harbour. **Bateman's Bay**, another 85 km (53 miles) south, is a crayfishing and oystering centre at the mouth of the Clyde River. Offshore are the **Tollgate Islands**, a wildlife refuge frequented by penguins. **Mogo**, 12 km (7½ miles) south of Bateman's Bay, was struck by gold fever in the 1870s. Today, a working gold mine east of the Princes Highway, near **Tomakin**, and a century-old battery stamper attract late 20th-Century fortune seekers.

**Moruya**, like Nowra to the north, is established several kilometres inland on the tidal waters of a river mouth. Its first home, Francis Flanagan's Shannon View (1828), is still lived in, and the Wesleyan (now Uniting) Church was built in 1864 of local granite. The 60-year-old granite quarry on the north side of the Moruya River once supported a town of its own. Among its notable "clients" has been the Sydney Harbour Bridge.

### Mort-ified Cheese

As the Princes Highway winds through the hills into **Bodalla**, 38 km (23 miles) south of Moruya, it's hard to miss the little town's Big Cheese. Some 4½ metres (15 feet) high and an equal

Hang-gliding off the Pacific Coast.

dimension wide, it was sculpted from metal in early 1984 to bolster the community's image as a cheesemaking centre, and to generate some extra tourist revenue. Adjoining facilities include a souvenir shop, cafeteria and ice-cream parlour, as well as an audio-visual presentation on cheesemaking. Visitors were once freely invited to tour the factory of the Bodalla Co-op Cheese Society, which produced about $2.2 million worth of cheddar annually, but health inspectors frowned upon that unsanitary approach. Today special arrangements must be made.

The town's growth and success in the dairy industry can be largely attributed to Thomas Sutcliffe Mort (1816-1878), who established a 5,200-hectare (12,850-acre) dairy farm and introduced such modern innovations as refrigerated cargo ships and—lo and behold—the finest cheese factory in the colony of New South Wales in 1861. Mort's diverse empire also included shipyards, a steam navigation company, a wool-broking agency, gold and copper mines and sugar refineries. All Saints Church (1880) was erected in his memory, built of local granite and sandstone.

American Western novelist Zane Grey made the Eurobodalla coast towns of **Narooma** and **Bermagui** famous in the 1930s as a base for his legendary big-game fishing expeditions. Today, the waters off these two small resorts—especially those around **Montague Island**, eight km (five miles) offshore Narooma—yield record marlin, tuna, shark and kingfish.

**Central Tilba**, 29 km (17 miles) southwest of Narooma, is a community in which time has stood still. Each of the two dozen wooden buildings in this village, classified and protected by the National Trust, are just as they were in the late 19th Century. The A.B.C. Cheese Factory closed in 1980, but its ancient equipment is still there for public inspection. Central Tilba was established in the 1870s when gold was discovered on Mount Dromedary; outstanding coastal views can be obtained from the 825-metre (2,706-foot) mountaintop, reached by a walking track.

**Bega**, population about 4,000, is generally regarded as the "capital" of the far South Coast of New South Wales. Settled in the 1830s, it lies 435 km (270 miles) by road south of Sydney. The Bega Co-operative Society cheese factory welcomes visitors for factory tours, cheese tasting and sales, while the adjoining Yarranung Farm gives milking demonstrations and allows children (and citi-fied adults) to wander through the paddocks with the animals.

**Kameruka Estates**, a few miles west, are listed by the National Trust Register as "the finest Australian example of an attempt to establish a small agricultural community based upon social ideas reminiscent of an English estate during the last century." A working enterprise that has been in almost continuous operation since 1834, most of its revolutionary ideas were introduced in the 1860s by Sir Robert Lucas Tooth of Australia's famous brewery family. The public are invited to a Folk Festival and Kameruka Garden Party every October; otherwise the 1845 homestead, church and school, and the 1,700 dairy and beef cattle and 8,000 Merino sheep, welcome visitors every day.

**Merimbula**, back on the so-called "Sapphire Coast," and its sister town of **Pambula** offer fine surfing, boating, fishing, prawning and oystering. **Eden**, the last sizable town before crossing the

ishing fleet
t Eden.

Victoria state border, is located on **Twofold Bay**, once a thriving whaling port. The Whaling Museum on Imlay Street recalls those 19th-Century days. Today Twofold Bay—the third deepest natural harbour in the world—is home to a fine fishing fleet. Industry has also become important to Eden, with a fish-processing factory, a petrol-distribution outlet, and the Japanese-sponsored Harris-Daishowa Chipmill on the south shore of the bay. Wednesday afternoon tours show how low-quality pulpwood logs are converted to small chips and shipped to Japan for making paper.

During its whaling era, Eden had stiff competition as a port from **Boydtown**, established in 1842 by banker-adventurer Ben Boyd on the south side of Twofold Bay. Boyd dreamed out loud that his settlement would one day become the capital of Australia. He established a steamship service to Sydney and erected many buildings. But in 1850 his empire collapsed: Boyd went bankrupt and fled Australia to the cannibal-populated Solomon Islands, and was never heard from again. All that remains of the grand scheme today

is the Seahorse Inn, a magnificent building with stone walls a metre thick, hand-carved doors and windows, and Gothic arches; and Boyds Tower, a 31-metre (102-foot) sandstone lighthouse built in 1846 but never lit. The latter is now part of the 8,950-hectare (22,115-acres) **Ben Boyd National Park**, encompassing the coastal headlands north and south of Twofold Bay. Its highlights include stunning red sandstone cliffs, a rich animal and bird life, and lovely wildflowers.

### Victorian Secrets

Just across the forested state border, at the hamlet of **Genoa**, a sealed side road turns south toward **Mallacoota Inlet**. This tiny resort town, much beloved by fishermen and nature lovers, is a one-way 24-km (15-mile) journey off the Princes Highway at Victoria's south-easternmost tip. It is surrounded by **Croajingolong National Park**, 86,000 hectares (212,500 acres) of rocky cliffs and open beaches, rainforest, open woodland and heath, stretching some 100 km (62 miles) from the New South Wales border to Sydenham Inlet. Mallacoota.

Numerous nocturnal mammals (including possums and gliders) and many snakes, some venomous, make their homes in the park; birds include lyrebirds, oyster catchers, pelicans, sea eagles and kingfishers. The pub at the charming village of **Gipsy Point**, overlooking the inlet between Mallacoota and Genoa, has a number of marsupial patrons, including one tame kangaroo considered a regular: there are photos of him standing at the bar and playing pool!

West of Genoa, the Princes Highway winds through its most remote stretch, 208 km (129 miles) of mountains and rainforest to Orbost. Other than the Monaro Highway junction town of **Cann River** and the **Alfred and Lind national parks**, both popular with bushwalkers, the main attractions are logging trucks. They seem to congregate at **Orbost**, a prosperous town of about 3,000 near the banks of the lower Snowy River. **Snowy River National Park**, in the mountains above Orbost, is popular with whitewater canoeists.

Another timber town, 93 km (58 miles) northwest of Orbost by winding, rugged road, is **Buchan**. It hosts a rodeo over Easter, a lumberjacks' contest in May. But its main attraction is its limestone caves, unquestionably the finest in Victoria. There are 350 caves here, but only three open to the public, including the Fairy Cave, whose numerous honeycombed chambers are embedded with ancient marsupial bones. In some of the off-limits caves, explorers have found tools and rock engravings dated to prehistoric habitation 17,000 or more years ago.

### The Gippsland Lakes

At **Lakes Entrance**, the Princes Highway offers its only ocean glimpse west of Eden. The resort here—arguably the most popular in all of Victoria—is situated at the narrow manmade inlet to the Gippsland Lakes, a long string of interconnected lagoons stretching west along the inner shore of the bass Strait for some 80 km (50 miles). They are separated from the sea only by a narrow band of dunes and hummocks called **Ninety Mile Beach**.

The year-round population of Lakes Entrance (about 3,000) increases to more than 20,000 in summer as holiday

West from
Lakes
Entrance.

makers pack the motels and caravan parks. Fishing, boating and swimming are the main draws; cruise boats offer regular sightseeing tours of the Lakes, which cover 388 square km (150 sq miles) of area. sometimes called the "Victorian Riviera," temperatures here consistently range about 20°C (68°F) in the middle of winter. The **Gippsland Lakes Coastal Park**, a reserve of dunes and heath along the lakes' seaward edge, and the **Lakes National Park**, a bird-filled woodland on a sandy peninsula between Lake Reeve and Lake Victoria, help protect natural features.

The commercial centre of East Gippsland is **Bairnsdale**, 285 km (177 miles) east of Melbourne via the Princes Highway. A sheep, dairy and timber centre, it is best known for its fine botanic gardens and the "Sistine Chapel" murals in St. Mary's Catholic Church. Nearby **Paynesville**, a boating resort, features the bizarre Church of St. Peter: a sailors' house of worship, it has a spire like a lighthouse, a pulpit shaped like the bow of a boat, and a sanctuary lighting fixture that was once a ship's riding lamp.

A 45-minute drive northwest of Bairnsdale is **Glenaladale National Park**, mythical home of an aboriginal monster called Nargun. This demon had an appetite for young children, whom he enticed to his den then devoured. The Den of Nargun, hidden behind the mist of a waterfall, has formations of stalactites and stalagmites.

Past the dairy and livestock town of **Stratford** (site every November of the Stratford Shears, a national sheep-shearing competition), at the junction of the Princes and South Gippsland highways, is **Sale**, which proudly lets itself be known as Australia's "Oil City." Since oil and natural gas were discovered in the Bass Strait in 1965, the industry has developed rapidly in this region, with processing plants and supply ports onshore, numerous rigs offshore. Esso Australia and the Broken Hill Proprietary Company (BHP) have developed the offshore Gippsland Basin under a two-decade-old working agreement. Today their major processing plant is near **Longford**, southeast of Sale. Known as the Gippsland Gas Processing and Crude Oil Stabilisation Plant, public visits can be arranged.

Gippsland, Victoria,

## The Latrobe Valley

The Princes Highway proceeds more or less directly west from Sale to Melbourne, a distance of about 215 km (134 miles). The string of small cities through which it passes comprise the Latrobe Valley, whose coal produces about 90 percent of the electricity for Melbourne and Victoria state. The valley sits upon the world's largest deposit of brown coal—about 60 km (37 miles) long, 16 km (10 miles) wide, and 140 metres (460 feet) thick. Open-cut mines and the steaming towers of power stations are everywhere. Public mine tours are offered at **Morwell** (where mining began in 1916) and the model town of **Yallourn**, built by the State Electricity Commission. **Moe**, the valley's largest (over 20,000 population) and most modern city, is the site of the Old Gippstown open-air folk museum and gateway to the mountain communities of **Walhalla** (a veritable ghost town that once boasted Victoria's richest gold mine) and **Mount Baw Baw** (the nearest ski resort to Melbourne).

For those with time to spend, the south Gippsland Highway from Sale offers a much more scenic alternative route to Melbourne. About 30 km (19 miles) northwest of **Yarram**, in the heart of the dense and rugged Strzelecki Ranges, the tiny twin national parks of **Tarra Valley** and **Bulga** feature primeval fern gullies, waterfalls and a plethora of plant species. South of Yarram are the historic townships of **Port Albert** and **Tarraville**. The Port Albert Hotel (1842) may be the oldest continuously operating licensed hotel in Victoria, while the old timber jetty—at which eager 19th Century Chinese gold miners once disembarked— is now crowded with yachts and motorboats. The Port Albert Maritime Museum is housed in the old Bank of Victoria. Tarraville was Gippsland's largest town in 1851, with nearly as many breweries as people (219). Perhaps it is divine justice that the Tarraville Anglican Church, a wooden structure held together without the use of nails, should outlive every one of those drinking establishments.

**Port Welshpool**, on Corner Inlet, is a key supply terminal for the Bass Strait oil rigs. Just west, at **Barry's Beach**, these marine platforms are constructed. Unobtrusive visitors can also see the leg

jackets being built: these are floated to the chosen ocean site, stood upright, then anchored to the ocean floor.

### Wilson's Promontory

There is good reason why Wilson's Promontory, a huge granite peninsula that represents mainland Australia's furthest thrust toward Antarctica, is the most popular national park in the state of Victoria. "The Prom," as it is affectionately called by regular visitors, features more than 80 km (50 miles) of walking tracks to long sandy beaches, forested mountain slopes, and heath and marshes packed with bird, animal and plant life. An estimated 100,000 people visit the park each year. Environmentalists are concerned with the impact they may have on the fragile ecology; for that reason, most of the park is inaccessible even by footpath. The most frequent memory taken home by many visitors is of the huge flocks of flamboyantly coloured rosellas and lorikeets which mischievously invade campsites in summer. Access to Wilson's Promontory is via the South Gippsland Highway, with a turn south-

ward either at Foster (from the east) or Meeniyan (from the west).

Further west on the South Gippsland Highway, closer to Melbourne, the town of **Korumburra** is wedged in the foothills of the Strzelecki Ranges. Although the name Korumburra is unfortunately derived from the aboriginal for "blowfly," the pesky insects seem no worse here than elsewhere. Korumburra is an old coal town whose last working mine closed in 1958. On its site, the Coal Creek Historical Park—a faithful reproduction of a coal-mining and railway town of the 1890s—has been constructed. It incorporates many buildings and furnishings transplanted from elsewhere in Victoria; craftsmen and others in period costumes help lend an air of authenticity to the park.

For many travellers, the most interesting stop in this final stretch to Melbourne is **Phillip Island**. Seven km (4½ miles) off the Bass Highway southwest of Korumburra, it is connected to the mainland fishing community of **San Remo** by a bridge. In an area about 104 sq km (40 sq miles), most of it cleared for grazing and chicory growing, are a bewildering array of tourist attractions. Among them are koala and bird sanctuaries, scenic offshore rock formations, historic homesteads, pottery shops, an antique clock display at Rhylston Park Homestead (1886), Australia's first motor-racing circuit (1928) and still one of its best, and numerous sports facilities, from water sports (surfing, diving, sailing, fishing, boating) to golf, tennis, bowls and croquet. Tourist lodging is centered at the north coast summer resort town of **Cowes**—named after the main port of England's Isle of Wight.

Unquestionably the biggest single attraction for Phillip Island visitors is the colony of fairy penguins at Summerland Beach. Around dusk each day of the year, hundreds or even thousands of these little birds parade from the waters of the Bass Strait to their protected burrows in the sand. Wings outstretched, they waddle in small broups up a concrete ramp past throngs of curious human onlookers.

In fact, the fairy penguin, like all penguins, is more at home in water than on land, and spends its days scouring the surf for small fish and squid. But it returns ashore to nest and breed in this penguin reserve year after year.

Left, Fairy Penguins. Right, lighthouse, Wilson's promontory.

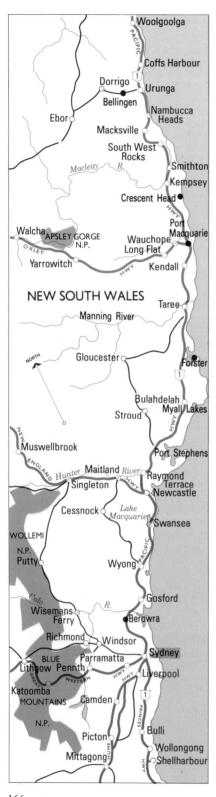

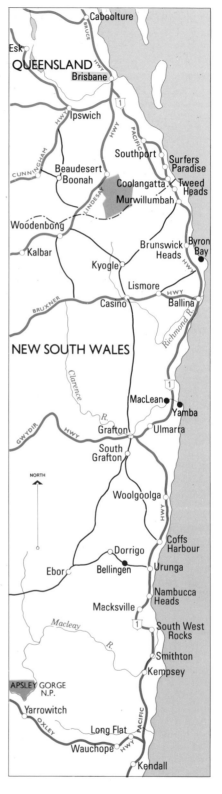

# SYDNEY-BRISBANE
# VIA THE PACIFIC

The ease with which the Sydney Harbour Bridge gives way to six free-flowing northbound lanes is a little deceptive. Within 15 minutes the escape route from Australia's largest city has slimmed down to the dual carriageway of the **Pacific Highway**, its traffic flow arrested at every suburban junction.

The leafy and often majestic avenues of Sydney's North Shore (there is, in fact, no shore but plenty of style) eventually give way to the more sparsely populated suburbs beyond Hornsby, and finally, to the **Hawkesbury Tollway**. But it is wise to bear in mind that, despite bicentennial promises, Sydney's arteries do not always flow freely. Begin your Pacific Highway adventures outside of peak hours.

It should also be pointed out that just before the entrance to the Hawkesbury Tollway, at Berowra, an unpretentious sign on the left indicates the proximity of the Berowra Waters ferry. This would be unremarkable were it not for the fact that the ferry crosses to the **Berowra Waters Inn**, unquestionably the finest restaurant in Australia.

### Rivers, Parks and Lakes

The Hawkesbury Tollway cuts through the heart of some of New South Wales' most beautiful and untamed national parklands. From the road you can occasionally catch glimpses of Cowan Creek meandering through the **Ku-ring-gai Chase National Park**; and when the tollway crosses the **Hawkesbury River** at Brooklyn a whole vista of dense scrub and opaque water opens up. This is oyster lease territory, and the home of the rented cabin cruiser, a popular weekend diversion for many Sydneysiders.

North of the Hawkesbury the road follows the rim of the **Brisbane Waters National Park** before heading back to the coast at Toukley. A stopover at the Central coast commercial hub of **Gosford** provides perfect access to the orchards and forests of the Mangrove Mountain area, and a string of beautiful beaches within minutes of the town. Also in the area is a reptile park and **Old Sydney Town**, an amusing if not

quite authentic recreation of the city's convict past—complete with painful daily floggings.

At the Doyalson power plant the Pacific Highway—back to a two and occasionally four-lane blacktop—heads along a narrow ridge between the ocean and **Lake Macquarie**. Frequently overlooked by tourists, the Lake (particularly its western shore) is a fascinating relic of a past age, when working folk could afford water frontages. The mining village of **Wangi Wangi**, for many years the retreat of the artist Sir William Dobell, is a classic example of the lakeshore charm.

### Steel City

The second city of New South Wales (and the seventh largest in Australia), **Newcastle** is a sprawling mass of people, commerce and industry which, because of the dominance in its workforce of steelworkers and miners, has long been considered a "blue collar" town of no sophistication. In the 1980s this is simply not true.

Newcastle has developed a city centre in which the cultural and aesthetic needs of its people are met within a dozen blocks. With the city's stately homes perched high on a hill which runs down to an industrialised but picturesque harbour, there are geographic similarities to San Francisco, and Newcastle shares with that city the bawdy charm of a seaport. Within easy reach of the wineries of the lower Hunter Valley, Lake Macquarie to the south and Myall Lakes to the north, not to forget the fantastic ribbon of surfing beaches, Newcastle is regarded by those who live there as a perfect compromise between city and country living.

For the visitor the temptation to bypass the city in favour of the warmer north may prove too strong. This won't worry "Novocastrians" in the slightest. They've been given short shrift by blow-ins for almost a century. Mark Twain, for example, spent a few hours in the town in 1895 and later declared that it was a town which consisted of "a very long street with at one end a cemetery with no bodies in it and at the other a gentlemen's club with no gentlemen in it."

North of Newcastle the Pacific Highway crosses the Hunter River at **Hexham** and skirts the western shore of

eceding
ges,
dists take
the water
Broken
ad,
S.W.

**Port Stephens** (another holiday centre with great fishing, swimming and oysters on a par with the Hawkesbury) before arriving at **Bulahdelah**, a town notable only for its phonetic pronunciation and the fact that it is the gateway to the beautiful **Myall Lakes**.

## The Holiday Zone

The Myall Lakes represent something of a victory for the conservationists of Australia; not on the scale of the Franklin River in Tasmania, but no less a victory for those who regard the unique features of the coastline as worthy of preservation. Here paperbarks, palms and other unusual swamp vegetation line the shores, while the waterways are filled with birdlife more exotic than any in the state. Surrounding the chain of lakes is national parkland where nature lovers camp in the wild.

At the northern end of the lakes is a string of beaches leading to the holiday resort of **Forster**, the southernmost of the beach towns which dot the eastern seaboard, and which Australians from southern climes refer to in general as "up north." Although there are beach resorts every few miles along the Pacific Highway north of Sydney, if you don't go as far as Forster you haven't really been "up the north coast."

**Taree** is the first major centre north of Newcastle, a thriving market town in the dairy-rich Manning Valley. The beautiful **Manning River** runs right through the middle of town, and on its banks huge crowds gather each Australia Day holiday to watch one of the best aquatic carnivals in the country.

As well as housing large and profitable dairies, the Manning and other valleys of the mid-north coast are timber centres providing cedar and pine from vast forests which stretch westward onto the New England Plateau. Here the highway winds through miles of forest, and it is worthwhile considering a detour along the well-made coast road from **Kew** to **Port Macquarie**.

These are some of the prettiest beaches in the state, with rocky outcrops and golden sands. On the western side of the road there is yet another chain of ocean lakes, ideal for fishing and boating. At Port Macquarie itself, once a picturesque former penal settle-

Barrenjoey Light and Pittwater.

168

ment full of historic sandstone buildings, the north coast tourist boom has taken its toll on the landscape. Garish motels, retirement villages and time-share resorts dot the headlands and red-brick suburbia has taken over the flatlands to the west. For all that, there is still much to like about Port Macquarie—good restaurants, top quality accommodation and easy access to superb uncrowded beaches or tranquil river valleys in the hinterland. At **Wauchope**, a few miles up the Hastings River, there is a fascinating replica of an old sawmilling village, **Timbertown**.

The highway again snakes inland and through the forests, but just before Kempsey it is worth making one 24-kilometre (15-mile) detour to take in the resort of **Crescent Head**, a pretty, peaceful town with fine surf and a good golf course.

**Kempsey**, another major dairy and timber centre, is almost as old as Port Macquarie and looks a good deal older. Its position 32 km (20 miles) inland, and the industrialisation which has occurred around it, have largely dissuaded tourists. Still, if you're sick of resort life and you want to sample bush normalcy, this town is for you. It is also a handy setting-out point for **Trial Bay**, to the northeast, home of an historic jail which held convicts, and, later, German internees.

### The Banana Coast

Beyond Trial Bay a distinctly tropical feel begins to permeate the air, and from **Macksville** on banana plantations are a common sight. Houses are built in the Queensland style, designed to catch the cooling breeze and keep things dry in the wet. More to the point, everywhere you look, the dominant colour is lush green and the roadside signs tell you this is paradise. It isn't, but it's a step in the right direction.

The timber port of **Coffs Harbour** is a sprawling centre of north-coast tourism and decentralised light industry. The growth which has occurred inland has somewhat overshadowed the continuing business of the port, but both tourism and industry manage to co-exist, largely because the lush hills can house a condominium resort on one side of the slope and a banana plantation or timber mill on the other with a minimum of intrusion.

Coffs is more or less the midway point between Sydney and Brisbane. Road travellers often set out to stay here overnight en route, and wind up staying a week or more. The town is alive with restaurants and pubs, bars and discos, particularly in the strip from the jetty to **Park Beach**. While it poses no threat to the nightlife supremacy of Queenland's Gold Coast (about which more later), Coffs is more upbeat than country, more mellow than the bright lights. It is a pleasant vacation mix.

Behind the town, the Bellingen Valley and the beautiful village of **Bellingen** offer a variety of scenic pleasures quite different to the coastal views. Some parts of the valley, particularly the pebbled river banks, look more like Canada than east-coast Australia. And as the valley gives way to the hills nearer **Dorrigo**, there is excellent trout fishing.

Just north of Coffs Harbour, at the oceanfront town of **Woolgoolga**, the large Sikh community has put its unique stamp on the topography with a lavish temple and a superb curry restaurant. Good curry houses are a rare thing in Australia. Don't drive past.

Again the Pacific Highway swings inland through the forests, this time emerging at **Grafton**, a lovely old town lined with jacaranda trees and situated on a bend of the big Clarence River, some 65 km (40 miles) from its mouth. Grafton boasts some delightful 19th Century architecture enhanced by its wide, tree-lined streets. Furthermore, this is flood country, and the houses close to the river are tropical bungalows on stilts. Like several north-coast towns away from the coast, Grafton has been bypassed in the tourist boom, and prices for food and accommodation are still quite reasonable. And although the fare may be plain, the service will be from another more gracious age.

### The Big River Coast

North of Grafton the highway follows the line of the Clarence River across flatlands to the coast at **Yamba**, with rambling old houses on stilts peering out from behind fields of sugar cane. Although summer flooding has been rare in the drought-stricken Eighties, it pays to keep watch on the long-range weather forecast between December

Surfboards receiving expert attention.

170

and February. Floods are usually just swollen river banks, down within 24 hours, but they can be a nuisance to the unwary traveller, trapped overnight on the high ground between two bridges.

The village of **Maclean**, built on several hills a few miles upriver from Yamba, is quaint, quiet, and a great spot from which to view the workings of the Clarence with its fishermen and cane haulers. Twenty minutes down a straight bitumen road is the resort of Yamba, filled with shoddily built "weekenders" and garish motels. The pub on the headland and the beaches spread below, however, are first-rate.

At the time of writing (mid-1984), construction is underway on a huge Japanese-financed resort village on the banks of the Clarence just out of town, a development seen by locals as a mixed blessing. It means new employment opportunities in a dying local economy, but for all its faults, Yamba had been a great place for snoozing in the sun with a fishing line. Now they'll have to thrive.

Across the Clarence, just up from its mouth at Yamba, the river divides into channels around a series of islands linked by the highway. Here, amidst the sugar cane, is a restaurant worthy of special note. The only true gourmet restaurant between Sydney and Brisbane, the **Chatsworth Island Restaurant** is a visual and culinary delight, making full use of the abundance of local seafood delicacies.

### The Summerland Coast

After a stretch of boring scenery, the Pacific Highway again clips the coast at **Ballina**, the southernmost beach town in a string reaching to the Queensland border, collectively known as the Summerland coast. Ballina, scene of a minor gold rush last century when the precious metal was found in beach sand near the mouth of the Richmond River, is now a bustling tourist centre and fishing port. It is currently being subjected to a mammoth canal development which is doing wonders for real-estate prices and who-knows-what for riverside ecology.

Although the highway heads due north through the magnificent rolling hills of the **Rainbow Region** (see box), the alternative coastal route takes in some equally breathtaking scenery and

# LIFESTYLES OF THE 'RAINBOW'

West of Cape Byron, Australia's most easterly point, a series of narrow and winding roads leads through the rolling hills to the lush hinterland which has become known as the Rainbow Region.

Over the past two decades this lovely area has attracted a large population of disillusioned city dwellers who have sought to build new and simpler lives using the technology and philosophy of the counterculture.

Dotted about the hills and rainforests are various communes, cluster housing projects, experimental domes and the like. Towns such as Nimbin and The Channon have been all but taken over by New Settlers, and the streets are filled with craft shops and colourful murals. They also now have representatives on councils and local government bodies, and have been able to get certain laws changed, like the easing of restrictions on communal land ownership.

Of course it hasn't all been peace, love and brotherhood in the Rainbow Region. When the New Settlers first began to arrive—for an alternative lifestyles festival in 1973—there was considerable opposition to them from locals. Although many of them eschewed the use of drugs for one reason or another, the New Settlers were all branded as marijuana cultivators. In 1976 police raided the Turntable Falls commune and arrested most of its population on pot charges, most of which were dropped after a lengthy court battle.

In the 1980s, however, there is widespread acceptance of the New Settler lifestyles and recognition of their achievements. The greatest compliment of all came in 1984, when the Hawke Labor Government proposed lump-sum unemployment benefits to enable young city people to establish alternative lifestyles at places like the Rainbow Region.

Wool spinne at work.

the picturesque town of **Byron Bay**.

There is a similar option an hour farther up the coast at **Mooball**. Here the coast road is not so well made but it avoids the commercial centre of **Murwillumbah** and passes some superb, almost virgin, beaches before meeting the highway again near **Tweed Heads**.

### The Gold Coast

The border town of Tweed Heads has only recently emerged from the shadows cast by its sister across the border, **Coolangatta**, but the tourist boom now proceeds apace. The town coffers are helped along by the fact that Queenslanders flock across the border to play slot machines in licensed clubs, these devices being illegal in the northern state.

The 32-km (20-mile) stretch of coast from Coolangatta to **Surfers Paradise** — bushland just a generation ago — is now the fastest-growing tourist area in Australia. And despite the recent recession, real-estate millionaires are as common as cases of sunburn. The city of the Gold Coast is hideous in parts, beautiful in others, but it is never dull. The

beaches, particularly **Burleigh Heads**, set in a national park, are strikingly beautiful. The high-rise skyline of Surfers Paradise, holiday headquarters for Australia's rich and powerful, must now rank with Ipanema, Miami and Cannes for architectural overkill. But at street level after dark it doesn't really matter that the high-rises tend to blot out the sun. That's the way the disco kings and queens of Surfers like it.

Holiday makers looking for diversions will find plenty on the Gold Coast. Surfers has performing dolphins at **Sea World**, and **Marineland of Southport** is another finny frolic. The **Currumbin Bird Sanctuary** is overwhelmed by flocks of lorikeets at feeding time; **Fleay's Fauna Reserve** near Tallebudgera is the place to pamper platypuses. There are antique cars at **Gilltraps Yesteryear World** in Coolangatta, model trains at **Traintasia** at Nobbies Beach, and a boomerang factory at **Mudgeeraba** inland from Burleigh Heads.

Between Surfers and Brisbane there is straight road and little else, and if you've sampled all that the Gold Coast has to offer that'll do you just fine.

Surfers
Paradise.

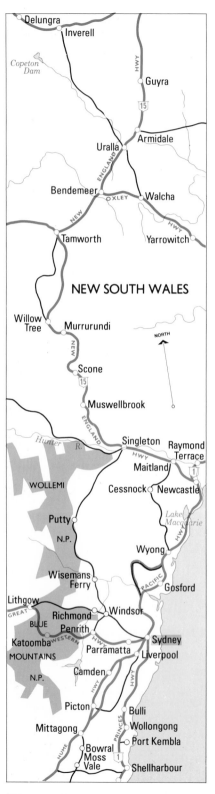

Delungra
Inverell
*Copeton Dam*
Guyra
15
Uralla  Armidale
ENGLAND
Bendemeer  OXLEY  Walcha
NEW
Tamworth  Yarrowitch  HWY

# NEW SOUTH WALES

Willow Tree  Murrurundi
NEW
NORTH
Scone
15
ENGLAND
Muswellbrook
*Hunter R.*
Singleton  Raymond Terrace
HWY
Maitland  1
WOLLEMI  Cessnock  Newcastle
Putty
N.P.  *Lake Macquarie*
Wyong  HWY
Wisemans Ferry  PACIFIC
Lithgow  Gosford
GREAT  Richmond  Windsor
BLUE  Penrith
Katoomba  WESTERN  HWY
Parramatta  Sydney
MOUNTAINS  Liverpool
N.P.  Camden  HWY  HWY
Picton  Bulli
Mittagong  Wollongong
HUME  Bowral  PRINCES  Port Kembla
Moss Vale  1
Shellharbour

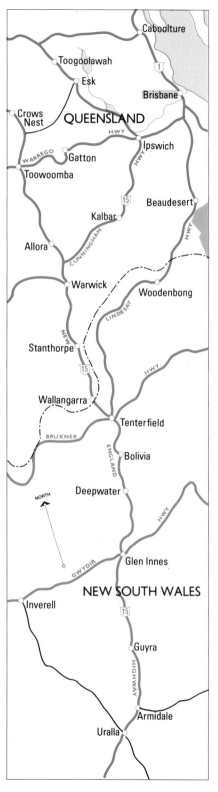

Caboolture
Toogoolawah
Esk  1
Brisbane
Crows Nest  # QUEENSLAND
HWY
WARREGO  Gatton  Ipswich
Toowoomba
15  Beaudesert
Kalbar
Allora  CUNNINGHAM  HWY
Warwick  Woodenbong
LINDESAY
NEW
Stanthorpe
15  HWY
Wallangarra
Tenterfield
BRUXNER  Bolivia
ENGLAND
NORTH  Deepwater
HWY
Glen Innes
GWYDIR  # NEW SOUTH WALES
Inverell  15
Guyra
HIGHWAY
Armidale
Uralla

# SYDNEY-BRISBANE VIA NEW ENGLAND

Just north of Newcastle the New England Highway leads off the Pacific Highway and heads northwest into the rich upper Hunter Valley. This narrow but well-made highway is the inland alternative route to Brisbane, slightly longer but often faster than the Pacific because of its long, straight stretches, and passing through some of New South Wales' most beautiful pastoral land.

Past the city of **Maitland**, the route leads through the wineries of the **Hunter Valley** where some of Australia's finest wine is produced (see box). The old mining villages of this area retain the look and feel of their 19th-Century origins, but the lower Hunter is about to undergo a metamorphosis which will drag it, kicking and screaming perhaps, into the 21st Century. Aluminium smelters, giant open-cut mines and power stations are part of a government masterplan to turn the area into the "Ruhr of New South Wales," and despite opposition from conservationists, the influential wine industry and many residents, the plan seems certain to go ahead.

As the highway heads deeper into the valley, the pace of life seems to slow. At **Singleton**, the giant $240 million Liddell power station on its outskirts notwithstanding, time seems almost to have stopped. The ornate buildings of the town's main street have changed very little in the past century, and it is a delightful place to while away a few hours.

Next stop is **Muswellbrook**, another picturesque mining and agricultural town about to undergo a disturbing facelift as part of the "Ruhr plan." Situated on the banks of the Hunter River, the town features some superb examples of colonial architecture.

A little farther, as the highway approaches the foothills of the Great Dividing Range, is the town of **Scone** which is pretty but unremarkable save for its "horsiness." This is the home of thoroughbred stud farms, horse shows and the sport of polo. Much of New England is squatter territory, where the sons of rich landed gentry continue the traditions of Mother England in respect of horsemanship, political conservatism

and bad dress sense. Clad in moleskins, R.M.Williams elastic-sided riding boots, tweed jackets and Wool Board ties, these sons of the soil play polo by day and womanise by night, before accepting adult responsibility in the form of a safe National Country Party seat in federal Parliament.

Scone hosts a major polo tournament each July, at which the French champagne flows freely between chukkas.

## Onto the Great Divide

At **Murrurundi** the highway finally leaves the Hunter Valley and enters the Great Dividing Range, the vast upheaval which separates the coastal plains from the tablelands along the entire length of New South Wales. The town itself is set in a valley of the Liverpool Ranges, and seems constantly to be shrouded in mist.

The road winds farther into the ranges and onto the New England plateau, eventually reaching the city of **Tamworth**. This pretty centre, surrounded by hills, is the largest in the northwest, with a population of more than 30,000 and a thriving local econ-

Fox hunting in the Hunter Valley.

# THE WINE INDUSTRY OF THE HUNTER

Although the state of South Australia now produces more than half of Australia's fine domestic wine, the Hunter Valley is the next most important wine region in terms of size and quality.

A few years ago the area specialized in particularly dry reds and whites, but with the expansion of the vineyards to the Upper Hunter, there is now Rhine Riesling and full-bodied red produced. And despite the threat of heavy industrialisation in the area, the wineries are expanding and thriving.

The Australian wine industry actually had its beginnings 160 kilometres (100 miles) to the south, in Sydney. But there is virtually no evidence left of the vineyard which flourished in the heart of that city. By 1827 the Macarthur family was making wine in considerable quantities at Camden, west of Sydney, but real commercial production of Australian wine did not begin until the later 1830s—in the Hunter Valley.

Those who make such judgements maintain that Australian wine consumption has more than doubled in the past 15 years. The annual Aussie intake is now around 18 litres of fermented grapes—still only about one-fifth of the amount of wine put away each year by French and Italians, but indicative of more sophisticated palates Down Under.

The wineries are spread over a large area around Pokolbin, and now some 80 km (50 miles) further up the valley near Muswellbrook. Most offer wine-tasting facilities and some, such as the Rothbury Estate in Pokolbin and Black Hill Cellars at Muswellbrook, also have restaurants.

A pleasant way to discover the valley is to tour the wineries of the lower Hunter, spend the night at Pokolbin or Cessnock, and drive on for a second bout of liver and brain damage at Muswellbrook the next day. The table wines of the region are uniformly good, and an ideal lubricant for picnic lunches in the rolling hills. You can also buy mixed dozens at very reasonable prices—a prospect worth considering if you intend to spend a week or more on the road. Australian country restaurants usually welcome people who "BYOG" (bring your own grog) and a good bottle of Draytons Bellevue can disguise a very ordinary mixed grill.

The most tourist-oriented of the wineries is Hungerford Hill Wine Village near Pokolbin, which boasts a restaurant, adventure playground for the kids, barbecue facilities, wine tastings and so on. There are some very good Hungerford wines but you'd have to be keen to queue for them. People do. Rothbury Estate, while also tourist-conscious, caters more for the connoisseur. You don't have to be particularly knowledgeable about wine, but if your tastes run to Pineapple Pearl or Blackberry Nip, you might not find what you're after.

omy based on sheep and cattle. Tamworth's role as a commercial centre for outlying farms and ranches prompted a local radio announcer to establish a promotion on the cowboy theme. In the early 1970s he organised a country music festival and started referring to Tamworth as "the country music capital of Australia."

At the time of its inception, most Tamworth residents were appalled at the thought of being typecast as hillbillies. But the annual CM Festival has come to be the town's major tourist drawcard, and has brought it fame of sorts. While not even its organisers would compare Tamworth's festival to anything Nashville could dream up, the 10-day festival each January attracts more than 30,000 visitors and adds millions of dollars to local revenue. Although some of the music is authentically Australian, the most common sound heard during CM Week is an American twang—usually false. And the country-music tourist attractions, such as the **Hands of Fame Park** (yes, folks, just like Mann's Chinese Theatre) and the **Hall of Fame Wax Museum**, are slavishly American. The prodigious quantities of beer consumed during the festival, however, are always 100 per cent Australian.

Off the highway, but not far from Tamworth along a road which follows the bends of the Peel River, is the old gold mining town of **Nundle** Abandoned diggings and the ghost town atmosphere make it well worth the detour.

North of Tamworth the New England Highway passes through spectacular country, with rugged peaks and long plains dotted by quaint old mining towns. As well as gold diggings, there have been numerous gem fossickers' settlements in the area over the years. Now, most of the fossicking is confined to places like Inverell and Glen Innes to the west, where sapphires are mined commercially. The town of **Uralla**, once a thriving gold centre, houses the grave of the legendary bushranger Captain Thunderbolt, shot during a battle with police at nearby Kentucky Creek in 1870.

As its name suggests, the New England tableland bears striking similarities, both in topography and climate, to "the old country," England. Its altitude

gives it frosty mornings nine months of the year, occasional snow and a year-round freshness. The graceful charm of the towns is also very English, and nowhere is this more evident than in the city of **Armidale**.

A university town filled with parks and gardens, cathedrals and tree-lined streets, this could be Oxford on a summer day. As well as the **University of New England** Armidale has two other colleges and five boarding schools, establishing it as the major NSW seat of learning outside Sydney. The student population has given Armidale an air of youthfulness in contrast to its stately Victorian architecture, and the downtown area is a crazy mixture of refined clothing stores and stock and station agents on the one hand, and health-food bars and funky bookshops on the other.

Armidale is worth exploring in some detail, on foot. A wander through the streets can result in the discovery of little pieces of colonial history and an appreciation of the many influences on Australian architecture. There is no other Australian city quite like it.

The highway out of Armidale leads along a ridge to the watershed of the Great Dividing Range, 1,320 metres (4,330 feet) above sea level, at **Guyra**, then on to the junction with the Gwydir Highway at **Glen Innes**. Glen Innes, as previously mentioned, is famous for its gemstones. Almost a third of the world's sapphires are mined in this area and, although most of the good spots are on commercial lease, you can fossick for sapphires, garnets, jasper, agate and numerous other stones at many places. The town itself features ornate buildings and is fringed by five lovely parks.

**Tenterfield** is the next major town along the route, once chiefly famous as "the birthplace of Federation" (because Sir Henry Parkes first called for it in a speech made in the School of Arts here), but now more famous as the birthplace of Peter Allen's grandfather. The expatriate singer, a very popular figure in Australia, topped the charts a few years back with a eulogy of his grandfather called "Tenterfield Saddler." For all that, it is a rather ordinary town in which there is not a lot but memories.

North of Tenterfield the highway

View to the southeast from Bald Rock.

crosses the border into Queensland before reaching the town of **Stanthorpe**, notable for the fact that it invariably makes the evening weather report with the coldest temperature recorded in the northern state. With the exception of the Atherton Tablelands near Cairns, it is the highest point in Queensland and holds the record for Queensland's coldest recorded temperature—minus 14.6°C (5.7°F).

At **Warwick** the tableland gives way to the **Darling Downs**, a vast area of beautiful, rolling plains and rich soil. The city of Warwick is the southernmost point of the Downs and its commercial hub, serving as a base for the dairy, beef and horse stud industries. It is a pretty and interesting place, on the banks of the Condamine River. There are some beautiful buildings but the town's most famous feature is its annual month-long rodeo festival, which attracts the best of Australian cowboys—the real ones as opposed to the plastic replicas found a couple of hundred miles back down the road at Tamworth.

From this point there are several alternative routes to Brisbane, some three hours away. Each has its own points of interest.

The New England Highway continues north to **Toowoomba**, Queensland's largest inland city and a garden one at least. Situated on the rim of the Great Dividing Range, with the Darling Downs laid out before it, Toowoomba is colourful year-round but sensational in spring. In addition, within a few minutes' drive of the downtown area there are parks and lookouts with superb views.

From Toowoomba the quickest route to Brisbane is the Warrego Highway through the coal mining town of **Ipswich**. However, should you choose to bypass Toowoomba, the Cunningham Highway leads directly to Ipswich from Warwick, and on into Brisbane. If time is of no consequence, there is a well-made minor road leading to the spectacular **Lamington National Park** in the McPherson Ranges. This vast and dramatic rainforest park offers some of the best bushwalking to be had anywhere in Australia.

The Gold Coast beckons below Lamington, or the traveller can take a direct route into Brisbane through the Numinbah Valley.

t. Warning
ational Park
fers some
the best
shwalking
Australia.

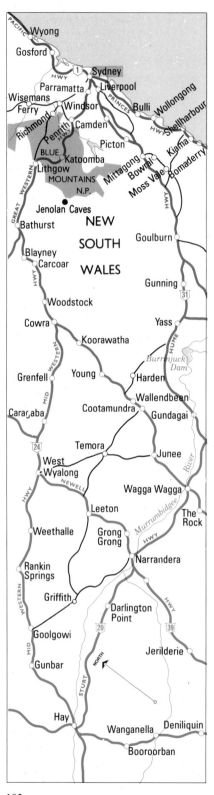

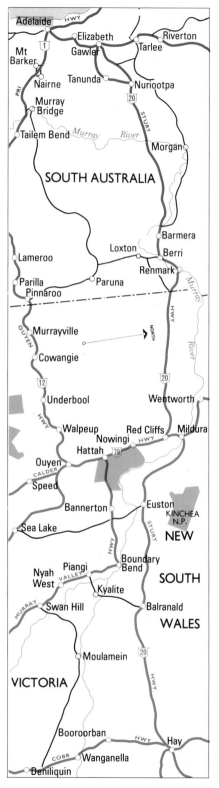

# SYDNEY-ADELAIDE:
# TWO INLAND ROUTES

Just west of Sydney hangs the low blue curtain of eucalyptus haze that has given the **Blue Mountains** their names.

It's the curtain that cuts the populous, beach-fringed coastal plain from Australia's notorious flat, harsh interior. And it was tightly drawn against the colony's first settlers as they struggled for more than two decades to squeeze through in a search for the broad acres they knew must be there for cultivation.

The first explorers' efforts to push through with the established techniques of full frontal attack were thwarted by the rugged sandstone cliffs. The footsteps of the successful ones who sought out the narrow passes are now followed westward by the main route out of Sydney, the Great Western Highway, as it joins the Mid-Western and Sturt highways on the most direct route to the South Australian capital of Adelaide about a third of the way across the country's southern seaboard. Even that comparatively small 1,400-kilometre (870-mile) nibble at a corner of the red continent is enough to open the curtain on the great Outback, where the crows fly backwards to keep the dust out of their eyes and the kids learn to swim in the mirage of the homestead paddock.

Today those explorers—Blaxland, Wentworth and Lawson—are remembered in the names of towns along the highway as it winds up into the mountains which, despite the difficulty they presented early travellers, are in fact a sandstone plateau reaching a height of only about 1,100 metres (3,600 feet). Erosion has let the stone fall away to form sheer cliff faces punctuated by picturesque waterfalls. The **Blue Mountains National Park** is the second largest in New South Wales, its rugged valleys are well served by bushwalking tracks and picnic and camping spots.

The Mountains' main town, **Katoomba**, is perched on the edge of the Jamison Valley, and shows off its natural wonders to the best from a cablecar running 275 metres (about 900 feet) above the valley floor. Also high on the list of breathtaking trips is the **Scenic Railway** which shafts down into a tree-clad gorge and is claimed to be the steepest railway in the world. As at most of the world's mountain resorts, there's an **Echo Point**. Katoomba overlooks one of the state's most photogenic and recognisable rock formations, the **Three Sisters**.

As the road drops from the mountains down the steep **Victoria Pass**, it narrows to cross a convict-built bridge which was part of the first road through to the rich wool, wheat, cattle and sheep country. A little way on, and 46 km (29 miles) south of the highway, are the magnificent **Jenolan Caves**, a mighty series of underground limestone halls and stalactite and stalagmite structures. A mock Olde English hotel, **Cave Houses**, tucked away in the canyon at the entrance to the caves, offers first-class accommodation.

### Bathurst and the Gold Rush

There's a monument to the ingenuity used in solving one of last century's great engineering problems at **Lithgow**, 12 km (7½ miles) on from the Jenolan Caves turnoff. It's the railway line which originally conquered the steep descent out of the Blue Mountains, known as the **Zig-zag Railway** for its unique method of overcoming the almost sheer mountainside. The zig-zag line was finished in 1869, but abandoned in 1910 for a more modern descent. Nostalgia and the dedication of train buffs eventually saw the line restored to give day excursions travelling back into railway history.

The city of **Bathurst** was a major pastoral centre even before it boomed with gold discoveries in the area in the 1850s. Its importance is once again based on rural production, although to the visitor its main interest is its link with the romantic Goldrush days. There's a packaged Gold Rush experience at **Karingal Village** on the city's scenic Mount Panorama, where an old-time diggings has been set up and gold-panning demonstrations are given. A bit more authentic is do-it-yourself fossicking at **Hill End**, a near-ghost town north of Bathurst.

Back in Bathurst, the scenic drive around **Mount Panorama** becomes a world-class motor racing circuit for two weekends of the year for two of Australia's most important motor sport events—in October for the Hardie 1000 production car race and at Easter for the annual motorcycle race meeting.

eceding ges, a farm ar Burra, uth stralia.

## Route One: the Mid-West

The Mid-Western Highway begins at Bathurst, veering off towards the Riverina district in the south of New South Wales. Just over 50 km (31 miles) from Bathurst is the photogenic and much-photographed village of **Carcoar**, where more than 20 restored colonial buildings with National Trust classification nestle in a picturesque little valley.

The highway runs through mainly sheep and wheat country to **Cowra**, a prosperous agricultural centre on the Lachlan River. Cowra has strong links with Japan. During World War Two, Japanese prisoners of war were interned in a camp there. The care local people gave to the graves of servicemen who died in an escape attempt impressed the Japanese, who later repaid them with the gift of several hectares of classically laid-out Japanese garden a colourful oriental showpiece in the gold-brown central west of New South Wales.

At Cowra the road runs out of overtaking lanes on hills and bends, and stays a basic two-lane blacktop for the next thousand-odd kilometres until the four-lane divided road approaches Adelaide. Actually, the road just about runs out of hills and bends anyway, as it gets into the true "sunburnt country" and "land of sweeping plains" of Dorothea Mackellar's evocative poem. The kangaroo warning signs aren't there just to give a bit of local colour or to provide target practice for frustrated shooters, although they do both—mostly the latter. 'Roos, cute and picture-postcard though they may be, are a serious driving hazard at night.

The harshness of the elements is burnt into the wild-west appearance of **West Wyalong**, 161 km (100 miles) west of Cowra. Motorists should avoid the bypass and drive down the main street of the former gold mining town.

It's a desolate drive on to **Hay**. The inspiration for Banjo Paterson's bitter poem, "Hay, Hell and Booligal," is apparent in the almost treeless horizons and the sun-parched tedium, broken only by the sight of an occasional emu or big lizard and the thudding sound of driving into a flock of feathered budgerigars.

Hay, about halfway to Adelaide, is a well-watered oasis on the banks of the **Murrumbidgee River**. For many years

Zig Zag Railway, Lithgow.

an important river crossing on the stock route to Victoria, it also served as a major link in the legendary Cobb and Co. coach network and is now the centre of an extensive wool-producing area. A century-old Cobb and Co. coach, used on one of the runs through the town until 1901, is featured at Hay's **Jail Museum**.

### The Sturt Highway

The route joins the Sturt Highway at Hay and continues on through more seared countryside to **Balranald**, another spot of green on the Murrumbidgee. About 150 km (93 miles) north of Balranald are the **Walls of China**, a geological phenomenon of 30-metre (98-foot) high walls of white sand running for 30 km (19 miles) across Mungo Station. They can only be seen by prior arrangement with the station owners. Another 80 arid km (50 miles) on from Balranald is another verdant spot as the highway touches the **Murray River**— the state border with Victoria—at **Euston**.

The highway crosses the Murray a further 80 km on and enters Victoria at the city of **Mildura**, a veritable Riviera of the state's northwest. While many Australian tourist-oriented centres claim the biggest or the longest of something, Mildura does itself the disservice of claiming the most of the biggest from the longest bar in the world (91 metres [298 feet] long at the Workingman's Club), to the largest fruit juice factory in Australia, to the largest deckchair ever built (in front of a main street motel), to the world's biggest talking Humpty Dumpty (at a poultry farm).

Despite the kitsch, Mildura is an exceptionally pleasant and friendly city, and its tourist orientation combines with its inherent water pastimes of fishing, swimming and boating. Irrigation has given the district a wealth of orchards and vineyards, and among the wineries offering tours and tastings are the Mildara and Karadoc wineries.

The Murray River, of course, is the dominant attraction, and it's easy to relive the days when the mighty paddlewheelers, laden with cargo and passengers, made the river a busy thoroughfare. Even a brief visit allows a taste of this stately cruising along the lazy Murray, lined with tall red gums, and

Three isters," lue ountains.

through one of the river's series of locks. There are two-hour trips on the steam-driven *Melbourne*, lunch and dinner cruises on the 1877 vintage *Avoca*, and five-day, fully catered cruises on the *Wanera* and the *Coonawarra*. For the more independent, there's a wide range of houseboats for hire.

But the water that has been the lifeblood of Mildura and other irrigated areas has brought the Murray itself to the brink of death. Farther downstream the silted shallows and skeletons of dead gums are evidence of the damage done in just over 100 years. Irrigation water flowing back into the river contains huge amounts of salt which had previously been held in the soil by trees cleared for growing crops. However, concerned governments have recognised the problem and are working to avoid the level of pollution which would turn Australia's greatest river into its greatest ecological disaster.

### Into South Australia

From Mildura it's a flat and straight drive through scrubby Mallee country to **Renmark**, on the Murray in South Australia. The fruit-fly inspection station at the border, where travellers are required to declare any plants or fruit they are carrying, is also the point where Eastern Standard Time ends, and clocks and watches go back 30 minutes.

Renmark, the first of the irrigation towns on the Murray, marks the start of the productive area (stretching to **Blanchetown**) which has been designated South Australia's Riverland. The area's orchards produce 2 million tonnes of fruit a year, and its 16 wineries include such names as Angoves and Renmano at Renmark, Berri Estates at **Glossop**, and Penfolds at **Waikerie**.

River transport is prominent here, too, with the paddleboat days remembered in the old steamer *Industry* moored as a floating museum. The 128-passenger *Murray Explorer* runs five-day cruises and there are lunch cruises and dinner dances on the cruising restaurant, the *Barragul*. Houseboats can be hired at Renmark, Loxton, Berri and Waikerie.

The air currents from the plains around Waikerie have made it a leading gliding centre and a venue for gliding competition. Its apt Aboriginal name, which means "anything that flies,"

however, refers to the abundant birdlife in the nearby **Hart Lagoon**.

After so much level country, the **Mount Lofty Ranges**, about 100 km (62 miles) from Adelaide, soon loom strangely in the distance. On the other side of the mountains the highway touches the wine area of the **Barossa Valley** (see box) at **Nooriootpa**. After passing through undulating wheatfields to **Gawler**, it links up with a four-lane divided road through to the outskirts of Adelaide.

### Route Two: via the Barrier

*On Western plains, where shade is not,*
*'Neath summer skies of cloudless blue,*
*Where all is dry and all is hot...*

These are apt lines to describe the longer alternative route from Sydney to Adelaide by the Mitchell and Barrier highways. They were written by a man born within a "coo-ee" of the Mitchell Highway—Banjo Paterson, author of Australia's best internationally known verse in "Waltzing Matilda" and "The Man From Snowy River."

Below, the paddlesteamer *Melbourne* on the Murray River Right, European elegance in the Barossa

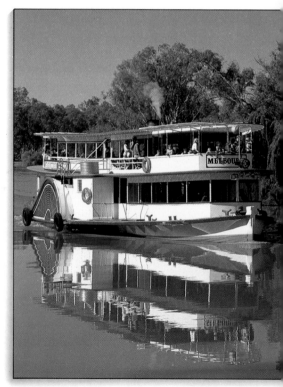

# GERMANY IN THE BAROSSA

It's debatable whether the dour Lutheran settlers of the Barossa Valley would approve of the goings-on there these days. But Australia's wine drinkers certainly do.

It's all *oom-pah-pah* and over-indulgence every second April for the Vintage Festival in the Barossa, a 30-km (19-mile) long hollow in the rolling wheatfields an hour-or-so's drive north of Adelaide. (The rest of the time the German heritage is as strong, but more subdued—in the proliferation of Lutheran churches, the place names and the mouth-watering wares in the bakery and delicatessen windows.) Thousands of hectares and row after row of grapevines, comprising nearly 40 vineyards, keep the Barossa's name at the top of sophisticated wine lists. The valley is the nation's biggest producer of award-winning wines.

With wine the main attraction, the valley does its best to keep the visitor's cup overflowing, literally as well as figuratively. Nearly all the wineries have tasting and sales rooms, and many have barbecue and picnic areas complementing the range of restaurants and pubs. Like a well-stocked cellar built up over many years, the wineries are spread the length of the Barossa Valley Highway as it winds from the major agricultural centre of Gawler, through Lyndoch in its forest setting and Tanunda, the most distinctly traditional German town, to the commercial and service centre of Nuriootpa, which is situated on the Para River.

Many of the wineries not only boast excellent produce, but have magnificent grounds and picturesque buildings, like the palm groves at Seppetsfield (which date back to 1852), the battlemented Chateau Yaldara, and the two-storey blue-marble buildings at Yalumba. For German-style cooking there are a number of restaurants; probably the best known are Die Galerie (a combined bistro and art gallery at Tanunda) and the Weinstube (on the Sturt Highway between Tanunda and Nooriootpa).

And to spiritual matters of another sort, the old Lutheran churches are of abiding beauty, with spires rising above quaint bluestone villages. Foremost among them are Langmeil at Tanunda, famed for its tree-lined Long Walk and where Pastor Kavel, founder of the church in Australia, is buried; the nearby St John's, dedicated in 1868 by dissidents from Langmeil; and Herbige Christe at Bethany where the Germans settled in 1842.

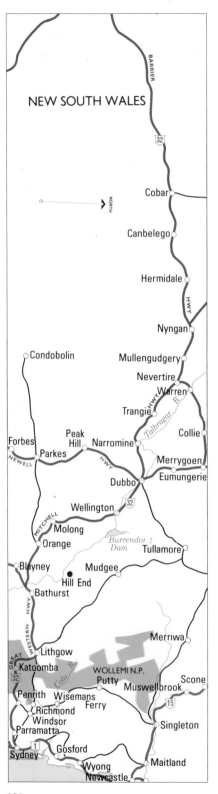

NEW SOUTH WALES

32

Cobar
Canbelego
Hermidale
Nyngan
Condobolin        Mullengudgery
                  Nevertire
                  Warren
         Trangie
Peak          Collie
Forbes  Hill  Narromine
Parkes        Merrygoen
       Dubbo   Eumungerie
    Wellington    32
      Molong
      Orange    Burrendong    Tullamore
                Dam
Blayney     Mudgee
         Hill End
    Bathurst
                    Merriwa
   Lithgow
Katoomba
  32    WOLLEMI N.P.
       Putty          Scone
Penrith  Wisemans  Muswellbrook
   Richmond  Ferry
   Windsor
Parramatta            Singleton
Sydney  Gosford
     Wyong      Maitland
     Newcastle

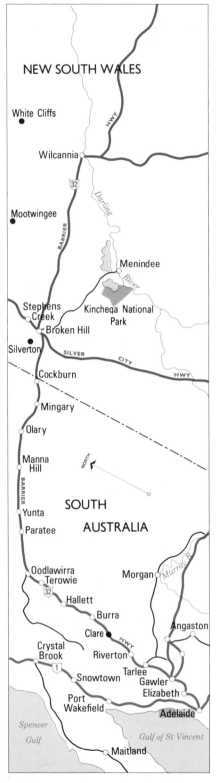

NEW SOUTH WALES

White Cliffs
Wilcannia
          32
Mootwingee
                   Menindee
          Stephens   Kinchega National
          Creek      Park
   Nyngan    Broken Hill
Silverton   SILVER   CITY
       Cockburn      HWY
       Mingary
Olary
Manna
Hill
       Yunta       SOUTH
       Paratee     AUSTRALIA

Oodlawirra      Morgan
 Terowie
  32
   Hallett
      Burra
   Clare        Angaston
Crystal
Brook   Riverton
       Snowtown   Tarlee
             Gawler
Port          Elizabeth
Wakefield
          Adelaide
Spencer
Gulf        Gulf of St Vincent
        Maitland

The 1,900-km (1,180-mile) trip veers north of the Mid-Western Highway route, starting in Bathurst and curving through the centre of New South Wales before dropping through the arid west of South Australia to Adelaide. It's a more typically Outback journey, taking in such character-laden towns as Cobar and Wilcannia and the independent-minded city of Broken Hill, all redolent of the pioneering spirit that still lives in the parched red land around them.

The route follows the Great Western Highway from Sydney to Bathurst, then forks northwest on the Mitchell Highway into hilly country and the town of **Orange** on the slopes of the extinct volcano, Mount Canobolas. Orange is, predictably, a fruit-growing centre; not so predictably, however, the crops are apples and cherries rather than any citrus fruits.

**Mount Canobolas** itself, 14 km (nine miles) southwest of Orange, is a 1,500-hectare (600-acre) flora and fauna reserve with walking trails, picnic areas, waterfalls and a 360-degree view of the countryside from the summit. The **Ophir Goldfields**, 27 km (17 miles) northeast of the city, were the site of the discovery of the first payable gold in Australia in 1851 and are now an official fossicking area. Banjo Paterson's birthplace is marked by a memorial three kilometres off the highway on the Ophir Road.

On its way into more undulating terrain around **Wellington**, the Mitchell Highway, like the Mid Western Highway, runs out of overtaking lanes and is a modest two-lane blacktop all the way to Gawler, 42 km (26 miles) from Adelaide. The **Wellington Caves**, eight km (five miles) southwest of the town, have huge stalagmite formations in their limestone caverns.

About the most westward of the well-watered and obviously productive areas is near the thriving city of **Dubbo**. It is in the middle of the wheat belt and is an area of large sheep and cattle properties and irrigated farms. There's a sampling of all this rural richness at the **Merrilea Farm Museum** a few kilometres out of town; this working farm has displays of antique machinery, Australiana, minerals and fossils.

Dubbo's main attraction for tourists is the **Western Plains Zoo**, a world-class wildlife park associated with Sydney's Taronga Park Zoo. Animals are placed in settings as near as possible to their native conditions, and penned by moats rather than cages or fences, giving an illusion that they are roaming free.

It may be a sign of an unconscious national obsession with a convict and bushranging past, but Australia has an inordinate number of jails as tourist attractions. Dubbo is no exception: the **Old Dubbo Gaol**, which was closed in 1966 after almost 80 years, has been restored complete with gallows and is open for self-guided inspection tours.

**Narromine**, 39 km (24 miles) on from Dubbo and on the edge of the Western Plains, is a major citrus growing area, and the local Citrus Packers Co-Operative will let visitors have a look around. The terrain provides thermal lifts to make the area ideal for gliding.

On into the Macquarie Valley Irrigation Area, the town of **Trangie** is the centre of a large cotton-growing industry, and visits can be arranged to the nearby Auscott Cotton Farm. Harvesting and ginning takes place from late April to June, the best time to visit.

## A Petrol Drought

The scenery starts to take on the inland's dry brownness heading to **Nyngan** on the Bogan River, where the Barrier Highway begins. Here motorists should decide whether they have enough confidence in their vehicles to push on, and start keeping an eye on the petrol gauge. There's no petrol available over the 128 km (80 miles) to Cobar; only one petrol station, at Emmadale, betwen Cobar and Wilcannia; petrol available only at little Topar between Wilcannia and Broken Hill; and few service stations from there to Yunta in South Australia.

**Cobar**, on the fringe of the Outback, typifies the resilience of the area's people as well as its hardy flora and fauna. From being a rip-roaring town of 10,000 people and 14 hotels not long after copper mining began there in the 1870s, its fortunes have varied; 100 years later its population was less than 4,000 and only one mine was operating. But the 1983 opening of the Eleura lead, zinc and silver mine has boosted the town's population and economy. The CSA copper mine, seven km (4½ miles) out of town, holds inspections every Friday; and the Pastoral, Mining and Technological Museum, in an old two-storey mining company office, gives a fascinating insight into the area and its people.

Another old building which can provide glimpses of old-style bush living is Cobar's Great Western Hotel. It's the epitome of country hotels with its massive first-floor verandah. It gives a chance to sample the character of the ubiquitous two-storey pub, found on at least one corner of any large town, but without the inconvenience of the old-style sagging bed and bathroom down the corridor. Classification by the National Trust means the exterior retains its original timberwork and iron lace, but on the inside accommodation has been transformed into modern motel-style units. It didn't need the National Trust to keep history alive in the Great Western's public bar, where the regulars lining the counter are always ready for a yarn with strangers.

### Aboriginal Cave Paintings

About 40 km (25 miles) along the highway to Wilcannia is the turnoff to the **Mount Grenfell** Aboriginal cave paintings. The caves—really shallow overhanging rock shelters—are a rare example of the primitive painting techniques with pigments applied by finger in human, bird and animal outlines. There are excellent examples of hand stencil paintings, made holding a hand against the rock and outlining its shape by blowing a mouthful of pigment around it. Visitors have to call at the Mount Grenfell Station homestead, about 30 km (19 miles) off the highway by good dirt road, for the key to the cages which have been built around the caves to prevent damage from vandalism or animals brushing against the easily erased paintings.

The highway continues on with long straight stretches to the sleepy town of **Wilcannia**, where a number of historic buildings and wharf remnants are reminders of the days when its position on the **Darling River** made it the third largest inland port in the country and earned it the title of "Queen City of the West." The lift-span bridge on the approach to the town is an interesting relic of those days: machinery lifted the roadway straight up to allow the paddlesteamers to pass underneath.

Travelling into **Broken Hill** there's a

Slagheaps a Cobar.

symbolic recognition of the city's individuality; although it's in New South Wales, watches and clocks are turned back 30 minutes to South Australia's time zone. Broken Hill lives in N.S.W. geographically and administratively, has most of its trade and communication through South Australia, but very much retains a mind of its own.

### Broken Hill's Mining Empire

The city looms large in Australia's industrial history, with legendary union-mine management confrontation resulting in the domination of the city by the unions' Barrier Industrial Council. Its mineral wealth played the largest part in changing the nation from being a strictly pastoral one. It all began in 1883 when a boundary rider and amateur geologist stumbled across a lump of silver ore on a rocky outcrop he described as a "broken hill." From the claim he pegged grew the nation's largest company, the Broken Hill Proprietory Co. Ltd. Although it diversified and had completely moved out of Broken Hill by 1939, BHP is still spoken of with distaste in the city for its attitude to the work force.

"The Hill" turned out to be the world's largest silver, lead and zinc lode, and while other mining towns have tended to peter out over the years, this one is still going strong. It has yielded more than 145 million tonnes of ore from its eight-km (five-mile) long lode. It has also become the centre for two of Australia's greatest institutions—the Flying Doctor Service, which carries medical attention across the vast distances of the Outback by aircraft, and the School of the Air, conducting classes by two-way radio for children on remote properties.

Broken Hill is also the focus of a school of painters calling themselves The Brushmen of the Bush and including such recognised names as Pro Hart, Jack Absalom and Hugh Schulz. Among the half-dozen or so galleries in the city, the one opened in the middle of town by Pro Hart—naive in style but not in self-promotion—complements the delightfully eccentric display at his suburban gallery.

Delprat's Mine, a disused mine in the almost black hill that dominates the city, gives the non-claustrophobic a

North Mine, Broken Hill.

chance to don hardhat, lamp and boots for a guided tour 120 metres (394 feet) underground in drives started in the early, evil days of hand drilling. With former miners as guides, it shows the terrible hardships of miners of the past and the still-hard conditions of today's underground workers. There are also surface tours of another mine, the North Mine, and reproductions of mine workings at the Gladstone Mining Museum.

Anyone who doesn't go down a mine can still "go down the mine" figuratively on the poker machines in the wide range of Broken Hill's licensed clubs. A lot of the city's social life revolves around the clubs and some of the bigger ones, such as the Musicians, Sturt, Legion and Social Democratic clubs, welcome visitors and have good dining and bar facilities.

## A Beach and a Ghost Town

In red, rocky country it may be, but Broken Hill still has its beach resort at **Lake Menindee**, 110 km (68 miles) away. This is the city's part-natural and part-man-made water-supply system. The lake, and a system of other lakes and channels, caters for yachting, power boating and swimming, and combines with the adjacent **Kinchega National Park** as a home for a wide variety of water birds.

The ghost mining town of **Silverton**, 23 km (14 miles) from Broken Hill, with its restored buildings is not just an attraction for tourists; it's becoming a regular star in Outback movie epics. With repainted shop and hotel signs, it's appeared in *A Town Like Alice, Mad Max II* and *Razorback*, and the predictable result is that an Outback Hollywood is evolving. also in the Silverton area is the 100-year-old Day Dream Mine, where inspections include walking down into the workings the way the pioneer miners did.

For the braver traveller with a bit more time, the Wilcannia-Broken Hill section can be done right off the beaten track with a detour through the **White Cliffs** opal field and the **Mootwingee** historic site. It's a rewarding diversion, but not one to be taken lightly because of the lack of sealed roads, petrol, water and creature comforts.

The opal field of White Cliffs, 98 km (61 miles) north of Wilcannia, is a lunar landscape of diggings craters. Many residents live underground to escape the scorching winds and extreme temperatures. Fossickers with permits can have a scrounge around; some of the locals don't mind showing off the interiors of their subterranean settlement. Accommodation at White Cliffs consists of a hotel and a camping area.

Looping around about 160 km (100 miles), a road leads to Mootwingee, a surprising area of greenness in the barren Bynguano Ranges. The strange and colourful rock formations surround ancient Aboriginal campsites, tools, engravings and paintings, which are outlined in films shown at the visitors centre. It's necessary to check with the resident ranger on arrival. There are camping facilities but no power.

Fifty km (31 miles) from Broken Hill, the Barrier Highway crosses into south Australia with a fruit-fly check at **Cockburn**, and unrolls through arid, scrubby country and a series of one-pub, one-shop towns into the wheatlands of the state's mid-north.

The first sight of a major town is at **Burra**, 150 km (93 miles) from Adelaide. An old mining town, Burra originally yielded copper to Welsh and Cornish immigrants who brought their mining traditions with them. The mines were closed in 1877 and re-opened in 1970; much of the original architecture remains, including a few of the dugouts along the banks of Burra Creek which at one stage housed about 1,500 miners. They can be inspected, along with other picturesque and historic buildings—this time including two jails, the Redruth Gaol and the Burra North Court House and Gaol.

On from Burra, 30 km (19 miles) off the highway, is **Clare**, the centre of the leading wine area of the Clare Valley. Fifteen wineries in a 25-km (15-mile) strip open to the public for sales. Among those which hold inspections are Quelltaler, established in 1870 and with original stone architecture intact; Sevenhill Cellars, established in 1851 by German Jesuit priests; and the well-known names of Taylor's Chateau Clare, Robertson's Clare Vineyards and the Stanley Wine Company.

The highway gets a little busier as it winds its way through sheep and cattle country to the agricultural centre of Gawler, where it joins the Sturt Highway for the run into Adelaide.

Right, a "road train."

# MELBOURNE TO ADELAIDE

The two most popular road routes between the capital cities of the states of Victoria and South Australia offer dramatic contrasts in terrain and scenery. One is partly a seaboard route that takes in some of Australia's most spectacular coastal terrain. The other carves through the history and heartland of Victoria's old goldfields, an area that has since given way to the golden yield of the wheat crop. The natural and historical aspects encountered along both routes say much about the history and settlement of the region.

**Around Port Phillip Bay**

From the fringe of Melbourne the Princes Highway speeds through the flat plains along the northern shore of Port Phillip Bay. For a glimpse of an era of opulent elegance just minutes from suburbia, take the turnoff to **Werribee Park**. In a 60-room Italianate mansion built in the 1870s by the Chirnside family, who migrated from Scotland and created a pastoral empire, visitors can see a vivid example of flamboyant wealth.

Another half-hour's drive, with the volcanic You Yangs dominating the skyline, brings you to the heart of Victoria's second city. In its early days **Geelong** rivalled Melbourne as an outlet for the wool of the Western District and the landfall for thousands who tramped northwards to the goldfields at Ballarat. From Ceres Lookout you have a view of a park-filled city curving around Corio Bay. A drive along the waterfront shows Geelong past and present, at work and at play—the old mansions, woolstores and piers and the new industries, wharves and container terminal; the fishing boats and the palm-treed lawns and pools of Eastern Beach. Along the Barwon River are fine homes such as the National Trust's Barwon Grange, refurnished in the period of 1855 when it was built by a merchant ship-owner.

For a whiff of nostalgia, take the Bellarine Highway out of Geelong and join the coast at **Queenscliff**. This was the "Queen of the Watering Places" in the 1880s when the great paddlesteamers brought the fashionable of Melbourne to stay at the handsome turreted hotels, today being restored to their brass-bed elegance. The Queenscliff fort, with its red brick walls, loopholes and polished cannon, was built in the last century to defend Melbourne against a possible Russian invasion. Now it is the Australian Army Command and Staff College. Its black lighthouse still guards The Rip, the treacherous entrance to Port Phillip Bay.

The road from Queenscliff to Anglesea meanders through small seaside settlements, sleepy in winter and pulsing with life in summer. Below the lighthouse at **Point Lonsdale** is the cave of William Buckley, an escaped convict who lived and hunted with an Aboriginal tribe for 32 years. He was the only white man in an Aboriginal world until the first settlers arrived in 1835. Near **Torquay**, the surf centre of Victoria, is Bells Beach, famed for the Easter surf contest which attracts the cream of the world's wave-riders.

**The Great Ocean Road**

Beyond **Anglesea**, where kangaroos share the golf course with the players, is the start of the Great Ocean Road, built by returned soldiers as a memorial to their comrades after World War One. It replaced an often-impassable track and opened up 200 kilometres (125 miles) of the state's most spectacular coastal scenery.

A favourite spot is **Lorne**, set on a picturesque bay with a bush backdrop. The slopes, once blackened by a devastating bushfire which swept through here on Ash Wednesday, February 1982, are again washed with green.

In the **Lorne Forest Park**, walking tracks wind along rivers and creeks to waterfalls and lookouts, through eucalypt forest and fern gullies. The walks vary from the gentle stroll along the St. George's River to rock-hopping along the craggy Cumberland to the Cascades. A three-hour hike up the Erskine River to the falls can be strenuous. The less energetic can reach the site by car. Along the coast at Kennett River, a six-km (3½-mile) drive will take you to the **Grey River Scenic Reserve**. It's a short walk (1½ km return) up a fern-filled gully amid towering blue gums, one of the best of its kind in Victoria.

receding
ages, The
welve
postles.

From Apollo Bay, the Great Ocean Road leaves the coast to wind through the forest behind **Cape Otway**, where the lighthouse has watched over the hazardous entrance to Bass Strait since 1848. For an alternative panoramic view of the ranges, turn inland at Skenes Creek and drive up into the hills. After 15 km (9½ miles), turn left into the delightful fern-and-mountain ash forest along Turton's Track. When the country opens out again you are on a high ridge. On the left, wooded spurs reach down to the sea; on the right are the volcanic lakes and plains of the Western District.

### The Twelve Apostles

Just south of **Lavers Hill**, take a breather under the tree ferns and myrtle beaches of Melba Gully before dipping down to the coast. Beyond Princetown lies the spectacular coastline of **Port Campbell National Park** where breakers have battered the soft limestone cliffs, creating grottoes and gorges, arches and sea-sculptures rising from the surf. The clifftop road gives only glimpses of the drama below, which includes tne stark rock stacks of the Twelve Apostles and the spray billowing through the arches of London Bridge. So take the time to turn off to all the vantage points.

The **Loch Ard Gorge** is a reminder of the dangers of this "shipwreck coast" where many a sailing ship has been pounded to pieces on the unforgiving reefs. The clipper *Loch Ard* hit the reef off Mutton Bird Island on June 1, 1878. Of the 54 people on board, only two survived. Tom Pearce, a young apprentice, saved the life of 18-year-old Eva Carmichael who, clinging to a spar, was washed into the gorge. He dragged her to safety and then climbed the sheer cliff to find help.

Beyond Peterborough and the dramatic Bay of Islands, the road turns inland to **Warrnambool**, once a busy port and now a progressive pastoral and holiday centre. Around the original lighthouse complex is the Flagstaff Hill Maritime Museum, a recreated 19th-Century port with its ship's chandlers, shipwrights and sailmakers. Among relics of wrecks is the *Loch Ard* peacock, an 1851 Minton porcelain statue miraculously washed up (still in its packing case) in Loch Ard Gorge.

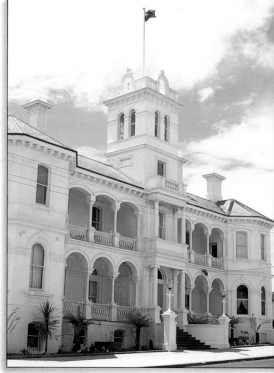

Near Warrnambool is **Tower Hill**, a volcanic crater containing smaller cones and lakes. Once a lush oasis of bush and swamp life, it was destroyed when the land was cleared for grazing and cultivation, but is being restored to its original beauty. A one-way road takes you through the centre of the crater where ducks once more nest on the lakes and emus enthusiastically share your picnic. Once back on the rim, turn left to circle the crater before rejoining the main road at Killarney.

### Sealers and Whalers

Along the coast is the fishing-village charm of **Port Fairy** where brightly painted boats tie up at the jetty with their catches of lobster and crab. Traditionally the birthplace of Victoria, Port Fairy was named by Captain James Wishart who brought his tiny cutter, the *Fairy*, into the Moyne River to find shelter during a sealing expedition in 1810.

Sealers and then whalers built quaint stone cottages which still nestle under the tall Norfolk Island pines shading the streets. You can still drink at the

Caledonian Inn which opened in 1844 and is said to be the oldest continuously licensed hotel in Victoria.

**Griffiths Island**, at the mouth of the river, was a whaling station, but is now a rookery for thousands of mutton birds which return each September from the North Pacific. The young hatch in January; every evening till they leave in April you can watch the adult birds swoop from the sea at dusk to feed their chicks.

On the way to Portland look in at **The Crags** for unusual rock scenery and a view of flat-topped **Lady Julia Percy Island**, where a colony of fur seals breed. **Portland**—big wharves on a broad bay and solid 19th-Century bluestone buildings—was a whaling station when Edward Henty arrived in 1834 and ploughed the first furrow in Victorian soil. The Henty family pioneered not only Portland but the wool-clip country to the north.

Around Portland gentle beaches contrast with the rugged rockscapes. Take the cliff walks at **Cape Nelson** and view the moonscape bluff of **Cape Bridgewater**, where wind and water have fashioned a petrified forest from scrub.

e coast at
ort
ampbell
ational
ark.

## Volcanic Flowers and Lakes

The coast road to South Australia skirts **Mount Richmond**, a sand-covered volcano ablaze with wildflowers in spring. It's a perfect spot for picnics and walks at any time of the year, and borders **Discovery Bay Coastal Park** with its vast rolling sand dunes and stretches of unspoilt beach. It runs along the southern margin of **Lower Glenelg National Park**, known for the scenic Glenelg River Gorge and the delicate limestone formations of Princess Margaret Rose caves. You can drive there or take a guided boat tour from Nelson up the gorge to the caves. The park is very nature-rich with 700 species of native plants but most of it can only be explored by river or on rough, sandy tracks.

Crossing the South Australian border you are into pine plantation country. At **Mount Gambier**, the centre of this large softwood industry, you can see the mills at work.

The city nestles on the side of Mount Gambier, a 5,000-year-old extinct volcano. Within its rim lie three craters, four crater lakes and a mystery: the Blue Lake that each November turns from winter grey to brilliant azure.

Outside the city are the **Tantanoola** limestone caves. Tantanoola became famous in the 1890s for the legendary "tiger" which terrorised the district. When shot, it proved to be an Assyrian wolf; the stuffed carcass now gazes glass-eyed at drinkers in the bar of the local hotel.

At Millicent take Alternate Route 1 to **Robe**, a once-important port that has retained much of its early character. The Caledonian Inn, licensed in 1858, still caters to weary travellers. A stone near the harbour commemorates the thousands of Chinese who disembarked at Robe in the 1850s and tramped hundreds of kilometres through bush to the Victorian gold-diggings, to avoid the £10 arrival tax imposed at Victorian ports.

This part of the coast is renowned for its shellfish. At **Kingston** you can buy delicious fresh lobster at the jetty.

### Waterfowl of The Coorong

Beyond Kingston lies **Coorong** (*karangh* or "narrow neck" to the

Ballarat.

Aborigines), a long thin neck of water stretching 135 km (84 miles) from the mouth of the Murray River to the saltpans and marshy ponds at the southern end. The crossing takes you across to the massive sand dunes of the **Younghusband Peninsula** that separates The Coorong from the Southern Ocean. If you don't have a four-wheel drive vehicle, it's a half-hour walk across the dunes to the ocean beach, an endless arc of golden sand left mostly to the seagulls, pied oyster-catchers and occasional fishermen. For thousands of years the Aborigines lived in this environment, netting fish in the lagoons, collecting cockles on the beach and fashioning reeds for rafts and baskets.

Pelicans, terns and seagulls have permanent breeding colonies on the small islands that dot The Coorong. A great number and variety of waterfowl feed on the seeds and tubers of the waterplants in the lagoons and drink at the freshwater soaks. For a closer look you can still travel part of the old bullock cart track that winds along the water's edge and camp anywhere in the national park. But to fully explore The Coorong you need time; preferably a

boat; and in the heat of summer near the drying saltflats, a strong nose!

From the Coorong, the Princes Highway wends its way past **Lake Alexandrina** at the mouth of the Murray, joining the Dukes Highway at Tailem Bend for the drive to Swanport and the gentle ride along the freeway to Adelaide.

### Gold Rush Memories
### On the Western Highway

Soon after shaking off the suburbs, the Western Highway winds westward from Melbourne into the bare, rolling Pentland Hills. Becoming a freeway, it brushes the orchards and market gardens of **Bacchus Marsh** where the notorious bushranger Captain Moonlight was once a lay preacher. It whisks you past the Lion Park, through farming country, past a mock castle and into **Ballarat** within an hour—a far cry from the jolting day-long journey along potholed tracks that faced the miners bound for the gold-diggings in the 1850s.

On the way into Ballarat a signpost points to **Eureka**, a name etched into Australian history. At the site, a diora-

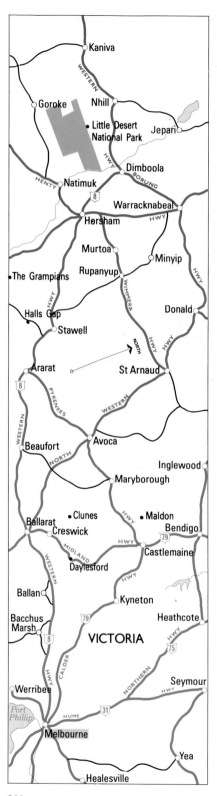
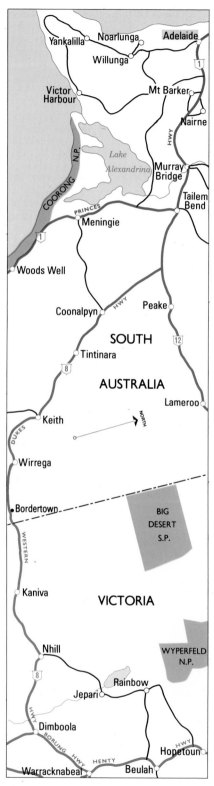

ma brings to life the day in December 1854 when the diggers, angered by government oppression, stood up for their rights at the Eureka Stockade. When troops stormed the stockade, 22 diggers lost their lives. Their sacrifice gained a new deal for their mates and provided a pivotal point for Australian republicanism that still burns today.

The rumbustious life of those times is recreated in the gold-mining town of **Sovereign Hill**. In the main street, re-sembling Ballarat in the 1850s with its old-fashioned wooden shops, apothe-cary and confectioners, you can watch craftsmen—blacksmiths, tinsmiths and potters—at work; have your own *Wanted* poster printed by the old press in the *Ballarat Times* office; sample a digger's lunch at the New York Bakery; or have a drink at the United States Hotel next to the Victoria Theatre where Lola Montez danced her famous "spider dance." Take a ride on a Cobb & Co. coach and pan for gold in the creek. After a look around the Red Hill gully diggings, slake your thirst at the "lemonade" tent—the sly grog shop where diggers celebrated their luck or drowned their sorrows. Then walk along the underground tunnel of the Quartz Mine, typical of the company mines where in the later years the real money was made.

### Golden Elegance

Today's Ballarat was born in the boom time and its wide streets, veran-dahs and lace, towers and colonnades give it grace and charm. The fine Art Gallery is renowned for its Australian paintings and the Botanic Gardens be-side Lake Wendouree sport Italian stat-ues and a blaze of begonias, at their best for the Begonia Festival in March.

Worth exploring are the other "gold-en" towns to the north of Ballarat, where once thousands of men dug into their eight square feet of dirt with ant-like ardour. **Clunes**, the scene of the first Victorian gold strike on July 1, 1851, boasts an ornate town hall, ele-gant banks and bluestone churches standing beside vacant verandahed shops. **Daylesford**, a picturesque town on Wombat Hill, is known (along with its neighbour **Helpburn Springs**) as the spa centre of Australia. In **Castlemaine**, the Greek temple-style market (now a museum) and other fine buildings date

from an era of promise never quite fulfilled. **Maldon** was selected as the National Trust's first "notable town in Australia" for its well-preserved goldrush-era streetscapes.

In **Bendigo**, some of the richest quartz reefs in the world created a Victorian extravaganza. The scarlet Joss House is an interesting reminder of the many thousands of Chinese who came to the "Big Gold Mountain," bringing with them their temples, tea-houses and fes-tivals. Their colourful Chinese dragon, Sun Loong, is 100 metres (328 feet) long and the star of the Bendigo Easter Fair.

The road west from Ballarat passes **Lake Burrumbeet** and **Beaufort**, notable for its beautifully preserved lacework band rotunda topped with a clock tow-er, then continues past forested hills to **Ararat**. The town's first settler named a nearby peak Mount Ararat "for like the Ark, we rested there." The town has indeed become a comfortable country centre for the surrounding farmers. Between Ararat and Stawell vines were first planted in 1863 by two French settlers who saw that the soil and climate resembled that of France. The vines flourished and fine wines have been produced at Great Western ever since. At Seppelt's, guided tours show you the champagne-making process and the long underground galleries, dug by ex-miners, where millions of bottles of champagne are maturing.

**Stawell** developed from gold finds at Pleasant Creek. Scenes of its pioneering days are among the exhibits at the town's "Mini World." The big event on the calendar is the Stawell Easter Gift, one of the richest footraces in the world, attracting entrants from many different countries.

### The Grampian Wonderland

Turn left at Stawell towards **Halls Gap** and the craggy face of the **Gram-pians** rises abruptly to dominate the surrounding plains. These mountains, named after the Scottish Grampians, are a series of rocky ranges thrown up by the folding of a sandstone mass into an uncommon cuesta formation—spectacular escarpments on the east side and gentle slopes to the west. Weathering has shaped bizarre rock sculptures and waterfalls cascade over the sheer face.

Spring brings a splash of colour as

wildflowers burst into bloom: the gold of wattle and guinea-flower, red grevilleas, pink heaths, blue lilies and orchids of every hue. More than a thousand species of native plants provide a year-round garden, at its best from August to November.

Vehicle-bound mountaineers can drive to many scenic points but there is still wilderness aplenty for the more adventurous and walking tracks to suit all sorts. You can drive past **Lake Bellfield**, where koalas feed in the manna gums, to the highest peak in the ranges, **Mount William** (1,167 metres or 3,829 feet). A 1½-km walk takes you to the summit. Return to Halls Gap via the Silverband Road to take in some of the highlights of the Wonderland Range.

Many of the outstanding features of the Grampians are woven into the Dreamtime legends of the Aborigines who lived in a land of plenty under their shadow. One such tells of Tchingal (the monstrous emu) who chased War (the crow) from her home in the Mallee. When War took refuge in a tunnel under one of the Grampian Ranges, Tchingal struck it with her foot, splitting it in two and so forming Roses Gap.

More than 40 Aboriginal art sites have been found in caves and rock shelters in the Grampians. Some of the more accessible are in the Victoria Range, where you can see hand stencils in red ochre in the **Cave of Hands**, and a variety of paintings including animals, human figures and a kangaroo hunt in the Glenisla Shelter. This site was found in 1859 by the owner of **Glenisla Station**, a sheep run (established in 1836) which once covered most of the Western Grampians. Today guests can stay at the century-old stone homestead and at several other farm properties around the district.

To continue your westward journey, set off from Halls Gap on the Mount Victory Road, taking the short detours to Boroka and Reid lookouts for magnificent but different views. From **Reid Lookout** high over the Victoria Valley, the home of kangaroos and emus, a 15-minute walk along the clifftop brings you to **The Balconies**, outcrops of sandstone that hang like giant jaws over the precipice.

As the road winds through the forest, stop at the viewpoint for the **McKenzie Falls** or take the walking track to the

Snow in the Grampians.

falls along the river, before going on to Zumsteins. Walter Zumstein, the beekeeper and bushlover who pioneered this valley, befriended the kangaroos and each afternoon their descendants still come from the forest to be fed.

From here, head for Horsham through flat farming country beneath the jagged outline of the Northern Grampians. They have their own charms: at **Flat Rock**, in spring, miniature rock gardens grow in the crevices; and the white pipeclay figures are on view in the Aboriginal **Cave of Ghosts**.

The Western Highway travels the heart of the **Wimmera**, the granary of Victoria, a sweep of golden wheatfields as far as the eye can see. This area, the size of Wales, stretches from the Grampians west to the South Australia border and north to the sand dunes and dry lakebeds of **Wyperfield National Park**. It is dotted with put-and-post office townships, soaring silos and more sheep than people.

**Horsham** is its hub and here on the banks of the Wimmera River is held one of the largest and richest fishing competitions in Australia. On Labour Day in March, thousands of fishermen line the river banks to try their luck at catching the biggest redfin.

For a change of scene, turn off the highway at Kiata and drive 10 km (six miles) south to the picnic ground at the edge of the **Little Desert National Park**. It's the desert that isn't, where in spring the heathland plants are a riot of colour. The Little Desert got its name from the poor sandy soils that made it useless farming country. But it is home to a wide variety of plants from mallee eucalypts to the silky tea-tree, desert banksias to orchids. Its wildlife ranges from the black-faced kangaroo to the silky desert mouse and the painted and bearded dragons.

From Kiata the road strides westward through the country centres of **Nhill** and **Kaniva** to the South Australian border.

### Charming Emptiness

With a couple of hundred kilometres of pancake country still to go before you reach the Murray River, your view of the Australian landscape might well begin to resemble that of actor Robert Morley when he wrote: "It's so empty and featureless, like a newspaper that has been entirely censored. We used to drive for miles always expecting that round the next corner there would be something to look at and there never was. That is the charm of Australia."

But there are diversions! Forty minutes' drive south of Bordertown lies **Padthaway Homestead**, an imposing stone mansion in an oasis of green English garden. The property was taken up as a sheep run in 1847 and the original cottage and outbuildings are still there. Today a number of vineyards spread over the acres where sheep once grazed.

South of Padthaway are the **Naracoorte Caves** containing not only beautiful limestone formations but a fossil cave where the traces of many extinct animals are being unearthed. They include giant kangaroos, a wombat the size of a hippopotamus and a marsupial "lion."

Returning to the Dukes Highway, the road crosses the Murray River at Swanport where a freeway winds in sweeping curves through the Adelaide Hills. Stop at **Eagle on the Hill** for sweeping views of Adelaide, a city set between amber hills and a sapphire sea.

"The balcony," a unique rock outcrop in the Grampians.

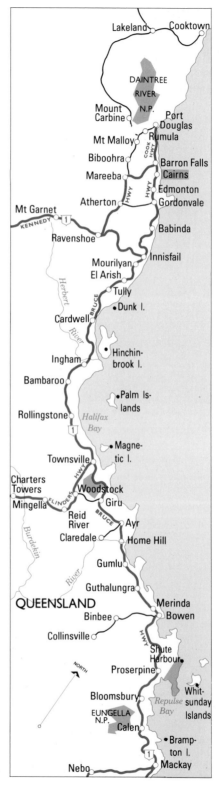

# BRISBANE-CAIRNS: QUEENSLAND COAST

First, the bad news. the main coastal route from Brisbane to Cairns (1,822 kilometres; 1,132 miles) is—in many places—little more than a track for athletic goats.

Your map will call it Highway One, but don't be fooled into thinking of it as a conventional highway, and don't—if you can avoid it—negotiate its pitfalls in your own vehicle. A sturdy hire car (with air-conditioning) offers the most peace of mind, especially on those northern sections of the route where cavernous potholes, crumbling edges and suicidal wildlfe conspire to line the pockets of mechanics and panelbeaters.

It may seem peculiar, in a state as prosperous as Queensland, to find a main arterial road in such poor condition. But distances between coastal centres can be vast and by comparison with more populated areas in the south of Australia, northern Queensland in particular remains very much a frontier.

Compensating for these little setbacks, the route north from Brisbane offers access to magnificent uncrowded beaches, pristine rainforests, tropical islands (from deserted to overpriced), authentic country pubs, splendid fishing and diving, mouth-watering local tucker and—consider this a bonus of what we call the Deep North—encounters with people and objects both unconventional and downright bizarre.

### Sunshine and Big Things

An early example: on the **Sunshine Coast**, 90 minutes north of Brisbane, tourism interests have a peculiar but effective preoccupation. It's called Big Things.

Unique in Australia, and probably the world, spectacular and varied roadside leviathans have been erected by competing tourist attractions as a means of luring the tourist inside to see the show. Don't be alarmed, for instance, to confront a 9.1-metre (30-foot) high dairy cow looming above the highway between **Nambour** and **Yandina**. It promotes a model farm and dairy display; and such is the good-natured curiosity of passers-by that a steady stream of them can been seen climbing a ladder and disappearing inside the cow via a trap door near the udders.

Nearby is an enormous fibreglass pineapple, inside which entrepreneurial vendors retail souvenir T-towels bearing the images of HRH Prince Charles and Lady Diana. Until a few years ago, the cow and the pineapple were acrimonious rivals whose public slanging matches—"I was the FIRST Big Thing!" fumed The Pineapple. "Sour grapes!" retorted The Cow—were consistently entertaining. Now, alas, peace reigns in the valley of the giants—and that includes a monstrous shell, an enormous bottle of beer and an oversized lawnmower.

Aloof from such down-market bickering, **Noosa Heads** (a short detour from the highway through the sleepy hollow of Yandina) has been called the Cannes of Australia, a heady blend of beauty, sophistication and high finance. Nestling beside the usually tranquil waters of Laguna Bay at the northern end of the Sunshine Coast, Noosa comes close to distilling the essence of the Australian Dream.

But the scope of the dream is dictated by the means of the dreamer, and Noosa has become known as the playground of the rich. This is misleading: a large measure of Noosa's charm lies in the fact that the hoi polloi share in the magic of a resort which 15 years ago was theirs alone.

When surfers from all parts of the world began discovering Noosa it was a sleepy little settlement, the weekend haunt of local farmers and fishermen. A few rough beach shacks, a post office and a shop—that was it. But the perfectly cylindrical waves which wrap around the points of Noosa's national park soon changed all that.

Because of its rare northerly aspect, Noosa's waves rank among the world's finest. Through the 1960s and early 1970s, surfers made the resort their mecca. Names of local beaches—Ti-Tree Bay, Granite Beach, Fairy Pool, Devil's Kitchen—captured, for them, the enchantment of Noosa.

Later, publicity about the place captured the imaginations of a different clique—the wealthy early retirees of Sydney, Melbourne and Adelaide. And from the moment they saw Noosa Heads, these refugees from commerce and the rat race began buying it. They snapped up large tracts of the best land

and dashed back south to wind up their affairs in preparation for living The Dream.

Sheltering the pleasure people of Noosa from prevailing southeasterly winds is the headland, a 334-hectare (825-acre) national park of high, silent rainforest cirsscrossed by walking tracks and bountiful with wildlife. On the soft white sand of numerous coves fringing the headland, normal inhibitions don't exist and all-over tans are commonplace. Even on the sand a few metres off Hastings Street (Noosa's main business street), topless girls soak up the sun or float listlessly in a sea so clear you can see whiting and flathead scudding across the bottom.

### Of Sand and Rum

Enjoy your share of Noosa's cosmopolitan pleasures, because the next stage of the route north is—by comparison—somewhat lacking in *a la carte* cuisine and beautiful people.

Highway One takes you through **Gympie**, a one-time gold mining town, then to **Maryborough**, known mainly as the departure point for barge trips to **Fraser Island**. A four-wheel-drive vehicle is necessary to explore the island; these can be hired locally.

One of the largest all-sand islands in the world, Fraser in the late Seventies became a battleground between mining interests and a brave band of conservationists led by local schoolteacher, John Sinclair. Against all odds, Sinclair won his fight to stop a mining company ripping up the island's mineral sands. But don't mention Sinclair's name in Maryborough—loss of jobs caused by the termination of mining caused such bitterness in the town that he and his family were forced to decamp straight for Brisbane.

The next major town north of Maryborough is **Bundaberg** (involving a 45-minute each-way detour from Highway One), recognised by most Australians only because it nestles in the heart of sugar country and produces an invigorating dark rum, sold locally in whopping half-gallon jars and affectionately known as "Bundie."

Pass up the next detour, to **Gladstone**, unless you happen to be interested in the world's largest alumina plant ($355 million to construct) and the general dreariness of this intensely industrial centre.

A few kilometres after crossing the Tropic of Capricorn, the northward traveller enters **Rockhampton**, sprawling commercial heart of central Queensland and the centre of the state's beef industry.

### Tropical Beef

Colourful local identity Rex Pilbeam, a former mayor who achieved national prominence by taunting enraged feminists in televised debates, himself resembles the baggy-necked Brahman bull he had cast in bronze and erected at the northern entrance to the city. The Brahman symbolises the hardy breed preferred by cattlemen to the north of "Rockie." At the southern end of town Pilbeam, as mayor, erected a bronze Hereford to represent the British breed crosses favoured by farmers in the south.

When the bronze beasts were cast, Pilbeam—anticipating playfulness by young lairs around town—had several spare sets of testicles of each animal placed in storage. Souvenir-hunters struck the Brahman almost immediately. They were dumbfounded when the

The Big Pineapple.

mayor ordered his workmen to bolt on a replacement appendage the very same day.

The anecdote demonstrates the practicality of frontier thinking. Although Rockhampton is a sprawling city of 53,000, with modern pubs and office blocks interspersed among the old, it remains on the edge of nowhere, flanked to the west by thousands of square kilometres of flat grazing country where heat, drought, floods and fires have shaped a hardy breed of remote survivors. Their isolation, like the remoteness of north Queensland itself, generates fiercely parochial attitudes, a point worth bearing in mind should the traveller catch himself discussing Sydney or Melbourne (or even Brisbane) in terms too complimentary for local tastes.

### The Japanese Connection

Rockie itself can be insufferably hot, but don't mention this. Just slip quietly away on a 40-kilometre (25-mile) detour to **Yeppoon** on the coast for a dip, some excellent local seafood and a look at the controversial Iwasaki tourist de-

velopment. Just north of Yeppoon, it adjoins an uninspiring tidal beach and has been the subject of more than a decade of outlandish rumour, prejudice and even a bomb attack.

It all began when Yohichiro Iwasaki, multi-millionaire Japanese resort mogul, announced plans to transform Yeppoon with a self-contained resort development of such vast dimensions it would make Disneyland seem small-time. Through the unflagging efforts of his friend Joh Bjelke-Petersen, Queensland's long-serving conservative premier, Iwasaki was able to acquire freehold title to a considerable chunk of waterfront land.

But when the resort did not proceed—and hundreds of beef cattle belonging to Iwasaki grew fat grazing on the site—the rumours and ill-will began. Wartime hatreds were revived with claims that the Japanese entrepreneur planned to use the land ("a foothold on our soil") to breed beef for the Japanese market. This, it was said, would threaten Australia's beef exports to Japan. Yeppoon became known as "Jappoon" and locals formed lobby groups dedicated to fighting the Iwasaki

Divers off Milne Reef, Cairns.

project via public meetings and the media.

The venerable Mr. Iwasaki, in his eighties when the project was announced, repeated assurances that the resort would be completed. He described the benefits: millions of dollars would be introduced to the local economy; he would subsidise a new airport at Rockhampton to accommodate big jets bringing in thousands of well-heeled Japanese tourists; innumerable jobs would be created. At public meetings of his own, Iwasaki distributed digital watches and transistors to soothe suspicious minds. He sent local councillors to visit his resorts in Japan and a local high school began a Japanese language course to give potential Iwasaki employees a comfortable edge on their competition.

A few years ago, when the opposition had lost momentum and the Yeppoon resort was finally under construction, an explosion severely damaged the first uncompleted block of Iwasaki units. A local fisherman was charged with the crime but later acquitted.

From Rockhampton, an adventurous traveller might consider a lengthy (but reasonably fast) detour west to **Emerald** and the famous central Queensland gemfields, where scores of latter-day pioneers fossick for precious stones on fields like The Willows, Tomahawk Creek, Glenalva, Sapphire, Rubyvale, Anakie and Reward.

There's nothing fancy about the gemfields: in tents, caravans and tumbledown tin shacks the miners have traded traditional comforts for the freedom and excitement of their own frontier. Ignoring a century of progress, they've converted to the lifestyle of the country's first hardy colonists.

The obvious rewards are sapphire, topaz, amethyst, jasper. Some fossickers have struck it rich in their first week ("Come stub your toe on a fortune!" urge the tourist pamphlets) but most small-time operators make a modest living selling gems to Thai businessmen who operate from pre-fabricated sheds dotted around the digs.

Refugees from the rules and restrictions of suburbia, complete families dropout here, battling to compete nowadays with big-league open-cut mining companies whose presence will eventually destroy the fossickers' addic-

Shute
Harbour,
Queensland

tive game of chance.

Although it is very much the long way around, a detour via Emerald—rejoining Highway One near Mackay—means avoiding the worst section of the Brisbane-Cairns route: 398 bone-jarring kilometres (247 miles) between Rockhampton and Mackay. Isolated, hot, dusty and monotonous, this stretch is known as Murder Highway because of the grim tally of unsolved killings that have occurred there.

If you do travel this road, try to avoid overnight stops in lonely areas. Take plenty of fresh water and a spare can of gas. And, no matter how miserable they might look out there in the heat, don't ever *think* about picking up hitchhikers.

### Roadside Junk

When you spot a full-sized Taiwanese fishing junk mounted on a rock pedestal beside the highway, breathe easy. Murder Highway is behind you and **Mackay** is just around the bend.

Why a fishing junk ?

Well, it's really just another example of Deep North pragmatism. Caught poaching clams within Australian ter-

ritorial waters, Taiwanese fishermen are regularly arrested by navy patrols (usually in the vicinity of the Great Barrier Reef) and their boats are confiscated. Since 1969 Australian taxpayers have spent more than $2 million to pay for the business of apprehending renegade junks, dragging their crews through the courts and then repatriating them by air to Taiwan.

The upshot of this frustrating but necessary procedure is that Australia now owns more than 30 junks, useless in Commonwealth waters because they don't meet requirements of safety and comfort. Sold at public auction for between $10 and $100, some of them have been broken down for parts. But most rot gently in tidal creeks around Mackay.

The most famous junk, *Shin Hsun Yuan No. 3*, captured by a navy cruiser in 1976, became Mackay's official tourist information centre. The Whitsunday Wonderworld Travel Council paid $10 for it, then fit volunteers with gas masks while they toiled for two months ridding the vessel of decaying clam meat. After a new paint job, the junk was hoisted onto its roadside pedestal and Australia

On a farm near Airlie Beach, Queensland.

at last had something to show for its long and costly battle against the clam pirates.

If you're tempted to outlay $10 for a junk, consider the words of a government officer who inspects the vessels: "They're rotten, waterlogged death-traps. I wouldn't go to sea in one for a million dollars."

Fanned by tropical breezes and surrounded by a gently rustling sea of sugar cane, Mackay is a pleasant city of wide streets and elegant old hotels. Round-the-world sailors wait out the cyclone season in its peaceful harbour and kids with backpacks—usually trying for jobs on nearby **Whitsunday Islands** resorts—pool their resources to rent gracious old colonial homes with views of the river.

There are flights in **Proserpine** and it takes only about 40 minutes (130 kilometres, 80 miles north) to reach **Shute Harbour** and **Airlie Beach,** where azure sea and glimpses of islands in the beautiful Whitsunday Passage give the traveller his first real taste of what the long trek has been leading to.

From Airlie Beach, boats of all shapes and sizes—including sail-yourself yachts—take passengers on idyllic cruises around the Great Barrier Reef (see following story) or deliver guests to islands such as Hamilton, Hayman, Day-dream, Hook and Lindeman. (See page 219 for details of some of these.)

Ideal for a day visit, Airlie Beach and Shute Harbour both offer fine restaurants and a degree of sophistication reminiscent of Noosa (but neither spot comes near matching Noosa's natural charms). Airlie Beach, in particular, has become cluttered with competing tourist traps whose lust for publicity gives the place the atmosphere of a circus-by-the-sea in the on-season.

**Hayman Island** is closest to the Reef and offers an all-round holiday including a nightspot right on the sand, superb cuisine and regular fishing trips from which guests often return with Spanish mackerel, which the island chef will cook to your liking.

Back on Highway One you'll find the road as torturous as ever, but the scenery much improved. In the cane harvesting season the skyline at night glows with myriad fires as farmers rid their crops of undergrowth. At such

Windsurfers

times it's worth keeping an eye peeled, at picnic areas and during those quick roadside stops, for irate venomous snakes.

**Townsville**, the state's second largest city, is built around a picturesque harbour at the base of Castle Hill, a tourist lookout. A few years ago, in a typical display of civic pride, a retired resident deduced that if Castle Hill were just a few metres higher, it could officially be called a mountain. As this seemed unlikely to occur without human intervention, the resident began carting dirt up the hill and dumping it on top. He is still busy with this project, which in itself is a kind of monument to obscure endeavour everywhere.

It may also have something to do with the fierce spirit of competition between Townsville and Cairns; both these delightful tropical cities go to great lengths to convince visitors of their superiority over the other.

From Townsville north the highway sticks pretty well to the coast, offering plenty of peaceful little spots for picnics, fishing and water sports. Most maps of the north carry a warning to beware of marine stingers (jellyfish) in summer months. Despite attempts by some vested tourist interests to play down the danger of stingers, it's best to take these warnings very seriously. In extreme cases jellyfish stings can even be fatal.

### Beware The Boulders

Another warning: about 45 minutes south of Cairns, in some of the most ruggedly beautiful terrain along the route, you'll come across a little town call **Babinda**. If it's hot, and it usually is, the traveller may be tempted to detour from the highway through Babinda to the much-signposted mountain picnic and swimming area called **The Boulders**. After a short walk through rainforest, he may be tempted to plunge into the gurgling stream for a refreshing dip.

Good advice is to do no such thing. The Boulders has claimed at least 25 lives this century. It's breathtakingly lovely, but it's also one of the most naturally dangerous spots in the country—and that's saying something. Unfortunately, tourism being such a competitive business, The Boulders' grim toll has not led to the closure of these drowning pools but to the hatching of a so-called Aboriginal legend, wherein the spirit of a beautiful Aboriginal princess is said to lure young male travellers to their destruction. Sadly, the legend seems to be self-perpetuating. This is one tourist trap that plays for keeps, as its list of young victims attests.

And so to **Cairns**.

Only a few years ago, it seems, Cairns was a sprawling country town. Now it's a tropical city of such diversity that visitors have a real problem deciding what to do first. Launching place to the northern islands of the Barrier Reef, home of the marlin fishing fleet and of some of the best hotels and eateries in Queensland, Cairns is also a radiating point to hinterland beauty spots such as the **Atherton Tableland**.

For those who investigate all these possibilities and still have time to spare, the road north to **Port Douglas** and **Cooktown** is worth exploring. The last leg into Cooktown (340 kilometres, 221 miles, from Cairns) can be rough at times, but after surviving the main highway from Brisbane, you'll be used to it.

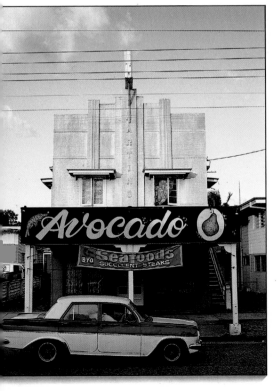

afood
staurant,
airns.

# THE GREAT BARRIER REEF

One of the natural wonders of the world, the Great Barrier Reef holds a fascination much greater for foreigners than for Australians. But this is no slur on the beauty of the Reef; rather, it is an indictment of the prohibitive internal airfares which have created holiday markets in places like Bali and Fiji while placing Australia's own tropical paradises beyond the budget of most wage-earning Australians.

In recent years, however, with the acquisition of offshore islands by Australia's two major domestic airlines, the Reef has become a more viable holiday option. But it must be understood that, despite rather misleading publicity, the resort islands off Central and North Queensland are not necessarily—and in fact are unlikely to be—on the actual reef.

The Great Barrier Reef stretches 1,930 kilometres (1,200 miles) from Bundaberg to near the coast of New Guinea, and actually comprises two reef systems—one extending as far as 350 km (220 miles) into the Pacific and the other hugging the shore, but dividing into more than 200 separate small reefs.

The reef comprises layer after layer of polyps—tiny, rapidly reproducing marine invertebrates which secrete limestone. Large colonies of polyps are connected horizontally; a thin film forms over their hard protective skeletons binding them together and eventually building into a reef.

Although parts of it have been attacked by the crown-of-thorns starfish, the Reef is still "alive," its myriad colours being determined by the state of decay of the coral. There are some 300 or more species of coral, ranging from the common blue and brown staghorns to incredibly intricate pink and purple sea fans, some of which resemble flowers.

There is also a fantastic variety of sea life, including more than 1,400 species of fish whose colours often rival those of the coral for brightness and brilliance. The northern part of the Reef is home to some of the biggest black marlin to be found anywhere in the world, while the entire reef is abundant with game fish, sharks and rays. The unwelcome intrusion of Japanese long-line trawling fishermen has now come under government control, ensuring that the waters of the inner reef are well-stocked with marine life.

As yet there are no strict controls over the sport killing of marlin, but an increasing ecological awareness among the fishermen themselves has seen fewer fish killed with each season.

The islands of the Great Barrier Reef are of two distinct types—continental and coral cay. The former make up the vast majority of the populated islands, and have nothing to do with coral. They were formed by separation from mainland Australia at the end of the Ice Age, as isolated mountaintops full of greenery. The cays, on the other hand, are sandy knobs in the coral, dotted with palm trees and a variety of other tropical vegetation.

Regardless of your reason for visiting the Reef, weather will play an important part in your enjoyment of its scenic attractions. A dull day in the Whitsundays can be like a dull day anywhere else where there's no choice of movies, no Bonwit Teller and no job to go to. Fortunately, Reef weather is fairly predictable. From late April through to

October it is at its best, the clear skies and moderate breezes offering perfect conditions for coral viewing, diving, swimming, fishing and sunning.

When the marlin season begins in mid-October the first signs of the approaching wet can be seen—variable and stronger winds, increasing cloud and occasional showers. By January there are few days without some rain, but the wet season is by no means totally inhospitable. Cyclones are uncommon and, if you can put up with the high humidity, you may see quite a bit of sun. In the southern winter, however, you can be assured of clear, warm days.

Another hazard of summer in northern Queensland is the annual invasion of sea wasps, or box jellyfish. The venom from these wasps can be fatal, and mainland beaches all carry signs warning against ocean swimming. The island beaches do not attract the swarms of wasps, and are relatively safe even during these months.

The popular resort islands inside the Reef offer a variety of attractions. They all operate good charter services and can be reached by air, seaplane or light plane.

**Fraser Island:** A continental sand island at the southern end of the Reef; in fact the largest sand island on earth. It features rainforests and varied wildlife. Strictly speaking this is not part of the Reef, but it is close enough. Reached by sea or air from Maryborough, Fraser has a number of accommodations and restaurants.

**Lady Elliot Island:** A quietly beautiful coral cay at the bottom of the Reef with camping and bungalow accommodation. Reached by sea or air from Bundaberg.

**Heron Island:** Best diving on the Reef. Where the beach ends the coral begins. Abundant marine life, all kinds of coral, easy sea and air access from Gladstone. Special packaged diving trips are available on the island.

**Great Keppel Island:** The resort here has the wildest nightlife and among the best facilities but the terrain is hardly tropical. A big selection of white sandy beaches, views to the mainland and plenty of social activities. Access from Rockhampton.

Hardy Reef, Whitsunday Island.

**Brampton Island:** Another popular resort set in a tropical garden surrounded by coral and calm seas. Sailing and water skiing in the bay, good beaches and rainforest walks. Access from Mackay and Shute Harbour.

**Lindeman Island:** Well-established resort with an airstrip right in the middle of the golf course. Also tennis, bushwalks, swimming, fishing and a favourite with families, its own adventure bush camp. Good views over other islands of the Whitsunday group. Access from Mackay and Proserpine.

**Hayman Island:** Resort set in a coral-trimmed lagoon at the northern end of the chain and closest to the outer Reef. Large entertainment complex, fine beaches and fishing. Access from Proserpine, Shute Harbour and Townsville.

**Hamilton Island:** The largest and most luxurious resort complex in the heart of the Whitsunday Passage. It boasts a floating marina; a jet air strip with non-stop flights to major cities (also servicing the surrounding islands); a unique fauna park featuring Australian animals; and a comprehensive sports complex. In addition, at Hamilton Harbor, boat charters and gamefishing facilities are available.

**South Molle Island:** Self-contained resort on a grassy, hilly island. Extremely popular but less expensive resort with diving, swimming, sailing, golf and fishing. Access from Proserpine and also Shute Harbour.

**Long Island:** Modest resort and camping. Lovely beaches, clear water and coral make this an idyllic getaway place for those who like solitude. Not much to do but a great environment for doing it. Bring a good book. Access from Proserpine and Shute Harbour.

**Daydream Island:** Just off Shute Harbour, a reasonably priced but popular resort that offers all the necessities for a good time. Fine bushwalks through dense tropical forest and great beaches. Access from Shute Harbour and Proserpine.

**Magnetic Island:** The largest of the northern islands and a national park, this haven just off Townsville houses a number of accommodations.

**Orpheus Island:** In the Palm group northeast of Townsville and very close to the outer Reef. Wonderful sea shells to be found on the beaches. A recently renovated resort offers good accommodation and entertainment. Access from Townsville.

**Hinchinbrook Island:** Large national park featuring rainforests, mangrove swamps and superb beaches. Only a small resort but ideal for the serious bushwalker or naturalist. Access from Townsville or Cardwell.

**Bedarra Island:** Small island with a new resort just established. Lovely white beaches and tranquil coves. Access from Dunk Island.

**Dunk Island:** Rainforest national park with a large resort nestled in one corner. Fine facilities and entertainment. Access from Townsville and Cairns.

**Fitzroy Island:** Totally surrounded by coral reef, a great place for diving and fishing. Resort recently extended. Access from Cairns.

**Green Island:** A tiny coral cay just off Cairns with a wonderful underwater observatory. Mostly for day trippers but there is some resort accommodation available.

**Lizard Island:** The most northerly of the resorts and home, during the season, to the marlin boats. The small resort caters to the tastes of the wealthy sports fishermen from all over the world.

coral
and.

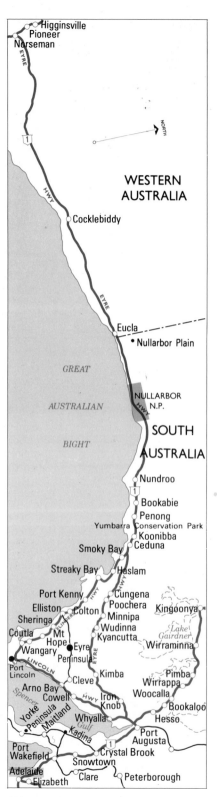

Higginsville
Pioneer
Norseman

WESTERN
AUSTRALIA

Cocklebiddy

Eucla
• Nullarbor Plain

GREAT

AUSTRALIAN

BIGHT

NULLARBOR
N.P.

SOUTH

AUSTRALIA

Nundroo

Bookabie
Penong
Yumbarra Conservation Park
Koonibba
Smoky Bay  Ceduna
Streaky Bay  Haslam

Port Kenny  Cungena
Elliston  Colton  Poochera  Kingoonya
Sheringa  Minnipa
Coutla  Mt  Wudinna
Hope  Kyancutta
Wangary  Eyre  Wirraminna
Peninsula
Port  Cleve  Kimba  Pimba
Lincoln  Wirrappa
Arno Bay  Woocalla
Cowell  Iron
Yorke  Knob  Bookaloo
Peninsula  Maitland  Hesso
Whyalla
Kadina  Port
Port  Augusta
Wakefield  Crystal Brook
Snowtown
Adelaide  Clare  Peterborough
Elizabeth

Lake
Gairdner

Spencer
Gulf

Gulf

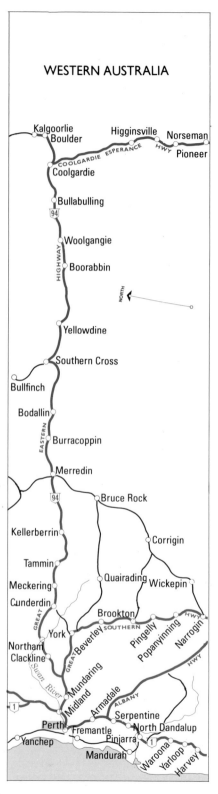

WESTERN AUSTRALIA

Kalgoorlie  Higginsville  Norseman
Boulder  Pioneer
COOLGARDIE ESPERANCE HWY
Coolgardie

Bullabulling
94

Woolgangie

Boorabbin

Yellowdine

Southern Cross

Bullfinch

Bodallin

Burracoppin

Merredin

Bruce Rock
94

Kellerberrin  Corrigin

Tammin

Meckering  Quairading  Wickepin
Cunderdin
Brookton
York  Pingelly  Narrogin
Beverley SOUTHERN  Popanyinning
Northam
Clackline
Mundaring
Midland
Armadale  ALBANY
Serpentine
Perth  North Dandalup
Fremantle
Yanchep  Pinjarra
Mandurah  Waroona  Yarloop
Harvey

Swan River

222

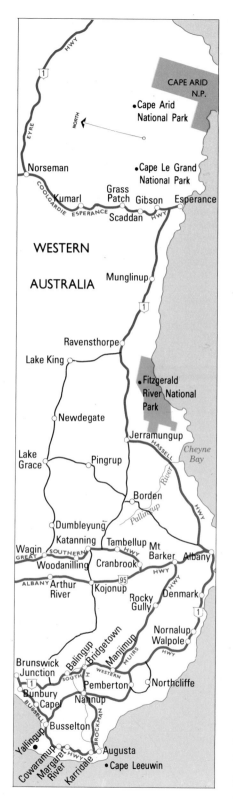

# ADELAIDE-PERTH: THE NULLARBOR

Of all the great Australian highway routes, the 2,000-plus kilometre (1,250-mile) stretch from Adelaide to Perth is considered the most daunting. The reputation is no longer deserved; since the upgrading of the Eyre Highway there are far more arduous routes around the continent. In reality, what is most likely to trouble the driver on his haul across the Nullarbor Plain is neither shoddy road surfaces nor unexpected weather conditions, but the mind-numbing straightness of the road, the sameness of terrain and the risk of falling asleep at the wheel.

But all that is a long way down the track as the motorist points his wheels northwest on Route 1, heading out of Adelaide. The haste to come to grips with the Nullarbor's vast dry reaches should be tempered by the realisation that there is plenty to see along the way.

The country of **Gawler** is an obvious place to take a break just a short hop from Adelaide. Like the South Australian capital, it was designed by Colonel William Light. In the old centre of Church Hill are most of the fine churches and beautifully architectured residences that gave Gawler its reputation as the "Athens of the North" (Adelaide itself being the "Athens of the South"). The beauty of old Gawler is enhanced by its proximity to the junction of the North and South Para rivers. South Australians make some fine beers, and Gawler's old pubs are an ideal place to sample them. The Railway Hotel, the Old Bushman and the Kingsford are all more than 120 years old and portray much of the history and character of the town.

A lengthier diversion draws the traveller down to the picturesque **Yorke Peninsula**, a miniature geographical replica of Italy seemingly kicking **Kangaroo Island** into the Southern Ocean. A loop of the peninsula takes in the east-coast port of **Ardrossan**, with its attractive water access. Down the coast is **Edithburg** with its splendid clifftop views and its famous old pub, the Troubridge Hotel. The town's cemetery includes the graves of the 34 victims of the 1909 wreck of the *Clan Ranald*. The scenic route south to **Yorketown** is a magical drive offering great coastal views of offshore reefs that are popular with local scuba divers. Yorketown is a small farming town surrounded by a series of salt lakes.

Towards the southwestern extremity of the peninsula is the great horseshoe-shaped sweep of **Pondalowie Bay**. Located in a national park, the bay is a fishing, diving and surfing paradise made even more appealing by its remoteness. A full seven hours' drive from Adelaide, it is a great place to camp and enjoy the beauty of the Southern Ocean coastline.

### A Little Patch of Cornwall

The ports of the Yorke Peninsula's west coast indicate its importance as a barley-growing area. It was from such places as **Port Victoria** that the early sailing ships left to race back to Britain and Europe with their cargoes of grain. Barley and fishing still play important parts in the peninsula's modest economy but mineral wealth contributed one of the more colourful chapters in the area's history. The discovery of copper at **Kadina** and **Moonta** led to the

mass migration of Cornish miners and their families from southwest England. Along with the port town of **Wallaroo**, the two hamlets grew as solid Cornish communities with strong Methodist church influences catering to a population of 30,000. The boom period of the 1860s has long since passed but the contribution of the Cornish Cousin Jacks and Cousin Jills, as they were known, is an indelible part of the peninsula's heritage.

Rejoining the route proper, the traveller encounters the large industrial city of **Port Pirie**. The cityscape is dominated by the chimneys of the world's largest lead smelter with the plant handling the smelting of silver and lead from Mount Isa in Queensland. Port Pirie, situated on the Port Pirie river, forms with **Whyalla** and **Port Augusta** the basis of South Australia's industrial heart known as the Iron Triangle.

Port Augusta is at the northernmost extremity of **Spencer Gulf** and marks the point where the Eyre Highway hooks west for the run towards the Nullarbor. If you can afford to resist the call of the west yet again, then blaze a

Preceding pages, the old telegraph station at Eucla, midway between Adelaide and Perth. Below, bowling at Port Augusta.

trail northeast and discover the natural wonders of the **Flinders Ranges**. The rugged grandeur of these mountains, with their striking contrasts of plunging gorges, stands in contradiction to the idea of Australia's interior being nothing but a sunburnt wasteland.

It's a long trek to the Flinders centrepiece—**Wilpena Pound**—but for sheer natural wonder it's worth the effort. The Pound is like a giant natural pit surrounded by the great protective walls of the range. From the high points on the pit's vast rim, awe-inspiring scenes of mountains, valleys and plains are the rewards to the trekker. The 35-km (22-mile) rim has St. Mary's Peak as its highest point; during winter, snowfalls have been recorded in the area.

The Flinders Ranges figure prominently in Aborginal folklore. Legend has it that the volcanic rim of Wilpena Pound was formed by the combination of two snakes. The area is a paradise for bushwalkers, but a measure of experience is advised. Access to the bowl is via Sliding Rock along Wilpena Creek. Once inside, visitors can't help but be impressed by the flora and fauna sustained by the well-watered lowlands.

The return to the Eyre Highway poses another option—whether to get stuck into the westward journey or take the southern diversion via **Eyre Peninsula** and the attractive township of **Port Lincoln**. Explorer John Eyre ploughed through the area in 1841, and although burnt almost to a frazzle by the harshness of the hinterland, he was impressed by the spectacular coastline. The peninsula has its own historical charm and romance in places like **Coffin Bay** and **Anxious Bay**.

### In the Footsteps of Eyre

The Eyre Highway hugs the coastline on its long route to Western Australia. That doesn't mean much today, but for the pioneers, the coastal route was much more harsh than the alternative of the interior. While vast stretches of the coastline are devoid of fresh water, limestone sinkholes in the **Nullarbor Plain** might have provided ready supplies. The Aboriginals had been aware of this for centuries, but the early white explorers learned the hard way.

John Eyre made the overland trip

from Adelaide to Albany, to become the first person to enter the western part of the continent other than by ship. He followed the **Great Australian Bight**, not realising how much water lay under the limestone table of the Nullarbor, just a few miles inland. There are no trees on the Nullarbor's surface as the limestone is unable to hold rainwater. Below the surface, however, underground streams have carved out huge caves in the limestone, in which French and Australian exploratory teams have set world cave-diving records. The Nullarbor is dissected by the trans-Australia railway, one of the world's great rail journeys with one straight length of track that stretches 479 km (298 miles).

The arc of South Australia's coastline is known as the Great Australian Bight. If you can imagine a giant continent-chomping creature taking a munch on Australia's southern shore, the result would be something like the familiar outline of this coast. The first impression of the coastal landform is that of the kilometres of sand dunes stretching along the great expanses of beach. These dunes suddenly give way to the sheer cliff formations that make the coastal strip near the West Australian border one of the most spectacular along the continent's great shoreline.

**Ceduna** is South Australia's most westerly town. From here to Norseman on the Nullarbor in Western Australia it is 1,232 km (765 miles). Any other pinprick along the way is nothing more than a water storage or petrol station. It's that sort of information that makes the Nullarbor an intimidating prospect.

Ceduna is the centre of a large pastoral industry. Moreover, surfers from both the east and west coasts know it as a favoured stopping-off place in their pursuit of waves. It's blessed with golden beaches; Cactus is perhaps the break surfers speak of with the greatest reverence. The navigator Matthew Flinders gave nearby **Denial Bay** its name when he realised it was not the access to the elusive Inland Sea that the early white explorers were certain existed. Inland from Ceduna is the 106,000-hectare (262,000-acre) tract of the **Yumbarra Conservation Park**. Its sandy ridges and granite outcrops appear inhospitable to man but the local wildlife (particularly emu and kangaroo) find it an ideal habitat.

Gold nugge from the Western Australian goldfields.

Pieter Nuijts, the Dutch navigator who charted so much of the southern Australian coastline, named the nearby islands of **St. Peter** and **St. Francis** after the patron saints of himself and his ship's captain. It was at Denial Bay that Nuijts decided he had sailed as far east as he dared and in 1627 made the decision to turn back westward.

### Kalgoorlie and the Goldfields

**Norseman**, a gold town, marks the end of the Eyre Highway. Here the traveller has the option of heading north on the Coolgardie-Esperance Highway or taking the road's southern route towards the coast. We've taken the northern way first, plunging the traveller into the golden heartland of Western Australia's mineral wealth.

This area, with **Kalgoorlie** as its hub, is a region of boom and bust, thriving settlement and ghost town. **Kambalda** is a rich nickel town whose proximity to Kalgoorlie has helped ensure the mining value of an area which had relied principally on gold production. This relatively new centre is notable for the emphasis its environmentally conscious

administrators have placed on design, planning and the benefits of minimal tree clearance.

By contrast, Kalgoorlie was established in more boisterous days when it was acceptable to denude the countryside in the mad search for gold. During the great gold strikes of New South Wales and Victoria in the 1850s and 1860s, Western Australia lagged behind. But when Irishman Paddy Hannan discovered gold in 1893, it was soon realised the wealth of the Kalgoorlie find far exceeded anything else in Australia. The Golden Mile became the richest bit of real estate in the world and the area went on to give up gold at a rate that still yields 112,000 ounces per year. The town's architecture retains much of its early charm with The Palace Hotel being a fabulous example of the Edwardian excesses of the day. The business district of Kalgoorlie is a leafy refuge from the moonscape of the diggings; the continuing trade in beer, prostitution and minerals still reflects much of the town's earlier intrigue.

**Coolgardie** was Kalgoorlie's twin in the Western Australian gold boom, but it is now a ghost town. This once-

gold-town
bar.

thriving community of 15,000, prospered from the tremendous bounties created by the gold rush. Three breweries thrived on the thirsts and payrolls of hard-working miners, two stock exchanges flourished and seven newspapers conveyed the news of the day. While the recent nickel finds revived towns such as **Laverton**, it was all too late for Coolgardie.

### Ghost Towns and Wheat

A survey of the area reveals other ghost towns. **Gwalia** and **Kanowna** are examples but there are many whose populations have dwindled to such a level that they, too, are certain to soon join the ghost brigade. In these centres stand the imposing relics of prosperous days. Visitors can explore the stately hotels and business offices and fantasize about the days when the west was the focus of the nation's last gold rush.

Due west of the goldfields, farmers harvest the state's other golden bounty—wheat. **Merredin** is a busy town at the heart of one of the world's great grain belts. The town was founded in 1891 around a waterhole on the way to the goldfields; it has since become a research centre for improving the yield of the vast wheat properties of the surrounding area. Merredin's claim as an agricultural hub makes the town's annual show one of the most prestigious in the state. The town's tree-lined main street is a showpiece seen at its best during November when the jacaranda is in bloom.

**Northam** is the central hub of the western wheatfields. Situated on the Avon River which runs through the Avon Valley, the town is part of an area of great historic importance. It wasn't until Robert Dale led an expedition over the Darling Range and into this 150-km (93-mile) stretch of fertile valley that the early settlers could be certain that the west held land capable of sustaining livestock and crops. The valley's towns were settled soon after the establishment of Perth. For an insight into the pioneering history, **York**, with its extravagantly designed town hall, **Toodyay** and **Mahogany Creek** are well worth exploring.

From the Avon area the journey into Perth is straight forward; all the motorist has to do is complete the short final

Eucla, Western Australia.

228

haul along the Great Eastern Highway. For the benefit of those who would rather opt for the coastal approach to the W.A. capital, we'll backtrack to Norseman to pick up Route 1 again as it dips south towards the coast.

### The Coastal Route

From Norseman, Route 1 becomes the southern arm of the Coolgardie-Esperance Highway. **Esperance** is a resort town and port with a name taken from the French frigate *l'Esperance* which moored in the bay while on a survey mission in 1792. Local attractions include the salt-rich Pink Lake and the grave of Tommy Windich, an Aboriginal guide who accompanied John Forrest on his two overland treks to Adelaide. The town has prospered since the establishment of the Esperance Plains agricultural project turned the area's semi-arid interior into fertile farmland.

The sheer beauty of the area is evident when the visitor examines the nature and bushwalking attractions of the nearby national parks. **Fitzgerald River National Park**, with its amazing seascapes and group of mountains known as the Barrens, is possibly the most spectacular. **Cape Arid** and **Cape Le Grand** national parks offer untainted coastal strips, an abundance of birdlife and some terrific campsites.

As the road swings southwest towards Albany and King George Sound, the opportunity for idyllic camping, fishing and surfing presents itself at almost every turn.

**Albany** appears in the state's history as the site where white settlement was first established in the west. It was on Christmas Day 1826 that Major Lockyer arrived in the brig *Amity* to open the early chapters in white history of the west. He was probably attracted by the splendid expanses of **King George Sound**, an enclosed waterway twice as big as Sydney Harbour. At nearby Strawberry Hill stands the state's oldest house, built in 1836 for Government Resident Sir Richard Spencer. In fact, Albany is half-circled by hills and if you can stand the climbing, there is plenty of exploring to be done. the post office with its shingled tower is the oldest in Western Australia, and the church of St. John the Evangelist, built in 1848, is

xchange
otel,
algoorlie.

the earliest house of worship in the state. Overlooking King George Sound is a memorial to the Light Horse cavaliers who served at Gallipoli during World War One. The memorial once stood in Port Said, Egypt, but was brought back to Australia after being damaged during the 1956 Suez war.

Westward is **Cape Leeuwin**, the southwest extremity of the continent and junction of the Indian and southern oceans. It is a point written into the marine lore of many navies and marked the start of Matthew Flinders' odyssey when he set out to explore and chart the entire Australian coastline. Just north is **Margaret River**, a great surfing location, and the resort town of **Busselton**, with its fine setting on the Vasse River. Locals point with pride to their two-kilometre-long jetty which took them 96 years to build. Near the pleasant resort town of **Yallingup** is a series of great caves created by erosion of the soft sandstone and limestone. There are about 120 in the chain but the four major ones open to the public are worthy of a visit.

**Cape Naturaliste** is the northern spur of Western Australia's great southern

cape. It almost embraces **Geographe Bay**, the large sheltered waterway just to the south of the city of **Bunbury**. This port, with its industrious harbour, owes its existence to Lt. Henry St. Pierre Bunbury who travelled overland to the coast from Pinjarra in 1836. The subsequent establishment of the nearby timber industry meant the town prospered and became the state's first country city. The famous jarrah and blackbutt hardwoods abound in the area and accounted for much of the early architecture. Explorer and politician Sir John Forrest is the city's most famous son; local memorials ensure he will not be quickly forgotten. There are plenty of smaller towns in the area that warrant closer inspection.

The **Donnybrook** Apple Festival is held each Easter to celebrate that town's reputation as one of the oldest orchard areas in the state. In spring the area resembles parts of the English west country, which is something that can't be said for **Collie**. Set amid thick forest, this coal-mining town is the only one in W.A. The open-cut mine and its attendant power station are outside the town, giving the visitor no indication of the area's source of prosperity. The hills of the **Darling Range** offer great views to the sea and the locals enjoy weekend picnics by **Wellington Dam**.

Up the coast is the green dairy town of **Harvey**, dating back to 1890. The nearby **Yalogrup National Park** can be reached by the old coast road for a solitary roam among the sand dunes.

Immediately north is a series of beaches and bays known as Perth's resort coast. For fishing, boating and surfing the area is blessed with such places as **Mandurah** on the Harvey Estuary and the sleepy resort town of **Rockingham**. In high season the towns and campsites are busy with holidayers but for the rest of the year they can be enjoyed in relative peace.

Back from the coast is the **Serpentine Falls National Park**. Those who can still enjoy the thrill of it all can take a slide on the steep rock face down which the falls tumble to a cool pool.

The huge industrial base of **Kwinana**, with its massive oil refinery and terminal plus wheat, nickel and alumina handling facilities, marks the obvious end of the country road. Immediately beyond lies Fremantle and Perth and the conclusion of the east-west odyssey.

Left, Cactus Beach on the Great Australian Bight. Right, a face from the Nullarbor.

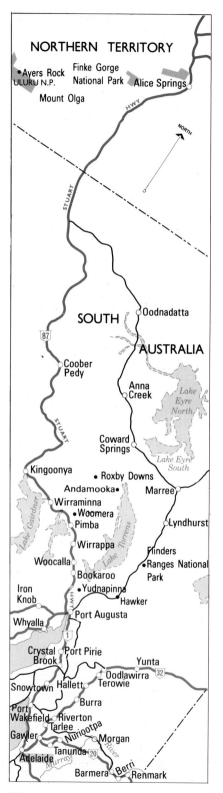

# NORTHERN TERRITORY

●Ayers Rock
ULURU N.P.

Finke Gorge
National Park

Alice Springs

Mount Olga

NORTH

SOUTH

Oodnadatta

AUSTRALIA

87

Coober
Pedy

Anna
Creek

Lake
Eyre
North

Coward
Springs

Lake Eyre
South

Kingoonya

● Roxby Downs

Andamooka●

Marree

Wirraminna

●Woomera

Pimba

Lyndhurst

Wirrappa

Woocalla

Flinders
●Ranges National
Park

Bookaroo

●Yudnapinna

Iron
Knob

Hawker

Whyalla

Port Augusta

1

Crystal
Brook

Port Pirie

Yunta

Snowtown

Hallett

Oodlawirra
Terowie

32

Burra

Port
Wakefield

Riverton

Tarlee

Gawler

Nuriootpa

Morgan

Tanunda

20

Adelaide

Murray

Barmera

Berri

Renmark

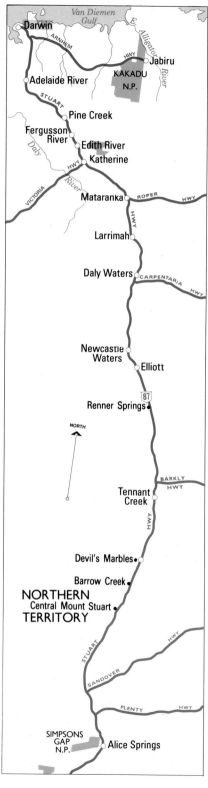

Darwin

Van Diemen
Gulf

ARNHEM

HWY

Jabiru

Adelaide River

KAKADU
N.P.

STUART

Pine Creek

Fergusson
River

Daly

Edith River

Katherine

VICTORIA

River

HWY

Mataranka

ROPER

HWY

Larrimah

Daly Waters

CARPENTARIA
HWY

Newcastle
Waters

Elliott

87

Renner Springs ●

NORTH

BARKLY
HWY

Tennant
Creek

AMH

Devil's Marbles●

Barrow Creek ●

NORTHERN
Central Mount Stuart ●

TERRITORY

STUART

HWY

SANDOVER

PLENTY

HWY

SIMPSONS
GAP
N.P.

Alice Springs

234

# ADELAIDE-DARWIN: THE RED CENTRE

The Adelaide-to-Darwin route is one of the great Australian bush journeys, but if you intend doing it by car, make sure you prepare adequately. The condition of road surfaces is indicated on most comprehensive maps, but it's imperative you obtain full information on the track ahead before tackling the journey. The most obvious hazard occurs during the wet season—October to May—when vast sections may be flooded, making roads impassable.

A glance at a map of the Stuart Highway carving northward through the heart of Australia depicts vast sections of lake country bordering the road in the South Australian outback. The majority of these do not hold permanent water, being little more than saltpans for much of the year. Remember, this is not Europe or North America. It's a route that takes in one of the world's oldest landforms, touching on such features as Ayers Rock, the mystical Olgas and some of the driest tracts of terrain in a very dry continent.

The run northward up the Princes Highway is pleasant enough, but it is not until the traveller reaches **Port Augusta**, 317 kilometres (197 miles) from Adelaide, that the real journey begins. It's here that the Stuart Highway starts the long trail northward. Ahead is almost 3,000 km (over 1,800 miles) of road, a good part of which is unsealed and certain to shake out any flaw in your car and the fillings from your back teeth if you're unprepared.

### Leaving the Ocean Behind

Before departing the Port Augusta area, it's worth taking in a few of the reminders of the town's role as the stepping-off point for pioneers of the Outback. Yudnapinna Homestead has been rebuilt as part of Homestead Park pioneer museum. Greenbush Jail (1869) is a reminder of the role law and order played in white man's attempt to tame the interior. Hancock's Lookout offers superb views of the surrounding terrain. Not far away is **Mount Remarkable National Park** with its beautiful wildlife.

Port Augusta is South Australia's most northerly port and the Stuart Highway traveller has his last glimpse of the coast for 3,000 km.

Ahead is saltpan country. If you're wondering why the road does not spear directly north instead of cutting a zig-zag course, it's because the surveyors had to find the most suitable route through the maze of lakes and lagoons. Bordering the region to the east are the **Andamooka Ranges**, the line of high country that separates the vast reaches of **Lake Torrens** from the other salt lakes of South Australia.

### Woomera and the Uranium Debate

The tiny settlement of **Pimba** marks the turnoff to **Woomera**, Australia's rocket and research base. Pimba is actually on the edge of the huge Woomera Prohibited Area which extends hundreds of kilometres into the heart of South Australia. Entrance to the town is permitted in daylight hours only, such is the level of secrecy surrounding the area.

The base and rocket station were set up soon after World War Two with the Australian Government working in league with Britain on a number of projects. It is thought that the base's main function involves the tracking of satellites but in the past the area has been used for the testing of some less-healthy technology. Atomic tests conducted at the Maralinga Restricted Area to the west are currently the subject of investigations involving suspected radiation illnesses of ex-servicemen who participated in the testing. Fortunately, the Stuart Highway does not run close enough to the testing sites to cause contemporary travellers any concern.

Inside the restricted area, Stuart Highway travellers are not permitted to deviate from the road unless authorised to do so. This means that you probably won't be able to drop in on **Roxby Downs**, a one-time semi-desert station that has become a focal point in the Australian uranium debate. Concentrated within just a few square kilometres of the Downs is the world's richest uranium lode. The decision whether to exploit and export the ore has become the subject of great political debate. The Australian government finds itself caught between its mild anti-nuclear stance and the economic benefits of cashing in on a resource sought by the energy-hungry countries of the Northern Hemisphere.

There is some compensation in the fact that not only is Roxby Downs rich in uranium, it also holds copper reserves rivalling those of Mount Isa. Other minerals, including gold, are believed to exist in quantity.

## Opal Country

**Coober Pedy** is the first town beyond the northern perimeter of the restricted area and earns an entry in the catalogue of mineral wealth as the world's largest opal-producing centre. At first glance, Coober Pedy looks like a battlefield from the Iran-Iraq war. The almost-treeless terrain consists of hundreds of mounds of upturned earth and abandoned mines where fossickers have rummaged through the landscape in search of the stones.

If you should arrive in Coober Pedy during one of the regular duststorms which sweep across the area, you could be excused for believing the apocalypse was nigh. With its backdrop of the Stuart Ranges, and sometimes no visible signs of life, the town looks like the last outpost of civilisation awaiting the holocaust.

There are a few more buildings than there were a decade ago, but most of the population lives underground in the remnants of former shafts carved out to provide comfortable space and fitted with modern household conveniences. These dwellings offer escape from the hot dust-laden winds and the high temperatures, which above ground soar to 50°C (122°F).

If you have the opportunity to visit these homes, you'll be surprised how cool it is below the surface and how elaborate the occupants have made the interiors. Should you feel the need to thank your God for your safe delivery to this point, there is even an underground church in which to perform the deed.

Coober Pedy is famous for its attractive white opals. The irony of the town's establishment is that the first opal lode was spotted by a youth who was *prospecting* for gold with his father in 1915. The town's name is an Aboriginal dialect word meaning "white feller's burrow."

## Stuart's Oodnadatta Track

From Coober Pedy the road darts westward to avoid the Stuart Ranges. It picks up the northern thread again when it meets the Alice Springs rail link. On the long dusty run towards the Northern Territory border, rail line and road regularly cross as they race towards the Alice. The opening of the 830-km (516-mile) all-weather track from **Tarcoola**, on the Indian-Pacific transcontinental link, to Alice Springs has changed the style of Outback rail travel. Gone is The Ghan, the famous old train that made the trip from Port Augusta to Alice Springs via **Oodnadatta**. In fact, the Oodnadatta Track was carved by John McDouall Stuart on his expedition to cross the continents in 1861-62. The Overland Telegraph route later followed the path pioneered by Stuart and when the railway arrived, Oodnadatta was established as the railhead for Central Australia.

Oodnadatta is now well to the east of the current north-south route, yet it retains a place in the psyche of most Aussies, who imagine the town with its Aboriginal name and complete remoteness as the epitome of the spirit and desolate nature of Outback living.

The Ghan line crossin a wildernes

An important part of Outback travel involves keeping an eye on the fuel gauge and being aware of your vehicle's facility to gulp the gas. Gas stations can be few and far between and if you are uncertain how far you have to go between stops, be sure to check with a local service station owner or police before you leave each town. For instance, there are no gas stops between Kingoonya, on the southerm border of the Woomera prohibited area, and Coober Pedy, 285 km (127 miles) to the north. And Coober Pedy is the only petrol stop between Kingoonya and the Northern Territory border. So when you are stocking up on opals, be sure to leave enough cash to fill the tank plus the spare fuel supply should you require it.

### Ayers Rock and the Olgas

Having driven this far, you are not going to dash across the border and make a beeline for the relative civilisation of Alice Springs without considering a visit to one of Australia's greatest landmarks, **Ayers Rock**, and the nearby jumble of massive boulders known as **The Olgas**. Of course, you do have the option of driving through to Alice Springs and catching one of the tourist flights out to the **Uluru National Park** in which stands the Rock and the Olgas. But if you've got the stamina and your car has the legs, take the 246-km (153-mile) diversion westward to the Rock. The turnoff is clearly marked; although the road traverses some unsealed sections, it poses few difficulties.

Ayers Rock is wondrous for a variety of reasons, the two most important being its physical beauty and its importance in the Aboriginal spiritual framework and folklore. It is the world's greatest monolith, standing 384 metres (1,260 feet) above the broad, sandy plain. Australians are familiar with the Rock's many moods from the huge variety of photographs taken from every angle of its nine-kilometre circumstances. As the sun moves across the sky, the Rock undergoes a multitude of colour changes from bright reds through delicate pastels, deep blues, greys, pinks and browns. During rainfalls it can appear silver as water cascades down its many furrows.

Uluru is the Rock's Aboriginal name

other form transport.

and it is a site very sacred to the Loritja and Pitjanjatjara tribes, who thousands of years ago daubed the walls of its caves with paintings. According to Aboriginal lore, almost every major physical aspect of the Rock can be traced to encounters between man, animals and the elements. It sits well with the Aboriginal theory that the land itself has life. Some of the features include Mutidjula or Maggie Springs, Djudajabbi (Cave of the Women) and Ngaltawadi (Kangaroo Tail), a giant slab of elongated rock attached like a huge handle at top and bottom only to the monolith's wall.

In keeping with the Rock's deep mystical nature, an event in 1980 served to bring the site into prominence in the most bizarre fashion. While staying in the nearby camping ground during a visit to the Rock, Mrs. Lindy Chamberlain reported that a dingo (wild dog) had entered the family's tent and taken her baby daughter, Azaria. The baby was never found but after some of her bloodstained clothing was recovered, a coroner's inquiry ruled that Azaria had indeed been taken by a dingo. The police, however, were not satisfied with that finding; the discovery of new evidence resulted in Lindy Chamberlain being found guilty of murder and her husband Michael of being an accessory.

The case received saturation media coverage and the subsequent sentencing triggered a "Free Lindy Chamberlain" campaign. Having exhausted the due process of appeal, Mrs. Chamberlain was still serving a life sentence in a Northern Territory jail at the time of writing. To this day public, if not judicial, opinion is still divided as to whether the mother was really guilty of the murder.

At a distance designed not to intrude on the Rock's visual majesty are accommodation sites including motels and a camping ground. The nearby airstrip provides a light plane link with Alice Springs.

The 28 boulders that form the Olgas squat about 32 km (20 miles) to the west of Ayers Rock. The Aboriginal name is Katatjuta, meaning "place of many domes." According to the Aborigines, some of the domes represent Pungalunga men, giants who fed on Aborigines. Ernest Giles, the first white man to view the Olgas, did not have the same

Aerial view
Ayers Rock

strength of imagination. He named the biggest dome—Mount Olga—after a Russian duchess, but was at least moved enough to describe the domes and columns as "huge memorials to the ancient times of the earth."

### 'A Town Like Alice'

**Alice Springs** is at the heart of Australia's great Red Centre and a suitable launching pad for visiting the wonders of "Centralia." This town of 15,000 sits amid the **MacDonnell Ranges**, almost at the geographical centre of the continent. The town is rich in Outback history, Aboriginal cultural reminders and the pervading theme of the Centre that white settlement was steeped in hardship.

Both road and rail entry to the town is via **Heavitree Gap**. Until the visitor cuts through the cleft in the range, Alice Springs is almost hidden from view. A few days in the town leaves you wondering about the time of the Neville Shute book, *A Town Like Alice*, because you soon realise there could be very few towns like Alice.

The Alice's role in pioneering the

Territory became apparent from the establishment of the first Overland Telegraph station in 1871. The station was established beside a spring named after the wife of the South Australia Postmaster-General. The station operated until 1933; it has been restored and is popular with tourists.

There is plenty to see in and around Alice but it might be advisable to settle into the town before planning day or half-day trips to various regional points of interest.

### Meteorites and Monoliths

At **Henbury** is a site where 2,000 to 3,000 years ago a shower of meteorites produced a group of 13 craters. The area covers 20 hectares (49 acres) with the largest crater being almost twice as long as a football field and about 12 metres (40 feet) deep. The smallest crater is barely six metres wide.

West of Alice is **Kings Canyon**, a precise cut in the surrounding 270-metre (886-feet) high red walls from which water tumbles during wet spells. In the gorge below are waterholes which support lush palm growth. For

erial view of
e Olgas.

the more intrepid is the route to the Garden of Eden, high in the canyon, where a series of waterholes support plant life.

Other local features include ancient Aboriginal artwork at **Ewaninga** and the red and ochre majesty of **Chambers Pillar**, a landmark by which the early explorers took their bearings.

In the town itself are museums depicting Alice Springs' role in pioneering the Outback, establishing the world-famous flying doctor service, and cataloguing white man's awkward and often tragic contact with the Aborigines.

Near the **Hermannsburg Mission** is a memorial honouring the great Aboriginal artist Albert Namatjira, who became a victim of the gulf between black and white cultures. He died a penniless drunk in 1959 after reproducing in his unique style the brilliant landscapes of the surrounding region.

A feature of the MacDonnell Ranges is the tremendous array of gorges. these include **Standley Chasm**, **Trephina Gorge**, **Simpsons Gap** and **Ormiston Gorge**. All are worth visiting along with **Finke Gorge National Park** with its surprising Palm Valley.

## Boat Races and Secret Bases

Alice is a relaxed town noted, among other things, for the thirst of its populace and such strange events as the Henley-on-Todd regatta. Each August, crews carry their boats through the dry bed of the **Todd River**. Don't be surprised if you run into a disproportionate number of Americans. They probably belong to the nearby **Pine Gap** communication and tracking base, an ultra-secret installation considered to be a vital link in the U.S. early-warning defence system.

On this reasonably symmetrical continent the closest you are going to get to dead centre is **Central Mount Stuart**, up the highway from Alice Springs. Stuart named the place Central Mount *Sturt* after the explorer he had accompanied 15 years earlier, but somehow the name became confused. (There was a lot of exploring and naming going in those days.)

It's not far to **Barrow Creek**, a tiny settlement with its backdrop of red mesa slope snuggled among the Watt and Forster Ranges. Barrow Creek station was one of 11 links along the

The Devil's Marbles.

stretch of the overland telegraph. Midway between Barrow Creek and Tennant Creek are the impossible-to-miss **Devil's Marbles**, a series of granite boulders that litter either side of the highway for several kilometres. Some of the larger ones stand balanced on tiny bases. It's thought they were part of one solid block, broken and gradually rounded into balls by wind and water erosion.

**Tennant Creek** is a gold town, although there is only one major mine still in production. After gold was discovered in 1932, the rush was short-lived, and it seemed the Creek was destined to become a ghost town. But the discovery of copper in the 1950s produced new prosperity. The town is 11 km (seven miles) from the creek. The story goes that a cart carrying timber to build the first pub became bogged and, thirst being one of the great Territory cravings, it was decided to erect the hotel on the spot. With its tree-lined double highway, the Tennant Creek of today bears few signs of such a haphazard beginning.

Just north of the Creek is the turnoff to the Barkly Highway, waiting to convey tourists and cattle trucks east to market and the Queensland border. Up here on the vast dry expanse of the **Barkly Tableland**, cattle is still king.

**Renner Springs** marks a geographical and climatic end to the long, dry journey, even though the tiny township is many kilometres from our destination. Just north of Lubra's Lookout, the Springs represent the end of the higher country and the southern extremity of the monsoon-affected plains. Ahead is savannah of the coastland and behind the inhospitable dryness of the vast interior.

**Newcastle Waters** is an historic stockroute junction town established as a telegraph station. In 1872 at Frew's Ironside Ponds, 50 km (31 miles) north of Newcastle Waters, the respective ends of the telegraph wire were joined to establish the overland communication link.

And that signals an appropriate point to terminate this description of the Stuart Highway run. The section detailing the road between the Carpentaria Highway turnoff (near Daly Waters) and Darwin is dealt with in the Darwin to Townsville route.

# PERTH TO DARWIN: THE LONG HAUL

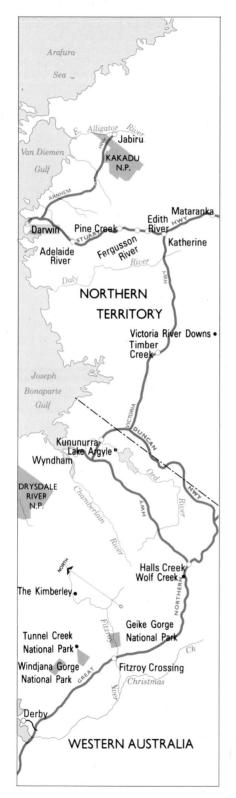

The Perth-to-Darwin route via Western Australia's Northwest Coastal Highway and Great Northern Highway is Australia's longest capital-to-capital haul. At 4,342 kilometres (2,698 miles) it is even longer than the Melbourne-to-Darwin trek.

It is a journey on which towns are infrequent, fuel stocks critical and water supplies sparse. After heavy rain, sections of road which are unsurfaced can be impassable. Spare parts for your car are often difficult to obtain so it is advisable to be aware of your vehicle's durability and the condition of the road ahead.

Heading for Geraldton, 503 km (312 miles) up the Brand Highway, the tiny town of **Gingin**—82 km (51 miles) north of Perth—is a good first stop. There are excellent fishing grounds off the coast, estuaries such as the mouth of the Moore River at **Guilderton** are ideal for casting a line. Just to the south of Guilderton is the **Yanchep National Park**. **Sun City**, tycoon Alan Bond's tourist resort, is nearby.

As the highway heads north, flanked on the east by the Darling Range, the traveller has the option of taking one of the turnoffs to the left which lead down to coastal attractions like **Nambung National Park** or the tiny town of **Jurien**. This lobster-fishing centre is set on the shores of an attractive, sheltered bay framed by an arc of sand dunes.

**Geraldton** supports a population of about 20,000 and is important as an administrative centre for West Australia's mid-coast region. A near-perfect climate enables visitors and locals to take advantage of the superb fishing conditions and fine sandy beaches that stretch north and south of **Champion Bay**. Geraldton is a modern, flourishing city noted for its beautiful surrounding countryside, agricultural wealth and rich lobster harvest.

This stretch of coast historically saw many shipwrecks, when mariners heading for the Dutch East Indies were swept too far east and struck the West Australia coast. In the 16th Century, the **Houtman Abrolhos Islands**, 64 km (40 miles) off the coast were first sighted and named. The islands and nearby waters claimed many ships over the years; relics from the wrecks are on view in Geraldton's Maritime Museum.

For panoramic views of the surrounding area, head for Waverley Heights. Fishermen can be seen trying their luck at Sunset Beach, Greenough River or Drummond's Cove. The river offers another picturesque aspect and has safe swimming and picnic areas. Ellendale Bluffs are notable for their sheer cliffs, at the base of which is a permanent waterhole. Locals will advise you to visit Chapman Valley or Kalbarri National Park, most spectacular in spring when the wildflowers are in bloom.

Geraldton is a favoured holiday destination for Perth families, but out-of-season accommodation is plentiful and relatively inexpensive.

A century ago **Northampton**, 48 km (30 miles) north of Geraldton, was an important outpost. Local buildings such as Chiverton House Museum were built by convict labour and the cemetery in the grounds of Gwalia Church records the passing of the convicts and free settlers who first settled the area. Twenty km (12 miles) away is **Horrock Beach** with its fine sand expanses and bays. Don't be surprised to see **Lake Hutt**, near Port Gregory, turn pink in the midday sun—it's just another of one of those bizarre natural phenomena caused by light, water and mineral content.

### Hutt River's Royal Family

In this neck of the woods you'll no doubt hear of the local "royal family." Prince Leonard and Princess Shirl are the self-appointed regents of **Hutt River Province**, a 7,400-hectare (18,000-plus-acre) property that "seceded" from Australia and established "self-rule" in 1970. The royal family holds court to an estimated 60,000 visitors each year and sells souvenirs such as tea towels, postage stamps and even currency. Only the tea towels are recognised by other governments.

Sandwiched between coast and highway is **Kalbarri National Park**, possibly the state's most outstanding park. The park's 190,000 hectares (469,000 acres) are set around the lower reaches of the Murchison river as it weaves its way to the Indian Ocean where multi-hued sandstone formations make up the im-

Preceding pages, Mour Newman iron mine. Below the Pinnacles.

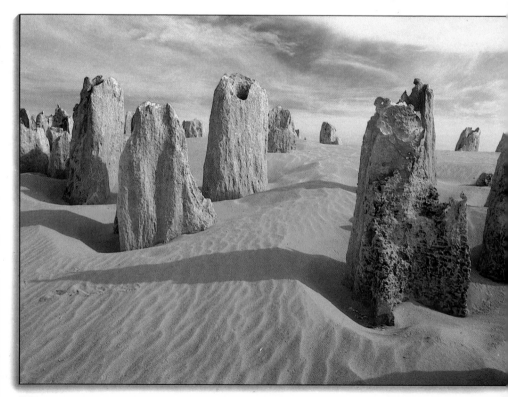

posing landmark of Red Bluff.

South of Carnarvon is the great system of peninsulas and inlets of **Hamelin Pool** and **Denham Sound**. These two huge expanses of water are protected in the northeast by **Dirk Hartog Island**, so named because a pewter plate, nailed to a post on Cape Inscription by the Dutch explorer, marks the first-known landing of Europeans on Australia's west coast. Hartog's landing took place in 1616, more than 150 years before James Cook explored the east coast.

**Carnarvon**, as might be expected of a town almost 1,000 road kilometres (625 miles) north of Perth, is blessed with tropical weather which occasionally turns monsoonal. Situated on the beautiful Gascoyne River, Carnarvon is colourful and rich in agriculture. Like towns of a similar latitude on Australia's east coast, it is warm in winter and tropical in summer, yields a huge banana crop and is known for the vibrance of its tropical wildlife.

Dutch explorer Willem de Vlamingh landed at **Shark Bay** to the south of Carnarvon in 1697. The first settlers, however, did not arrive until 1876 and Carnarvon was established seven years later. The town's main street was laid out in the 1880s; its width can be explained by the fact that camel trains returning from the interior were required to turn in the space. The port is popular with game fishermen while locals and vacationers swim at picturesque Pelican Point. **Miaboolya Beach**, 22 km (14 miles) outside the town, is worth visiting; so is **Bibbawarra** artesian bore, where the water surfaces at 70°C (158°F).

The coast to the north is quite spectacular, encompassing the land-locked **Lake McLeod** (famous for its salt production), coastal blowholes, sheltered beaches, wild seascapes and Cape Couvier with its fishing attractions.

The Gascoyne River sometimes flows beneath its bed giving the impression of being empty, but it's still capable of irrigating much of the surrounding agricultural area.

### The Pilbara's Mineral Wealth

North of Carnarvon and across the Tropic of Capricorn lies one of Western Australia's most interesting regions. **The Pilbara** is the focal point of the

state's mineral wealth and is unquestionably one of the world's richest patches of real estate. Here, iron ore is king. Exploration springs out of company towns which seem to appear overnight amid the spinifex. Ore mined at such places as **Tom Price** and **Mount Newman** is freighted by vast rail systems to the coast where it is loaded for shipping to local or overseas markets.

The magnificent **Hamersley Range National Park** can be found in this area. Head for Wittenoom for access and explore the park's gorges and awesome bluffs.

**Exmouth** is another of the "instant" towns but it was built for a very different reason. The town was established as a service centre for the nearby U.S. Navy's North West Cape installation. the super-sensitive base is part of the U.S. early-warning and tracking network and is considered one of the most vital links in the West's defensive communication network.

Superb big game fishing can be enjoyed in the sheltered waters of Exmouth Gulf and visitors should not leave the area without taking in the rugged beauty of **Cape Range National Park**.

**Karratha** is 40 km (25 miles) from the port town of **Dampier** and has been developed as the work base for the mighty Hamersley Iron concern. Other industries have established bases in the town; today Karratha, set on the shores of Nickol Bay, has developed as the regional centre of Roebourne Shire.

The name Dampier bobs up in the geography of the area by virtue of the voyage of English buccaneer William Dampier, who plotted that section of coastline in 1699. Dampier wasn't impressed with what he saw—little fresh water, no grass-skirted maidens nor beckoning palm fronds—so he considered it unfit for white settlement. His name also appears in the Dampier Archipelago, of which **Barrow Island** is part. The island is the centre for the North West Shelf oil and gas fields. Far from being an environmentally threatened area, it is classified as a wildlife sanctuary and boasts some unusual animal, bird and plant life.

**Roebourne** is the oldest town in the northwest but in recent years its importance has been losing way to the clout of the newly established mining

Hamersley Range National Park.

248

towns. The nearby ghost town of **Cossack** is a reminder of the one-time might of the local pearling industry, while a jaunt up the Fortescue River reveals the lush area surrounding the **Millstream**, a bountiful supply of fresh water for many Pilbara towns. The **Chichester Range National Park** is a fine outing for naturalists or hikers.

For an indication of just how much ore might be coming out of the ground, take a look at the loading facilities at **Port Hedland**. This seaside town, which copes with more tonnage than any other port in the country, is almost exclusively geared to handle the ore from the huge open-cut and strip mining centres of the Pilbara. Port Hedland is built on an island linked to the mainland by three long causeways. Visitors can view the loading from the wharves where some of the world's largest ocean going ore carriers dock. The Mount Newman Mining Company has organised bus tours to inspect its operations.

Port Hedland is really a mixed bag. Its tropical setting makes it prone to cyclones; its seas are considered unsafe for swimming because of the threat of sharks, stone fish and other nasties; and

its industrial and mineral predominance might not be to everyone's liking. But the local fishing is good, there are nearby Aboriginal carvings, birdlife is abundant, and you can cool off in the town swimming pool or at Pretty Pool. If you choose to stay, the town has plenty of accommodation from camping grounds to modern motels.

For a sampling of a real Western Australian outback town, detour 193 km (120 miles) southeast to Marble Bar. This town, with a population of about 300, is reputedly the hottest place in Australia. It owes its existence to the discovery of gold in 1891 and again in 1931. Daytime temperatures regularly soar past 38°C (100°F).

### A Pearl of a Town

Along the vast sameness of the road between Port Hedland and **Broome**, the highway carves a gentle arc to describe a stretch of coastline known as **Eighty Mile Beach**.

During the 1920s, Broome was the capital of the world pearling industry, with more than 300 luggers competing for finds off the northwest coast of

Millstream
Falls.

Australia. The fleet has since dwindled to just a few luggers but there are still strong reminders of Broome's multiracial heritage and the days when six hotels, three movie houses and a well-paid populace made it a boisterous town. A stroll through the timber dwellings and businesses of Chinatown provides an insight into what the town was once like.

Those left in the town talk about such attractions as the "Golden Staircase to the Moon," a phenomenon viewed when moonlight reflects on the ocean bed at low-water spring tides. The 22-km (14-mile) long **Cable Beach** was so named when the underwater communication link between Broome and Java was established. The area is known for its radical tides. At **Gantheaume Point**, when the tide is low, giant dinosaur tracks considered to be 130 million years old can be viewed.

Broome comes alive each August when fishermen, farmers, drifters, miners, drovers and even tourists swell the town's population ten-fold for the *Shinju Matsuri*, Festival of the Pearl.

Along the highway from Broome is **Derby**, the administrative centre and port for the huge cattle-producing region of the West Kimberley. It's located near King Sound, 216 km (134 miles) east-northeast of Broome. For people approaching from the south, it is the logical gateway to the huge area of rivers, gorges, wildernesses and cattle runs known as the Kimberley.

### The Kimberley

Seven kilometres outside town is a strangely shaped baobab tree with a bulbous base that is said to have been used as a prison for Aborigines during colonial times. **Windjana Gorge** and **Tunnel Creek**, with their wildlife attractions, are 96 km (60 miles) to the east and are worth a visit.

It has been only recently that the Kimberley became accessible to people other than the toughest pioneers, cattlemen or prospectors. If you've planned your trip well you will arrive in this region sometime between autumn and spring to avoid the peak summer temperatures and the wet season. The roads are constantly being improved as the area opens up to tourism and development, but take heed of local

Manning Gorge in the Kimberleys.

warnings about road conditions.

To the west of Derby, on the Fitzroy River, is **Geike Gorge**. Like Windjana Gorge, Geike is one of the most spectacular in the northwest.

The meteorite crater at **Wolf Creek** is the second largest in the world while at **Halls Creek** remnants of the 1884 gold rush can be seen. The gold-rush made few prospectors rich but the harsh environment and shortage of water claimed the lives of many diggers.

The Great Northern Highway cuts along the southern perimeter of the Kimberley before heading north towards **Wyndham**, the most northerly port in the state and a-link supply port for the gigantic **Ord River Scheme**. This project to dam the Ord River and so harness the monsoon runoff for irrigation has opened up the region for the cultivation of tropical crops. In 1963, **Kununurra** became the focal point for the scheme with the opening of the nearby Diversion Dam. **Lake Argyle** is the main storage reservoir and is situated in the Carr Boyd Range south of Kununurra.

The **Argyle Downs Homestead**— historic home of one of the northwest's great pioneering families, the Duracks—was moved to a new location to escape the rising waters. It shows how life once was for the early settlers of the Kimberley.

From here it is an easterly run to the Northern Territory border. This is where the Victoria Highway carves clear across the northwest of the Territory, fording the dozens of creeks that form the Victoria River system. To the south is the great cattle property of **Victoria River Downs** while to the north and west are the coast and the numerous river mouths and estuaries which abound with wildlife, including crocodiles. The more you head towards the Top End, the more you will learn about crocodiles and water buffalo (an unwelcome introduction from Indonesia). Like kangaroos, water buffaloes can be a particular threat to motorists, who have been known to collide with them at night.

Although Darwin is the target for this trip, Katherine, where the Victoria Highway meets the Stuart, is the terminus for this description. We've plied the Katherine-to-Darwin stretch in another chapter.

Windjana Gorge in the Kimberleys.

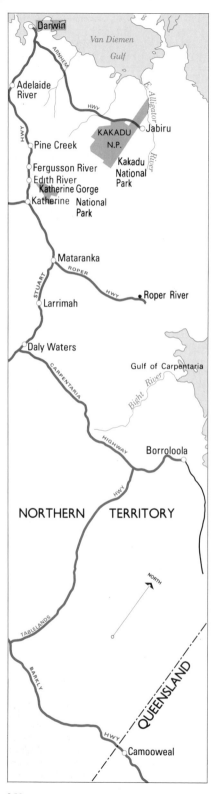

# FROM DARWIN TO TOWNSVILLE

The ragged and lengthy arc that plots the route from Australia's northernmost city to the Queensland coastal city of Townsville is prescribed travelling for anyone aspiring to see the interior by car.

It's a route that plunges south then east through vast tracts of country that embrace the northern elements of Centralia, the crocodile-ridden tropicana of the Gulf country, the slab-like flatness of the Barkly Tableland and the lushness of the Queensland coastal hinterland. On completing the journey, the traveller arrives at a coastal city established as an ideal stepping-off place for exploring the Great Barrier Reef and its beautiful islands, and placed on the jetset route with the recent development of an international airport.

Like any journey that involves Outback driving, this route requires ample preparation and a vehicle capable of going the distance. Australia's vast expanses have their own way of punishing those who don't heed the warnings.

## Arnhem Land

Before starting on the route proper, time should be taken to visit **Kakadu National Park**. It is one of Australia's greatest and most sensitive wilderness areas with its 6,000 square kilometres (2,300 sq miles) bordering the western edge of Arnhem Land. The park, with its diversity of terrain ranging from flood plain to plateau, is a natural habitat for almost 250 bird varieties and more than 100 species of animals and reptiles. The flora is equally impressive, with no less than 1,000 different types of plants.

Heading south on the Stuart Highway, **Katherine** looms as the Top End's second most important town. White settlement records its importance as a telegraph station and cattle centre but the area boasts older, more intriguing attractions. **Katherine Gorge** is a great canyon of sandstone cliffs that is best explored by boat. Boats operate mostly on the lower two gorges but the more inquisitive traveller can explore the other 11 upstream. The gorge is part of an 1,800-sq-km (695-sq-mile) national park that sees little human intrusion on its unspoiled plateaus.

It's worth remembering before you explore the **Cutta Cutta Caves** south of Katherine that this is some of the oldest terrain on our planet. The series of five limestone caves were hollowed out almost 500 million years ago and form part of a selection of ridges and depressions unique to the area.

Southward the road plunges on through arid plain boasting anthills and spindly scrub as its only significant features. The anthills are usually about 3 metres (11 feet) high and point north-south, a position which allows them the maximum benefit of heat and shade.

## An Unlikely Oasis

**Mataranka** is a small town that gained its name when the railway arrived in 1928. It was once part of the huge Elsey property. In 1916 Mataranka station was established as an experimental sheep run, a project doomed to failure in this classic cattle country. The surprise attraction is the nature park, the feature of which is a four-hectare (10-acre) section of tropical forest comprising palms and paperbark trees surrounding a sparkling thermal pool. The pool, with its water temperature of 34°C (93°F) is a real oasis amid the north's arid surrounds.

**Daly Waters** comes as a suitable warning for the traveller to be alert for the Carpentaria Highway intersection. It's here the route takes its eastward turn towards the coast. Daly Waters itself is worth a pause for a drink at the oldest pub in the Territory. The low stone building, once a refreshment stop for drovers on the overland cattle drives, was first licensed in 1893. But the droving days have since given way to the era of the road train, and the north is now criss-crossed with a network of routes by which these huge trucks convey the cattle to market or railheads.

The traveller has the option of continuing south on the Stuart Highway to just north of **Tennant Creek**, where the Barkly Highway intersection marks the way to Queensland. The alternative is to turn off the Stuart farther north, near Daly Waters, and probe towards **Gulf of Carpentaria** country via the Carpentaria and Tablelands Highway. This route finally connects with the Barkly Highway, so named for the vast, flat expanse of the **Barkly Tableland** that dominates the terrain.

### Mount Isa's Mineral Might

From **Camooweal**, a small town just over the Queensland border, it is 188 km (117 miles) east to **Mount Isa**, the giant mining town seemingly in the middle of nowhere but providing jobs and a measure of prosperity from the 334 million tonnes of copper mined there each year. The area is also rich in lead, silver and zinc deposits, so making Mount Isa one of the bonanza stories of Australia's mineral economy.

"The Isa" is Queensland's largest single industrial enterprise. The company employs 20 per cent of the city's 27,000 populace. The rich lode was discovered in 1923 by prospector John Campbell and the tiny tent settlement rapidly developed into the nation's largest company town. Away from the mines, the Mount Isans relax at man-made **Lake Moondarra** or socialise in any of the hundred or so licensed clubs. This is also rodeo country and during August, Mount Isa hosts a three-day event said to be Australia's richest rodeo.

**Mary Kathleen** is a uranium-mining town which was established in 1950, suspended operations in 1963, resumed in 1976 and finally halted again in 1982. The prosperity may have gone but the town's ample water supply and nearby Lake Mary Kathleen make it a lush green relief from the harsh surrounding country.

**Cloncurry's** historical significance is evidenced in the area's many memorials to the pioneering days. It was here the Royal Flying Doctor Service established its first base, and here that drovers drank with copper and gold miners during the thriving 1860s. A Stockmen's Hall of Fame has been established through national sponsorship.

From Cloncurry, the Flinders Highway forges east through **Julia Creek**, notable for its massive shale-oil deposits, and **Hughenden**, centre of the large Flinders River pastoral district. Nearby, in a 3,000-hectare (1,200-acre) national park, is the majestic **Porcupine Gorge** with its sheer 120-metre (400-foot) high walls.

**Charters Towers** owed its era of

Katherine Gorge.

prosperity to Jupiter, an Aboriginal boy who in 1872, while on an expedition with prospector Hugh Mosman, found gold in the area. The good times transformed a tiny town into a truly commercial showplace boasting splendid architecture. The recently restored Chareters Towers Stock Exchange in the historic Roya Arcade is one of the city's splendid 19th Century landmarks. Many fine period residences still stand with Ay Ot Lookout being one of the most notable.

**Townsville** is a relaxed and graceful coastal city. The red granite of Castle Hill forms an impressive backdrop to Flinders Street, Townsville's main thoroughfare, notable for its fine late 19th-Century architecture. The city is the commercial hub for the area's rich sugar, copper, beef and refining industries. But for the visitor, it's the region's natural bounties that appeal most.

Immediately to the east is the **Great Barrier Reef**, deserving of its status as one of the world's natural wonders. Its nearby islands, including picturesque Magnetic, can be reached by ferry or charter boat. The rich, green hinterland is bordered by steamy mountain ranges

and hide jewels such as **Valley of Lagoons**, acclaimed by explorer Ludwig Leichhardt as the most picturesque landscape he encountered on his treks.

Notable attractions within easy reach of Townsville include the **Crystal Creek-Mount Spec National Park**. This spectacular site, with its tracts of rainforest, is dominated by the mountain which offers sweeping views over Halifax Bay. Crystal Creek is flanked by inviting lagoons, creating an image of unblemished tropical paradise.

The natural barrier of the blue Pacific is the most significant natural aspect. Townsville itself sits by Cleveland Bay with the tree-lined Strand providing access to the shoreline.

Wildlife abounds along the banks of the area's many streams, rivers and lagoons. For bird fanciers, the mangrove and marsh reserve known as **Town Common** is the natural habitat for many species of water fowl. Boating in its many forms is a great attraction along this stretch of coast, but some visitors might find the simple pursuits, such as a leisurely stroll through downtown Townsville's tropical Victoriana equally appealing.

Left, view of Townsville. Right, finding the way at Mount Isa.

# HOBART: THE ISLAND CITY

Hobart, capital of an island state, is as removed climatically from the other capitals as it is by time and distance. Here is a riverside city whose cooler climate and low-profile buildings offer the impression of a small European city. With its mountain backdrop and the water aprons of the **Derwent River**, it appears a comfortable community, secure in its location and the size of its population (160,000).

The first attempt at settlement was made in 1803 at Risdon Cove, about eight kilometres (five miles) from the Hobart of today. Tasmania was then known as Van Diemen's Land; it was to this remote corner of the British Empire that Governor King sent Lt. John Bowen with a party of 35 convicts and 10 officers to establish a penal settlement. Risdon Cove proved unsuitable, so in 1804 the settlement moved downstream to the site of Hobart. The hamlet of 433 dwellers was named after Lord Hobart, the Secretary of State for the British colonies.

The civilised tranquility of modern Hobart almost conceals the fact that the site and neighbouring locations were once the dumping grounds for some of the worst of Britain's criminal class. When Governor Macquarie arrived in 1811 to inspect Hobart, he was horrified at the disorderliness of the place and immediately proceeded to draw up a plan for settlement that included the offer of free land grants, loans and cheap convict help for free settlers.

Macquarie's initiative helped open up the fertile farming district of the Derwent Valley. It was not long before Hobart's wharves were busy loading wool bales and cargoes of grain bound for Britain. The Derwent soon became one of Australia's most significant ports. Whalers and sealers used it as a base to launch expeditions into the southern Pacific and Southern Ocean.

To this day, Hobart's sailing dependence is fittingly remembered each December 26 when the yachting fleet leaves another great port 1,000 kilometres (620 miles) north for the Sydney-to-Hobart Blue Water Classic. Through repeated telecast finishes of the race, those Australians who have not been to Hobart have come to admire its beautiful river setting. The cooler climate gives the area a scenery more frequently associated with England. The sight of gently sloping pastures and woodland against the brilliant blue of the Derwent provides one of the most idyllic introductions any city could offer.

In places the river is unusually broad; at the city dock its depth plunges to 20 metres (65 feet). Straddling the expanse is the graceful arc of the **Tasman Bridge**, showing few scars of the 1975 tragedy when it was struck by a ship, causing the roadway to collapse and killing a dozen people.

Like so many other river cities, Hobart stands against a spectacular backdrop of mountains. The squat bulk of **Mount Wellington** looms to 1270 metres (4,166 feet). Beside it stands the equally imposing **Mount Nelson**. Their heights are often shrouded in clouds; in winter, snow crowns their peaks. The lowlands are a paradise for bushwalkers, and motorists can explore the heights via 20 km (12 miles) of roadway that twists up and around Mount Wellington.

Preceding pages, Twisted Lal with Cradle Mountain in the background

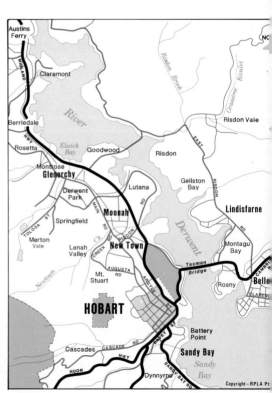

258

## Colonial Relics

**Old Hobart** is a project to be tackled on foot. Abandon the car to explore such fine old haunts as **Battery Point**, still looking much as it did a century or more ago. Local historians say this area is Australia's most complete colonial village. The area has the feel of an Old England or Maine maritime village with its maze of old houses, uneven streets and quaint businesses. In a sloping park stands the gun battery which gave the area its name.

A row of old sandstone warehouses along the waterfront at **Salamanca Place** was the business headquarters for Hobart's wealthy merchants who transported their wares via the tall sailing ships which once moored nearby. The point's dominating edifice is **St. George's Church** with its colonial spire. It was designed by Tasmania's two fine colonial architects, Blackburn and Archer, and still contains its 19th-Century box pews.

**New Town** is an old inner suburb that developed as a village apart from the original town but has since been absorbed by Hobart. It contains many historic buildings including **St. John's Church**, one of Australia's oldest.

**Anglesea Barracks**, the nation's oldest military establishment still used by the forces, is notable for its 18th Century naval guns and buildings which date back to 1814. History abounds in the city's fine old buildings, many of which were erected by convicts. The lake in the grounds of **Government House** was formed when convicts quarried on the site to remove sandstone used in the building of the Customs House, later to become **Parliament House**.

In all, Hobart has almost 80 buildings that rate National Trust "A" classification, making the town a haven for students of colonial architecture.

Hobart is so much smaller than most of the mainland capitals that it is fair to say the people who live by the Derwent retain many of the hospitable traits associated with country dwellers. Conservation rather than development is seen as the target of tourism and, despite the establishment of modern attractions like the **Wrest Point** gambling casino, the focal point of civic pride is the past.

obart with
Mount
Wellington.

# TASMANIA: AN IDYLLIC ISLE

Australia's island state of Tasmania, only 296 kilometres (184 miles) from north to south and 315 km (196 miles) east to west at it's widest point, is shaped like a shield. Its population of less than half a million enjoys an uncrowded environment amid Tasmania's natural beauty and fascinating history. Touring the isle is a treasure hunt whose rewards are found in every village, valley and street. The journey should be taken slowly in order to soak in the atmosphere of peace and old-worldliness, and the untrammelled beauty of Tasmania's wilderness.

A great highland plateau, rising from the western and the southern coasts, sprawls across two-thirds of the island. Much of the land is elevated at 900 metres (3,000 feet) with peaks rising to over 1,500 metres (5,000 feet); it embraces an area spangled with lakes. Here rise the streams and rivers which run off in every direction plunging through deep gorges on their way to the sea.

The tour route described here covers the alluring northern and eastern coasts, part of the central highlands—with an excursion to the rugged West Coast—and the main population centres of Tasmania.

## Devonport and Launceston

Situated centrally on the North Coast, astride the Mersey River, the city of **Devonport** is home to 23,000 people and is the obvious base from which to explore much of northern Tasmania.

Within easy day-trip distance, the rugged valleys of the Mersey and Forth Rivers provide spectacular scenery. The coastline, with its attractive beaches, is served by a good highway passing through gently undulating country. The northern entrance to Tasmania's most famous national park—**Cradle Mountain-Lake St.Clair**—is approximately 100 km (62 miles) by road from Devonport or can be reached by charter plane.

Heading east from Devonport on the Bass Highway, **Launceston** is only 98

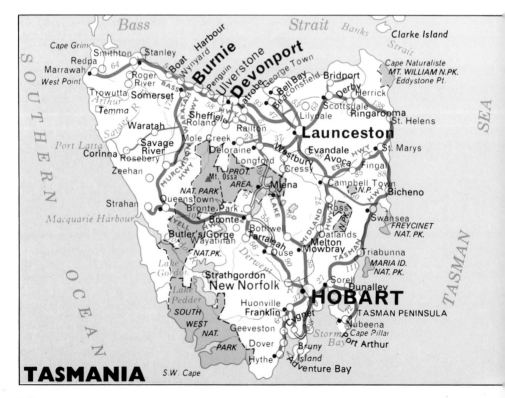

km (61 miles) away. The historic town of **Deloraine**, midway between the two cities, nestles in a valley of the Meander River surrounded by Quamby Bluff 1,226 metres (4,022 feet) and the Western Tiers. Settled in 1823 and containing many buildings of early colonial architecture, the township has been classified by the National Trust of Australia. Worth a visit, about 20 km (12 miles) from the town, is **Mole Creek** with its limestone caves, Tasmanian Wildlife Park, fascinating Mole village and leatherwood honey factory.

Situated at the head of the idyllic Tamar River, is a rich agricultural area; Launceston is both Tasmania's second largest city and the commercial nerve centre of almost half of the state.

Launceston is graced with parks and gardens and boasts magnificent attractions including **Cataract Gorge** and **Cliff Gardens**. A chairlift linking these two fine recreation areas also spans the gorge through which surge the waters of the South Esk River.

Another popular attraction is the **Penny Royal Mills** complex. These restored and rebuilt structures from the early 19th Century have been converted into two comfortable motels and an entertainment centre and are connected by their own vintage tramway.

A round trip of about 65 km (40 miles) skirts one side of the Tamar River to the new and spectacular Batman Bridge, over the river to return by the other side through scenic orchard country. A half-day excursion to **Notley Fern Gorge** provides a surprising diversion. Here, just a stumble from the carpark, a path dips out of the sunlight into a subtropical fern glade and leads for a short distance by a crystal-clear stream and on through a forest of ferns where the silence is broken only by the sounds of water and occasional bird calls.

## The East Coast

The Tasman Highway runs east from Launceston and then winds south down almost the entire length of the East Coast to Hobart. The 434-km (270-mile) road has a good bitumen surface, is mainly two lanes wide and, although some sections go over mountain passes, can be covered in one day.

The East Coast claims the mildest climate in the state and some of its finest scenery, ranging from rugged mountains to long white sparkling beaches with prime facilities for fishing, surfing, boating or just lazing. Add to this a good range of accommodation in peaceful holiday towns and the traveller will be tempted to spend several days on the journey.

The coast is also steeped in Australia's history. It was not long after a permanent settlement was established in Hobart in 1804 that the East Coast was explored. Rich grazing land was discovered and fishing and whaling along the coast brought settlement to Georges Bay and Bicheno by the 1930s. Maria Island, was settled as a convict station in 1825, pre-dating Port Arthur.

Leaving Launceston on the 169-km (105-mile) leg to **St. Helens**, the road heads northeast through lush farmlands, then winds through forest and fern-covered hills by a pass known as The Sidling to **Scottsdale**. Farther on is **Derby**, on the Ringarooma River. It's now an historic shanty town and was a prosperous tin-mining town between 1876 and 1929.

Soon after leaving Derby the Tasman Highway turns southeast and descends via the Weldborough Pass to **Pyengana** where a side road leads 10 km (six miles) to the picturesque **St. Columba Falls**. It's a further 20 km (12 miles) to St. Helens, largest of the East-Coast towns. Heading south the road follows a magnificent surf beach for 20 km to **Scamander**, then turns inland, climbs a mountain pass to **St. Marys** and descends again to the coast by the serpentine Elephant Pass, with glimpses of the ocean seen at every turn.

### Bicheno and the Hazards

The road then follows the coast to Bicheno, flanked by characteristic mountain and forest scenery on one side and an impressive seascape on the other. Now a thriving holiday resort and port for a small fleet of fishing vessels, Bicheno's history began in 1803 when the harbour was used by whalers and sealers. It was then known as Waub's harbour.

A local story relates that the name Bicheno honours an aboriginal slave woman who saved her *de facto* husband and another sealer from drowning in the bay. Her grave is located in the township.

A turnoff 10 km (six miles) south of Bicheno, leads 26 km (16 miles) on good gravel road to **Coles Bay**. The charm of this tiny holiday town, and the **Freycinet National Park** just beyond, makes ample amends for having to return over the same road to the highway.

The fantastic **Hazards**—300-metre (1,000-foot) hills of solid red granite rising from the ocean—form a dramatic backdrop to the snowy beaches, ocean pools and quiet bush paths where native animals and birds can be seen.

**Swansea**, on Great Oyster Bay, is another popular holiday and fishing resort. A number of historic homes and buildings are located in the area including the original Council Chambers built in 1838 and still in use as a general store.

The highway then follows the coast south to **Triabunna**, port for a commercial fishing fleet and a giant wood-chip industry using timber from nearby forests. The coast here is dominated by **Maria Island**, 21 km (13 miles) offshore. Used as a penal settlement from 1825 to 1832, the island is now a wildlife sanctuary and it can be visited by charter flight or ferry. At the nearby village of **Orford** are the ruins of the early settlement where convicts were loaded for passage to Maria Island.

### Inland to Hobart

After crossing the Prosser River the highway follows it through a rugged gorge to the old village of **Buckland**.

The remaining 62 km (39 miles) of the Tasman Highway cross a range of hills before descending to **Sorell** and approaching Hobart through its eastern suburbs and over the Tasman Bridge.

Tasmania's capital, **Hobart**, on the broad estuary of the Derwent River, has a magnificent deep-water port where overseas ships moor almost in the centre of the town.

Hobart's part in the founding of Australia, although it post-dates Sydney by 15 years, gives it reason to claim the title of Australia's most historic city. Gracious Georgian buildings were erected in that period and a number have survived, adding old-world charm to a modern and carefully planned city.

By way of contrast with the city's colonial past the modern **Wrest Point Hotel-Casino** in the suburb of Sandy

Tasmanian Devil.

262

Bay has become Hobart's best known feature. Apart from gaming, the hotel stages a variety of live shows in their cabaret room. There are few better places from which to view the city's aesthetic beauty than the top floor of the Wrest Point. The 64-metre (210-foot) tower offers guests (who have 195 self-contained rooms from which to choose) panoramic views of the Derwent estuary and parts of the city. On the expanse of water below, fleets of tiny sailing craft, some with the colourful splashes of spinakers evident, bob and dart in the channel which once conveyed the convicts to their island prison.

One excursion that must be mentioned is to **Port Arthur** on the Tasman Peninsular, 110 km (68 miles) from Hobart. Now under control of the National Parks and Wildlife Service, Port Arthur was a penal settlement between 1830 and 1877. Apart from the stone reminders of a dreadful past, the Tasman Peninsula is a most picturesque area with many and varied attractions for the visitor: bushwalking, tennis, golf, fishing, animal park, marine park and steam timber mill.

The village of **Nubeena**, once a convict farm, has become a popular holiday resort. At **Eaglehawk Nest**, where the rocky coastline displays several geological curiosities such as the Tasman Arch and Tessellated Pavement, game fishing is organised for groups or individuals.

A visit to **Lake Pedder** and **Lake Gordon** in the wild southwest requires a 2½-hour drive each way from Hobart on a bitumen highway, and the spectacular beauty of the area makes it worthwhile. Lake cruises are available and fishing licences can be purchased at **Strathgordon**.

### Along the Lyell Highway

From Hobart to Queenstown the 250-kilometre (155-mile) Lyell Highway follows Derwent River for about 80 km (50 miles) to **Ouse**, then climbs up to the central highlands and winds past power stations, lakes, diversion canals and pipelines of the Hydro-Electric Commission.

Side roads lead to scenic spots and trout fishing waters, and chalet accommodation is provided at **Bronte Park** and **Tarraleah**. Access to **Lake St. Clair**

in Cradle Mountain National Park was limited to intrepid bushmen until the Lyell Highway was built in the 1930s.

Heading west from **Derwent Bridge**, last outpost of civilization before you reach the West-Coast mining towns, the Lyell Highway climbs to cross King William Range before snaking down again through **Mount Arrowsmith Gorge**. The road suddenly descends from an open plain into a gap, dramatically zigzagging down into a deep chasm with the road clinging to a precipitous slope. The walls are dark green with treetops and gradually a great valley begins to open out below. A glance back will reveal the deep ravine cut by the Surprise River between the King William and Loddon Ranges.

The highway then follows the valley between two rows of mountains, often with ice-covered peaks. Away to the south, **Frenchman's Cap** 1,411 metres (4,629 feet) can be seen on a clear day. The road skirts the Raglan Range then descends via the Victoria Pass. The final stage reveals the most spectacular sight to be found on any Australian highway as the narrow road winds down the steep slopes of Mount Owen, its edges skirting the bare, eroded gullies that plunge down into **Queenstown**.

Were it not for enormous mineral deposits in the region, the West Coast with its awesome wilderness would probably, even now, be uninhabited and inaccessible. The discovery, in 1871, of a vast wealth of tin and copper in the mountains surrounding Queenstown brought mining development— and fortunes that have boomed and waned.

### Zeehan's Silver Mines

The port of **Strachan**, 40 km (25 miles) away, no longer used by cargo ships, is a quiet town depending on its fishing fleet and the thousands of visitors who come each year to join cruises up the Gordon River. Two cruise vessels operate from September to June taking passengers some 30 km (19 miles) along Macquarie Harbour and the same distance up the Gordon River. On the way they pass an uninhabited island whose serene appearance gives no hint of the brutal torture for which it was once infamous. **Sarah Island** was Tasmania's first, and most inhuman, convict penal station and the scene of Marcus Clarke's story *For The Term Of His Natural Life*.

**Zeehan**, lies 37 km (23 miles) north of Queenstown. A rich silver town in the 1880s with 8,000 people, 26 hotels and its own stock exchange, Zeehan was once booming. Shares in the Silver King mine jumped from £19 to £95 in a few months. But Zeehan's ride at the top was short-lived. In August 1881 the Bank of Van Dieman's Land closed its doors and 27 of Zeehan's mines, with their funds locked up, ceased operating.

The road from Zeehan to **Burnie** consists of the 90-km (56-mile) Murchison Highway to **Waratah** and the 72-km (45-mile) Waratah Highway and traverses rugged mountain country, passing the lakes and dams of the Pieman River Power Development.

The Waratah Highway twists its way through the Hellyer Gorge, another of the deep wooded ravines in which Tasmania abounds, before arriving in the gentle green farmlands of the North-Coast strip. The tour around Tasmania can be completed with a 54-km (34-mile) drive from Burnie to Devonport on the Bass Highway.

Left, punishment irons from Port Arthur. Right, Cape Raoul.

269

# Searching High And Low:
# Australian Cultural Forms

Australian culture, like the culture of most nations, has two sides to it —popular culture and "high" culture. They aren't entirely separate, of course; there is more transfusion between the two than people are usually aware of. A great many recent films of the spectacular film-industry revival, from *Picnic at Hanging Rock* to *Newsfront* to *Gallipoli*, manage to be both works of art and popular at the same time. Nevertheless, the division between the two is just as persistent as it is in Europe and America.

When most people talk about Australian culture they tend to think of the traditional "high" arts such as literature, drama, music, painting, opera, ballet and sculpture, with perhaps architecture and films thrown in. Australia has a rich history of achievement in all these areas. As usual, the different arts have flourished and waned at different times; Australian film-making is experiencing a tremendous resurgence at the present time and Australian films have become widely admired in other countries. While dance (including ballet) and playwriting have experienced a similar surge in energy, the visual arts such as painting and sculpture have suffered something of an eclipse after the remarkable development of the 1970s.

But to restrict culture to these traditional arts is absurd. When one talks of the culture of the American Indians, or the Australian Aborigines, or the British people, one is really talking about their characteristic way of life: the rituals, ceremonies, sports, activities, myths, pastimes and popular arts as well as their high culture. The same is true of Australia, and because the nation's history of "high art," less than 200 years old, is so short, it is perhaps even more true than in Western countries. The culture of Australia is best thought of as a mix of all the things which help identify Australian life as Australian: Patrick White's novels *and* Australian-made TV soap serials; the Sydney Symphony Orchestra *and* rock groups such as Men At Work; Fred Williams' landscapes *and* daily newspaper cartoons; the Sydney Opera House *and* the Melbourne Cup. Australian culture is made up of a multitude of arts, artefacts and activities.

## Artists in Exile

Though many Australian artists have won international acclaim, the best and most characteristic creation in the arts takes place within Australia itself. In the 1940s and 1950s many local artists had to go overseas to make a name for themselves: Joan Sutherland, the opera singer, Patrick White, the novelist, Sidney Nolan, the painter, Robert Helpmann, the ballet dancer, Clem Meadmore, the sculptor, and many others. They became expatriates, though Sutherland, White and Helpmann have since returned home. Audiences then, the artists lamented, showed a general lack of sophistication and appreciation for the "high" fine

arts. This trait had developed long before; the literary needs of early settlers, for example, were few and simple, and the fictional tradition accorded itself to such simplicity for a long time. Success seemed to come to a writer only if he relinquished his Asutralianism and opted for exile.

Outside influences accounted for many achievements. Outstanding works such as *Voss* and *Riders In The Chariot*, by modern Australian novelist Patrick White, are,

Preceding pages, opening of the 1982 Commonwealth Games; a mural marking the tenth anniversary of Sydney Opera House. Above, racegoers enjoy lunch in the members' car park before the Melbourne Cup.

strictly speaking, set in the Dostoyevskian tradition. It was a source of humiliation to Australian literateurs that one of the finest novels about Australia was written by a mere visitor—Kangaroo (1923), by D.H. Lawrence.

These days, however, most Australian artists tend to remain in Australia, partly because their audiences have grown to the point where it is now possible for artists to make a living in Australia as performers or creators, and partly because mass communications have made it possible for them to stay in Sydney or Melbourne and still, sometimes, reach an international market.

Take cartoonists as an example. There are some brilliant artists operating in this medium in Australia today, including Bruce Petty, one of the few Australians to win an Oscar (for his animated film *Leisure*), Patrick Cook, Mike Leunig, Peter Nicholson, Victoria Roberts, Ron Tandberg and Tony Edwards, creator of *Captain Goodvibes*, the surfing hog. A generation ago they might have had to go overseas to carve out a career for themselves: Petty, in fact, did. But nowadays Petty lives in Sydney, draws for Melbourne and sends his films off to London and Los Angeles; Roberts draws occasionally for the *New Yorker*; and Cook's work involves daily cartooning, satire for the theatre, and illustrating books on the British elections. It's a pretty electric scene.

Nor is it a recent development. Australia has a long and illustrious tradition of cartooning and black-and-white art stretching back to the 1890s with artists of the calibre of David Low, Phil May and Norman Lindsay. The intense activity which characterizes Australian culture today—and it is an extremely lively time in the "high" and popular arts—is really the result of a long history of development. To understand Australian culture now it is necessary to understand what it has come from.

## The British Cultural Model

The first century of Australian white culture was basically derivative. The white convicts and their white jailers took little notice of the black Aboriginal culture which had been in existence for at least 40,000 years before their arrival. It was European art, artefacts and activities which were transplanted to Australian soil at the same time as

European crops. For European read British; British institutions, British justice, British government and British concepts dominated the colonies for the first 100 years.

There is little in the painting or poetry of the time which reflects an indigenous Australian approach; in early colonial landscapes even the trees look English! This British substructure still underlies a great deal of Australian culture, in everything from a night at the opera to the national passion for cricket or to the snow, holly and ivy which still decorate Australian Christmas cards, even though the temperature on Christmas Day may be over 100°F and the family might spend the day at the beach.

Most Australian poetry is still based on English models and rhyme schemes while English TV comedies are more popular than ever. The Australian flag still has a Union Jack on it, and many Aussies still leap to their feet whenever they hear *God Save The Queen*. It's what you'd expect of a culture which was brought out from England in the first place and, though it has changed, still bears the mark of its origins very clearly.

The great turning point in Australian cultural history was the 1890s. It's easy to make too much of this period, and there's been some attempt in recent years to modify the "myth of the nineties," but it's true nonetheless that the end of the 19th Century saw a tremendous upsurge in Australian nationalism which was reflected in the arts, especially literature.

This was the period when the *Bulletin* school of balladists and short-story writers got under way, helped by balladists such as Banjo Paterson, who wrote *The Man From Snowy River* (recently made into a film), and Henry Lawson, the finest short-story writer to emerge from this country. Many of them celebrated the bush, and its traditions such as mateship, Aussie nationalism and the underdog at the expense of the "bunyip aristocracy." Joseph Furphy wrote his famous novel *Such Is Life*, said to be the last words, before he was hanged, of Ned Kelly, the bushranger and folk hero. Today one of Australia's leading literary magazines, *Overland*, still has Furphy's self description *Temper democratic, bias Australian* on its masthead.

At a more popular level, Steele Rudd began writing his *On Our Selection* series, about life on poverty-stricken bush properties, which led to decades of *Dad and Dave* serials, radio shows, yarns and jokes.

A little later C.J. Dennis started celebrating city larrikins in his poems about Ginger Mick and The Sentimental Bloke. The 1890s saw the start of a distinctive Australian literature which has continued strongly through the novels of Henry Handel Richardson, Christina Stead and Eve Langley (all of them women), the short stories of Barbara Baynton, Gavin Casey and Peter Cowan, and the poetry of Christopher Brennan, Kenneth Slessor, R.D. Fitzgerald, Douglas Stewart and Judith Wright, to the writers of the 1980s . . . of which more later.

## Australia Comes Into Its Own

The same thing happened, though less dramatically, in the other arts at the turn of the century. Louis Esson began writing plays in self-consciously Australian idiom. A recognisable Australian school of landscape painting began to emerge and crystallized later in the work of Sir Arthur Streeton, Tom Roberts and the Heidelberg School. Dame Nellie Melba, the first of a long line of opera stars, made an international name singing French arias in Italian in British concert halls and gave her name to an ice-cream dessert, Peach Melba. Low, May and Hop began drawing for the *Bulletin*. Australians made *Soldiers of the Cross* which is said to be the first feature movie in the world, and the film industry flourished.

Australian architecture had long since developed an indigenous style based upon the bush homestead with high-pitched galvanized roofs and shady verandahs. By about 1910, however, most Australians were living in the terrace houses, decorated with cast-iron balconies, which still predominate in the inner suburbs of Melbourne and Sydney, or in the suburban red-brick or fibro bungalows, which were to become the dominant local architectural style.

## 'Americanization'

By the end of the first two decades of this century the Melbourne Cup horse classic was established and Australians had fought at Gallipoli and on the Western Front in the 1914-18 war. The words *digger* and *cobber* had entered the Australian language and startled outsiders had begun to comment on the Australian accent, which sounded as though Aussies were trying to speak with their mouths closed! The political Commonwealth of Australia began at the turn of the century; a cultural commonwealth was also

beginning to grow up.

In the late 1920s and early 1930s, however, another change took place. At the very time that Australia was beginning to break free, politically and culturally, of British domination it came under the influence of the United States, which was emerging internationally and possessed, through the mass media, immense cultural as well as economic and political power. In this Australia was taking part in the internationalization of culture which has occurred throughout the entire Western world, a process which, however much cultural nationalists might dislike it, is absolutely inevitable in an age of mass communications and which has enriching as well as destructive elements.

America's dominance and, in some cases, control of the media—the Australian film industry virtually disappeared halfway through the century because of U.S. control of the local film distribution networks— meant that internationalization was often indistinguishable from Americanization. As the century wore on, American movies, American pop songs, American radio shows, and quiz shows and, later, American TV shows took over much of the media. American slang crept into the language,

The unconventional with the conventional. Above, sheep take a tumble at an exhibit of contemporary Australian art, Victorian Arts Centre. Right, inside Sydney Opera House.

American idioms crept into advertising, business and finance, and American ideas influenced house design, shops, petrol stations, hoardings, motels, supermarkets and much else; hence the feeling that Australia often gives today's visitors of being part British, part American and part Australian. It is. An American company, General Motors (Holden), began manufacturing the first local car after World War Two and called it the Holden. "Australia's Own Car."

Radio became a tug-of-war between Australian Broadcasting Commission (ABC) announcers, who kept to an impeccable British accent, and commercial disc jockeys who adopted phony American accents and became known as "Woolloomooloo

ance to some of the American input; the mass media was very vulnerable to U.S. influence, but the traditional arts, especially the performing arts such as music, drama, opera and ballet, kept very close to their British and European sources. American culture, its high culture included, was regarded as inferior. Between 1939 and 1945, when large numbers of U.S. soldiers were stationed on the mainland, there were open fights between Australian and American servicemen and "Yanks Go Home" graffiti decorated the factory walls. Things American had a certain glamour about them but they met with a lot of scepticism as well. Big U.S. cars were known as Yank Tanks; there were a lot of anti-American jokes around. Sometimes the Australian cultural resist-

Yanks." It was years before a genuine broad Australian accent became acceptable on the air, and then only after the horse-racing announcers had paved the way. While American writers topped the bestseller lists and American comics took over the news stands, American movie stars became the cultural heroes and heroines of the nation.

### An Australian Cultural Resistance

Despite this, a native Australian culture continued to develop and strengthen itself. In a sense it had merely added the American to the British, European and Asian ingredients which had been stirred into the local cultural mix. There was considerable resist-

ance took strange forms. By the 1930s, for instance, many of the old bush songs and ballads which had developed during the 19th Century had either died out or faded into the background and American Country-and-Western music (or Hillbilly Music, as it was called on the radio) became popular in the bush and in country towns and villages. Local hillbilly singers began imitating the American singers, adopted names like Tex Morton, Buddy Williams and Slim Dusty ... and then began writing their own songs about local rodeos, outlaws, bush picnics, pubs, bushrangers, tall tales, yarns and country myths. Before long Australia had developed its own style of country music— as unmistakable as a Queensland cane toad (another import)—along with its own travelling music-and-rodeo shows and its own country music stars, records and radio stations.

If you asked most Australians these days to name a typical Aussie song more than likely they'd reply "The Pub With No Beer," a smash hit and eternal bestseller by Slim Dusty. Dusty's real name is Gordon Kirkpatrick, and he was born and bred in the bush, learnt to yodel by listening to American records, wrote his first song ("When The Rain Tumbles Down In July") in the country-and-western style, sells more records than any other artist in the nation (including local rock groups) and is as genuine and pleasant an Aussie as you could wish to meet. Now there's a cultural mix!

which had contained Australian life for so long, being broken open. Australians suddenly learned what delicatessens, white wines, rock 'n' roll, pizzas, hippies, surfboards, women's lib and student power were about and soon had their own versions. The traditional connection with British high culture was weakening, and the American input seemed to have been partly absorbed. Phrases like "crisis of identity" and "the Australian character" were in the air. In retrospect, all the conditions seemed to be there for a cultural take-off.

### Vietnam, Balmain and Drugs

The efflorescence, when it did occur, was remarkable. In the last 10 to 15 years, the

### New Migrant Influences

If the 1890s was the first great period of Australian cultural growth, the 1960s and 1970s was the second. The reasons are complex. The World War Two, and the end of the Depression gave a clear fillip to Australian nationalism; the 1960s and early 1970s were a time of steady economic growth and growing self-confidence. Also, the nation's isolation seemed to have come to a decisive end: a massive immigration program brought millions of migrants from Britain and Europe, including a hefty influx of Italians and Greeks and other Southern Europeans.

There was a sense of the old, stale moulds,

arts, "high" and popular, have flourished as never before and the culture of the nation has never seemed more self-confident.

The poets, as usual, led the way. At first they were dominated by the academic poets—A.D. Hope, James McAuley, Evan Jones, Chris Wallace-Crabbe. Professor Hope's erotic yet intellectually disciplined poetry, in particular, has had a profound impact on Australian literature. They were followed by a loose collection of poets such as David Malouf, Bruce Dawe, Les Murray

Above, rehearsal at the Opera House. Right, Australia has made well-known contributions to rock music worldwide. Sydney and Melbourne are breeding ground for talent.

and Bruce Beaver who adopted a freer and more vernacular approach to their verse and concentrated more on specifically Australian themes. Murray has borrowed from Aboriginal techniques to celebrate his "roots' in the mid-north New South Wales coast. Dawe has achieved remarkable popularity with his sardonic and sometimes highly political poetry commenting upon contemporary urban life as in his poem "ICI building":

*What goes on behind this bland display*
*of rock-bottom confidence, these seventeen*
*storeys*
*of kept stenographers, lavender-smocked*
*concubines and white shirt-sleeved*
*Rothman's smoking eunuchs?*
*(Human affections like investors pause*

that the best writing in Australia today is in this form. Earlier writers such as Hal Porter and Peter Cowan led the way, but they hardly prepared Australia for the sudden burgeoning forth of writers such as Frank Moorhouse, a cool ironist, Peter Carey, concoctor of bizarre and eerie fables, Morris Lurie, a Jewish joker, Murray Bail, Michael Wilding and James McQueen. Women writers have always been prominent in 20th-Century Australian fiction, and this is the case with modern short-story writers too; Thelma Forshaw and Judith Wright have been followed by Helen Garner—better known for her novel *Monkey Grip*—Andrea Stretton and others.

In the novel the progress has been much steadier, perhaps because it has been domin-

*seeking a sign where no sign will be given).*

If Dawe is the most "Australian" of the nation's contemporary poets, another group which sprang up in the 1970s in response to the Vietnam war and the sudden fracturing of poetic idioms which had occurred overseas was openly influenced by modern American poets. They include Robert Adamson, a stalwart of the "Le Ghetto de Balmain" literary push, John Tranter, Barry Breen, Vicki Viidikas, Michael Dransfield (the best of the drug poets but who died an early death; the casualties among poets have been high), Andrew Taylor, Robert Gray, John Forbes and Kate Jennings.

The short story, too, has suddenly returned to prominence. It could be argued

ated for so long by Patrick White, Nobel Prize winner and author of several major novels including *Voss*, *Riders in the Chariot* and *Fringe of Leaves*, as well as of many plays and short stories. White has influenced younger novelists such as Randolph Stow, especially through his poetic and elaborate prose style. A younger generation of novelists, such as Peter Mathers (*Trap, The Wort Papers*), David Ireland (*The Glass Canoe, Woman of the Future*) and Thomas Kenneally (*Bring Larks and Heroes, The Chant of Jimmie Blacksmith, Schindler's Ark*) have taken their own idiosyncratic and more social approach.

The revived Australian film industry has drawn, in part, upon the work of these writers for scripts; *Monkey Grip* launched Noni Hazelhurst on a spectacular acting career and *The Chant of Jimmie Blacksmith* took director Fred Schepsi to Hollywood. But the film makers have drawn more heavily upon the dramatists who emerged in Melbourne and created a lively, radical, political theatre in Australia for virtually the first time.

## Film Dramatists

There had been, once again, some harbingers—Ray Lawler and his *Summer of the Seventeenth Doll*, and Alan Seymour's *One Day of the Year*, about the Anzac Day celebrations in which the nation ritualistically celebrates its defeat at Gallipoli in World

Romeril, author of *The Floating World*, and Barry Oakley, a very funny playwright whose works include *The Feet of Daniel Mannix* and *Scanlon* were also involved in the new theatre.

In Sydney, Alex Buza and Steve J. Spears have written less political plays. Such are the film and stage possibilities in Sydney that Williamson and Oakley have both moved there, confirming the view of some artists that Sydney is a sort of antipodean New York, annexing the best work in the country through its cultural (and financial) power.

## Images on Canvas

Painting and sculpture enjoyed such popularity in the mid-1970s that it was common-

War One, a remarkable act of catharsis closely linked to the old Australian traditions of mateship and sympathy for the loser or underdog.

Melbourne's experimental theatres La Mama's and The Pram Factory provided the artistic focus. Among the playwrights they encouraged were Jack Hibberd, author of *Dimboola*, the most successful piece of restaurant theatre ever staged here; and *Stretch of the Imagination*, a great one-man play by David Williamson. Williamson has written a series of highly successful topical plays such as *Don's Party*, *The Club* and *The Perfectionist* (the first two have already been made into films) and the scripts for movies such as *Gallipoli and Phar Lap*. John

place to talk of an "art boom," with buyers and business investors paying very high prices for local works. This local activity was partly reflected in the construction of the new National Art Gallery in Canberra and the spectacular million-dollar purchases of its director, James Mollison. Since the economic recession the art boom has slackened and painting seems to be going through one of its periodic crises, with the abstract movement having lost some of its energy and many artists being unsure as to where to

Australia has developed a number of characteristic pursuits which might come under the label of "low" culture. Left, Surf Carnival at Sydney's Bondi Beach. Right, log-sawing.

move next. But if this is a period for recouping and consolidating, it follows one of sustained expansion.

Once again, Melbourne was the early focus; after World War Two a group of imagist, or figurative, painters emerged which for a long time was indentified as "the Australian school." Its practitioners included Sidney Nolan, whose series on Ned Kelly the bushranger have become national icons; Albert Tucker, whose gnarled Aussie faces helped make Donald Horne's *The Lucky Country* (meaning Australia) a phenomenal bestseller; Arthur Boyd and Clifton Pugh. But there never was an Australian *school*; local painting was far too diverse for that.

In the 1960s and early 1970s Sydney

death, Williams always joked that he was wary of the bush, but his re-creations of it have given Australians a powerful image of their own country to replace the earlier visions of Streeton and Drysdale.

## Music, Crafts and Architecture

Music in Australia has always been a matter of performance rather than composition. The nation has several well-established symphony orchestras, chamber groups and opera companies, including The Australian Opera. A tradition of local music-making at *eisteddfords* and concerts has been strong; Joan Sutherland made her way to the top from exactly that background. Despite the lack of opportunities, however, composers

became the centre for an abtract expressionist movement which drew upon earlier painters such as Ian Fairweather and Godfrey Miller, and was soon experimenting with hard edge, colour field and lyrical expressionist modes. John Olsen painted a landscape series called *The You Beaut Country* which seemed to summarize his own, and the nation's optimism. Eric Smith, William Rose, John Coburn and Stanislaus Rapotec were followed by younger painters such as Brett Whiteley, David Aspden, Michael Johnson and Tim Storrier.

In Melbourne, Fred Williams established himself as the most important landscape painter of the post-war years, or even in the history of Australian painting. Before his

such as Richard Meale, Peter Sculthorpe, Nigel Butterley, George Dreyfus, Anne Boyd and Moya Henderson have had their work performed here and in other countries. Ballet has shared in the recent growth in the "high" arts, helped by such dancer choreographers as Graeme Murphy.

The crafts have expanded to cover everything from kitchen pottery to gallery exhibition pieces by such craftspeople as Milton Moon, Les Blakeborough, Marea Gazzard, Heather Dorrough and Jutta Feddersen. Local architects have created the National Art Gallery and the High Court in Canberra, the Arts Centres in Brisbane and Melbourne and the Festival Centre in Adelaide. A recognizably Australian style of domestic architecture has emerged using traditional bush materials—such as timber and galvanized iron, but the country's best-known architectural symbol, the Sydney Opera House, was designed by a Dane, Joern Utzon.

## Jingles and Jingoism

Australia has produced some fine rock bands but, like some of the country's other popular arts, they are inevitably derivative. While Men At Work, The Little River Band and Air Supply have topped the charts overseas, and are backed up by literally thousands of local groups which play at dances, pubs, clubs and rock venues all over

## Ockerism and Satire

A few years ago, John Singleton, the ad agency man, began using working class "ocker" figures in his campaigns—brash, likeable blokes with broad Australian accents and a trad, down-to-earth Aussie style instead of the rather smooth, British-oriented operators who had previously dominated the TV ads. The results were sensational. Paul Hogan, a former Sydney Harbour Bridge rigger, became a national TV star and the cult of the "ocker" took over the TV channels and radio waves.

It has since subsided, but the success of a satirist like Barry Humphries is linked to the same sense of national self-awareness. Humphries has created on stage, on film and in

the country, they play within American and British idioms. Goanna and Redgum, as their names imply, are more self-consciously Australian groups and, along with Midnight Oil, draw upon local folk music and write their own very contemporary lyrics.

The new wave of Aussie nationalism has produced some bizarre results. Many advertising campaigns draw so manipulatively upon national pride that it's hard to tell the jingle from the jingoism: *C'mon Aussie C'mon* became a national bestseller. Political parties, insurance companies, banks and building societies use the same advertising agencies to produce indistinguishable, glossy TV images of Australian beaches, bush and sporting heroes.

comic strips some of the enduring stereotypes of contemporary Australianess: Bazza McKenzie, the globetrotting Ugly Aussie; Sandy Stone, the archetypal suburbanite; and his most famous creation of all, Dame Edna Everage, the bitchy blue-rinse drag queen who has become an international figure and these days purveys everything from sell-out stage shows to Malleys washing machines to a peculiar brand of right-wing politics. Phillip Adams, head of the Australian Film Commission, announced

Above, sculpture within the Victorian Arts Centre, Melbourne and right; a reminder of another strand to Australia's artistic heritage Aboriginal art on Bathurst Island, off Darwin.

not long ago: "I believe that Barry Humphries is more important than Patrick White (the novelist) and that Bruce Petty (the cartoonist) is a more important artist than Sidney Nolan (the Ned Kelly artist)." Whether Adams is right or not, his stance is a confirmation of the remarkable importance of the popular arts in Australia.

## The Power of Sport

Most popular culture, however, is focused on less demanding and more hedonistic activities—sport, drinking, clubs, pubs, gambling, beaches, the bush. In all these areas Australians have created their characteristic rituals and way of life.

The beaches which line the coast led to the

evolution of the surf life-saving movement, the surf ski, the surfboat and the current Australian domination of the world surfboard championship contests.

Australians are sometimes said to be the heaviest gamblers in the world. The dogs, the trots and the races figure heavily in working-class life and the poker machines which subsidize the nation's sporting, service and social clubs are patronised by everyone; the nation's estimated betting turnover for one year was twice as high as its expenditure on social services and three times as high as its defence bill!

Sport is so strong, both as a mass entertainment spectacle and a leisure activity, that the best-known national figures tend to be Test cricketers such as Dennis Lillee who has since retired and gone over to the TV ads. Crowds of more than 100,000 pack into the Melbourne Cricket Ground to watch the Aussie Rules Grand Final, a spectacular local form of footie which is *the* mass spectator obsession of the southern states.

Australians are also among the heaviest drinkers in the world; each year they consume 144 litres (38 U.S. gallons) of beer per head, which puts them behind only the Czechoslavakians and the West Germans in the world beer-drinking stakes.

## The Great Outdoors, An Australian Art Form

The bush, like the beaches, is the home of an entire spectrum of activities: bushwalking, camping, barbecues, swimming, shooting, off-roading, touring, caravanning, bush holidays, canoeing, skiing, mountain climbing and conservation work. They provide a good example of how everyday things like that can spread out into politics and the arts, and, in its broadest sense, culture.

In the alternative lifestyle communities on the New South Wales north coast, for instance, subsistence living in the bush, involvement in the politics of the conservation movement and the songs, music and parable-plays that grow up, all merge into one another. It illustrates how activity art and culture, ultimately, are inextricable.

As this author himself has written in *The Australian People*:

"Australians have always had to create their culture by adapting and modifying overseas cultures. The surprising thing is that, after so short a time, Australian habits and institutions should be so instantly recognizable.

"The range is wide: Saturday morning shopping, Saturday afternoon on the beach, Sunday driving in the car, thongs and T-shirts in St. Kilda and Sutherland, bush picnics, Christmas barbecues, kids clutching sample bags at the Show, roadside fireplaces, galvanized-iron changing sheds, jacarandas and flame trees in the back garden, the footie final, headlines about drought and the Davis Cup, race broadcasts on the radio, the Golden Casket Lottery, the Melbourne Cup, the Sydney-Hobart yacht race, the local Leagues club, surf carnivals, holidays on the coast ... this is the stuff of Australian life, the forms and ceremonies through which Australians have finally managed to create an idiosyncratic culture of their own."

# A SOCIETY CONSUMED BY SPORT

The importance of sport to the Australian way of life can never be overestimated. In this young, assertive society sport has become more than an outlet for any excess energy.

The physical culture, which might have lapsed when machinery took the hardship out of pioneering and settling the vast land, has manifested itself in competitive sport. Sport has become the language in which the brash newcomer to the family of nations shouts: "Hey world, here I am, look at me!"

In the psyche of the emerging nation sporting success has become confused with prosperity. Social or economic problems seem miniscule when the media is consumed with reporting the might of Australian sportsmen and women. Successive prime ministers have appreciated sport's welcome intrusion as the great common denominator and have adapted it to suit their own political ends.

Sir Robert Menzies, Australia's longest-serving prime minister, was a genuine cricket fan and never missed an opportunity to watch the Australian team in action. Malcolm Fraser, on his ascent to power in 1975, vowed to "put sport back on the front page," a reference that voters were supposed to relate to the return of the good times.

But neither of those leaders tapped the Australian appetite for sport as well as the incumbent, Robert James Lee Hawke. Whether hosting international cricket matches, celebrating yachting victories or forecasting football results, Bob Hawke has plundered the great common ground of the Australian people. No mean sportsman himself in student days, Hawke has used sport as a megaphone to middle Australia. It has worked. At one stage of the sporting romance the opinion polls rated him Australia's most popular prime minister ever.

### The Golden Fifties

The exercise might appear as one giant charade, were there not such a thing as the Australian sporting tradition and were it not based on the solid ground of achievement.

Preceding pages, start of the Sydney to Hobart Yacht Race at Watsons Bay and South Head. Left, taking the plunge; water sports are very much alive and well.

With the benefit of its superb climate, Australia produced a stable of champions whose single-minded competitive drive, innate aggressiveness and national pride crashed onto the world forum during the 1950s and has continued in different forms through to the present.

The Fifties signalled the start of Australia's dominance in world swimming and tennis, plus its arrival as a force in track and field, cycling, boxing, sculling and golf. The significance of these sports was that, unlike the British Commonwealth games or cricket or rugby, they were truly international and established the young nation's place on the world podium. To Europeans and Americans of the day, Australia might have been an unknown cultural wasteland on the other side of the world; but, boy, could its people run, swim and play!

Through sheer athletic ability, John Landy, Herb Elliott, Marjorie Jackson and Betty Cuthbert (track); Murray Rose, Dawn Fraser, John Henricks, Lorraine Crapp, John and Ilsa Konrads (swimming); Frank Sedgman, Lew Hoad and Ken Rosewall (tennis) made the Fifties an ongoing celebration of Australian sporting success. They created a tradition for generations to follow. The climax to this golden decade came in 1956; Australia dusted the United States 5-0 in the Davis Cup tennis final and at the Melbourne Olympic Games athletes from the host country won an astounding 35 medals—13 gold, eight silver and 14 bronze.

Yet, as much as sport has been a unifying factor in Australian society, it is also viewed as something strangely divisive. This observation is held not only by sport's detractors, who feel the sports pages serve no useful purpose save for the disposal of vegetable peelings, but also by the sporting cognoscenti. The problem is that despite the nation's small population, Australians are preoccupied with a vast range of different and often conflicting sports. Football, for instance, is by far the largest spectator sport; but "football" itself is really a broad term covering the codes of soccer, Australian Rules, rugby league and rugby union.

### The Cricket Mania

It is only in summer, when cricket grabs the public's imagination, that Australians are united in their sporting interest. Spectator interest settles predominantly on the efforts of the Australian team in its Test match encounters with sides representing the West Indies, India, Pakistan, New Zealand and traditional rival England.

A Test match might take five days to complete and even then can finish in a draw. To the detached observer, cricket's tactical intrigue is less than evident. But to Australians raised on the exploits of Don Bradman, Ray Lindwall, Keith Miller, Dennis Lillee or Greg Chappell, the proceedings are followed with religious zeal. The game receives saturation and sophisticated television coverage, making armchair experts of millions of Aussies.

In the more-than-100 years since Australia played its first Test series against England, nobody has been better at the game than a slightly built fellow by the name of Donald Bradman. "The Don," as he was known, was the greatest batsman who ever lived. During the 1930s and 1940s he was to cricket what Pele later was to soccer or Babe Ruth had been to baseball. It was unfortunate that the age of television did not arrive soon enough to accurately catalogue the man in his prime.

A Test series is played over three, four, five or sometimes six matches. In Australia, the battlegrounds are the large cricket arenas of Sydney, Melbourne, Adelaide, Brisbane and Perth. Ground capacities range from 30,000 to 90,000; lovers of the game say there are few greater sporting moments than to experience the opening over of an England vs. Australia Test before a capacity Melbourne Cricket Ground crowd.

### Fans and the One-day Game

The combination of sun, passion and beer can make cricket crowds boisterous, humorous and sometimes downright dangerous. For a sampling of cricket support in the raw, try a day out among the bare chests and beer on The Hill section of the Sydney Cricket Ground. This grassy embankment, so long a part of cricket lore, will soon be consumed by concrete stands. While there are those who think that's a pity, others will applaud.

Cricket has its variations, the most exciting being the "limited over" or one-day game. As the name implies, these are wham-bam affairs that come and go in a heated rush and often wring participants and spectators dry with their overload of tension and drama. These games are at their best when played under lights at night. Given the right circumstances and participants, a limited-over match at the Sydney Cricket Ground

can be a night of pure theatre with all the prescribed elements of tragedy, tension, climax and triumph.

### Aussie Rules Footie

While international cricket is the top of the pyramid, the game is played at multiple levels from Sheffied Shield (interstate matches) down through the district ranks to junior and social level. On any summer Sunday you'll find the social plodders, with their attendant picnics and barbecues, enjoying the game at an entirely different and less frenetic pace, some of them no doubt fuelling and foiling their Bradman fantasies with a can or four of Foster's beer.

On the surface it seems incongruous that

cricket, with all its traditions, could have given birth to Australian Rules football. The game originated from a crude brand of Gaelic football played by miners on the Victorian goldfields during the 1850s. In 1858 H.C.A. Harrison and T.W. Wills formed Melbourne Football Club after drawing up a set of rules borrowed liberally from other football codes. In 1866 the game's first official rules were established, only to be altered in subsequent years.

The Melbourne-based competition, in-

Above, cricket takes on an exciting variation with a game played under lights at night. Right, the crowd is more sedate in a Test series played in Melbourne.

volving a sport that is virtually unknown beyond Australia's shores, draws on support from a city with fewer than 3 million inhabitants, yet by any comparison it ranks among the most popular football leagues of *any* codes *anywhere* in the world. It's estimated that each winter Saturday in Melbourne one person in 16 attends a VFL game and thousands more follow the saturation television coverage. Crowds of almost 80,000 have attended important premiership games while 121,696 was the official attendance record for the 1970 grand final between Collingwood and Carlton.

A VFL grand final is one of *the* great sporting experiences, rivalling an English FA Cup Final or an American Super Bowl event for colour, emotion, passion and

by their beach-harbour lifestyle, cynically claim Melburnians have nothing better to do than go to the football. It's a comfortable put-down but there is more to the appeal of Aussie Rules than that. The game flows along with high scoring and spectacular marking (catching).

### The Art of Non-Compromise

In Sydney, and points north, footie of a different kind is the winter preoccupation.

Rugby league started as a professional alternative to rugby union. It's played in a half-dozen provinces of a half-dozen countries, and to that degree qualifies as an international sport, although 90 per cent of the world's best league players live within 30

atmosphere.

The power and wealth of the VFL clubs draws star players from other districts and states such as South Australia, Tasmania, Western Australia and, occasionally, New South Wales and Queensland. While Victoria is the showcase of Australian Rules football, the other states get a chance to flex their might during the State-of-Origin games. These are inter-state representative games in which each state picks its best players, including those who have departed for the glory and lucrative semi-professional pay packets offered by the VFL clubs.

The code's Melbourne popularity is truly an enigma, for it cuts across sex, age, and class barriers. Sydneysiders, perhaps spoiled

kilometres of Sydney Town Hall. Rugby league is essentially a physical rather than cerebral game. Modern strategy is based on an uncompromising masochist style of defence that prompted one American football coach to say: "Our guys could never stand up to that sort of constant punishment." You don't have to play this game to feel how much it hurts.

League attendances are nothing like those of the VFL, but the Sydney clubs keep the players in the style to which they can't afford to become accustomed through the revenue of slot machines and licensed clubs.

An overview of the game reveals some strange twists: the players are professional in their preparation and commitment yet they parade their stuff in arenas not fit for trading cattle; the performers take big health risks but get next to zilch in the way of "golden handshakes" or long-term security.

In Brisbane and Sydney, the game found its roots in the inner working-class suburbs and, despite media overkill, has not had too much success in broadening its social base.

Rugby league's appeal rests in its strong gladiatorial image, macho confrontationism and the belief that witnessing a dazzling backline movement resulting in a try (touchdown) is one of the real joys in this sporting life. Catch it in the treble delivery of television's action replay and you can happily hit the hay on a Sunday evening in the belief that rugby league might really be "the greatest game of all."

Union, or rugby, is strictly an amateur code, which means that instead of bucks you get free beer to take the pain out of the bruises. The game's popular interest is at representative rather than club level. Two or three times a year, the New South Wales and Queensland state teams engage in a battle that makes the Eureka Stockade seem like a church tea party.

If you enjoy football, take the opportunity to see the Wallabies (the national side) in action. The Aussies are acclaimed for combining the best of the combative spirit with a creative flourish that can make the game a joy.

At club level, rugby union projects a social spirit often lacking in the professional codes. Compared to league, the game has a

In the modern era, St. George has been the most winning club, Western Suburbs the most bad-assed, Manly the royal pretenders, and Parramatta the tramps shining. The Aussie national side is known as the Kangaroos, and when they last hopped through a tour of France and Great Britain unbeaten, even the lily-white English rugby union scribes acclaimed them as the best rugby outfit of either code to hit those shores.

### The Game They Play in Heaven

According to its devotees, rugby union is the game they play in heaven, which is quite remarkable considering its relative popularity in New South Wales and Queensland.

"silvertail" image based partly on its strength in the universities and private schools. The Ella brothers are a contradiction to the class rule, three gifted Aboriginal athletes from Sydney's inner southern suburbs who all wound up wearing the gold shirts of the Australian team. Mark, perhaps the most disciplined of the three, honoured his country and club by accepting the captaincy of both. His home club is Randwick, known internationally as one of the world's finest. They've plundered successive Sydney

Above, rugby—the game they play in heaven—is strictly an amateur code. Right, another popular sport, not normally involving beer or bruises, is bowling.

premierships in a style that has earned them the title of the "Galloping Greens."

## Soccer's Ethnic Melting Pot

The history and conduct of soccer in Australia bears little comparison to the other codes. Soccer's conduct in Australia defies all sense of reason. It was founded more than a century ago by earnest British migrants, then went through a steady transition until the post-World War Two period when the arrival of migrants from southern Europe threw the game into the melting pot. Now the majority of clubs in the National Soccer League are governed by ethnic minorities from the Italian, Greek, Croatian, Yugoslav, Maltese, Dutch, Macedo-

The transition to the round-ball craft brings us to basketball, a game professionally geared to make a run on the public imagination and hip pocket. The twin-conference National Basketball League has bolstered club standards and established the national team's rating in the world's top 10. The NBL has rocked the local cradle by restricting the intake of imported players to two per team. As a result, basketball has earned itself a clean-skin administrative image which is the envy of other sports.

## The Great Individualists

If Australia's rise to nationhood turned ordinary men and women into the most rugged of rugged individualists, it followed

nian and even Australian communities. Australia's most prominent players have names like Kosmina, Katholos, Bertogna, McCulloch, Senkalski and Soper.

Australia's most impressive international result came with the Socceroos's successful qualification for the 1974 World Cup Finals in West Germany.

Club soccer is best with ethnic rivalry, administrative heartache, poor media coverage and the unwillingness of the public to accept the multi-cultural melange. Other than that, the sport is okay.

At junior level, the code claims the strongest participant push in Australia and occasionaly throws up a player of genuine class.

that the sporting zealots would not be far behind. Formal games gave rise to the tennis talents of Rod Laver, John Newcombe and Evonne Goolagong Cawley; and golfers Bruce Devlin, Graham Marsh, Peter Thomson, David Graham, Jan Stephenson and Greg Norman. Johnny Famechon, Lionel Rose and Jimmy Carruthers punched portholes in the fabric of world boxing; McKay and Hunt squashed while Anderson, Mockridge, Sutton and Bishop cycled.

But it has been those sports which pit the individual against the elements which have brought out the best in Australians. They have ruled international surfing almost since its inception as a competitive sport, with Mark Richards' four world titles marking him as the greatest surfboard rider of all time. In surf lifesaving nobody has epitomised the breed better than multiple ironman champion Grant Kenny, an athlete also destined for Olympic glory in kayaking. Hang gliding and sailboarding are two relatively new sports in which Aussies have also excelled.

Although Australia has produced Formula 1 world champions in Jack Brabham and Alan Jones, the real heroes of the sport are the touring car drivers. The class attracts heavy sponsorship and wide television coverage for its championship series, which has been dominated in recent years by Peter Brock. Highlight of the calendar is the Bathurst 1000 held in October. This rich endurance event for production sedans

de Castella, as it was by the anti-establishment larrikinism of swimmer Dawn Fraser and cricketer Ian Chappell. At spectator level, the public feeds off this vast mixture of emotions.

From childhood every budding athlete absorbs the fantasy of representing his country. In Australia to be chosen to wear the national colours of green and gold is almost akin to being accepted into heaven.

During the 1970s it was perceived that Australia's climate and the natural health and athleticism of its people were no longer enough to guarantee international success. In fact, Australia had fallen behind not only the United States and the Eastern Bloc countries, but also most of Western Europe.

The most positive step to bring Australia

attracts superb live television coverage and an international field of drivers. The talented Brock has won it more times than any other driver.

### The Sporting Attitude

The Australian sporting attitude is a complex and often elusive animal. At competitor level it is a blend of anti-establishment nationalism, cheek, aggressiveness, fair-mindedness and a deep hatred of losing. It's a creed that allows for sometimes-bitter enmity in the arena, but genuine camaraderie after the encounter.

It is as much epitomised by the spartan excellence of runners Herb Elliott and Rod

in line with modern sport coaching, psychology and medical techniques was the establishment of the Australian Institute of Sport in Canberra. The AIS caters for a multiplicity of sports and students on a part or full-time basis. Its graduates headed Australia's medal challenge at the Los Angeles Olympics and its staff not only includes some of the world's best coaches in sports ranging from field hockey to swimming, but marathon champ Rob de Castella in the biophysics department and his coach Pat

Above, clearly unaware that it carries a large number of Australian dollars on its back, this horse would rather give the race a miss. Right, New Zealand-bred Phar Lap.

Clohessy as head of the distance running program.

## A Nation of Punters

Australians have been described as a nation of punters. It's true that the average Aussie likes to gamble. His interest can extend from plunging the pay packet on the toss of the coins in a two-up game, to a once-a-year flutter on the Melbourne Cup. The sporting punter can risk his money on horse, harness or greyhound racing, but there is one race in the year that captures the imagination of all and puts millions of dollars through the bags of bookmakers and the agencies of the Totalizator Agency Board (TAB).

At 2:40 p.m. Melbourne time on the first Tuesday in November, the nation stops for the running of the Melbourne Cup. This 3,200-meter (two-mile) event has become an international thoroughbred classic since it was first held at Melbourne's Flemington course in 1861. No other classic, including the Kentucky Derby and English Derbies, exercises so strong a hold on the public. Only wowsers (killjoys) do not have a punt on the Melbourne Cup. It's a public holiday in Victoria and even the process of government is suspended so the nation's decision makers can watch the live telecast.

The Cup has been dominated by New Zealand-bred horses with perhaps the most famous being the mighty Phar Lap. The "Red Terror," as he was known, was Australasia's greatest racehorse, and included among his greatest wins the 1930 Cup. He started 51 times for 37 wins, his last being a record time in the Agua Caliente Handicap in America. He died in mysterious circumstances soon after that win and although an autopsy failed to reveal the cause of death, anti-American feeling ran high at the time. Phar Lap was a symbol of hope and courage in Depression-hit Australia. His heart was 1½ times the size of a normal thoroughbred's and veterinary surgeons claimed it as the reason for his strength and valour. The expression, "a heart as big as Phar Lap," is a clichéd accolade for a human or animal with more than its share of courage.

### Breeding and Betting

The Australian thoroughbred industry is one of the world's most sophisticated. International owner-breeder Robert Sangster rates Australian brood mares among his best stock and bases part of his racing empire on the Australian racing calendar which operates in opposite seasons to that of the Northern Hemisphere.

Capital city racetracks are superbly planned and appointed, offering a range of on-course betting. There are no private betting shops in Australia although illegal or starting price (SP) bookmakers run flourishing telephone services. The TAB is the national agency and offers a multiplicity of computerised ways to relieve the punter of his cash. You can bet on horses, dogs or trotters; and if you have a phone account, you can take on the TAB without having to step outside your front door.

The real punter, of course, is the person who goes to the track and takes on the bookmakers. The "track" can mean a night trot meeting at Sydney's Harold Park, a country greyhound venue, or something as exotically Australian as the Birdsville picnic races.

At the track you'll observe a different slice of Australiana. It's big on brash and cash and thrives on a level of street savvy you will not encounter anywhere else. At Sydney's Randwick or Melbourne's Flemington, the atmosphere on race day is electric. The sense of energy and expectation is almost overpowering regardless of whether you've wagered five bucks or fifty grand. Here the colourful character is commonplace and the battle of wits with the bookmakers is never ending. The sight of thoroughbred horseflesh parading among the manicured lawns and gardens, jockeys in their brilliant silks and the well-shod punters in their fashions, makes a day at the races anything but dull.

In some societies there is a certain stigma attached to gambling, but in Australia it's a way of life. The stars of the industry are the top trainers and jockeys, several of whom are millionaires. Tommy Smith has been Australia's highest-stake winning trainer. The nation's greatest jockey was George Moore, whose career stretched over 22 seasons; he rode 2,278 winners in seven different countries. In 1967 he went to England and won the first three classics of the season—the 1,000 Guineas, the 2,000 Guineas and the Derby. Ironically he never won a Melbourne Cup, having been robbed of his best chance in 1957 when connections scratched his mount, the champion, Tulloch.

Contemporary stars are Roy Higgins, Ron Quinton, Darren Gauci, Wayne Harris and Brent Thomson. Horses who have retained the affection of punters are the great Kingston Town, Manikato (who died in 1984 and is buried at Moonee Valley racecourse), the gutsy grey Gunsynd, and Luskin Star, a two-year-old sensation who later became an outstanding sire.

### Television and Armchair 'Norms'

A working knowledge of racing, or any major sport, offers the easiest entrée to the still largely male-dominated Australian society. Wherever men gather—in pubs, clubs or the workplace—sport is the major topic

of conversation. Aussies bet on it and brag about it, they eulogise or verbally crucify its performers, analyse its conduct and speculate about its future. But one thing they never do is tire of it.

Through television, Aussies are watching more sport than ever before. This not only includes local sport, but international tennis, British and European club soccer, World Cup soccer, American football, baseball and basketball, plus summer and winter Olympics. The networks flash fat chequebooks to secure overseas and local television rights and the resultant ratings and advertising revenue justifies the outlay. Sport's sheer popularity and coverage make the tradition a self-perpetuating one, guaranteeing the Australian obsession with games and athletic endeavour a vibrant future.

Television's slick sports coverage is so complete that the "electric goldfish bowl" has been blamed for breeding a population of sedentary sportsmen and women. These armchair "Norms," as they have become known, are characterised by a beer-bellied character who in his own mind is a champion of everything. But the only real exercise he gets is when he beats a well-worn path between armchair and refrigerator to replenish his supply of beer. So concerned were government and health authorities about this character, that they launched an advertising campaign—called "Life, Be In It"—to get him out of his chair and into the great outdoors.

### Back Packs and Action Replays

Meanwhile, the networks are still competing for his downtime with more lavish sports productions. A glance at the TV sports calendar indicates the extent and professionalism of that coverage. Let's start in autumn with the kickoff of the football season. In capital cities, the studios are geared to go with prime-time delayed telecasts of their local match-of-the-day. In Melbourne and Sydney, this means multiple camera angles, portable backpack cameras, on-the-ground microphones and glimpses of the dressing-room drama. On grand final day in Sydney and Melbourne, the coverage and build-up, interviews and direct telecast consumes almost the entire day's programming on the networks which have bid successfully for the rights.

Left, 25,000 participants in the annual Sydney to Bondi Fun Run get off to a start. Right, rounding a corner in the Australian cycling championships in Sydney's Centennial Park.

# FOOD AND DRINK

The first thing one has to understand about an Australian national cuisine is that there really isn't one. There is a national dessert known as the pavlova—the invention of which is disputed by neighbouring New Zealand—and a few joke items invariably thrust in the faces of unsuspecting visitors. These include the quite appalling meat pie, a black sticky paste known as Vegemite, and an extremely curious confection called the Chico roll.

In addition, because of a bad attack of nationalism in hindsight, certain very odd dishes turn up from time to time in restaurants that give themselves such names as the Squatter's Retreat or the Jumbuck Inn. They serve things such as rack of lamb Bendigo (roast lamb), Hobart shoulder (roast lamb) and Beaudesert lamb (roast lamb). Lamb, in fact, still remains a slight obsession in this country, no matter what the dish may be called.

That's the bad news about the place. There is, however, a lot of good news: magnificent tropical and temperate-water fish, east coast rock oysters that are among the world's finest, a glut of fruit and vegetables from every climatic zone, excellent and cheap wines, and a variety of beers which are claimed by inhabitants of various states of Australia to be national treasures. In addition to this, because of successive waves of migration since World War Two, there is a wealth of foreign cuisines now available.

But to understand where "Australian" cuisine stands at this moment in time, a little culinary history is necessary.

## One Man's Meat

When Captain Arthur Phillip sailed his fleet into Sydney Cove in 1788 he found a race of people that no European could even begin to comprehend. The Aborigines were hunter-gatherers and always had been so. The land served them well. But to English eyes the land could offer very little that was even vaguely edible.

The Aborigines had no markets where exotic foodstuffs could be studied before they were tried and they had no European-recognised system of barter. Added to this,

Although some would argue that Australian national cuisine doesn't exist, fine fare is widely enjoyed. Left, Il Duomo, a seafood restaurant in Byron Bay, N.S.W.

because of the unrecognisable climate and soil peculiarities, almost all of the food plants brought by the First Fleet (either as cuttings or as seed) failed dismally. The First Fleeters, therefore, were forced to fall back on ship's rations—salt pork and beef, flour and blue boiler peas.

Apart from establishing a tradition of salt meat and soda bread (otherwise known as damper) that lasted for more than a century, this also established a second tradition that has lasted until the present day: anything imported *must* be superior.

There was also a certain reluctance on the part of the early white settlers to experiment with "native" foodstuffs when it was far easier to import known food plants and animals than to improve the local offerings.

An example of this is the Cape Barren goose, which breeds mainly on two small islands in the Bass Strait separating Tasmania from mainland Australia. Because the goose was indeed a delicious fowl, some attempts were made to domesticate it. But as one early experimenter ruefully remarked, it was extremely pugnacious, attacking other barnyard animals.

Had Australia been discovered in, say, 1600, because of the extreme isolation and the absolute need to make do with what was available, today the Cape Barren goose would be as domestic a bird (and as common on festive tables) as the American turkey. But in the 19th Century, who on earth was going to wrestle with the problems of breeding bad temper out of this feathered swine when tolerably docile European geese were available? The answer was, no one. In a culinary sense, Australia was discovered just a little too late.

## Cordon 'Roo

Of the other animals the country had to offer, the kangaroo was tolerated either roasted in the style of venison, jugged in the English fashion, or made into a "steamer," a dish with Scottish origins. The steamer was basically a kangaroo stew with the addition of red currant jelly (imported) and port (domestic).

But once again, any fool of a thing that bounced around like a pole vaulter, rather than walking on all fours like any other decent, law-abiding grass-eater from the Old World, presented certain problems. Fencing was one of them.

However, one kangaroo dish that survived well into the 20th Century and which—for a brief period in the 1960s—was a success in cans for export was kangaroo tail soup. The Anglo Saxons in the 19th Century deemed it to be, "far superior to oxtail in all respects." But by the 1970s a rash of mortification set in and it was declared to be unpatriotic to eat the country's national emblem. On the other hand, by a curious twist of Antipodean logic, to this day it is still quite okay to feed one-half of the nation's coat of arms to Spot or Rover, the family pet, and (if one can get away with it) export it to the United States or Japan as boneless beef.

Other marsupials fared less well at the hands of immigrant cooks who were forced

style of cooking was middle to lowerclass British. If not salt meat and damper, it was all roasts and spuds, pickled pig's trotters and pies. It is only comparatively recently that the standard entertaining dish of roast meat and three vegetables (usually made up of roast mutton or lamb, roast potatoes, roast pumpkin and something green) has been supplanted.

Another traditional dish that survives only in private households is the Australian mixed salad. This collation, once highly praised by French underwater explorer Jacques Cousteau, is an extremely complicated assembly. A slice each of corned beef, ham and steamed chicken breast are placed in the centre of a standard dinner plate. Three lettuce cups are then arranged in a semi-

to improvise from time to time out of sheer necessity. The most abused was the bandicoot, which was declared by all cookery writers of the late 19th Century to have "a most disagreeable odour." Emu needed "a sailor's digestion" and galah pie was regarded as a most menacing poultry dish indeed. Apart from wood-boring witchety grubs—which some people regarded with horror while others opined that if the feeling of eating worms could be overcome they would be "far more esteemed in delicacy than the whitebait of England"—that was just about the be-all and end-all of "native" fare.

Because of the class balance of the colony's first white-enforced immigrants, the

circle at the end of the plate facing away from the intended diner. Into one cup goes a scoop of potato salad. Into the centre goes a tomato, quartered and covered in a peculiar Australian mayonnaise made from sweetened condensed milk, vinegar and pepper. The third cup is filled with sliced pickled beetroot. Thick slices of processed cheese are placed between these cups and then slices of orange, cut in half are twisted and placed in position over the whole at decorative points.

While kangaroo meat was tolerated in the 19th Century, the picture above is today more representative. Right, wine matures in the Barossa.

One other traditional Australian dish that may occasionally be found in restaurants is Colonial goose. In Great Britain it has been variously claimed to be of both Yorkshire and Scottish origin. But it also turns up in a slightly different form in Provence, France. Basically it is a highly seasoned stuffed shoulder of mutton or lamb and can be very good indeed.

Apart from the meringue dessert called the pavlova (claimed with no authority whatsoever to be named after the dancer of the same name) and a pleasant sponge cake square covered with chocolate and coconut called a lamington (said with equally dubious authority to have been named in the honour of the 19th-Century governor of Queensland, Baron Lamington), that is the

the Australian eating public—they offer good value for money. Most have adapted somewhat to European tastes but if one tries, one can sample anything from *sashimi*, through beggar's chicken and Peking duck to Vietnamese *pho*.

Next in the cheaper scale of restaurant comes the cooking of the Levant, well represented in most capital cities and highly favoured by students. It is fairly impossible to muck up this style of cooking because in general it is a cuisine of poverty.

In other national styles the state of Victoria's capital, Melbourne, has always been known for middling to superlative Italian food which is at last breaking away from the pasta-with-everything school. However, even in the pasta division things are looking

country's Anglo Saxon heritage.

However, since 1960, because of the post World War Two waves of migration, that national culinary scene, as far as restaurant eating is concerned, has changed in a dramatic way.

### Eating Ethnic

Cheapest and most popular are the Asian eating houses of any style or form, ranging from Cantonese, through Indonesian, Thai, Burmese, Japanese and, most lately, Vietnamese.

Although it is impossible to give a national assessment of the quality of these places—thanks to a growing sophistication among

up and many restaurants are making their own.

Many other European styles are well represented. Greek and, more recently, Turkish restaurants have always offered honest fare with no frills. The cooking of the Balkan regions is usually basic but good—at least in Sydney and Melbourne. Because of the Lutheran tradition in South Australia, that state's Barossa Valley offers several German restaurants of more than tolerable standards.

And here and there one finds a smattering of Russian, Hungarian, Danish and Spanish-style eating houses, entirely removed from the steak, pizza and fast-food hamburger tradition.

There are gaps of course. The cooking of the Indian subcontinent is very poorly represented and where it is found is usually very bad indeed. This may have something to do with the fact that many Australians for a long time regarded a curry as a sort of hot meat jam and that early Cantonese-style restaurants pandered to this delusion.

Now one turns to French-style restaurants. Before 1940 there were a smattering of French chefs in Australia and a few large hotels in the capital cities claiming to offer true *haute cuisine*. Mostly, it was a colonial botch. Then in the late 1960s and early 1970s, the country suffered from a plague of bistro-style eating houses where the owner-chef seemed to believe that the only thing necessary for authenticity was a

magnificent. Until comparatively recently the capital cities at least were littered with fish and oyster bars. When they started to disappear because of soaring real-estate costs, they were replaced by up-market versions of the same.

Every Asian restaurant has at least one fish or crustacean speciality on its menu. The city of Melbourne at present probably offers the widest and most imaginative list of fish eating houses in the nation. There are several Italian-style restaurants, for example, which have carried the preparation and serving of anything from the sea to a high art form. Unfortunately, in these Italian establishments the decorations are often quite hair-raising; but one can put up with that lunacy for a taste of the product.

blackboard and a piece of chalk. Those that have survived are not half bad in a *Franglaise* bastardised sense (rack of lamb once threatened to engulf the continent).

Then came the oddity of *cuisine minceur*—the old less-is-more-principle, in other words. But those who could afford this new culinary fashion decided that less wasn't more at all and demanded plates of spuds (potatoes). So what now exists is *cuisine minceur* but-lots-of-it-otherwise-the-bastards-will-riot.

#### Another Man's Poison

In an eating-out sense one leaves the best to last. As stated earlier, Australia's fish are

There also remain a number of Australian-style fish houses where the product is served with absolutely no frills, quite often in waterfront or waterside surroundings (especially in Sydney), and these should be sought out. However. the visitor wants to take his or her seafood, he or she should at least sample, rock oysters, Australian crayfish (especially the Tasmanian variety), Queensland mud crabs, King George Sound whiting (which is no relation to the English fish of the same name), the all-pervading

Above, Doyle's seafood restaurant in Sydney is justly famous. Right, Australians themselves are now recognising the fact that the country produces some excellent wines.

snapper and the estuarine tropical barramundi.

To end this food lecture on something of a low note: excellent standards of any cuisine can be found only in the large cities. Apart from coastal resorts and known tourist spots, the Australian countryside is a culinary wasteland. It is still by-and-large steak and eggs and burnt sheep. Stick to the cities if you expect gourmet satisfaction.

### The Amber Fluid

Now to booze, grog, rum, mother's ruin and fourpenny dark. Beer, of course, is first and foremost. In 1983 an Asian travel magazine, in dubbing Australia "The Land of the Liquid Lunch," carried a cover

photograph of a fat, bearded gentleman surveying a couple of tinnies (cans) of frosty Foster's with a knife and fork. There is no doubt that Australians, while not quite reaching the top of the world's beer-drinking league, favour it over everything else alcoholic.

This was not always so. The colony of New South Wales was founded on rum. Before refrigeration was invented it was next to impossible to brew any sort of decent beer during the summer months when temperatures often reach 40°C (104°F). But once refrigeration was perfected around the middle of the 19th Century, rum—mainly from India and dubbed "odious Bengal"—lost out and the national fashion started.

While in the 19th and early 20th centuries almost every district had its favourite brewery and there was fierce partisanship over the merits of various brews, vast improvements in road transport coupled with mergers and takeovers saw the demise of the independent brewer with his distinctive regional beer. Now there are general differences between the beers of each state but like the hamburger they are approaching a national sameness.

Generally, the premium beer of the country as a whole is Foster's lager, which originated in Victoria but is now brewed in New South Wales as well. Queenslanders favour their own Castlemaine XXXX (pronounced "Four ex") and Western Australian fans demand Swan Lager (known derisively as "Black Duck" elsewhere). One of the last specialised beers in the country is Cooper's Sparkling Ale, made by the relatively small firm of the same name in Adelaide. It is unique in the world of Australian beers in that the bulk of the company's outlet is still bottle-fermented by a method similiar to that used in making champagne and familiar to all home brewers. It is certainly the heaviest and probably the strongest of all the country's bottled beers. Unlike most other Australian beers it can be bought only by the bottle and is not available as a bar draught beer.

In general terms all Australian beers are far higher in alcoholic strength than standard British or American brews, but lower than some of the stronger German. In pubs they are invariabiy served at temperatures that would make anyone with sensitive teeth scream in agony. In summer, in hotter areas, chilled glasses are *de rigueur*.

Visitors might as well give up on measures of beer served in hotels in each state. But the New South Wales *middy* (somewhere around the old half-pint measure) is known as a *pot* in Victoria, and the New South Wales *schooner* (somewhat less than an old English pint) is a completely different measure in Queensland where they don't drink it anyway but prefer something called a *five*. A lady's waist is at times called a seven which is Victoria's standard measure where it is simply called a beer.

### Stronger Stuff

Before getting into the subject of wine, that stuff that founded the nation—rum—is worth a mention. Australian rums, rather like Australian wines, have absolutely nothing in common with the liquids produced by other countries, especially those of

Jamaica and the West Indies in general. Although most Aussie rums are dark, they don't possess the underlying tar taste of those of the Caribbean, and most are smooth.

Bundaberg overproof is perhaps the most "fashionable" (although all rums suffer from their convict ancestry). It is commonly referred to as "Bundi." The second most esteemed is Red Mill overproof. Taken to excess, of course, either can be deadly, but they are extremely pleasant. There is a third rum, not easily obtainable but modelled on the rum that did what it did to the British Royal Navy. It is called Inner Circle. Remember that name and approach the bottle with extreme caution. Although the product is indeed smooth, excellent and induces good humour, the phrase "kill a brown dog" is not of Australian origins for idle reasons.

Other spirits and liqueurs are made in Australia but are in no way comparable to their imported counterparts. Australian whisky, if one can still find a bottle, is decidedly interesting.

### No Ordinary Wine

The Australian wine industry is not quite as old as the First Fleet (all the vine cuttings died) but it was not all that far behind, first moderate successes being achieved on the Liverpool Plains outside the town of Sydney. The area is now a suburb of that city.

But like everything else European, the vines had their problems with the Antipodean climate and soil. Although Australian winemakers attempted for decades to ape the styles of Europe and labelled their products accordingly, nothing could disguise the fact that the wines were indeed very, very Australian. A Californian winemaker perhaps put it best in recent years when asked by a breathless representative of the Australian wine industry on how the wines stood up to similar products in other countries. "I believe," he said "that Australians are very good at making Australian wines."

Australians themselves are now recognising the fact that the country produces excellent wines, which can stand on their own merits and are to be much-admired in their own right. But there is no way that an Australian red is going to taste like something that comes from Bordeaux nor is an Australian sparkling wine very much like a true champagne. Australians are beginning to respond to this new winemaking nationalism and enjoying more and more of their own excellent products. It was not always so. In its early years the industry was ham-

pered by the fact that the Currency Lads and Lasses (the native-born) regarded still red and white wines as something rather nasty that only foreigners drank. If they touched wine at all, it had to be port or muscat. Therefore, for years, the industry relied for profit on fortified wines. Most of them were coarse.

Matters have now changed and the country's *vin ordinaires*, usually sold by the flagon (two litres) or by the cask (4½ litres and upwards) are some of the best "simple" wines for money in the wine-drinking world. Those are the wines that one will invariably be offered if one wants a glass of white or red in a pub or wine bar, or a couple of glasses or a carafe at a licensed restaurant.

Above this level, and speaking very

broadly, Australian quality reds tend to be heavier and contain more oak than most European wines while the whites tend to be somewhat flatter in style.

The country's better fortified wines—although they continue to be labelled port and muscat—are not only unique but quite brilliant. The best come from Victoria's Rutherglen district from a series of relatively small winemakers, although some of the older offerings from South Australia's Barossa Valley are equally complex.

Both red and white still wines vary in style from state to state (region to region is the more correct phrasing, but wines in the country are invariably known by state). The softest and perhaps the most subtle in a good year come from the Hunter Valley area of New South Wales; while the most robust come from South Australia's Coonawarra region and the Southern Vales (or McLaren Vale). The country's most expensive premier red always has been Grange, originally from the Grange vineyard on the outskirts of Adelaide. A straight cabernet sauvignon, it can cost a king's ransom.

At times it is hard in Australia to procure a true regional wine. As the world's present most-quoted wine expert, Englishman Hugh Johnson, has testily remarked, Australian master winemakers will truck in material from almost anywhere to achieve a standard blend in any premium wine. Although Johnson may rage about this, what the great man has never understood is that Australia is

some smaller wine companies do have an attitude to "their" products that irritates almost everyone. Many wineries specialise in still red or whites to the exclusion of other types because, they claim, "cellar door demand" requires them to stock a full range of wines some of which have nothing to do with their own vineyards.

Another claim by Australian winemakers that infuriates both resident and visitor alike is the cry: "Every year is a vintage year in this country." This is, of course, so much rubbish; otherwise why the proliferation of blended wines? Every wine region in Australia has its year of total failure (the 1982 drought of the century virtually destroying the entire vintage in the east of the continent). But the wine novice or tourist has to

perhaps the only country in the world where vineyards can get regularly devastated by bushfires. Therefore, in certain seasons, one has to truck in if one is going to produce any wine at all and damn the fact that it is a mix. Mind you, it does lead to some odd statements on certain labels in which a wine is declared to be a blend of grapes from vineyards that are just about as far apart as Burgundy and Afghanistan.

Australians, used to this blending technique, don't worry overly much about it. But

Two unusual displays of food. Left, dried fruit and nuts. Right, an agricultural exhibit at the Royal Agricultural Show in Sydney.

fight his or her way through this tangle unaided.

At the end it can be said that most Australian wine is there to be enjoyed without a show of pretence. It really doesn't matter if the drinker decides to take a bottle of Grange in the company of an Adelaide Floater (a meat pie in a soup dish filled with a mush of blue boiler peas, the whole topped with tomato sauce). God alone knows if enough visitors to this country start demanding this bizarre creation it could start an international trend that could send cuisine into complete oblivion and even be gloomily, albeit reluctantly, noted by *Larousse Gastronomique*. That would be recognition enough for a simple nation.

# A UNIQUE FAUNA AND FLORA

Australia's splendid isolation has had a profound effect on the evolution of animals and plants in the southern continent. The sheer age of the land mass and its division by sea from other continents allowed Nature to have her way, independent of what was happening elsewhere. Consequently, Australian wildlife took on a unique character that prospered until the arrival of white man and the onset of the technological age.

In 200 years of white settlement, considerable damage has been inflicted on the environment. However, in the latter half of the 20th Century, the conservation movement has gathered such impetus that the continent's environmental future is starting to look more secure. Notable victories by the conservationists include the rescue of vast sections of the southwest Tasmanian wilderness from the threat of dam construction, the official protection of endangered plants and animal species, restriction on logging in the shrinking rainforests of the eastern seaboard, and the acceptance by most political parties of the growing power of the conservationist movement.

The need to preserve this uniqueness is becoming apparent as Australians grow more aware of their environment. In the bush, grasslands, oceans and desert, examples abound of what makes Australian wildlife so special.

### Amazing Mammals

There are no better examples than the Australian mammals. Mammals are warmblooded and furred, and almost all give birth to their young alive and suckle them. There are three groups of mammals—marsupials, monotremes and placentals. In Australia, marsupials are by far the most prominent. They give live birth, but their young are not fully developed, and are kept in a pouch until they develop enough to move around independently. Kangaroos, possums and wallabies are examples of Australian marsupials.

Monotremes are probably the most exotic type of mammals. Rather than giving birth

Preceding pages, Australia's splendid isolation has had a marked effect on its flora and fauna; the Boabtree is common in Australia. Left, kangaroos are also indigenous. Right, Possum at Gosford Reptile Park.

to live young, they lay eggs. However, they do suckle their young and display many other mammalian traits. The duck-billed amphibious platypus is a monotreme, as is the echidna or spiny anteater.

The placental group comprises all the familiar large mammals that exist on Earth. While they proliferate on most continents, very few examples can be found among the native Australian fauna. The native dog, the dingo, is a member of the placental group but naturalists are of the opinion it might be an introduced species.

Although scientists have found examples of marsupials in fossil form in many parts of the world, living species are known only in Australia and South America. The opportunity to study marsupials in large numbers in their own habitats exists only in Australia.

Most marsupials are herbivorous while others include insects, small reptiles or smaller mammals in their diets. The larger members of the carnivorous group are the native "cats" and "wolves." These bear no relation to the cat or canine families but their names do suggest some sort of confusion on the part of the early whites who attempted to classify these strange creatures. Examples include the Tasmanian devil and the Tasmanian tiger. The latter is a wolf-like creature thought to be extinct except by a few naturalists who have reported recent sightings in wilderness areas.

The herbivores abound and represent the cuddly postcard image of Australian wildlife. The shy, tree-dwelling koala is an example as are the many varieties of possum, including the ringtail and the glider. But undoubtedly the best known are the macropods, or hopping marsupials, such as the kangaroo, wallaby, wallaroo and kangaroo rat. The familiar kangaroo profile is the greatest Australian symbol of them all, which makes foreigners wonder just why Aussies seem bent on hunting the breed to extinction.

The great kangaroo debate has been waged on very emotional grounds that have

you consider a 'roo's ability to jump fences.

Now, licences are issued for professional shooters to cull the troops. Ironically, much of the kangaroo meat finishes up in the food bowls of family pets, a rather pathetic conclusion seeing that the woes of the native were caused by the introduction of "foreign" animals.

Today, the kangaroo populations are carefully monitored and, although some of the tinier species have been steadily losing out to such introduced species as rabbits and feral cats, there is little risk of the great bounding macropod disappearing.

The retiring koala, despite its often misused title, is not a bear but is yet another exotic example of Australia's herbivorous marsupials. Its habit of sleeping openly in

sometimes contrived to cloud the real issues. Before the arrival of the white man and his sophisticated agricultural techniques, the kangaroo population was controlled by the climate and environment. In times of drought, female kangaroos intuitively did not come into season, thereby putting restraints on the expansion of the herd. This helped preserve food supplies. In times of plenty, the kangaroo populations increased. However, this fine balance was altered when artificial irrigation of the grasslands created more food for the 'roo troops. While the kangaroos grew in number and competed with sheep and cattle for the available feed, farmers sought ways to keep the 'roo troops off their properties—no small task when

the forks of gum trees made it an easy target for hunters who valued it for its fur. So great was the slaughter that urgent steps were taken to save the koala. The shy marsupial is now completely protected.

The wombat is related to the koala; but instead of making its home up a tree and dining on gum leaves, it uses its powerful digging paws to make burrows under stumps, logs or in creek banks. It lives on roots, leaves and bark.

The rarer placental animals include the

Above, Koalas in the Lone Pine Sanctuary, Brisbane. Right, the emu and the blue-tongued lizard are part of the wildlife that can be seen while on the road.

fruit bats or flying foxes, rats and mice. These rodents are thought to have arrived rather than evolved on the continent, but they were certainly here centuries before the white man. When Europeans arrived with their own species of rodent, there were already more than 50 local types living in a wide variety of habitats.

The dingo, or native dog, was probably introduced to Australia via the migration of Aboriginals from Asia when man first came to the Great South Land.

### Reptiles and Amphibians

Australian reptiles are also unusual, whether it be for their appearance or fascinating habitats. Reptiles figure prominently

like a snake, they are often killed in error.

Many city dwellers welcome the presence of the blue-tongued lizard in their gardens. This character hunts snails and insects, may not be as faithful as a dog but is decidedly cheaper to keep.

Don't expect Australia's freshwater tortoise to pull his head in like others do. He has to twist his neck to one side to tuck the head inside his shell.

Two species of crocodile abound in the far north of the country. One is a native croc found in inland freshwater streams and lagoons. The other is the larger and far more dangerous saltwater crocodile of Southeast Asia.

Australia has more than its share of frogs and toads, many similar in appearance to

in Aboriginal legend and diet but whites do not hold them in such regard, particularly the venomous snakes such as the taipan, tiger snake, death adder and brown snake. Non-venomous varieties like the carpet snake and green tree snake abound.

Lizards, ranging from the tiniest of skinks to goannas more than two metres (6½ feet) long, proliferate in Australia. Perhaps the most exotic is the frill-necked lizard, which has a frock of skin around its neck erected into a broad collar when confronted with danger. It should not be confused with the bearded dragon, so named for his mane of spines.

Found only in Australia and New Guinea is a group of legless lizards that look so much

those of Europe and North America, and many peculiarly Australian. One type found in the drier climes of central Australia is known to inflate itself with water and burrow underground to survive long, dry periods. Sadly, the most infamous amphibian is the Queensland cane toad. This giant was introduced to eradicate a cane parasite but has become such an unwelcome intruder in his own right that environmentalists are currently examining ways to eradicate him. It's yet another example of the destabilising effect introduced species have had on the local environment.

The subject of amphibians returns this discourse to the sea where some of Australia's more intriguing animals thrive. The

Great Barrier Reef is a nature wonderland blessed with numerous fish, shell and polyp species peculiar to Australian waters. But one doesn't have to go snorkelling on the reef to sample the coastal wildlife. A scramble over any coastal rock platform will reveal shellfish, starfish, anemones, crabs and even the occasional octopus.

Take heed of warnings about the potential dangers of the blue-ringed octopus. This small coastal variety is known to be extremely venomous, but little has been learned about its toxin or why it can sometimes be handled without risk but very, very rarely might claim a victim.

Australia's early explorers were almost as intrigued by the strange birdlife as they were by kangaroos and koalas. Here was a land

The eccentric bowerbird builds a structure of bower on which he performs to win the attention of a female. He adorns his court with brightly coloured trinkets such as stones, glass or objects collected from gardens or houses. The mallee fowl places her eggs under a mound of sand that acts as an incubator. By varying the level of sand, the bird can keep the eggs at a regular temperature according to the heat of the day.

Eagles, hawks, crows and cuckoos of native origin can all be observed. The opening up of the southern continent helped map the migratory habits of numerous Northern Hemisphere species known to "fly south for the winter."

The vastness of the continent and the variety of habitats allows for numerous

where the swans were black instead of white, where a relative of the kingfisher that the Aboriginals knew as kookaburra peeled off a manic laugh, and where the great flightless emu could almost outrun a horse.

There were elegant magpies who signalled the start of day with their peculiar call, and strutting lyrebirds with their silver tails, exotic mating dances and ability to mimic the sounds of other animals, including humans.

On the east coast particularly, flocks of raucous parrots plundered the fruit trees. They included in their number the brilliantly plumed rosellas and lorikeets, displaying colours that suited their precocious personalities.

species of waterfowl. Some were hunted by the early settlers while development consumed coastal habitats. But protective measures and environmental awareness have saved many from the threat of extinction.

Visitors to Australia expecting to see kangaroos bounding through the streets of the cities and koalas scuttling up the nearest telephone pole will be disappointed. Like most wildlife, the Aussie animals are generally shy of man. Of course, you can go to any of the capital city zoos such as Sydney's

Above, Australia's Spear Lily followed by an avenue of jacaranda trees in full bloom. Right, Australian Banksia followed by the emblem of New South Wales.

306

Taronga Park and see most forms of local wildlife from platypus to black snake. But the best way to encounter them is usually in their own environment where, with a certain amount of stealth and respect, you might be fortunate enough to witness them going about their business.

Most people, including city-bound Australians, aren't afforded this privilege. A suitable compromise is a visit to any of the larger nature reserves that exist on the fringe of some of the cities. Here, in natural surroundings and often under the guidance of a park ranger, you can observe examples of Australia's wondrous animals.

As for the flora; well, it's almost everywhere. From a stroll through the leafy outer suburbs of Sydney or Melbourne, to a

encounter, but he and his assistants went to extraordinary lengths to collect samples, log descriptions and make detailed drawings. For Banks, it was a labour of love and it is fitting that he should hold such an important place in Australian history. Cook named Botany Bay after observing Bank's state of excitement at his botanic discoveries. The eye-catching banksia trees that proliferate along the coastline are sturdy reminders of the botanist's interest. It's a pity the settlers and farmers to follow did not share his respect for the local vegetation.

## A Land of Eucalypts

The range of Australian eucalypts is immense, ranging from low, stunted, scrub-like

bushwalk in the jarrah forests of Western Australia or a camping trip in the Tasmanian wilderness, you can easily expose your senses to the great Aussie bush. Unlike the animals, it will not run away at your approach despite the early white man's efforts to kill off as much of it as possible.

Whereas the first white settlers might have been intimidated by the unfamiliar eucalypt forests, the Aborigines saw them as perfect habitats and sources of food.

The first white to appreciate Australia's unique flora from an academic viewpoint was the great botanist Sir Joseph Banks, who sailed with Cook on the *Endeavour*. Banks was not only intrigued by the incredible variety of new plant life he was to

bush to the great towering varieties of the highland forests. There are ghost gums, so named because under the light of the moon they appear silvery-white; and rock-hard ironbarks, capable of blunting the toughest timber saws. The name eucalypt is all-embracing and even includes larger varieties of wattle.

It is from the gold and green of the wattle that Australia draws its national colours. So hardy is the wattle that it is usually one of the first varieties to rejuvenate after a season of bushfires. There have been many bushfires since white settlement and while some plant types have suffered, the wattles have thrived. In season, they bathe the bush in gold with their blossoms.

Unlike the softwood varieties of Europe and North America, most Australian natives have very hard timber. This made clearing the land an extremely arduous task for the early settlers. When the pioneers encountered softer dress timber, they were often ruthless in their zeal to lop it down. The virtual disappearance of cedar from the rainforests of the coastal hinterlands is witness to their efforts.

In Tasmania, the mighty Huon pine was found to be one of the best building timbers in the world. It is especially prized by boat builders. The jarrah forests of south Western Australian are currently under threat from mining and earlier culling. Jarrah and the tough Karri are also superb building timber and foresters are exploring ways to

guarantee their proliferation and combat a disease called "die-back."

A concerted drive to replant some of the tree life laid waste in the name of agricultural development is currently in train. As shade for stock, protection against soil erosion, enrichers of soil and friends of man, trees are making a comeback.

The Australian deserts might appear vast infertile wastes in the dry season, but it only takes a good downpour to turn them into a paradise of wildflowers. The seeds can lie dormant in the soil for years waiting for moisture to bring them to life.

One section of Australia noted for its variety of wildflowers is the southern corner of Western Australia. The area has become

so famous that commercial growing of some of the more exotic types has become a minor local industry. The best-known plant of the area is the kangaroo paw, appropriately named for its resemblance to the hind paw of the kangaroo. Among the semi-desert plants is the Sturt pea, which proliferates with the slightest hint of moisture.

An understanding of Australia's vast climatic and geographical differences provides an insight into the wealth of plant life. From the tropical growth of northern Queensland's steamy jungles, to the delicate blossoms of New South Wales' cool southern tablelands, there is seemingly no end to the variety.

There are some types of plants that thrive almost anywhere in Australia, regardless of climate, soil type or man's presence. The most abundant of these is the acacia, or wattle. Visitors might also note the presence of grass-trees in almost all areas. These are sometimes called black boys because of the spear-like vegetation that juts from the centre, often to a height of five metres (16 feet).

The presence of some plants common only to South America, South Africa and Australia has led observers to believe the great land masses of the Southern Hemisphere were once joined.

Like many of the continent's animals, Australian flora has been affected by the introduction of foreign trees, grasses, shrubs and plants. In some instances these types have flourished unchecked, completely altering the ecological balance of entire regions. However, many city and country-dwellers have become aware of the importance of native plant life. In the cities, the replanting of native trees has seen bird and insect life return to these areas with the resultant re-germination process for which birds and bees are so famous. More than 200 years after Banks went into raptures about this botanic wonderland, teachers are leading Australian children out into the wild to experience and appreciate the beauty and uniqueness of the local wildlife.

Australia can be a harsh mistress, as it has proven by the ferocity of its great bushfires. It also has some of the finest wilderness regions left on this planet, and some of the most exotic animal and plant life. It is an awesome responsibility to preserve it as such.

Left, bushfires such as this in North Queensland can have a devastating effect. Right, a gum tree in the Snowy Mountains.

311

# GUIDE IN BRIEF

# Travelling to Australia

## By Air

Sydney and Melbourne are the two major international airports with flights from Asia, the Pacific (including New Zealand), Europe and North America. Adelaide, Darwin, Perth, Brisbane, Cairns, Townsville and Hobart also have international airports, so check on the gateway options available. Twenty-three international airlines service Australia frequently. (See Appendix.)

A variety of discount fares is now available: there is certainly a lot more competition than there used to be. But the basic problem with travelling to Australia is that because it is a long way from anywhere, it is expensive to visit. Travellers can take advantage of Apex (advance purchase excursion) fares, but the price is dependent on the time (or season) of travel. Different low, shoulder and peak-season rates exist for different directions of travel, so it is wise to seek the advice of a knowledgeable travel agent before purchasing a ticket.

## By Sea

Travel patterns over recent years have changed considerably and most visitors to Australia now travel by air. The traditional method of travel to Australia was by ship. Several companies however still offer infrequent and expensive cruises to Australia, or which include Australia. (See Appendix.)

# Travel Advisories

## Immigration

Visitors require a passport and visa to enter Australia. Exception is made only for New Zealanders, who require a passport but no visa. Visas are free and valid for up to six months. Applications should be made to the nearest Australian or British Government representative. (See Ap-

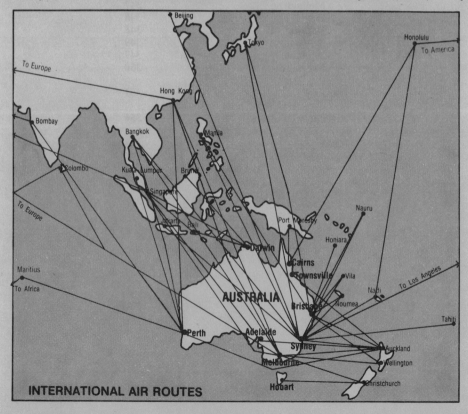

**INTERNATIONAL AIR ROUTES**

pendix for a list of Australian Consular offices overseas.)

Visitors must also produce an onward or return ticket and must have sufficient funds to enter Australia. British, Canadian, Irish and Japanese visitors who are between 18 and 30 years old are eligible for a working-holiday visa. This entitles a maximum stay of three years and employment during that time. Such visas can only be applied for in the home country.

## Health Precautions

Vaccinations are not required if you are flying direct to Australia and have not come from an endemic zone or from a smallpox, yellow fever, cholera or typhoid-infected area in the 14 days prior to your arrival in Australia.

## Customs

For visitors over 18 years of age the usual regulations apply to Australia. There are no customs charges on personal belongings which you intend to use for your stay. In addition you may import 200 cigarettes or 250 grams of cigars or tobacco, one litre of alcoholic liquor, and goods to the value of A$200 in personal baggage.

On arriving in Australia the interior of your aircraft will be sprayed with a particularly foul-smelling substance. This is not a happy introduction to Australia, but is just part of the strict control on the importation of flying insects, animal or plant products fruit, vegetables and seeds. Australia is free from many exotic insect pests and intends to stay that way. Visitors should also note there are various restrictions on taking fruit or vegetables between states.

Australia is rabies-free and all incoming animals are placed in quarantine. Dogs and cats travelling from England and Europe must spend one-month quarantine in England and five months in Australian quarantine. Those from America and Hawaii are placed in one-month quarantine in Hawaii and four months in Australian quarantine. From the Pacific countries, dogs and cats are placed in Australian quarantine for nine months. If you have any other type of pet it would be best to check with customs in your home country well in advance.

## Departure Tax

The departure tax of A$20 has to be paid (in local currency only) by all travellers departing Australia. This is one of the highest departure taxes in the world and leaves visitors with a nasty taste in their mouth.

## Currency and Exchange

Australia's currency, you will be glad to know, is dollars and cents. Coins come in one- and two-cent copper pieces; five-, 10-, 20- and 50-cent silver ones; and a new dollar coin was introduced in 1984.

Notes are $1, $2, $5, $10, $20 and $50. Bring in as much foreign currency as you like but don't leave with more than A$250 in cash.

In mid-1984, foreign currency conversion rates for every A$1.00 were as follows: 1.16 Canadian dollars, 1.39 New Zealand dollars, .64 pounds sterling, .90 US dollars, 2.41 German marks, 7.42 French francs, 207 Japanese yen and 1.89 Singapore dollars.

Travellers' cheques (whatever currency) can be readily cashed at international airports, banks, hotels, motels, and other similar establishments. All well-known international travellers' cheques are widely used in Australia, and all major credit cards are accepted. The most widely recognized and accepted are American Express, Diners Club, Mastercard, Visa Card and Carte Blanche. You could encounter difficulties with other overseas cards.

# Getting Acquainted

## Government and Economy

Since 1901 Australia has been governed as a federal commonwealth with a parliamentary system of government based on a mixture of British, American, Canadian and Swiss democracies. The prime minister heads the national government and is the leader of the party holding the greatest number of lower house seats. The lower house is the House of Representatives, the upper house the Senate. Voting in Australia is compulsory and also somewhat complicated as a preferential voting system is used, whereby each candidate is ranked in order of preference.

To prevent the rival cities of Sydney and Melbourne from battling for the honour of being the nation's capital, the city of Canberra was founded. The federal parliament is based here and like Washington, D.C., in the United States, Canberra is in its own separate area of land, the Australian Capital Territory.

A premier leads each state government. There are two main political groups, the Australian Labor Party and the coalition of the Liberal

Party and the National Party. The current prime minister, Mr. Bob Hawke, is the leader of the Labor Party. Governors in each of the states. along with the governor-general, represent the British Crown in Australia.

## Geography

Australia is the smallest continent in the world, and is believed to be the oldest continent on earth. It is roughly 4,000 km (2,500 miles) from east to west, and 3,200 km (2,000 miles) north to south. The coastline measures 36,735 km (22,826 miles) and is washed by three oceans and four seas. About 40 percent of the continent lies in the tropics. Separated from other land masses early in its geologic youth, Australia developed by

itself, resulting in a unique flora and fauna.

Comparable in size to the United States (excluding Alaska), Australia is the only continent with just one nation on it. The population of Australia is approaching 15 million, about 160,000 of whom are Aboriginals. Almost the entire population is crowded into a narrow strip along the east coast and in a small section around the southwest corner of the continent.

The Great Dividing Range, stretching almost the whole length of the continent, separates a narrow fertile strip on the east coast from the red centre. West of the range the country becomes increasingly flat and dry, habitation virtually ceases, and the horizon is broken only by occasional mysterious protuberances like Ayers Rock and the Olgas, and some starkly beautiful mountains like the Flinders and the Macdonnell ranges. In the far south of Western Australia a repeat of

# Meteorological Chart

| Major Cities | | Jan | Feb | Mar | Apr | May | June | July | Aug | Sep | Oct | Nov | Dec |
|---|---|---|---|---|---|---|---|---|---|---|---|---|---|
| **Sydney** | Maximum °C | 26 | 25 | 25 | 22 | 19 | 17 | 16 | 17 | 20 | 22 | 24 | 25 |
| | Minimum °C | 18 | 18 | 17 | 15 | 11 | 9 | 8 | 9 | 11 | 13 | 15 | 17 |
| | Rainfall mm | 98 | 113 | 128 | 127 | 124 | 131 | 105 | 81 | 70 | 75 | 78 | 80 |
| | Water Temp. °C | 22 | 22 | 22 | 21 | 14 | 17 | 16 | 16 | 16 | 17 | 19 | 20 |
| **Melbourne** | Maximum °C | 26 | 26 | 24 | 20 | 17 | 14 | 13 | 15 | 17 | 20 | 22 | 24 |
| | Minimum °C | 14 | 14 | 13 | 11 | 9 | 7 | 6 | 6 | 8 | 9 | 11 | 13 |
| | Rainfall mm | 48 | 50 | 54 | 59 | 57 | 50 | 48 | 49 | 58 | 67 | 59 | 58 |
| | Water Temp. °C | 18 | 18 | 17 | 16 | 15 | 14 | 13 | 13 | 13 | 14 | 15 | 16 |
| **Brisbane** | Maximum °C | 29 | 29 | 28 | 26 | 23 | 21 | 20 | 22 | 24 | 26 | 28 | 29 |
| | Minimum °C | 27 | 20 | 19 | 16 | 13 | 11 | 9 | 10 | 13 | 16 | 18 | 17 |
| | Rainfall mm | 162 | 164 | 145 | 87 | 69 | 69 | 57 | 47 | 48 | 75 | 95 | 130 |
| | Water Temp. °C | 25 | 25 | 25 | 24 | 22 | 20 | 20 | 19 | 20 | 21 | 22 | 24 |
| **Adelaide** | Maximum °C | 30 | 29 | 27 | 23 | 19 | 16 | 15 | 16 | 19 | 22 | 25 | 28 |
| | Minimum °C | 16 | 17 | 15 | 13 | 10 | 8 | 7 | 8 | 9 | 11 | 13 | 15 |
| | Rainfall mm | 19 | 20 | 24 | 44 | 69 | 72 | 66 | 62 | 51 | 44 | 31 | 27 |
| | Water Temp. °C | 19 | 20 | 20 | 18 | 16 | 15 | 14 | 14 | 14 | 15 | 16 | 17 |
| **Perth** | Maximum °C | 30 | 30 | 28 | 24 | 21 | 18 | 17 | 18 | 19 | 21 | 25 | 27 |
| | Minimum °C | 18 | 18 | 17 | 14 | 12 | 10 | 9 | 9 | 10 | 11 | 14 | 16 |
| | Rainfall mm | 8 | 11 | 20 | 40 | 124 | 186 | 174 | 139 | 81 | 55 | 21 | 14 |
| | Water Temp. °C | 20 | 20 | 21 | 21 | 20 | 19 | 18 | 18 | 18 | 18 | 19 | 20 |
| **Darwin** | Maximum °C | 32 | 32 | 32 | 33 | 32 | 31 | 30 | 31 | 33 | 34 | 34 | 33 |
| | Minimum °C | 25 | 25 | 25 | 24 | 22 | 20 | 20 | 21 | 23 | 25 | 25 | 25 |
| | Rainfall mm | 391 | 330 | 260 | 103 | 14 | 3 | 1 | 2 | 13 | 50 | 126 | 243 |
| | Water Temp. °C | 29 | 29 | 29 | 28 | 28 | 26 | 26 | 24 | 27 | 27 | 29 | 29 |
| **Hobart** | Maximum °C | 22 | 22 | 20 | 17 | 14 | 12 | 11 | 13 | 15 | 17 | 19 | 20 |
| | Minimum °C | 12 | 12 | 11 | 9 | 7 | 5 | 4 | 5 | 6 | 8 | 9 | 11 |
| | Rainfall mm | 45 | 41 | 44 | 52 | 50 | 57 | 54 | 49 | 53 | 61 | 61 | 56 |
| | Water Temp. °C | 15 | 15 | 15 | 14 | 13 | 12 | 12 | 11 | 11 | 12 | 12 | 13 |
| **Canberra** | Maximum °C | 28 | 27 | 24 | 20 | 15 | 12 | 11 | 13 | 16 | 19 | 23 | 26 |
| | Minimum °C | 13 | 13 | 10 | 6 | 3 | 1 | 0 | 1 | 3 | 5 | 9 | 11 |
| | Rainfall mm | 59 | 57 | 52 | 47 | 52 | 38 | 37 | 45 | 48 | 69 | 64 | 58 |
| **Cairns** | Maximum °C | 32 | 31 | 30 | 29 | 27 | 26 | 25 | 27 | 28 | 29 | 31 | 31 |
| | Minimum °C | 24 | 24 | 22 | 22 | 20 | 18 | 17 | 18 | 19 | 21 | 22 | 23 |
| | Rainfall mm | 399 | 441 | 464 | 177 | 91 | 51 | 30 | 26 | 36 | 35 | 84 | 167 |
| | Water Temp. °C | 28 | 28 | 28 | 26 | 26 | 23 | 22 | 23 | 24 | 25 | 27 | 28 |
| **Alice Springs** | Maximum °C | 37 | 36 | 33 | 29 | 23 | 20 | 19 | 22 | 26 | 31 | 34 | 35 |
| | Minimum °C | 22 | 21 | 18 | 14 | 9 | 6 | 4 | 7 | 10 | 15 | 18 | 20 |
| | Rainfall mm | 34 | 39 | 22 | 12 | 17 | 16 | 13 | 12 | 6 | 20 | 23 | 32 |

the mountain range-coasted strip pattern heralds the Indian Ocean. In the north-central part the dry country runs to the sea and in the extreme north a tropical area lies within the monsoon belt.

## Climate

Anytime is the right time to visit. Australia has perfect weather for touring, particularly in the capital cities which lie outside the extreme hot and cold belts. The seasons in Australia are the converse of the Northern Hemisphere. September to November is spring, December to February summer, March to May autumn and June to August winter.

The seasonal variations become smaller as you head north, until in Darwin (in the monsoon belt) there are only two seasons: hot and dry, or hot and wet. North of Brisbane things are pretty hot most of the year. As a rule you can assume that from November to March it's warm to boiling everywhere. You are advised to stay away from Darwin during the monsoon season but the northern winter offers ideal touring weather—warm days, clear blue skies and cool nights.

In the south, winters tend to be chilly with plenty of snow on the mountain ranges. You may head south for the skiing but otherwise, Melbourne can be rather cold, grey and miserable in winter. It's best to avoid Melbourne in July/August. Tasmania, the island state off the southern tip of the continent, is the coolest.

The summer temperatures in central Australia are far too high for comfort. In winter, the nights may be cool but the days are clear and warm.

Apart from climatic seasons, visitors should bear in mind the holiday seasons, too. Christmas is not only the regular holiday season, but is also the middle of the long summer school holidays. Other school holidays are in May and August/September. If travelling during these seasons, make sure everything is booked well in advance.

For more information on Australian weather conditions, refer to the chart on page 316.

## Clothing

Generally, Australians are informal dressers. However, for special occasions like dining at better-class hotels or restaurants in the larger cities, a tie and jacket are recommended. If you visit Australia during summer, include at least one warm sweater or jacket for air-conditioned rooms and the occasional cold snap. Your swimsuit, sunglasses and suntan lotion are a must.

If travelling to the southeastern states during winter, include warm clothing, a raincoat and an umbrella. You'll need a sun hat and good strong walking shoes if you intend to do some bushwalking. And if exploring the Great Barrier Reef, an old pair of sneakers is suggested.

## Time Zones

Australia has three time zones. Eastern Standard Time is 10 hours ahead of Greenwich Mean Time (Tasmania, Victoria, New South Wales, Queensland). Central Australian Time is 9½ hours ahead (Northern Territory and South Australia) and Western Standard Time is eight hours ahead (Western Australia). So when it is noon in Perth, it's 1.30 p.m. in Darwin and Adelaide, and 2 p.m. from Cairns to Hobart.

During the summer things go slightly haywire as daylight saving does not operate in Western Australia or Queensland so those two states are one hour behind.

Not taking Daylight Savings into consideration, international times are staggered as follows:

When it's noon in Sydney and Melbourne, it's
11:30 a.m. in Adelaide/Darwin
11 a.m. in Tokyo/Seoul
10 a.m. in Hongkong/Manila/Singapore/Perth
9 a.m. Jakarta/Bangkok
7:30 a.m. in Delhi/Calcutta
3 a.m. in Paris/Rome/Frankfurt/Amsterdam
2 a.m. in London/Lisbon
11 p.m. yesterday in Buenos Aires
9 p.m. yesterday in New York/Washington
8 p.m. yesterday in Mexico City/Chicago
6 p.m. yesterday in San Francisco/Los Angeles
4 p.m. yesterday in Honolulu

## Weights and Measures

Australia operates under the metric system of weights and measures. Fruit and vegetables are bought by the kilogram, petrol and milk by the litre, distance by the metre or kilometre, and speed limits in kilometres per hour.

Despite it being some two decades since the change from the imperial system to the metric system, a 183 cm person is still referred to as being six-foot tall. The main conversions are:-
1 metre = 3.28 feet
1 kilometre = 0.62 mile
1 kilogram = 2.20 pounds
1 litre = 1.5 pints (US) = 1.8 pints (UK)
0°Centigrade = 32°Fahrenheit; 25°C = 77°F

## Electricity

The domestic electrical supply in Australia consists of 240 volts and five hertz alternating current. Universal outlets for 110 volts (for shavers and small appliances) are usually supplied in leading hotels and motels. For larger appliances such as hairdriers you'll need to bring along or buy a converter and a special flat three-pin adaptor plug to fit into outlets.

## Business and Banking Hours

General retail trading hours for Australian stores are from 9 a.m. to 5:30 p.m. Monday to Friday, and 9 a.m. to noon Saturday. Late shopping on Friday is available in Melbourne, Adelaide, Brisbane, Hobart and Darwin, and on Thursday until 9 p.m. in Sydney, Canberra and Perth.

Restaurants and snack bars, bookshops and local corner stores are open until later in the evening and sometimes all weekend. Australians still enjoy the tradition of the holiday weekend and most businesses are closed on Saturday and Sunday.

Banks are open from 9:30 to 4 p.m. Monday to Thursday and until 5 p.m. on Friday. All banks, post offices government and private offices, and most shops close on public holidays. (See below).

Transport reservations and hotel bookings can be affected by these holidays and many restaurants and hotels raise their prices.

## Public Holidays (1985)

| | |
|---|---|
| Jan. 1 | New Years Day |
| 28 | Australia Day Holiday |
| March 4 | Labour Day—W.A. & Tas. |
| 11 | Labour Day—Vic. |
| 18 | Canberra Day (A.C.T.) |
| Apr. 5 | Good Friday |
| 6 | Easter Saturday |
| 8 | Easter Monday |
| 9 | Easter Tuesday (Vic.) |
| 9 | Bank Holiday (Tas.) |
| 25 | Anzac Day |
| May 6 | Labour Day (QLD) |
| 6 | May Day (N.T.) |
| 20 | Adelaide Cup Day (Adelaide area) |
| June 3 | Foundation Day (W.A.) |
| 10 | Queens Birthday (except W.A.) |
| July 5 | Alice Springs Show Day—N.T. (Alice Springs area only) |
| 12 | Tennant Creek Show Day—N.T. (Tennant Creek area only) |
| 19 | Katherine Show Day—N.T. (Katherine area only) |
| 26 | Darwin Royal Show Day—N.T. (Darwin area only) |
| Aug. 5 | Bank Holiday—N.S.W. |
| 5 | Picnic Day—N.T. |
| Sept. 26 | Melbourne Show Day—Vic. (Melbourne area only). |
| Oct. 7 | Labour Day—N.S.W. & A.C.T. |
| 7 | Queens Birthday—W.A. |
| 14 | Labour Day—S.A. |
| Nov. 4 | Recreation Day—Tasmania only) |
| 5 | Melbourne Cup Day—Vic. (Melbourne Area only) |
| Dec. 25 | Christmas Day |
| 26 | Boxing Day (except S.A.) |
| 28 | Proclamation Day—S.A. |

## Embassies and Consular Services

If you are anxious to see how your taxes are being spent abroad or to read the latest newspaper from home, most countries have diplomatic representations in Australia. Diplomatic missions are located in Canberra. (See list in Appendix.)

There are also consular representatives in other major cities and the larger ones have nearly as many consular offices as Canberra. The address and telephone numbers are easily found in the Yellow Pages under "Consulates and Legations."

## Health Services

Doctors, dentists and hospitals all have modern equipment, highly trained skills, extensive facilities, and are very expensive. Health insurance cover is available but there is usually a three-month waiting period after you sign up, before any claims can be made. A wise investment is a health and accident insurance policy.

Chemists or pharmacies have fully qualified professional who dispense medication according to doctor prescriptions. These stores also carry familiar brands of general medications, cosmetics, toiletries and other personal needs.

## The Media

Each major city has at least a "good" daily as well as a tabloid and evening papers. The Sydney Morning Herald and the Melbourne Age are two of the most important dailies. The only nationwide daily paper is The Australian. Numerous weekly newspapers and magazines are sold alongside South Pacific editions of international publications, such as Newsweek and Time. Airmail copies of overseas newspapers and journals are readily available at specialised newsagents and bookstores.

Around the country the number of television stations varies from place to place. In remote areas the ABC (Australian Broadcasting Commission) may be all you can receive. This is the national, advertising-free, television and radio network—the equivalent of the BBC. Sydney and Melbourne also offer three commercial stations and a government sponsored station.

Radio also has the ABC plus a whole host of AM and FM commercial stations, offering everything from rock to classical, and talkback to "beautiful music."

## Photography

Australia is a photographers delight and the cost of film is not expensive, compared to the rest of the Western world. If bringing your own film, be careful not to have it ruined by the airport X-rays. Whether black-and-white or colour, developing is no problem, and many places now offer instant developing of print film.

# Tourist Information

If you are gathering information as a potential visitor to Australia, contact the Australian Tourist Commission office where brochures with lots of lowdown are readily available:
Australian Tourist Commission,
324 St. Kilda Rd.,
Melbourne, Victoria 3004,
Australia
tel. (03)690-3900;
tlx. AA 31911 AUSTOUR
Make sure you obtain the literature before you make your trip.

Tourist information within Australia is handled by the various state and local offices. Every region has its own tourist offices:

**Australian Capital Territory**;
ACT Government Tourist Bureau,
London Circuit & West Row,
Canberra City 2601.

**New South Wales**;
NSW Government Travel Centre,
16 Spring St.,
Sydney 2000.

**Queensland**;
Queensland Government Tourist Bureau,
Adelaide & Edward streets.
Brisbane 4000.

**Victoria**;
Victorian Government Travel Centre,
272 Collins St.,
Melbourne 3000.

**South Australia**;
South Australian Government Tourist Bureau,
18 King William St.,
Adelaide 5000.

**Western Australia**;
Western Australia Government Travel Centre,
772 Hay St.,
Perth 6000.

**Northern Territory**;
Northern Territory Government Tourist Bureau,
9 Parsons St.,
Alice Springs 5750.

**Tasmania**;
Tasmanian Government Tourist Bureau,
80 Elizabeth St., Hobart 7000.

These offices are generally open 9 a.m. to 5 p.m. weekdays plus Saturday mornings. They will supply you with brochures, maps, price lists and other information and very often book accommodations, tours and transport for you. Most towns have a tourist information office of some type and these can be very helpful with suggestions on local attractions and places of interest.

## National Parks

If you intend to visit some of the national parks in Australia, obtain information on them from the state-operated National Parks Organisation. Its offices are found in:
(National Parks and Wildlife Service),
189–193 Kent St., Sydney 2000;
138 Albert St., Brisbane 4000;
16 Magnet Court, Sandy Bay (Hobart) 7005;
129 Greenhill Rd., Unley (Adelaide) 5061;
(National Parks Service),
240 Victoria Parade, East Melbourne 3002;
(National Parks Authority),
Hackett Drive, Crawley (Perth) 6009;
(Conservation Commission of the Northern Territory),
Gap Road, Alice Springs 5750.

## Historic Buildings

To visit some of Australia's many historic buildings, it is well worth to consider obtaining a membership from the National Trust, which is dedicated to preserving historic buildings in all parts of Australia. The Trust owns a number of buildings throughout the country which are open to the public and as a trust member, you are entitled to free entry to any of their property. Annual membership costs A$18 for single and A$27 for families. Especially if you are doing much travelling around Australia, you'll soon find this pays off. National Trust has offices at:
42 Franklin St., Manuka, ACT 2630;
Observatory Hill, Sydney, NSW 2000;
Old Government House, George St.,
    Brisbane, Queensland 4000;
Tasma Terrace, Parliament Place,
    Melbourne, Vic. 3000;
Ayers House, 288 North Terrace,
    Adelaide, SA 5000;
Old Perth Boys School, 139 St. George Terrace,
    Perth, WA 6000;
74 Esplanade, Darwin, NT 5790;
81 St. Johns St., Launceston, TAS 7250.

# Transportation

## Domestic Air Travel

It is more than likely that during your holiday you will have to use one of Australia's two national domestic airlines. TAA (Trans Australia Airlines) is government-owned while Ansett, its competitor, is private.

Both operate regular scheduled flights between all capital cities and tourist/regional centres throughout Australia. Flying is very expensive but safe. Both Ansett and TAA have their own terminals and commuter buses run regularly between these and the airports. A few examples of fares and flying times (one way, economy class) include:

Sydney—Melbourne $133.30 (1½ hours)
Sydney—Perth $346.40 (4½)
Melbourne—Adelaide $125.90 (1)
Melbourne—Canberra $105.30 (1)
Brisbane—Sydney $137.90 (1¼)
Brisbane—Melbourne $202.90 (3)
Adelaide—Alice Springs $197.20 (2)
Perth—Adelaide $266.50 (3 hr 5 min)
Canberra—Sydney $75.70 (35 min)

Booking is advisable on all domestic airline services unless you want to take advantage of the standby fares that are available on most routes. You have no guarantee of a seat when travelling standby, but it can save you around 25 percent of the regular economy fare. You buy your ticket at the airport and fly when there is a seat available. If you don't get on the first flight you may wait for the next one. A discount up to 35 per cent is available when purchasing return economy fares in advance. You have to book and pay for these Apex tickets 30 days in advance and you cannot alter your booking in either direction, losing 50 percent if you do.

Students under the age of 26 get a 25 percent discount on the regular economy fare if an international student identity card is shown when purchasing the ticket.

Both Ansett and TAA offer a 30 percent discount on internal fares to international visitors as long as the distance to be travelled is more than 1,000 km. Bookings may be made before or after arriving in Australia. If booking after arrival in Australia an identification and international airline ticket must be produced.

Round Australia fares are offered by both domestic airlines and are excellent value if you want to see a lot of Australia in a short time. A number of round-trip routes are available and may be started at any city or town en route. Stopovers can be arranged to suit your itinerary, provided the round trip is completed in 90 days.

Other bargain fares, excursion fares and package holidays are available. Consult TAA or Ansett directly as the offers seem to vary from week to week.

A number of secondary airlines operate scheduled flights from the main country areas and towns in the various states, to link with the major trunk services. The major secondary airlines are Air New South Wales and East-West Airlines (New South Wales); Ansett Airlines of South Australia; Airlines of Western Australia; Air Queensland; and Airlines of Northern Australia (Northern Territory).

In addition to the major and secondary airlines mentioned there is a third group of smaller regional and local airlines. These mainly fly intra-state routes and give access to more remote destinations, islands and tourist areas.

## Buses

Competition between the two major bus companies and numerous independent competitors has meant lots of bargains are to be had when travelling by bus in Australia. The two major nationwide bus operators are Ansett Pioneer and Greyhound Australia. The standard of coaches is high with most incorporating lay-back seats, washrooms and air-conditioning. Some companies are now even screening video movies during overnight journeys in a bid to attract passengers.

If you plan extensive bus travel in Australia there are several discount plans available. Greyhounds Eaglepass offers unlimited travel on Greyhound routes for either 30 days at $465 or 60 days at $690. Ansett Pioneer's Aussiepass allows 15 days unlimited travel for $240.00, 30 days for $430, and 60 days for $640. In some cases these passes allow free access to local bus services and sightseeing tours and also offer discounts on accommodations and rent-a-cars. Although both companies go to all major centres Greyhound has a more extensive network and more frequent services. Bus terminals are well equipped with toilets, showers, shopping facilities and are generally very clean.

There are many other bus companies in Australia although none have as comprehensive a route network as Ansett or Greyhound. A variety of package tours which include transportation and accommodation departs regularly from capital cities. These tours can range from three to 50 days and are run by a number of different bus companies. Another bus tour features camping out; rather than hotels you stay in a tent, and this proves considerably cheaper than overnight stops in motels.

## Railways

A vast network of railways operates from one end of the nation to the other. You can get around Australia, around the coasts and into the Outback on modern air-conditioned trains. The principal lines follow the east and south coasts linking the principal cities of Cairns, Brisbane, Sydney, Melbourne and Adelaide. Lines from Adelaide connect with the line between Sydney and Perth—the famous Indian Pacific run.

During its 3,955-km (2,457-mile) journey, the Indian Pacific crosses the Nullarbor Plain with the longest stretch of straight railway track in the world, where nothing exists except reddish-brown scrub, blue sky and telegraph poles. Passengers making this 65-hour journey from coast to coast are well catered for, with luxuries such as an observation lounge, bar and music room complete with piano.

If you plan to travel widely on Australia's trains an Austrailpass is recommended, which entitles you to unlimited first-class rail travel on interstate and metropolitan trains. The pass is for purchase overseas only and for foreign passport holders only. These passes are available for 14 days at $290 to three months at $750, and do not cover meals or sleeping berth charges. More information is available from Railways of Australia, 325 Collins St., Melbourne, Victoria 3000.

## Waterways

The once-busy coastal shipping service where you could take a comfortable and leisurely sea journey from one Australian port to the next has long gone. The only regular maritime service is the ferry operating between Melbourne and Tasmania. The trip is often very rough and if you are taking a car, it's not very cheap compared to the air fare. The trip takes about 14 hours; for more information contact Australia National Line, 65 Riverside Ave., South Melbourne, Victoria 3000.

## Rental Cars and Motorcycles

Australia has three nationwide car rental companies and numerous local ones, and competition between them is fierce. The big three are Avis, Hertz and Budget and their rates are just about identical. The small outfits are cheaper and offer special deals but they don't give you the service and extras of the major companies. The big companies have offices in almost every town and at the airports and rail terminals. Approach them if you want to pick up a car or leave a car at an airport, or if you want to do a one-way rental trip—pick up in Sydney or leave in Melbourne. Whatever your method of travel on the long stretches it is very useful to have car for local travel. The major companies offer unlimited kilometre rates in the city but when travelling outback it's usually a flat charge, plus so many cents per kilometre. When you collect the car, rental firms ask for a deposit of $100 payable by cash or credit card, this deposit is refunded on return of the vehicle.

Car rental rates in Australia as elsewhere rise and fall daily but examples of rental rates are:-
For a small car, you pay about A$20 (per day) plus 14 cents (per km);
for compact, A$23 plus 15 cents;
for medium, A$26 plus 20 cents; and
for large, A$38 plus 25 cents.
(Rates vary with operators, higher in country areas.)

Compulsory third-party insurance is included in car rentals and comprehensive insurance plans are available for an additional fee. You usually must be over 21 to hire a car although some companies have 25 as the minimum age requirement. Always look for special deals such as weekend rate where you are offered an extra 24-hour rental at no added cost. Budget even offer a standby rate.

Lots of other vehicles are available for rent in the warmer climates of Alice Springs, Cairns or the Gold Coast. You might like to rent a Moke. This open air jeep-like vehicle can be a lot of fun

on short trips and very economical on petrol. Camper-vans are available for hire in most large cities and they are particularly popular in Tasmania. Motorcycles are also available in a number of locations and many Australian cities now offer bicycle hire if you are feeling energetic.

## Motoring Advisories

If you are thinking of exploring Australia by car keep in mind that beyond cities, distances are long and towns get few and far between. Major highways linking capital cities are sealed and of a good standard. However you don't have to get very far off the beaten track to find yourself on dirt roads. Driving in Australia won't cause you many problems as long as you drive on the left-hand side of the road and keep your seat belt fastened at all times, whether driving or occupying the front seat.

The speed limit in a built-up area is 60 km/h (37 mph) and in the country 100 and 110 km/h (62–68 mph) depending on the state. Australian drivers are certainly not the best in the world, although the once-appalling accident rate is now being lowered by the introduction of random breath testing in most states. If you exceed .05 percent blood-alcohol level, a hefty fine and loss of licence is automatic.

Petrol comes in regular and super grades and is sold by the litre. All the well-known international brands are available and prices vary between 45 to 50 cents a litre. Overseas drivers licences are valid throughout Australia although an international driving permit is preferred. For extended touring you may want to buy a new or used car and this involves much the same hassles as anywhere in the Western world. New cars have a 12-month, 20,000-km warranty, and if buying a used vehicle reliability is all important.

Each state has an Automobile Association and will readily supply you with excellent maps and literature. These associations are represented nationally by the Australian Automobile Association. All day-to-day operations are handled by the state organisations, who for a small membership fee will provide a free emergency breakdown service. If you intend travelling long distances by car, membership in a state Automobile Association is highly recommended. The addresses are:-

**Sydney**;
National Roads and Motorists Association (NRMA),
151 Clarence St., Sydney, NSW 2000.
Tel: (02) 236 9211, Tlx: AA 22348 NRMAS.
**Melbourne**;
Royal Automobile Club of Victoria (RACV),
123 Queen St, Melbourne, Vic. 3000.
Tel: (03) 607 2211, Tlx: AA 30223 RACV.
**Canberra**;
National Roads and Motorists Association (NRMA),
92 Northbourne Ave, Canberra City, ACT 2601.
Tel: (062) 43 3777, Tlx: AA 62278 NRMACA.
**Perth**;
Royal Automobile Club of Western Australia Inc.

(RACWA),
228 Adelaide Terrace, Perth, WA 6000.
Tel: (09) 325 0551, Tlx: AA 93106 RACWA.
**Brisbane**;
Royal Automobile Club of Queensland,
Pacific Highway and Levington Street, Eight-mile
Plains, Qld. 4123.
Tel: (07) 341 2555, Tlx: AA 41740 RACQNS.
**Adelaide**;
Royal Automobile Association of South Australia
Inc. (RAA)
41 Hindmarsh Square, Adelaide, SA 5000.
Tel: (08) 223 4555, Tlx: AA 82334 RAA.
**Darwin**;
Automobile Association of the Northern Territory (AANT)
79 Smith St., Darwin, NT 5790.
Tel: (089) 813837, Tlx: AA 85748 AANT.
**Hobart**;
Royal Automobile Club of Tasmania (RACT),
Corner of Patrick & Murray streets, Hobart, Tas. 7000.
Tel: (002) 34 6611, Tlx: AA 58071 RACT.

## Hitchhiking

Hitchhiking in Australia is discouraged by the police in some states, but it can be very easy. Successful hitching in Australia depends on your common sense. Don't carry much luggage, look clean, and display a sign announcing your destination. The best place to get rides is on the outskirts of a town at a junction where vehicles travel slowly and can stop easily.

# Communications

## Post

The postal service is the worst of Australia's public services. Post offices are open 9 a.m. to 5 p.m. Monday to Friday, and the service is only reasonably efficient while rates are not too cheap. Post offices will hold mail for visitors, as will the American Express offices for their members.

A standard letter within Australia costs 30 cents. Outside the continent, the rates are as follows (all amounts are in Australian cents):

|  | Airmail | Postcard |
| --- | --- | --- |
|  | (up to 20 gram) |  |
| United Kingdom & Europe | 85 | 50 |
| United States & Canada | 75 | 45 |
| Hong Kong & India | 60 | 40 |
| Singapore & Malaysia | 55 | 35 |
| New Zealand | 30 | 30 |

## Telephones

Public telephones are located throughout cities and towns and are found in most hotel rooms. Local calls from a public phone booth cost 20 cents for an unlimited amount of time. Or they can also be made from STD (Subscriber Trunk Dialling) phones and the red phones which are found in public places like shops, bars and hotels. STD, used for calling long distance to most Australian locations, is available for all private and some public telephones (the grey-green ones). STD calls cost up to one-third the normal charge after 9 p.m. and before 8 a.m.

## International Calls

When calling overseas, direct-dial calls may be made from any ISD-connected (International Subscriber Dialling) telephones. ISD public phones are not very common as yet but you will find them at city GPOs and airports. International calls may also be booked through the international operator.

## Telegrams and Cables

These can be sent by telephone through the operator or by lodging them at the post office. Cables can be sent at urgent rate, ordinary, or letter rate and the cost obviously depends on the rate used and the destination.

The front pages of the telephone directory give further information on all telegraphic services, in addition to telephone interpreter service, community service, and recorded information service. In an emergency for the police an ambulance or in the case of a fire, dial 000.

# Tours and Attractions

What follows is a mini guide as to where to stay, what to eat, and what to see when visiting a specified region or state in Australia.

## Canberra, Australia Capital Territory

There is something special about a national capital and Canberra is no exception. The city is unlike other large Australian metropolises both for its orderly neatness and because it is inland. Canberra is the meeting place of many cultures.

In 1912 an American architect, Walter Burley Griffin, won first prize in a worldwide competition for the design of Australia's new capital. The Depression and two world wars resulted in very slow development of the site and it wasn't until the Fifties, Sixties and Seventies that progress really got underway and the essential concept of Griffin's plan was realised.

The population today is over 230,000; about half of these are under 26 years of age. Canberra is principally a place of government and public services and there are few local industries. Canberra tourist offices are located in :

**Sydney**: 9 Elizabeth St., Sydney, NSW 2000, tel. 223 3180.

**Melbourne**: Harold Arcade, 247 Collins St., Melbourne 3000, tel. 637 737.

**Canberra**: Jolliment Centre, Northbourne Avenue, Canberra City, ACT 2601, tel. 497 555.

The Canberra Tourist Bureau is open from 9 a.m. to 5:15 p.m. Monday to Friday, and 9 a.m. to 11:30 a.m. Saturday. It will supply you with an excellent selection of brochures and leaflets, and will inform about latest tours available.

### Transportation:

The only way to get around Canberra is by road. Bus services are frequent and buses are modern. The bus information kiosk is on the corner of Alinga Street and East Road; it will supply you with maps and timetables and advise on special offer tickets. A free bus service is available in the inner city area around London Circuit. This only runs between 11 a.m. and 3 p.m. weekdays. Cycling is an excellent way to see Canberra and bicycles can be hired by the hour, by the day, or by the week. If you intend hiring a bike make sure you get a copy of the Canberra Cycleways map from the tourist office.

### Accommodations:

Canberra is amply supplied with all forms of accommodations although not particularly cheap ones. If your budget doesn't stretch to the officially recognised hotels listed in an Appendix, a number of options are available.

The **Canberra Youth Hostel** is at Dryandron Street, O'Connor, telephone 489 759, about seven km from the city centre. Nightly charges are $6 and to get there, take the 380 bus from Canberra City Post Office to the Scrivener and Miller Street stop. You can hire bicycles from the Hostel.

The **YMCA** at 2 Mont St, Canberra, telephone 473 033, takes both men and women. Essentially for solo travellers, an overnight stop including breakfast will cost you $13.50.

For those with a moderate budget, guest houses and private hotels on Northbourne Avenue offer bed-and-breakfast at a reasonable cost. The **Chelsea Lodge**, **The Blue and White Lodge** and the **Platon Lodge** are three of these. All are clean, quite comfortable and offer bed and good breakfast for around $12 single and $16 double.

Two camping sites close to Canberra are the **Canberra Lakes Carotel**, telephone 411 377 and the **South Side Motor Park**, telephone 806 176. Charges ranges from $6 for two people with a tent.

### Dining Out:

The embassy people keep Canberra cosmopolitan—and it shows in the menus. Local specialties are trout, lamb and beef. For lunch try the **Civic Hotel**. The **Ainsley Hotel** and the **Cock & Bull** offer pub-style food with good helpings at reasonable prices. For dinner, Canberra has a variety of ethnic restaurants. The **Malaysia Restaurant**, the **Vietnam Restaurant** and **Sinbads** are all recommended as good value. If you are out and hungry late at night watch for the "**Tucker-buses**." These are double decker buses that park anywhere serving hot dogs, hamburgers and the like till very late.

### What to see:

A look at the **Regatta Point Development** display is one way to put Canberra's development into perspective. It is open daily from 9 a.m. to 5 p.m. and houses a collection of models, photos and diagrams that explains how this planned city works.

For another way to obtain a full picture of the city, head for the top of Black Mountain or Mount Ainslie. From the **Black Mountain** summit, you can survey the Australian National University, the Civic Centre and Lake Burley Griffin with the Captain Cook Memorial water-jet in the distance. Black Mountain is topped by the 195-metre (640-foot) telecom tower with viewing galleries and revolving restaurant. The summit is open to the public from 9 a.m. to 10 p.m. and admission is $1.

Northeast of Civic Centre is **Mount Ainslie**. From here you can see Central Canberra, including Parliament House, the National Library, Australian War Memorial, Anzac Parade and Lake Burley Griffin.

From either summit, it is easy to see how the twin hubs of Capitol Hill and City Hill dominate the workings of Canberra and how Lake Burley Griffin neatly divides Canberra into two. The shoreline of the lake extends for some 35 km (22 miles), and although not recommended for swimming you can go bboating on the lake.

There are a number of places of interest around the lake. The **Carillon**, standing on Aspen Island connected to the shore by a footbridge, is one such. Marking Canberra's 50th Anniversary, it was presented by the British government to the Australian people. It is one of the largest free-standing bell towers in the world and its 53 bells are either played by hand or automatically; recitals and public inspections take place regularly.

Near the Commonwealth Avenue bridge, the **Captain Cook Memorial jet** hurls a column of water 140 metres (460 feet) into the air. It is one of the world's highest and at any one time there can be up to six tonnes of water "hanging." On the shore opposite the jet is a large metal globe on which are traced Cook's three great voyages of discovery.

The heart of Burley Griffin's plan was the parliamentary triangle. At the apex on Capitol Hill, Australia's new and permanent Parliament House is being built, while below it stands the long white structure of the present parliament. Nearer the lake are the other major elements of the plan—on the right, the classic lines of the National Library; and on the left, the High Court, with its new neighbour, the Australian National Gallery. These national monuments are briefly described below:

**Old Parliament House**—Australia's temporary Parliament House was officially opened by the Duke of York in 1927 enabling the Federal Parliament to move in from Melbourne. Sited on King Georges Terrace, the building includes a display on Australia's government structure. When parliament is not in session there are free tours every half hour 9 a.m.–12:30 p.m. and from 1 p.m.–4:30 p.m.

**New Parliament House**—The new Parliament House is currently being built on Capitol Hill. Described as "a building for the 21st Century and beyond," the building will only occupy 15 percent of the 32-hectare (80-acre) site. The remainder will be landscaped with formal and informal gardens. The building is due for completion in late 1988, in time for Australia's bicentennial celebrations.

**National Library**—Opened in 1968, the National Library is regarded by many as Canberra's most elegant building. Not itself a public lending library, it provides services for other libraries and students. Brilliant features of the foyer are three Aubusson tapestries and 16 coloured-glass windows by Australian artist Lenard French. The Library is open 9 a.m.–10 p.m. Monday to Friday and 9 a.m.–4:15 p.m. weekends and public holidays.

**High Court**—The High Court building is an impressive structure of ultra-modern design. Opened by the Queen in May 1980, the core of the design is a public hall 24 metres (79 feet) high, encircled by open ramps which rise to the courts. Open from 10 a.m.–4 p.m. daily it is linked to the neighbouring National Gallery by a pedestrian bridge.

**Australian National Gallery**—The ANG houses a $60 million art collection on three levels. Opened to the public in October 1982, the gallery has a superb collection of Australian Art and collections from the rest of the world.

**Australian War Memorial**—Canberra's biggest

tourist attraction, the War Memorial draws over 1 million visitors annually. Admission is free and the memorial is open from 9 a.m.–4:45 p.m. every day except Christmas Day.

**The Royal Australian Mint**—Just about the only big factory in Canberra, the RAM is one of the largest and most modern coin factories in the world. Built at a cost of $9 million, the mint produces metal currency for a number of other countries besides Australia. The mint is open 9 a.m.–4 p.m. Monday to Friday when coins are produced.

**Botanic Gardens**—Situated on the lower slope of Black Mountain the Botanic Gardens are devoted entirely to native Australian flora. Planting began in 1950 and the gardens were officially opened in 1970. The highlight of the garden is the rainforest zone, achieved in Canberra's dry climate by a special spray system. The gardens are open 9 a.m.–5 p.m. and entry is from Clunies and Ross streets.

**Embassies**—Over 60 countries maintain diplomatic representatives in Canberra and their mission buildings form a tourist attraction of their own. The British High Commission was the first diplomatic office in Canberra in 1936 followed in 1940 by the U.S. Embassy. The embassies are mostly south and west of Capital Hill scattered through the surburbs of Red Hill, Forrest and Yarralumla. Many of the buildings have been designed in the architectural style of the country the mission represents. Two of note are the U.S. Embassy in a red-brick Williamsburg Mission style and the Thai Embassy with its upsweep roof corners and gold-coloured roof tiles. See appendix for addresses of embassies in Canberra.

## Shopping:

Around City Hall is the civic and business heart of Canberra. A series of shopping complexes lie close to Civic Square and these house department stores, boutiques, cafes and gift shops. Canberra's city shops are open Monday to Thursday 9 a.m.–5 p.m. Friday from 9 a.m.–9 p.m. and Saturday 8:30 a.m.–noon.

## Night Life:

The Canberra Theatre complex in Civic Square contains the theatre, the playhouse and the centre gallery which puts on anything from Shakespeare to rock music. Most of the regular cinemas are around the Civic Square area too. Foreign-language films are mostly held at various cultural centres—the National Library, the Maison de France, and the Goethe Centre. The Monaro folk group holds a monthly woolshed dance on the last Saturday of each month at the Woolshed in Yarralumla. Resident jazz groups and rock bands can be seen just about every night of the week at pubs, clubs and discos. Consult the daily press or *This Week in Canberra* for what's on.

## Sydney, New South Wales

The heart of NSW is Sydney, the state's capital and the largest city in Australia, with a population of over 3 million people. First settlement in Australia was made in 1788 at Sydney Cove, now known as Circular Quay. Sydney today is a lively bustling centre for industry, business and manufacturing as well as a major port. It spreads over 1,736 sq km (670 sq miles), considerably larger in area than Rome or Los Angeles County, for example.

Geographically Sydney is divided by the harbour into north and south. The famous Sydney Harbour Bridge spans the bay to link these two areas. Most of the places of interest in the city area, including the city centre, are to the south of the harbour. Within minutes you can walk from Circular Quay to the Opera House, the Harbour Bridge and the Centrepoint Tower, Sydney's best viewing spot. If you want to go to the North Shore, catch a ferry from Circular Quay or go by train.

The NSW Government Travel Centre is at 16 Spring St., tel. 231-4444, open Monday to Friday, 9 a.m. to 5 p.m. It has the usual range of brochures, leaflets and accommodation details. Other NSW Government Travel centres are located in Brisbane, at the corner of Queen and Edward streets, tel. 311-838; and in Melbourne at 345 Little Collins St., tel. 601-378.

## Transportation:

**Trains and Buses**. Sydney is serviced by electric trains and these are by far the quickest way to get around. The service is frequent and noisy on the underground sections and no smoking is allowed on board.

Extensive bus services are mostly run by the Urban Transit Authority, with main bus stops at Circular Quay, Wynyard Square and at the Central Railway Station. A free city bus service (No. 777) operates from York Street on a loop around the Domain and back. The *Sydney Explorer* is a tourist bus service which operates a continuous loop around the city's tourist sights. From 9:30 a.m. to 5 p.m. daily, it leaves at roughly 15-minute intervals from Circular Quay. It costs $8 for the day and you can hop on and off whenever you like.

The Public Transport Commission offers several special deals; Day Rover tickets entitle holders to unlimited travel on any suburban bus, train or ferry (except hydrofoil) for $3.30, while Weekly Rovers are available for $16.50. Obtain more information on these and other deals from the Urban Transit Authority Travel & Tours Centre, 11–13 York St., Sydney, tel. 297 614.

**Ferries and Cruises**. However, the ferries are by far the nicest way of getting around Sydney. They all depart from Circular Quay; the Urban Transit Authority issues timetables free of charge. The longest regular ferry run is the trip from No. 3 jetty to Manly, covering 11 km in 35 minutes. The shortest ride goes to Kirribilli and offers a panorama of the city skyline, the Opera House and the Harbour Bridge within a 10-minute trip.

Apart from the harbour, services are also available at the Royal National Park to the south and on Pittwater to the north. There is a variety of more comprehensive harbour cruises, as well as lunchtime and supper cruises.

Generally cruises run by the Urban Transit Authority are far cheaper than those run by private agencies. At 10 a.m. and 2 p.m. daily you can take a *Captain Cook* 2½-hour coffee cruise from No. 6 jetty at Circular Quay. Although a little more expensive, this cruise offers an interesting commentary, unlimited coffee and biscuits and comfortable seating.

**Taxis**: These are more numerous in Sydney than anywhere else in Australia and the locals use them casually, stopping them for hire anywhere. Flag fall costs 90 cents and 55 cents per km thereafter. A phone booking costs an additional 50 cents, and two of the larger companies are ABC and Taxi Combined Services.

### Accommodations:

When deciding on a place to stay, always take into consideration the size of Sydney. The hotel you choose may be of the right price, but you don't want to spend all your time travelling to points of interest. If you are without accommodations the NSW Government Travel Centre or the Public Transport Commission will always find you a place to stay. See the Appendix for a listing of major hotels.

Sydney has two **hostels** operated by the Youth Hostel Association. One is located at 28 Ross St., Forest Lodge, tel. 692-0747; while the other, the larger of the two with 120 beds, is at 407 Marrickville Road, Dulwich Hill, tel. 569-0272. Both hostels charge $6 per night.

A brand new **YWCA** has just opened in the heart of Sydney—at 5 Wentworth Ave., Darlinghurst, tel. 264-2451. They have 100 beds. Single shared starts at $19, private $29. Twin shared is $30 and private $39.

Two privately run hostels in the Kings Cross area are recommended. The **Young Cross Country Travellers Centre**, 25 Hughes St., Kings Cross, tel. 358-1143 is well-run and good value, but occasionally gets a little overcrowded. The reception area has a notice board that offers items for sale, and useful tourist tips. The **Kings Cross Backpackers Hostel**, 162 Victoria St., tel. 356-3232, has 78 beds.

Budget hotels are mainly located in the city, Kings Cross or Bondi. In the city the **Peoples Palace** at 40 Pitt St., tel. 211-5777 is run by Salvation Army but strictly as a business venture. Rooms are from $14 a single or $24 a double. Directly opposite the Peoples Palace is the **CB Private Hotel**, tel. 211-5115. There are 200 rooms and daily rates are from $10 single and $15 double. In Kings Cross the **Gala Private Hotel** at 23 Hughes St., tel. 356-3406 and **Springfield Lodge** at 9 Springfield Ave., tel. 358-3222 are worth mentioning. Rates are $15 and $18 respectively for a single room and $25 and $24 for a double. Just a short trip from the city on the eastern suburbs railway will get you to Bondi. Here the **Phelellen Lodge** or the **Bondi Beach Guest House** are the places to stay. The Phelellen Lodge at 11A Consett Ave., tel. 301-521, whose room rates are from $11.50 offers a light breakfast for an extra $2. The Bondi Beach Guest House, tel. 371-0202 operates at 2 addresses: 124 Curlewis St. and 11 Consett Ave. Room-only rates are from $10 single and $16 double.

## Dining Out:

Thanks to the influx of new Australians, Sydney now boasts an astonishing variety of eating places. Sydney's restaurants are not found in any specific suburb; good restaurants are all over Sydney. Some of the ones you should try are listed below:

**French;**

L'Aubbergade,
353 Cleveland St.,
Redfern,
Tel. 699-5929

Bagatelle,
117 Riley St.,
Darlinghurst,
Tel. 357-5675.

**Chinese;**

Tai Yuen,
110 Hay St.,
Haymarket,
Tel. 211-3782.

**Italian;**

The Italo-Australian Club,
727 George St.,
City,
Tel. 211-5150

La Rustica,
435 Parramatta Rd.,
Leichhardt,
Tel. 569-2824.

**Greek;**

New Hellas,
287 Elizabeth St.,
Sydney,
Tel. 264-1668.

Diethnes,
336 Pitt St.,
Sydney,
Tel. 267-8956.

**Indian;**

Mayur,
MLC Centre,
Sydney,
Tel. 235-2361.

Shah Jehan,
79 Oxford St.,
Bondi Junction,
Tel. 389-7670.

**Lebanese;**

Emad's,
298 Cleveland St.,
Surry Hills,
Tel. 698-2631.

Abdul's,
Corner of Cleveland &
Elizabeth streets,
Surry Hills,
Tel. 698-1275.

**Seafood;**

Sails,
Sunderland Avenue,
Rosebery,
Tel. 371-6799.

Doyles on the Beach,
11 Marine Parade,
Watsons Bay,
Tel. 277-2007.

**Vegetarian;**

Zorba the Buddha,
2 Flinders St.,
Darlinghurst,
Tel. 357-6363.

The Whole Meal,
121 Pitt St.,
Sydney,
Tel. 233-2228.

Lots of pubs offer counter lunches on a barbeque type grill with as much salad as you can eat. The **Dolphin Hotel** in 12 Crown St., Surry Hills, and **The Oaks Hotel** at 118 Military Road, Neutral Bay, offer good food that can be eaten indoors or outside in the beer garden.

## What to See:

Sydneysiders have been referring to the area under the Sydney Harbour Bridges as **The Rocks** for more than 150 years. Sydney's first settlement was made here and it is truly the heart of Sydney. The best way to explore The Rocks is by foot,

starting at the Visitors Centre in 104 George St. North. You can obtain information and leaflets at the centre, and also see a short film about the area. The film and leaflets explain how old warehouses are being restored and turned into trendy and interesting places like the **Argyle Art Centre** and **The Old Spaghetti Factory**. Places to visit at the Rocks are the **Argyle Cut, Cadman's Cottage**, the **Argyle Tavern**, the **Geological and Mining Museum** and the **Hero of Waterloo Hotel**. Guided walking tours leave the Argyle Art Centre daily at 10:45 and 11:45 in the morning, and 12:45 and 2 in the afternoon.

Down at the end of the Rocks is **Sydney Harbour Bridge**. Called "The Coathanger" by Australians, it was completed in 1932 at a cost of $20 million. From the bridge it's just a short walk around Circular Quay to **Sydney Opera House**. This improbable collection of curving walls soar 67 metres (220 feet) and has become the international symbol of Australia. To get a feeling for the building take a stroll outside it to study its form and space. Then take one of the guided tours which operate every half hour from 9 a.m.-4 p.m. daily (except Christmas Day and Good Friday), costing $2. On Sundays there is free outdoor entertainment. You will see everything from street theatres to jazz bands.

The Opera House looks fine from any angle but the view from a ferry, coming into Circular Quay is probably the best. For the best view of Sydney take a trip up **Sydney Tower** on top of the Centrepoint complex. The tower is 305 metres (1,000 feet) high and opens from 9:30 a.m. to 9:30 p.m. Monday to Saturday, and 10:30 a.m. to 6:30 p.m. Sunday and public holidays. From the Tower you will see that Sydney has plenty of parks.

The eastern section of Sydney centre is dominated by three beautiful parks—Hyde Park, The Domain and the Royal Botanic Gardens. **Hyde Park** is the most central of the large city parks, and attractions here are the **Archibald Fountain** and the **Anzac Memorial**. The **Domain** is an open stretch of grassland where on Sundays after 2 p.m. some of Sydney's orators climb on their soapboxes to entertain anyone who will listen. The **Royal Botanic Gardens** was originally established in 1816. Stretching back from the harbourfront, more than 400 varieties of plants grow throughout the park's 27 hectares (67 acres). The park is open from 8 a.m. to sunset. Sydney's biggest park of ponds, grasslands, and bush is **Centennial Park** in the eastern suburbs. The park also has cycling and horse tracks and both can be hired nearby.

Situated on the Domain is the **Art Gallery of New South Wales**. The Gallery has an excellent permanent display of paintings by Australians as well as Europeans. You can visit the gallery Monday through Saturday from 10 a.m. to 5 p.m. and on Sunday from noon to 5 p.m.

The **Australian Museum** located at the corner of College and William streets, across from Hyde Park, features Australian natural history and includes an extensive Aborigine section. This is Australia's largest museum and is open Tuesday through Saturday from 10 a.m. to 5 p.m. and on Sunday and Monday noon to 5 p.m. Admission is free.

The **Museum of Applied Arts and Sciences** on Harris Street, Ultimo, is a totally different type of museum. Here you can operate working models of engines and see exhibits of early gramophones, keyboard instruments, cameras, model ships and clothing. Admission is free and the museum is open 10 a.m. to 5 p.m. Monday through Saturday and from 1 p.m. to 5 p.m. on Sunday

Beyond the city's central district you'll find other destinations worth visiting:

**Kings Cross** is Sydney's sin centre. Apart from strip joints and sex shops it has some good restaurants and lots of hookers. When it's working the El-Alamein Fountain at the end of Darlinghurst Road is attractive.

**Paddington** is a bit further out from the city centre. This suburb is some 5 km (three miles) southeast of downtown and the best way to see it is on foot. Called "Paddo" by locals, this community offers visitors narrow streets lined with beautifully restored Victorian terrace houses, as well as restaurants, antique shops and galleries.

A short ferry ride from No. 5 jetty at Circular Quay will take you to **Taronga Park Zoo**. The Zoo is open daily from 9:30 a.m. to 5 p.m. and admission is $4. The zoo has one of the most attractive settings of any zoo in the world. In fact *taronga* in aboriginal means "view over the water."

One of the best-known northern beach areas is **Manly**. With four ocean beaches this resort offers a variety of swimming and surfing possibilities. Those with a desire to see sharks close up can watch them at **Marine Land**, where there is a daily feeding. Beyond Manly a string of oceanfront suburbs stretch 40 km (25 miles) north to **Palm Beach** and the spectacular **Barrenjoey Heads**.

Along the south coast of Sydney harbour you'll find about 32 km (20 miles) of good beaches. The closest is famous **Bondi Beach** and the best surfing beaches are **Maroubra** and **Cronulla**.

The beaches within Sydney Harbour are sheltered and calm and generally smaller. On hot summer weekends they tend to get crowded. Two of them, **Reef Beach** on the north and **Lady Jane Beach** on the south, are nude beaches. You will find "topless" ladies on most Sydney beaches these days.

Two superb national parks are within easy reach of the city. **Kuring-gai Chase National Park**, on the southern banks of the Hawkesbury River, is only 25 km (15 miles) north of Sydney. There are many bush-walks and the park also has some magnificent aboriginal rock carvings. West Head offers a beautiful view across Pittwater. Thirty km (19 miles) south of the city is the **Royal National Park**. This is second oldest national park in the world and offers some superb bushwalks and good surfing beaches.

If you drive west of Sydney you can see three historic old towns: **Parramatta** and the sister towns of **Windsor** and **Richmond**. Among Australia's earliest settlements, they contain buildings dating back to the late 18th and early 19th centuries. Most of the historic buildings are open to visitors.

At **Doonside** near Parramatta there is a large collection of native birds and other wildlife at the **Featherdale Wildlife Park**. It's here you go to cuddle a koala.

There are many day-trips that can be made from Sydney. Sixty-five km (40 miles) west of Sydney are the **Blue Mountains**, part of the Great Dividing Range that runs along Australia's eastern seaboard. The Blue Mountains were once an impenetrable barrier to expansion inland. Today these mountains provide a popular nearby vacation retreat for Sydney residents. **Katoomba** is the main resort centre and trains operate there regularly.

It takes only three hours by car to drive the 161 km (100 miles) north from Sydney to the **Hunter River Valley** noted for its wineries, in the area located near Cessnock and Pokolbin. Visitors are welcome at most of the wineries. Some Sydney tour buses include the Hunter Valley. If possible, on the way to the Hunter Valley stop at **Old Sydney Town**. Seventy km (43 miles) north of Sydney, Old Sydney Town is a major reconstruction of early Sydney with replicas of early ships, houses and other buildings. It's open 10 a.m. to 5 p.m. Wednesday to Sunday, and every day during school holidays.

## Cultural Activities:

The theatre is alive and thriving in Sydney. The **Sydney Opera House** is of course the focal point of the theatre and the general arts scene, but it certainly isn't the only one. The **Seymour Centre** stages a variety of shows, but there are also top-rate companies and theatres such as **The Actors Company**, **Cell Block**, **Ensemble**, **Genesian**, **New Theatre** and **Nimrod**. Theatre is easy to locate as are films. As well as the scores of cinemas in and around the city, you'll find interesting films at the **Sydney University Union Theatre** and the Opera House.

Whatever your taste in music it can be satisfied in Sydney. The **Sydney Symphony Orchestra**, regarded as a first-class international group, appears regularly with leading Australian and international conductors and soloists at the Opera House and other venues. Sydney has a whole load of pleasant wine bars, where for a low entry charge you can catch some music and get a meal if you want. To listen to some good jazz **The Basement** at Circular Quay, the **Marble Bar** of the Hilton Hotel, **Soup Plus** at 383 George St. and the **Old Push** at 109 George St., are all worth a visit. For rock-n-roll try **Salina's** in the Coogee Bay Hotel, the **Musicians Club** at 94 Chalmers St., and the **Tivoli** in George Street.

A lot of Sydney's evening entertainment takes place in the Leagues Clubs or other private clubs, where the profits from poker machines finance big-name acts at low, low prices. They may be "members only" for the locals, but as an interstate or international visitor you're welcome to drop in. They are a Sydney institution, so if you get a chance to visit one, the most glittering and lavish of the lot is the **St. George Leagues Club**, known locally as the Taj Mahal. Other night spots worth checking in the local press are **Kinsela's** at 383 Burke St., Darlinghurst, and **Don Burrow's Supper Club** in the Regent Hotel.

## Shopping:

Sydney is a mecca of shopping centres. Nearly every new high-rise building in the city area seems to have an underground shopping arcade offering a variety of merchandise. Things to shop for in Sydney are opals and sheepskin products. Sydney's main shopping district is bounded by Martin Place, George, Park and Elizabeth streets. Within this area you'll find large department stores like **David Jones, Grace Bros** and **Waltons** as well as sprawling of the largest areas in the four-level **Centre Point** shopping arcade that runs between Pitt and Castlereagh streets.

Sydney's real centre is **Martin Place**. This pedestrian plaza provides seating for weary shoppers and at lunchtime on weekdays, works and shoppers alike gather to hear free entertainment. **Paddy's Market** at Darling Harbour offers a variety of merchandise including fresh produce, clothing, flowers, pets, jewellery and leather goods. The market is open Friday and Saturday from 7:30 a.m. to 5:30 p.m.

## Sports:

In Sydney you can sample a variety of sports, from water sports to those where both feet are kept on the ground. Besides surfing and swimming Sydneysiders also enjoy other water-oriented activities. Heading the list is **boating**; there are also **snorkelling** and **scuba diving, water-skiing** and **fishing**. For more information on these contact the New South Wales Government Tourist Bureau.

The **yachting** season runs from September through May. Races and regattas are held nearly every weekend. Races that are particularly popular are those between the "18-footers." These are perhaps the most exciting sailboats in the world and the competition is hard fought. Races are held every Saturday; the spectators ferry leaves Circular Quay at 2 p.m. Sailers turn out in full force each year for the start of the big Sydney-to-Hobart Yacht Race, December 26th. You can watch harbour races from a ferry that follows the boats.

An organized Surf Carnival is held at one of Sydney's ocean beaches on most Saturdays between October and March. The carnival consists of swimming competitions, surfboat races and board-riding events. There are also special surfboard-riding competitions in summer months, but the venues are often not selected till the day of the contest to take maximum advantage of surf conditions and wave formations of the day.

For the **golfer**, public courses are available and for the **tennis** player, Sydney has both public courts and private tennis clubs.

You also have a wide variety of spectator sports to choose from. Sydneysiders love a good **horse race** and the city has six race tracks to prove it. Randwick is the closest and principal track but races are scheduled throughout the year at Canterbury, Rosehill and Warwick Farm. Trotting races are held Friday nights under the lights at Harold Park a short distance from the city; and **greyhound races** on Saturday nights at Harold

Park or Wentworth Park.

Though four codes of **football** are played in Sydney the most popular is the Rugby League. Games are played during the winter months at the Sydney Sports Ground at Moore Park and at other ovals in Sydney.

Sydney's summer sport is **cricket**. The season runs from October to March and international and interstate matches are spread throughout this period. You can watch cricket being played at the Sydney Cricket Ground at Moore Park. This is one sport which is played quite often on Wednesdays as well as weekends, and sometimes in the evenings under lights.

## Melbourne, Victoria

Melbourne, as Australia's second city, is Victoria's prime attraction. Although it is not as intrinsically appealing as Sydney, Melbourne lays claim to being the fashion, food, cultural and financial centre of Australia.

Melbourne has always been the poor relation of Sydney and despite their fierce rivalry, Melbourne has always come off second best. In population there is little difference between them; they are both large cities in the 2½ million to 3 million bracket yet, somehow, Sydney is far more the metropolis than Melbourne. But don't let Melbourne's conservative appearance fool you; the city does hum.

The climate is totally undependable; it is possible to experience all four seasons in one day.

The heart of the inner city, called the "Golden Mile," contains the government and commercial hub of Melbourne, its chief shopping street, and the main hotels and theatres. The perimeters are the Yarra River on the south, Spencer Street on the west, La Trobe Street on the north and Spring Street on the east. For a bird's-eye view of downtown Melbourne go to the observation deck of the National Mutual Building at the corner of William and Collins streets; it's open weekdays.

For tourist information, maps and brochures on Melbourne, the Victorian Government Travel Centre is at 230 Collins St., tel. 602-9444, and is open 9 a.m. to 5 p.m. on weekdays and 9 a.m. to noon Saturday. The Melbourne Tourism Authority is on the 20th level Nauru House, 80 Collins St., tel. 654-2288. This office is only open weekdays 9 a.m. to 5 p.m. Further information on Melbourne and the state of Victoria can be obtained from the National Parks Service of Victoria at 240 Victoria Parade, and the Youth Hostel Association at 122 Flinders st., Melbourne.

## Transportation:

Melbourne's public transport system is by far the best and most comprehensive in Australia. Trams form the basis of the system. In all there are about 750 of them and they operate as far as 20 km (12 miles) out of the city. Buses are the secondary form of public transport and the train services provide a third link for Melbourne's outer suburbs. For information on Melbourne's public transport contact either the Victorian Government Travel Centre or phone the Transport Information Centre on 602-9011 between 7:30 a.m. to 10 p.m. Sunday. A complicated system of tickets and travel cards operate, offering concessions on travel by train, tram or bus. The Transport Information Centre will advise you on what tickets are best for your plans.

Melbourne's transport tend to curl up and die around midnight after which taxis are the only form of transport available. Two of the major cab companies are *Silver Top Taxis* 345-3455 and *Taxis Combined* 620-331.

## Accommodations:

Melbourne has a fairly wide range of accommodations, but it is not centered in any particular area. Most of the major expensive hotels are within the Golden Mile (see the Appendix for listing), but the seaside suburb of St. Kilda is probably the best for general accommodations. The classified columns of *The Age* newspaper on Wednesdays and Saturdays is the place to look.

Two Melbourne youth hostels is in operation. **The Hostel**, at 500 Abbotsford St., tel. 328-2880, has 44 beds. Two minutes' walk away, at 76 Chapman St., tel 328-3595, is the other hostel (100 beds). Both are about three km from the city centre in north Melbourne and easily accessible by tram 54 or 57 from Elizabeth Street.

The **YWCA** is at 489 Elizabeth St., tel. 329-5188, and caters for both males and females in a large downtown motel complex. All rooms have shower and toilet facilities and the rates are $19 single and $26 double.

Most of the moderately priced hotels in Melbourne are concentrated on the Spencer Street end of the city, around the railway station and close to the Greyhound bus terminal. The **Spencer Hotel Motel** at 44 Spencer St., tel. 626-991 offers accommodations from $10 per night in the old hotel section, and from $20 in the newer motel style rooms. Don't be put off by its somewhat gloomy exterior.

The **Great Southern Hotel** just down the road at 16 Spencer St., tel. 623-989, offers accommodations from $10 per night. It is an old-fashioned reminder of the days of rail travel and the rooms are pretty old-fashioned too. Other very basic cheap city hotels are the **City Lodge** (235 King St., tel. 676-679) and **Purnall's** (445 Elizabeth St., tel. 329-7635).

A bit up market from these hotels is the **Victoria** at 215 Little Collins St., tel. 630-441. You have a choice of rooms without private facilities for $21 single and $26 double or a room with private facilities, colour TV and other mod cons at $36 single and $43 double.

Melbourne has a dozen or so campsites but none of them are close to the city. The **Footscray Caravan Park** at 163 Somerville Road, tel. 314-6646, is the most centrally situated. There is no camping but they will rent you an on-site caravan for about $14 for 2 people. The **Melbourne Caravan Park**, 262 Elizabeth St., Coburg East, tel. 354-3533, is 10 km north of the city. Camping is allowed from $5 and on-site vans are available from $7.

## Dining Out:

Melbourne, as stated earlier, is Australia's culinary capital. The *Melbourne Yellow Pages* telephone directory has 26 pages of restaurants to prove it. The Victorian licencing laws make it very difficult and expensive to give a liquor licence. The alternative is the BYO (bring your own) which allows patrons to bring their own liquor to drink with their meal. The result is a considerable saving in meal expenses, since it is very rare to be charged corkage.

There are restaurants all around the city and there are often real national quarters: Go to Lygon Street, **Carlton**, for Italian food; Siva Street, **Richmond**, for Greek food; Sydney Road, **Brunswick**, for Turkish food; Little Burke Street in the **city** for Chinese food. If you are looking for suggestions for restaurants to visit the *Age Good Food Guide* is available from bookshops and is excellent value at $7.95. Below is a list of some of the recommended restaurants:

**Chinese;**
Nam Loong,
223 Russell St., BYO.

Asian Food Plaza,
Corner of Little Bourke and Russell streets,
tel. 663-3536, BYO.

Orchid Garden Restaurant,
119 Little Bourke St.,
City, tel. 662-3591, licenced.

**French;**
Escoffier,
328 Kingsway,
South Melbourne, tel. 690-1522, licenced.

Rogalski's,
442 Clarendon St.,
South Melbourne, tel. 690-1977, licenced.

**Italian;**
Tamani's,
156 Toorak Rd.,
South Yarra, BYO.

Alfio's,
164 Toorak Rd.,
South Yarra, BYO.

**Greek;**
The Likon,
272 Swan St.,
Richmond, BYO.

The Greek Inn,
105 Clarendon St.,
South Melbourne, tel. 905-684, BYO.

**Japanese;**
The Shogun Japanese Restaurant,
Coberlib Place,
City, tel. 662-2471, licenced.

Yamato,

28 Corrs Lane,
City, tel. 663-1706, BYO.

**Lebanese;**
Lebanese House Restaurant
268 Russell St.,
City, tel. 662-2230, BYO.

King Solomon's Restaurant
665 Nicholson St.,
North Carlton, tel. 387-3404, BYO.

**Indian;**
Rajah Sahib,
23 Bank Place,
City, tel. 675-521, BYO.

The Empress of India,
466 Swanson St.,
Carlton, tel. 347-8555, BYO.

**Vegetarian;**
The Wholemeal
52 Collins St.,
City, tel. 631-596, BYO

**Seafood;**
Melbourne Oyster Bar and Seafood Restaurant
209 King St.,
City, tel. 671-881, licenced.

Fish Exchange,
349 Flinders Lane,
City, tel. 627-808.

Melbourne's pub food is of a very high standard whether you're eating it at your corner local hotel or the latest "in" establishment. The **Palace Hotel** at 893 Burke Road, Camberwell, is regarded by the locals as one of the best food bargains in Melbourne. It can get very crowded and with the majority of the dishes costing from only $3.50 to $4.50, it is easy to understand why. The **Fawkner Club** at 52 Toorak Road West, has an open-air courtyard out front as its main attraction. Counter meals are in the $5 to $7 bracket, and include a serve-yourself salad table. Finally, in Albert Park, the **Victoria Hotel** at 123 Beaconsfield Parade is up-market but pretty good.

## What to See:

**City Square**, the new hub centre of the city, was opened by Queen Elizabeth II on May 28, 1980. It is kind of an architectural mishmash with lawns, shops, cafes, waterfalls and flower gardens, seemingly in no particular order. The real attraction of the square is the 25,000-bulb video matrix screen, with each bulb individually controlled by a computer.

The **National Museum of Victoria** is at 285 Russell St. The Museum is open from 10 a.m. to 5 p.m. Monday to Saturday and 2 p.m. to 5 p.m. Sunday. Admission is free. On display is a large collection of Australiana as well as the stuffed remains of the great Australian racehorse Phar Lap, which mysteriously died in the United States. A block farther up Russell Street, is the

**Old Melbourne Gaol** and Penal Museum. Built in 1841 it is now owned and operated by the National Trust. This is where the famous bushranger Ned Kelly was hanged. With its many penal relics on display it is an unpleasant reminder of Australia's early convict days. It is open from 10 a.m. to 5 p.m. daily and admission is $2.

The **National Gallery of Victoria**, 180 St. Kilda Road, is part of the eye-catching new **Victoria Art Centre**. The gallery has several floors and houses a very fine collection of local and overseas art. It is open 10 a.m. to 5 p.m. Tuesday and Thursday and 10 a.m. to 9 p.m. Wednesday, 10 a.m. to 5 p.m. Friday to Sunday. Entry is 80 cents. Beside the gallery is the recently opened **Concert Hall** complex. This houses an excellent concert hall, the state theatre, and a performing arts museum.

**Melbourne Cricket Ground** was the central stadium for the 1956 Olympics. It can accommodate over 100,000 spectators and is Australia's biggest sporting stadium. Within the cricket ground is the **Cricket Museum**, which houses cricket memorabilia including paintings, etchings, cartoons and scorecards. There are conducted tours of the museum on Wednesdays at 10 a.m.

**Melbourne Zoo** is just north of the city centre in Parkville. The zoo is open 9 a.m. to 5 p.m. every day of the week and admission is $4.

Victoria has named itself the "Garden State" and in Melbourne it is easy to see why. **Alexandra Gardens** is the popular lunchtime retreat for the city office workers. **Queen Victoria Garden** has a 10,000-plant floral display clock as its focal point. The **Royal Botanic Gardens** between Alexandra Avenue and Domain Road are arguably the finest gardens in Australia. They cover 41 hectares (101 acres) and there are some 12,000 plant species. The gardens are open Monday to Saturday 7:30 a.m. to sunset and Sunday 9 a.m. to sunset. The Botanic Gardens form just a part of the larger park known as **The Kings Domain**. This park contains the Shrine of Remembrance, **La Trobe's Cottage** and the Sidney Myer Music Bowl.

At the end of Collins Street are **Fitzroy Gardens** and the adjacent **Treasury Gardens**. Magnificent English elms provide shaded places for a quiet picnic lunch. In Fitzroy Gardens, surrounded by lawns and covered by ivy brought from England is **Captain Cook's Cottage**. It was brought from Yorkshire and reassembled in the park in 1934. It is open from 10 a.m. to 4:30 p.m. daily and admission is 60 cents.

**Day Tours around Melbourne**: While Melbourne's immediate setting is not spectacular there are places of interest all around. On the eastern edge of Melbourne, the **Dandenongs** are one of the most popular day trips from the city. You can clearly see the Dandenongs from central Melbourne and they are only about an hour's drive. They are cool due to the altitude and are lush green due to the heavy rainfall. One of the major attractions of the Dandenongs is **Puffing Billy**, a restored miniature steam train which runs along a 13 km track from Belgrave to Emerald Lake Park. The round trip takes 2½ hours and costs $5.60 for adults and $3.70 for children.

Tucked away beneath the foothills of the Great Dividing Range some 64 km (40 miles) northeast of Melbourne, **Healesville** is an idyllic pleasure resort in the valley of the Watts River. Healesville's top attraction is the Sir Colin MacKenzie Sanctuary. Internationally famous as a wildlife haven, the park is open 9 a.m. to 5 p.m. and admission is $4.

### Cultural Activities:

Melbourne is noted for good theatre. You'll find productions at the city's three major theatres—**The Princess Theatre**, 163 Spring St.; **Her Majestys**, 219 Exhibition St; and **Comedy Theatre**, 244 Exhibition St.

The peak month for theatre and almost every other kind of performance is March, during the great Moomba Festival. If you're visiting Melbourne during November and April, take advantage of free outdoor concerts, symphonies, ballet and rock groups, at the **Myer Music Bowl**. The Melbourne Symphony Orchestra performs at a variety of locations between March and October. For more information on Melbourne's lively arts pick up a copy of *This Week in Melbourne* from the Victorian Government Travel Centre.

There are an amazing number of theatre restaurants in Melbourne: some of them good and fairly expensive because you have to pay for an obligatory dinner as well as the show. The **Last Laugh Theatre** at 64 Smith St., and the **Naughty Nineties** at 675 Glenferrie Road, Hawthorne, are just two of the many.

Most of Melbourne's nighttime scene is tied up with rock pubs. *The Age Weekender* will tell you who's on and where. They range from small venues like the **Station Hotel** on Greville Street, Prahran, to the big hanger-size **Bombay Rock** on Phoenix Street, Brunswick. Cover charges vary widely depending on what night of the week it is and what band is playing. It's free on some nights, but generally it's from around $5.

Jazz action also takes place mainly in pubs—popular ones include **The Victoria Hotel**, Beaconsfield Parade, Albert Park; the **Anchor and Hope**, Church Street, Richmond;; and the **La Brasserie** at Prahran Market, South Yarra.

### Shopping:

As stated earlier, Melbourne is Australia's commercial capital and major fashion centre. Collins and Bourke streets are noted for department stores and boutiques. On Bourke Street, shoppers find many of the city's major department stores; **Buckley & Nunn**, **Coles** and **Waltons**. The huge **Myer** store on the Bourke Street Mall is the largest department store in the Southern Hemisphere. At the top end of Collins Street, between Spring and Swanston streets, Melbourne's most exclusive fashion boutiques specialize in imported designer clothes.

Then there are the shopping arcades; the oldest, the **Royal Arcade** dates from 1870. Other arcades include **The Block** and the **Australian Arcade** under the Hotel Australia. Street markets are also very popular in Melbourne. **Victoria Market**, Victoria Street, North Melbourne, is open on Tuesday, Thursday and Saturday morn-

ings and Friday from 6 a.m. to 6 p.m. This century-old market has everything—live poultry, vegetables, toys, clothing and much more. The **Flea Market**, Drummond Street, Carlton, opens Friday nights and Saturday mornings.

### Sports:

If you want to watch the locals cast away their Victorian reserve, any major sporting event will do but football and horse racing are the surest bets. **Australian Rules Football**, a mixture of rugby, soccer and Gaelic football, is at its best in Melbourne. Six matches are held each Saturday during the April-September season. The finals pit the two top teams at the Melbourne Cricket Ground before more than 100,000 fans.

Melbourne's other great passion is **horse racing**, held the year round on Melbourne's metropolitan courses at Flemington, Caulfield, Mooney Valley and Sandown. Flemington is the home of the Melbourne Cup, an internationally famous racing event held on the first Tuesday in November. On this day the entire nation grinds to a halt to hear the race on radio or see it on television. Meanwhile all Melbourne is at the track where huge amounts of champagne and betting money flow. It is also the fashion event of the season.

December to February is the season for international test **cricket** matches played at the Melbourne Cricket Ground.

## Brisbane, Queensland

The city of Brisbane is just a few degrees south of the Tropic of Capricorn. The best months to visit are from April through November when daytime temperatures range between 20 and 27 degrees Celsius (68 to 80°F). Most of the rain comes during the summer months of December, January and February. With a population of over 900,000 Brisbane is Australia's third largest city, but to some it is still a "large country town."

The busy port city is an ideal base from which to explore southern Queensland, and the best gateway to the attractions of northern Queensland. The centre of Brisbane occupies a stretch of land bounded by the sea on one side and the Brisbane River on the other. The main commercial streets follow a grid pattern. Streets running south to north have feminine names; those running west to east masculine. The Parliament buildings and the Botanic Gardens nestle in the bend of the river at the top of the peninsula. The usual selection of maps, leaflets and helpful information is available from the Queensland Government Tourist Bureau, on the corner of Adelaide and Edward streets, tel. 312-211. Opening hours are 8:30 a.m. to 5 p.m. weekdays and 8:30 to 11:15 a.m. on Saturday.

### Transportation:

Public transport within the urban area consists of buses and river ferries. For information on city buses it's worth visiting the information centre in the City Plaza behind the town hall. They will answer any queries you might have on concession fares or supply timetables. If phoning for information, call 225-4444.

Brisbane ferries are fast, cheap and clean, but Brisbane doesn't make as much use as it might of its river. Ferries do run from Eagle Street to East Brisbane and Hawthorne every half hour and across the river from Alice Street, by the Botanic Gardens. Fares are just 30 cents. Probably the most popular cruise is the trip to the Lone Pine Koala Sanctuary. It departs from the Hayles Wharf every afternoon at 1:30 p.m. returning at 5:30 p.m. and costs $8. Taxis are best booked by phone on the following numbers 320-151 or 391-1091.

## Accommodations:

Brisbane is not the best city for accommodations but it is improving slowly. Major hotels are listed in this book's Appendix. Although some distance from the centre, the **Brisbane Youth Hostel** at 15 Mitchell St., Kedron, tel. 571-245 is a modern pleasant hostel with room for 60 people at a cost of $5 per night. It is eight km from the city centre.

Probably Brisbane's cheapest lodgings are offered by the **Adventures Club** at 1 Annie St., Kangaroo Point, tel. 391-7309. For a list of other hotels and guesthouses see appendix.

You can forget about camping in Brisbane as there is a curious council regulation that forbids tent camping within a 22-km radius of the city centre. For an excellent guide to Queensland camping grounds ask for the brochure issued by the Government Tourist Bureau.

## Dining Out:

Brisbane possesses a number of good restaurants but culinary standards are well below those of Sydney, Melbourne and Adelaide. Queenslanders generally dine much earlier than other mainland Australians. Most restaurants are concentrated around the city in Fortitude Valley and near the University at St. Lucia. Local specialities are Queensland Mud Crabs and Moreton Bay Bugs (a king of crayfish cooked and served in its shell). Brisbane also has a wide range of ethnic restaurants and a good selection of the traditional steak and salad places.

## What to See:

Use your maps to find your way to the **City Hall tower**, as this is the best place to begin your tour of Brisbane. The observation platform is open from 9 a.m. to 4 p.m. and the lift to the top is 30 cents. The City Hall, built in 1930, is one of the biggest city halls in Australia. It also houses a museum and art gallery on the ground floor and the large open square that fronts the building makes it look even more impressive.

**Parliament House** at the corner of Alice and George streets was opened in 1868. This building is an imposing example of French Renaissance architecture that is now spoilt with the newer annex that towers above the original structure.

One of Brisbane's earliest buildings dating from 1829 is the **Old Observatory and Windmill**. Built by convict labour it was originally designed to operate as a windmill but the sails never worked, so it was converted to a convict-manned treadmill. It stands on Wickham Terrace, overlooking the city.

For a tour of Brisbane's other interesting early city buildings get yourself a copy of the National Trust's *Historic Walks* brochure. The National Trust have their headquarters at the end of George Street.

**The Queensland Museum**, at the corner of Gregory Terrace and Bowen Bridge Road, has a number of interesting exhibits on marine life of the Great Barrier Reef and also displays on the Aborigines and their customs and implements. The museum is open 10 a.m. to 5 p.m. Mondays to Saturdays and 2 p.m. to 5 p.m. Sundays and public holidays.

The **Botanic Gardens**, 20 hectares (50 acres) of flowers, shrubs and trees, borders the Brisbane River next to Parliament House. The Gardens are open daily from sunrise to sunset and it's a popular spot for bike and riding. **Newstead Park** is a pleasant riverside park and is the site of Newstead House, Brisbane's oldest residence. Farther downriver **New Farm Park** is a favourite with flower lovers.

One of Brisbane's top attractions at Fig Tree Pocket is the **Lone Pine Koala Sanctuary**. It was the first koala sanctuary established in Australia and its colony of about 100 is the largest on public display anywhere. The Sanctuary also has wombats, emus, Tasmanian devils, platypuses and a variety of other Australian animals. It's open from 9:30 a.m. to 5 p.m. daily and admission is $4.

Bus tours to the Lone Pine Sanctuary often stop on the way at **Mount Coot-tha Forest Park**. From here only eight km from the city centre you can look out over Brisbane and the surrounding countryside to Moreton Bay. Within the park are the Mount Coot-tha Botanic Gardens, a cactus garden, a Tropical Display Dome and the Sir Thomas Brisbane Planetarium.

## Shopping:

If shopping in Brisbane, you'll find the best selection of native handcrafts and artifacts at **Queensland Aboriginal Creatives** on George Street. Other souvenir items to be bought are rugs, garments and bags made from hides and skins; and jewellery from local gemstones (rubies, sapphires, opals).

## Nightlife:

Brisbane is not a lively nighttime city but it has all the usual pubs where rock, jazz and folk groups are featured.

The **SGIO Theatre** on Turbot Street, is the home of the Queensland State Theatre Company. Most overseas artists appear at **Her Majesty's Theatre** on Queen Street.

In late September–early October, Brisbane takes on a carnival air during "Warana"—a week-long spring festival with parades, arts shows, beauty contests and other events.

You'll find the full rundown on what's on and where in the weekend papers or in the free entertainment paper, *Time Off*.

## Adelaide, South Australia

Although its population is approaching 1 million, Adelaide manages to retain many of the charms of a much smaller city. It is a dignified and calm city in a superb setting. The city centre is surrounded by a ring of parks and further out the whole metropolitan area is rimmed by the Mount Lofty Ranges.

Adelaide is an easy city to get to know, with the streets being laid out in a straight-forward grid pattern, interspersed with several squares. The main street through the centre of the town is King William Street. The main shopping street is Rundle Street, with a mall closed to traffic, running from King William Street through to Pulteney Street. Circling the inner city area are the great parklands that dominate the shape of Adelaide. Through the northern section of these parks flows the Torrens River and beyond the river is North Adelaide.

The South Australian Government Tourist Bureau is at 18 King William St., tel. 212-1644. It is open Monday to Friday 8:45 a.m. to 5 p.m. and Saturday 9 a.m. to 11:30 p.m., Sunday and public holidays from 10 a.m. to 2 p.m.

### Transportation:

All information on the Adelaide transport system is available from the South Australian Government Tourist Bureau or the State Transport Authority, tel. 218-2345 until 10:30 p.m. daily.

Most travel within Adelaide is done by bus or train but there is one tram service that travels between Victoria Square and the beach suburb of Glenelg. Concession and special offer tickets are available and a free *Bee Line Bus* follows the city shopping circuit from Victoria Square to the railway station along King William Street.

### Accommodations:

A listing of major hotels can be found in this book's Appendix. cheap central accommodation is not easy to find in Adelaide, but if you are stuck for a bed, the South Australian Government Tourist Bureau can arrange. Most of the budget accommodation is to be found in the beachside suburb of Glenelg.

**Adelaide Youth Hostel** is very central at 290 Gilles St., tel. 223-6007. It only sleeps 16, so if it's full try the **Adelaide YMCA** at 76 Flinders St., tel. 223-1611. It takes guests of either sex and is a very modern building, boasting facilities such as squash courts and sauna.

### Dining Out:

You can eat very well in Adelaide. Adelaide may not have the volume or variety of restaurants found in Sydney or Melbourne, but the standard is remarkably high and the local wines are excellent.

Hindley Street is the centre for ethnic restaurants. Here you'll find Lebanese, Chinese, Greek and Italian restaurants interspersed with Adelaide's small and seedy collection of strip clubs.

Best of all there are many places in Adelaide where you can have lunch or other meals in the open air and the climate is so dry, it is unlikely you will get rained on.

### What to See:

Within the square created by Adelaide's park lands is the city central shopping and business district—a conglomeration of 19th-Century architecture and modern buildings.

**King William Street**, one of the city's main thoroughfares, is considered the widest capital city street in Australia. Here are most of the city's banks, insurance offices and post office.

Another main tree-lined boulevard is **North Terrace**. Important buildings along this thoroughfare include **Parliament House, Holy Trinity Church, Government House, South Australian Museum, Art Gallery, State Library** and the **University of Adelaide**.

Just north of North Terrace on the banks of the Torrens River is the **Festival Centre** complex. The centre was completed in 1973 and was built specifically for the Adelaide Festival, which takes place during March of every even-numbered year. It contains a main 2,000-seat auditorium, a smaller drama theatre, a 360-seat experimental theatre, a 2,000-seat open-air amphitheatre, an art collection, restaurants and a bar. Hourly guided tours are held weekdays from 10 a.m. to 3 p.m. and Saturday 10:30 a.m. to 3 p.m.

Showplace of Adelaide is the 688-hectare (1,700-acre) **Botanic Gardens**. Here you will find 16 hectares (40 acres) of native Australian vegetation and a world-renowned collection of water lilies (in the park's lakes).

On Frome Road next to the Botanic Gardens is Adelaide's **Zoo**. It's open daily 9:30 a.m. to 5 p.m. and on Sunday 10 a.m. to 5 p.m. The best way of getting to the zoo is aboard the launch *Popeye*, which sails along the Torrens River between the zoo and Festival Centre.

One of Adelaide's greatest attractions and Australia's most celebrated wine region is the **Barossa Valley**, just 64 km (40 miles) northeast of the city. Every touring company in Adelaide has a Barossa Valley excursion in its books. Most trips last a day and take in a number of stops for wine tasting. Fares are around $20 and that sometimes includes lunch The South Australian Government Tourist Bureau can supply you with a full list of tours available.

To the southeast, Adelaide is flanked by the **Mount Lofty Ranges**. Mount Lofty itself at 771 metres (2,529 feet) offers spectacular views over Adelaide; there are a number of parks in the hills with a wide variety of wildlife.

**Hahndorf**, just 29 km (18 miles) southeast of Adelaide, is a popular tourist destination. It is the oldest surviving German Festivals which include the Schuetzenfest Beer Festival, held each January on Australia Day.

### Cultural Activities:

The focus of Adelaide's entertainment scene is the **Festival Centre**, and many of Adelaide's cultural events are held in this complex. Both the Adelaide Symphony Orchestra and the State Theatre perform at the Festival Centre. International performers regularly appear at the centre.

The State Opera performs at the **Opera Theatre**, on Grote Street. Other playhouses are the **Sheridan Theatre** in North Adelaide and the **Q Theatre** on Halifax Street.

### Shopping:

Adelaide's main shopping area is concentrated on the pedestrian-only **Rundle Street Mall**. But the best shopping is done in South Australian wineries.

### Nightlife and Entertainment:

To find out what's on obtain a copy of the regular news sheet put out by the South Australian Government Tourist Bureau. There is always something on at the **Adelaide Festival Centre** and there are the usual pubs with rock, folk and jazz music. The sin center of Adelaide is **Hindley Street**. Interspersed with excellent restaurants you'll find strip clubs, bars, porno bookstores and the usual ladies of the night.

## Perth, Western Australia

Perth with a population of 870,000 is the capital of Western Australia. It is a beautiful city and enjoys a year-round average of eight hours sunshine a day. Perth lies astride the Swan River, some 19 km (12 miles) inland from her seaport of Fremantle.

Murray Street and Hay Street are the main shopping streets. The West Australian Government Travel Centre is at 772 Hay St, tel. 321-2471. The centre is open from 8:30 a.m. to 5 p.m. Monday to Friday, and 9 a.m. to 11:45 a.m. Saturday. The usual information and brochures are available. Be sure to pick up one entitled, *In and Around Perth*, which lists all the places of interest and tells you how to get to them.

### Transportation:

The Metropolitan Transport Trust operates bus, train and ferry services within the city and out to the suburbs. For maps and on-the-spot information the Metropolitan Transport Trust is at 125 St. Georges Terrace, tel. 325-8511.

### Accommodations:

See list of accommodation in Appendix.

### Dining Out:

Perth has a wide variety of places to eat. You can find restaurants with all sorts of international cuisines; and to make them easy to find they are all concentrated in one area. The region is James Street / William Street, where you'll find lots of ethnic family restaurants with good food at reasonable prices.

### What to See:

Some of the places to visit in and around Perth are:

**King's Park**, 504 hectares (1,245 acres) of natural bushlands, garden and wildflowers.

**London Court**, a central city shopping arcade recreated as a 16th-Century English street.

**The Western Australian Museum** on Francis Street with fine displays of whales and Aboriginal culture.

**The Art Gallery** at 47 James St., featuring contemporary and original Australian painting.

**The Old Mill** in South Perth, restored as a pioneer folk museum.

Suggested just out-of-town tours include the **Swan River Valley** with its vineyards and the Caversham Wildlife Park, and **Rottnest Island**. "Rotto," as it is known to the locals, is a popular summer resort just off shore from Fremantle, opposite the mouth of the Swan River. The tiny island offers beautiful beaches and the clear blue waters of the Indian Ocean.

### Shopping:

Distinctive local products to shop for are opals and other gemstones, aboriginal craft, and iron-ore jewellery.

**Hay Street Mall** is the most enjoyable place to shop without the noise and fumes of traffic. Branching away from this central mall are the six traffic-free shopping arcades: **Piccadilly, National Mutual, City, Trinity, Plaza** and **Wanamba.**

### Entertainment:

A useful source of entertainment possibilities is *This Week in Perth* available in hotels or from the West Australian Government Travel Centre. The 8,000-seat **Perth Entertainment Centre** is where most overseas artists perform. The **Perth Concert Hall** and the **Perth Music Shell** hold concerts by the Western Australian Symphony and other well known orchestras.

During the Festival of Perth—February and March—the city stages plays, films and music in both indoor and outdoor settings. But year round you will always find something happening. Perth has a busy selection of pubs, discos, nightclubs and theatre restaurants.

## Darwin, Northern Territory

The Northern Territory is one of the world's last frontiers. It is commonly referred to as the "Top End" by its residents. Nearly half of the Top End's residents (50,000) call Darwin home.

Darwin is an international gateway to Southeast Asia and a strategic commercial centre. When planning a trip to Darwin, take into account that it only has two seasons—the wet or monsoon season from November through April, and the dry from April to October.

The Northern Territory Government Tourist Bureau is at 31 Smith Street Mall, and is open from 8:45 a.m. to 5 p.m. Monday to Friday and 9 a.m. to noon Saturday. The Bureau will give you all the advice you need on places to stay and tourist attractions.

### Accommodations:

See list of accommodations in Appendix.

### Dining Out:

Darwin has always been a cosmopolitan city and this shows in its restaurants. You can eat just about any type of food you want, but the main source of protein in Darwin is liquid—beer. It has a reputation as one of the hardest drinking towns in the world. In an average year each Darwin resident consumes 230 litres (61 U.S. gallons) of beer. A Darwin stubie (the local beer bottle), contains 2 litres instead of the normal 375 milli-litres; this sums up Darwins' thirst.

### Shopping:

Darwin is probably the best place in Australia for buying Aboriginal artifacts and the best place to shop in Darwin is the **Arnhem Land Aboriginal Art Gallery** at 35 Cavenagh St.

## Hobart, Tasmania

Most of Tasmania's 413,000 residents prefer to be called Tasmanians rather than Australians, and Tasmania is very unlike Australia thanks to the high rainfall and dense vegetation. Hobart, with a population of 167,000, is the capital of Tasmania; it is picturesque and easy-going. Surrounding one of the world's finest deep-water harbours, the city covers the broad lower valley of the Derwent River. Mount Wellington provides a spectacular backdrop to the city and the view from the 1,270-metre (4,166-foot) pinnacle provides an unobstructed view of the harbour, and a good portion of south and central Tasmania as well.

First stop for visitors should be the Tasmanian Government Tourist Bureau, at 80 Elizabeth St., tel. 346-911. The Bureau is open Monday to Friday 8:45 a.m. to 5:30 p.m. and weekends and holidays from 9 to 11 a.m. Here bookings can be made for tours and accommodations and make sure you pick up your free copy of *This Week in Tasmania*.

Places of interest in Hobart can usually be taken in by a walking tour that is organised by the National Trust and the Tasmanian Government Tourist Bureau. Details can be obtained from the bureau. The walk takes in **Battery Point, Salamanca Place** and the **Maritime Museum**. Other places you'll want to visit are **Anglesea Barracks**, the **Tasmanian Museum and Art Gallery** and the **Wrest Point Casino**.

### Accommodations:

See list of accommodations in Appendix.

### Dining Out:

Most of the restaurants in Hobart are concentrated in three areas: the city, Sandy Bay and Battery Point. It is possible to walk through all three areas if you can't find what you want in one of the areas.

### Shopping:

Articles made from the island's natural resources make interesting mementoes. The usual gimmicky souvenir finds its way onto store shelves, but look for local gemstones, wooden products made from Huon Pine, shellcraft, and antiques around Battery Point.

### Entertainment:

Most of Hobart's nightlife is concentrated on the **Wrest Point Hotel Casino**. It was Australia's first casino and also houses a restaurant, hotel and nightclub. If you would like to do more than just gamble, the cabaret room regularly stages lavish floor shows with overseas entertainers. The casino opens at 1 p.m. and operates Sunday to Thursday to 3 a.m., Friday and Saturday to 4 a.m.

If your tastes in entertainment are a little more simple, check the *Hobart Mercury* for a guide to what's on and where. Hobart has the usual pubs and clubs with rock, jazz and folk groups.

# Festivals/Seasonal Events

Listed below are some of the varied and unusual events held in Australia.

## January

**Perth Cup**—A major horse racing event in the Australian racing calendar.
**Hahndorf Schuetzenfest** (near Adelaide)—Competitions in marksmanship, feasting with traditional German food and beer with singing and dancing.
**Royal Sydney Anniversary Regatta**—Sailing races on Sydney Harbour.
**Cricket Matches**—International and interstate matches in capital cities.
**Ocean Beach Surf Carnivals**—Held most

weekends in summer months at major Australian surf beaches.

**Festival of Sydney**—A month long Festival of Arts.

## February

**Royal Hobart Regatta**—An aquatic carnival on Hobart's Derwent River.

**Festival of Perth**—A month long festival of cultural events.

## March

**Begonia Festival** (Ballarat, Vic.)—Excellent flower displays in Ballarat gardens.

**Moomba**—Melbourne's 10-day festival of street parades, sporting events, cultural activities and a fireworks display.

**Canberra Festival**—A week of festivities to commemorate the foundation of Canberra; entertainment includes aerial displays, barbecues, pop concerts and fairs.

**Adelaide Festival of Arts**—A 21-day biennial presentation (even numbered years) of the **Arts of Australia** - music, opera, theatre, ballet, art, literature, and light entertainment.

## April

**Barossa Valley Vintage Festival**—Held every two years in the Barossa Valley, near Adelaide, to celebrate the grape harvest in the traditional German manner (held in odd numbered years alternating with the Adelaide Festival of Arts).

**Australian Gemboree** (Easter)—Promoting interest in gemstones - includes rock swaps, auctions, field trips, exhibitions.

**Sydney Royal Easter Show**—Australia's largest agricultural and industrial show featuring parades and varied entertainment.

**Sydney Cup Week**—A week of horse racing culminating in the running of the Sydney Cup.

## May

**Bangtail Muster** (Alice Springs)—A celebration including cattle round-ups, rodeos and parades.

**Camel Cup** (Alice Springs)—A fun filled series of camel races held in Alice Springs.

## June

5th: **Darwin Beer Can Regatta**—A boating event staged on Darwin Harbour for craft made almost completely from beer cans.

3rd-13th: **Townsville Pacific Festival**—A 10-day festival of arts; culture and exhibits centered on Pacific society.

## July

2nd, 9th and 16th: three major horse races—**Rothmans 100,000** and **Fourex** in Brisbane; and **Grand National Steeplechase** in Melbourne.

31st: **Trout Season Opens**, Tasmania

## August

11th-20th: **Brisbane Royal Show**—Agricultural displays, livestock and machinery.

Aug. 20-Oct. 29: **Royal South Street Competitions**—Staged in Ballarat, Vic. All forms of performing arts including the Grand National Eisteddfod.

27th: **Henley-on-Todd Regatta** (Alice Springs)— A fun festival; mock yacht races in bottomless craft on the dry bed of the Todd River. There are also "water" skiing events.

During Aug: **Australian Ski Championships**— International competitions at Thredbo, Snowy Mountains.

## September

2nd-10th: **Royal Adelaide Show**—Agricultural and horticultural exhibition.

14th-24th: **Melbourne Royal Agricultural Show**— A 10-day display of rural and industrial products, sporting events and amusements.

18th-25th: **Toowoomba Carnival of Flowers**— celebrations centered around floral displays.

Sept. 24-Oct. 23: **Horse Racing Carnival**, N.S.W.—with exhibitions and sporting events.

Sept. 19-Oct. 10: **Warana Spring Carnival**—A Brisbane festival with processions, Mardi Gras, arts and crafts, concerts.

Sept. 24: **Australian Rules Football Finals**—An exciting finale to the season of a fast moving game.

Sept. 30-Oct. 9: **Perth Royal Show**—An agricultural and horticultural exhibition.

30th: **Trout Season Opens**—Snowy Mountains.

## October

2nd: **Australian Grand Prix Motor Race**

19th-22nd: **Royal Hobart Show**—An agricultural exhibition.

Oct. 29-Nov. 5: **McLaren Vale Wine Bushing Festival** (Near Adelaide)—A week of winery tours, tastings, auctions, displays.

Oct. 29-Nov. 5: **Jacaranda Festival**, Grafton N.S.W.—Floral displays, garden exhibitions.

## November

Oct. 29-Nov. 5: **Victorian Spring Racing Carnival**—A week of horse racing events culminating in the running of the Melbourne Cup (Nov. 1); one of the major horse racing events of the year.

Oct. 30-Nov. 5: **Horse Racing Carnivals** (Vic.), in Melbourne and Sydney.

17th-20th: **Australian Open Golf Tournament**— Carrying over $A150,000 in prize money.

Nov. 27-Dec. 11—**Australian Open Tennis Tournament**

## December

24th: **Carols By Candlelight**—Held in city parks of particular note; carols at Melbourne's Sidney

Meyer Music Bowl, and Sydney's Hyde Park.

**26th: Sydney to Hobart Yacht Race**—Departs Sydney Harbour on Dec. 26 to cover the 1,000 km course to Hobart.

# Language

———by John Borthwick

Righto, for starters, Australians *don't* wander around yacking at each other like Pommie parodies. The following nonsense contains rhyming slang which *some* of the people *might* use *some* of the time, but if you use it like this—well, you'll make a mug of yourself.

"Take a Captain Cook (look) at the Coffs Harbour (barber) with his Malcolm Fraser (razor) giving that Werris Creek (Greek) a Dad n' Dave (shave). It'd give you the Hawkesbury Rivers (shivers)."

This is closer to Cockney rhyming slang than to the true Australian vernacular, or Strine, as it calls itself. Strine (the term for Australian) is a linguistic rebellion which goes back to the earliest Irish convicts in Australia and pokes its tongue at that most ubiquitous form of English colonialism, the English language.

Strine is not so much a dialect as a "slanguage." It is full of flash, filth and fun. It is ungrammatical and is spelt as phonetic as it is spoken; and the best way to do *that* is through the nose. [Some scholars claim this adenoidal enunciation arose out of a need to keep the trap (mouth) shut against blowies (blow flies).] Elocuting like a ventriloquist your "day" becomes "die," and if you "die," well, you've "doid."

Strine is rarely acknowledged in written form except by smart-aleck philologists like the bloke who coined the term "Strine," Professor Afferbeck Lauder (go on, say it: "Alphabetical Order"), hysterical etymologists and of course, speakers of *other* forms of English. A perfect phonetic transcription of Strine has been achieved by a Seppo mate ... (This is your translator speaking: Seppo = Septic Tank = Yank = American. Mate = friend, pal. *Not* lover.) ... of mine who for years has signed-off his letters to Australia with "Lighter mite" (viz. "Later, mate").

The Australian lingo is characterised by informality (you can use it anywhere except O.S.), a laconic, poetic originality ("she was uglier than a robber's dog") and a prolific profanity ("he's as thin as a streak of pelican shit"). A particular flair for the insult culminates in "knocking the Poms," that is, mocking the English—who are usually referred to as "whinging Pommies." (A recent advertisement for surfing holidays described the destination, Bali, as having "more breaks than a Pom in traction.")

An Australian accent varies more according to social class than geography. Even though dictions may range from silver-tail to Ocker, an honest Australian accent is no bar to social mobility—as long as you're not two snags short of a barby, that is, stupid. In fact, the current Strine Pry Minsta, Bob Hawke, sounds like a chainsaw in a bad mood, but voters from Bullamakanka to the Black Stump all know that he speaks, literally, the same language as they do.

So, there's a list of your basic Strine slang words and phrases on page 351. Without it you'll be up the creek in a barbed-wire canoe without a paddle. And *with* it you'll probably make a nong of yourself but 'avago anyway. Just don't strine (strain) yourself.

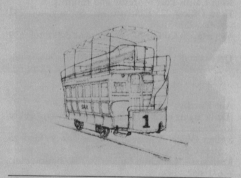

# Appendix

## Airlines Servicing Australia

**Air India;**
[Biweekly service Tuesday and Friday: Sydney-Perth-Bombay-Rome-Amsterdam-London.]
**Head Office**: 3 Elizabeth St., Sydney 2000, tel. 232 8477.
**Queensland**: 21st floor, Lennons Plaza, 68 Queen St., Brisbane 4000, tel. 312 194.
**South Australia**: 9th floor, TAA Bldg., 144 North Terrace, Adelaide 5000, tel. 516 525.
**Victoria**: 13th floor, Royal Globe Bldg., 444 Collins St., Melbourne, tel. 602 3933.
**Western Australia**: 7th floor, Elder House, 111 St. Georges Terrace, Perth 6000, tel. 222 511.

**Air Nauru;**
[Wednesday and Sunday: from Melbourne and Sydney to Nauru.]
**Head Office**: 80 Collins St., Melbourne, tel. 653 5709.

## Air New Zealand;

[Frequent Trans Tasman services linking Sydney, Melbourne, Brisbane with Auckland, Christchurch. Onward services to Fiji, New Caledonia, Norfolk Island, Cook Islands, Tahiti, Western Samoa, Hawaii, London, Port Moresby, Tonga, Los Angeles, Singapore, Hongkong, Tokyo. One weekly service from Perth to Auckland.]

**Head Office:** 115 Pitt St., Sydney 2000, tel. 233 6888.

**Queensland:** Watkins Place, 288 Edward St., Brisbane 4000, tel. 229 2799.

**South Australia:** 11th floor, National Bank Bldg., 22 King William St., Adelaide 5000, tel. 212 3544.

**Victoria:** 154-156 Swanson St., Melbourne 3000, tel. 636 221.

**Western Australia:** 11th floor, National Bank Bldg., 50 St. Georges Terrace, Perth 6000, tel. 325 1099.

## Air Nuigini;

[Three flights per week from Sydney-Port Moresby and return. Two flights weekly from Brisbane-Port Moresby and return. Three direct flights from Cairns-Port Moresby and return.]

**Head Office:** 225 Clarence St., Sydney, tel. 232 8900, 232 3100.

**Victoria:** 80 Collins St., Melbourne 3000, tel. 639 327.

**Queensland:** 127 Creek St., Brisbane 4000, tel. 229 5844, also at 4 Shield St., Cairns, 4870, tel. 514 177.

## Air Pacific;

[Daily flights except Friday to Nadi, twice weekly to Noumea, Honiara and Vila.]

**Sydney Office:** American Express Tower, George Street, Sydney, tel. 233 7877.

**Melbourne:** 450 Little Collins St., Melbourne, tel. 671 652.

**Queensland:** Corner of Edward and Elizabeth streets, Brisbane, tel. 229 6655.

## Alitalia;

[Saturday and Tuesday, Sydney-Melbourne-Singapore-Bombay-Rome.]

**Head Office:** 118 Alfred St., Milsons Point, 2061, tel. 922 1555.

**Victoria:** 143 Queen St., Melbourne 3000, tel. 676 865.

**Queensland:** 171 Edward St., Brisbane 4000, tel. 312 196.

**South Australia:** 150 North Terrace, Adelaide 5000, tel. 212 5333.

**Western Australia:** TAA General Agents, 32 St. George's Terrace, Perth 6000, tel. 323 0331.

## British Airways;

Sydney (daily), Melbourne (daily except Monday), Brisbane (Monday, Friday), Perth (Monday, Wednesday, Friday) and Adelaide (Monday, Friday) to Auckland, Brunei, Jakarta, Singapore, Kuala Lumpur, Bombay, Muscat, Abu Dhabi, Bahrain, and London.]

**Head Office:** British Airways House, Suite 4201, MLC Centre, 19-29 Martin Place, Sydney 2000, tel. 232 1777; also at Sixth Street Mascot, 2020,

tel. 699 5255.

**Victoria:** CML Bldg., 330 Collins St., Melbourne 3000, tel. 602 3500.

**Queensland:** 243 Edward St., Brisbane 4000, tel. 229 3166.

**Western Australia:** AMP Bldg., 140 St. Georges Terrace, Perth, tel. 322 6433.

**South Australia:** 33 King William St., Adelaide 5000, tel. 212 1022.

**Australian Capital Territory:** ASL House, 28 Ainslie Ave., Canberra, tel. 476 322.

## Cathay Pacific Airways Ltd;

[Sunday, Monday, Wednesday fly Sydney-Melbourne-Hongkong. Thursday fly Sydney-Hongkong. Saturday, Melbourne-Sydney-Hongkong. Thursday, Brisbane-Sydney-Hongkong.]

**Head Office:** Swire House, 8 Spring St., Sydney 2000, tel. 231 5122.

**Victoria:** Suite 7C, 343 Little Collins St., Melbourne 3000, tel. 601 156.

**South Australia:** 14th floor, 45 Grenfell St., Adelaide, 5000, tel. 212 1655.

**Queensland:** 8th floor, 40 Queen St., Brisbane 4000, tel. 229 9344.

**Western Australia:** 11 St. Georges Terrace, Perth, tel. 322 1377.

## Continental Airlines;

[Thrice weekly Sydney-Auckland-Honolulu-Los Angeles. Twice weekly Sydney-Nadi-Honolulu-Los Angeles. Once a week, Melbourne-Sydney-Honolulu-Los Angeles and Sydney-Melbourne-Honolulu-Los Angeles.]

**Head Office:** 54 Carrington St., Sydney 2000, tel. 290 1755.

**Victoria:** Suite 213, 343 Little Collins St., Melbourne, 3000, tel. 03/602 5377.

## Canadian Pacific Airlines Ltd;

[Twice weekly from Sydney (Friday and Sunday) to Vancouver and Toronto via Nadi, Honolulu.]

**Head Office:** 1 Castlereagh St., Sydney 2000, tel. 268-1861; also at 62 Pitt St., tel. 273 077.

**Victoria:** 500 Collins St., Melbourne 3000, tel. 625 457.

**Other states:** CP Air is represented in all other states by Ansett Airlines of Australia.

## Garuda Indonesian Airways;

[From Melbourne and Sydney (Monday, Wednesday, Saturday, Sunday) to Abu Dhabi, Athens, Amsterdam, Bombay, Denpasar, Frankfurt, Jakarta, Jeddah, Karachi, Kuala Lumpur, Paris, Rome, Singapore, Tokyo. From Darwin (Friday and Sunday) to Denpasar, Bali, Jakarta on to connecting flights.]

**Head Office:** 4 Bligh St., Sydney 2000, tel. 232 6044.

**Victoria:** 45 Bourke St., Melbourne 3000, tel. 654 2522.

**Western Australia:** 55 William St., Perth 6000, tel. 321 5213.

**Northern Territory:** 16 Bennett St., Darwin 5790, tel. 098/816 422.

**Japan Air Lines;**
[Tuesday, Thursday and Saturday, from Sydney to Tokyo.]
**Head Office:** Norwich House, 19 Bligh St., Sydney 2000, tel. 232 8655.
**Victoria:** 227 Collins St., Melbourne 3000, tel. 636 326.
**Queensland:** 243 Edward St., Brisbane, tel. 313 045.
**South Australia:** 9th floor, 144 North Terrace, Adelaide, tel. 212 3152.

**KLM Royal Dutch Airlines;**
[Friday, Sydney-Melbourne-Colombo-Dubai-Amsterdam.]
**Head Office:** 5 Elizabeth St., Sydney 2000, tel. 233 6255.
**Queensland:** Ansett Centre, 16 Ann St., Brisbane 4000, tel. 228 8222.
**South Australia:** 4th floor, 45 King William St., Adelaide 5000, tel. 217-7222.
**Victoria:** 80 Collins St., Melbourne 3000, tel. 635 111.
**Western Australia:** 26 St. Georges Terrace, Perth 6000, tel. 325 0201.

**Luthansa;**
[From Sydney and Melbourne Tuesday, and Saturday to Kuala Lumpur-Dubai-Frankfurt.]
**Head Office:** 143 Macquarie St., Sydney 2000, tel. 275 334.
**Queensland:** 380-386 Queen St., Brisbane, tel. 229 2666.
**South Australia:** IMFC House, 33 King William St., Adelaide 5000, tel. 515 239.
**Victoria:** 120 Collins St., Melbourne 3000, tel. 636 131.
**Western Australia:** 32 St. Georges Terrace, Perth 6000, tel. 352 1198.

**Malaysian Airline System;**
[Wednesday, Sydney-Melbourne to Kuala Lumpur-Kuwait-Frankfurt-London. Saturday, Sydney-Melbourne to Kuala Lumpur-Dubai-Amsterdam-London. Sunday, Sydney-Melbourne to Kuala Lumpur-Kuwait-Frankfurt-London. Wednesday and Saturday Perth to Kuala Lumpur.]
**Head Office:** American Express Tower, 388 George St., Sydney 2000, tel. 232 3377.
**Victoria:** Myer House, 250 Elizabeth St., Melbourne, tel. 663 2445.
**Western Australia:** Allendale Square, 77 St. George's Terrace, Perth, tel. 325 9188.
**Queensland:** TAA Bldg., corner of Greek and Adelaide streets, Brisbane, tel. 229 9888.
**South Australia:** TAA Bldg., 144 North Terrace, Adelaide, tel. 516 171.

**Pan American World Airways;**
[From Sydney (daily) and Melbourne (vis Sydney—Tuesday, Wednesday, Friday, Sunday) to Auckland, Honolulu, San Francisco, Los Angeles, Houston, New Orleans and New York. Direct from Sydney to Los Angeles Wednesday, Friday and Sunday.]
**Head Office:** 14 Martin Place, Sydney 2000, tel. 233 111.

**Melbourne:** 233 Collins St., Melbourne 3000, tel. 654 4788.
**Adelaide:** TAA Bldg., 144 North Terrace, Adelaide 5000, tel. 512 821.
**Brisbane:** 307 Queen St., Brisbane 4000, tel. 221 7477.
**Canberra:** 28-36 Ainslie Ave., Canberra 2600, tel. 476 763.
**Perth:** 178 St. George's Terrace, Perth 6000, tel. 321 2719.

**Philippine Airlines;**
[Monday, Melbourne-Sydney-Manila-Bangkok-Karachi-Frankfurt-London (Gatwick). Wednesday, Melbourne-Sydney-Manila-Bangkok-Bahrain-Rome (Fiumicino)-Amsterdam. Friday, Melbourne-Sydney-Manila-Bangkok-Karachi-Frankfurt-London (Gatwick). Saturday, Sydney-Brisbane-Manila-Bangkok-Dubai-Athens-Zurich-Paris (Orly).]
**Head Office:** AMP Bldg., 121 William St., Melbourne 3000, tel. 626 101 or 626 102.
**New South Wales:** 49 York St., Sydney 2000, tel. 294 123.

**Qantas Airways;**
KANGAROO ROUTE: nine flights weekly from Australia to the United Kingdom. Four flights weekly from Australia to Europe with flights originating in Sydney, Melbourne, Brisbane, Townsville, Adelaide, Perth and Darwin. Stopovers include Singapore, Bangkok, Bombay, Bahrain, Athens, Rome, Amsterdam with destinations like Belgrade, Frankfurt, London and Manchester.
ORIENT ROUTE: Thrice weekly to Tokyo. Five flights to Hongkong on Monday, Tuesday, Thursday and via Manila, on Friday and Saturday. Wednesday, Perth to Hongkong via Bangkok. Sunday, Perth to Manila direct.
INDONESIA ROUTE: Twice weekly to Jakarta, Denpasar, Melbourne and Sydney, and once per week between Perth and Denpasar.
SOUTHERN CROSS ROUTE: Daily from Sydney to Honolulu and San Francisco; two services per week extending to Vancouver. Five services per week to Los Angeles from Australian ports Melbourne, Sydney, Brisbane and Townsville.
PAPUA NEW GUINEA ROUTE: Friday and Sunday [via Brisbane].
PACIFIC ISLANDS ROUTE: From Sydney or Melbourne daily except Friday.
TRANS TASMAN ROUTE: From Sydney daily, from Melbourne Friday and Saturday. From Brisbane Wednesday, Saturday and Sunday. From Adelaide, Thursday.
**Head Office:** Qantas Hhouse, International Centre, George Street, Sydney 2000, tel. 236 3636.
**Melbourne:** CBA House, 114 William St., 3000, tel. 602 6026.
**Brisbane:** 288 Queen St., 4000, tel. 224 3711.
**Perth:** 93 William St., 6000, tel. 327 6222.
**Adelaide:** 14 King William St., 5000, tel. 218 8418.
**Hobart:** 77 Elizabeth Mall, tel: 345 700.
**Canberra:** 197 London Circuit, 2601, tel. 481 411.
**Darwin:** 50 Mitchell St., 5790, tel. 823 312.
**Townsville:** 280 Flinders Mall, 4810, tel. 716 901.

**Singapore Airlines;**
[Daily Melbourne-Sydney-Singapore. Thrice weekly Perth-Singapore. 22 services weekly Singapore-Europe. 12 services weekly Singapore-United States.]
**Regional Office**: Singapore Airlines House, 17-19 Bridge St., Sydney 2000, tel. 231 3522.
**New South Wales**: 456-458 Hunter St., Newcastle, tel. 24 511.
**Australia Capital Territory**: 211-219 London Circuit, Canberra, tel. 474 122.
**Victoria**: 416-420 Collins St., Melbourne, tel. 602 4555.
**Western Australia**: 172 St. George's Terrace, Perth, tel. 322 2422.
**South Australia**: 108-116 King William St., Adelaide, tel. 212 3656.
**Queensland**: 127 Creek St., Brisbane, tel. 221 6300; also at 346-352 Flinders St., Townsville, tel. 713 171.
**Tasmania**: 185 Liverpool St., Hobart, tel. 347 955.

**South African Airways;**
**Head Office**: 9 Elizabeth St., Sydney 2000, tel. 233 6855.
**Victoria**: 327 Collins St., Melbourne, Victoria 3000, tel. 625 341.
**Western Australia**: 68 St. Georges Terrace, Perth 6000, tel. 321 2435.

**Thai International;**
[From Sydney-Monday, Thursday, Friday, Saturday. From Melbourne - Monday, Thursday, Friday. From Brisbane - Saturday. From Perth - Friday.]
**Head Office**: 13 Bridge St., Sydney 2000, tel. 241 2171.
**Victoria**: 60 Market St., Melbourne 3000, tel. 626 132.
**Queensland**: 167 Eagle St., Brisbane 4000, tel. 229 3172.
**South Australia**: 32 Grenfell St., Adelaide 5000, tel. 212 5255.
**Western Australia**: 5 Mill St., Perth, tel. 322 4799.

**UTA French Airlines;**
[Sydney-Noumea, Thursday. Sydney-Noumea-Tahiti-Los Angeles, Friday. Sydney-Jakarta-Singapore, also direct to Bahrain, and to Paris, Sunday.]
**Head Office**: 33-35 Bligh St., Sydney 2000, tel. 233 3277.
**Queensland**: 331 Queen St., Brisbane 4000, tel. 221 5655.
**South Australia**: 45 King William St., Adelaide 5000, tel. 212 4466.
**Victoria**: 459 Collins St., Melbourne 3000, tel. 622 982.
**Western Australia**: 178 St. Georges Terraces, Perth 6000, tel. 322 1267.

**Yugoslav Airlines;**
[From Sydney and Melbourne (Sunday and Wednesday) to Dubai and Belgrade.]
**Head Office**: 126-130 Phillip St., Sydney 2000, tel. 221 2899, 221 1666.
**Victoria**: 124 Exhibition St., Melbourne 3000, tel. 636 017, 636 019.

# Sea Cruise Companies

**Blue Funnel**
*Princess Mahsuri*. Singapore, Bali, Fremantle, Adelaide, Melbourne and Sydney; Sydney, Brisbane, Hayman Island, Cairns, Ambon, Manila and Hongkong; New Guinea, Rabaul, Townsville, Hayman Island and Sydney.

**CTC**
*Turkmenia*. Jet/ship, London-Singapore-Fremantle.

**P&O**
*Canberra*. From England
*Sea Princess*. From England
*Oriana*. Cruises the Pacific

**Royal Viking Lines**
*Royal Viking Star*. Cruises around the world following the seasons sometimes taking in Australia, Sydney and Cairns during Australia's summer months of January, Februray and March.

**Sitmar Cruises**
*Fairstar*. Cruises the Pacific.

# Australian Missions Overseas

**Afghanistan:**
No Resident Representative—see Pakistan.
**Algeria:**
Australian Embassy, 60 Blvd. Colonel Bougara, El-Biar Algiers, tel. 602 804.
**Argentina:**
Australian Embassy, Santo Fe 846 Piso 8°, Buenos Aires, tel. 326 841 or 326 848.
**Austria:**
Australian Embassy, Mattiellistrasse 2-4, A-1040 Vienna, tel. 52 85 80.
**Bahamas:**
No Resident Representative—see Jamaica.
**Bahrain:**
Australian Consulate-General Bahrain Chamber Commerce Bldg., King Faisal Road, Manama, Bahrain, tel. 255 011.
**Bangladesh:**
Australian High Commission, Dhaka, 184 Gulshan Ave., Gulshan, Bangladesh, tel. 600 091, 600 095.
**Barbados:**
No Resident Representative—see Jamaica.
**Belgium:**
Australian Embassy, 52 Aven. des Arts, 1040 Brussels, tel. 511 3997.
**Bolivia:**
No Resident Representative—See Chile.
**Botswana:**
No Resident Representative—see South Africa.
**Brazil:**
Australian Embassy, SHIS QI 9, Conj 16, Casa 1, Brasilia D.F., tel. 248 6669.
Rio de Janeiro: Australian Consulate-General, Voluntarios da Patria, 45/5 Botafogo—RJ 22270 Rio de Janeiro, tel. 286 7922.

**Britain:**
Australian High Commission, Australia House, The Strand, London WC2 B4LA, tel. 01/438 8000.
Edinburgh: Australian Consulate, 4 Hanover St., Edinburgh EH2 2HG, tel. 031/226 6271.
Manchester: Australian Consulate, Chatsworth House, Lever Street, Manchester M1 2DL, tel. 061/228 1344.

**Brunei:**
Australian Commission, Teck Guan Plaza, Bandar Seri Bagawan, Brunei, tel. 27 272.

**Bulgaria:**
No Resident Representative—see Yugoslavia.

**Burma:**
Australian Embassy, 88 Strand Rd., Rangoon, tel. 80 711.

**Canada:**
Australian High Commission, The National Bldg., 130 Slater St., Ottawa K1P 5H6, tel. 613/236 0841.
Toronto: Australian Consulate-General, Suite 2324, Commerce Court West, Corner of King & Bay streets, Toronto, Ontario, tel. 416/367 783.
Vancouver: Australian Consulate-General, 800 Oceanic Plaza, 1066 West Hastings St., Vancouver B.C. V6E 3X1, tel. 684/1177.

**Chile:**
Australian Embassy, Santiago, 420 Gertrudis Echenique, Las Condes, Santiago de Chile, tel. 228 5065.

**China:**
Australian Embassy, 15 Donzhlmenwai St., San Li Tun, Beijing, China, tel. 522 331 or 522 336.

**Colombia:**
No Resident Representative—see Venezuela.

**Costa Rica:**
No Resident Representative—see Mexico.

**Cyprus:**
Australian High Commission, 4 Annis Komminis St., (corner Strassinos Avenue), Nicosia, tel. 73 001.

**Czechoslovakia:**
No Resident Representative—see Poland.

**Denmark:**
Australian Embassy, Kristianagade 21, 2100 Copenhagen, tel. 262 244.

**Ecuador:**
No Representative Resident—see Venezuela.

**Egypt:**
Australian Embassy, 1097 Corniche el Nil, Garden City, Cairo, tel. 983 939.

**Ethiopia:**
No Resident Representative—see Kenya.

**Fiji:**
Australian High Commission, Dominion House, Thomson Street, Suva, tel. 312 844.

**Finland:**
No Resident Representative—see Sweden.

**France:**
Australian Embassy, 4 Rue Jean Rey. 75724 Paris Cedex 15, tel. 575 6200.

**Gabon:**
No Resident Representative—see Nigeria.

**German Democratic Republic:**
Australian Embassy to the G.D.R., 111 Berlin— Niederschoenhausen, Grabbeallee 34-40, Berlin, tel. 480 0126.

**Germany, Federal Republic of:**
Australian Embassy, Godesberger Allee 107, 5300 Bonn 2, tel. 02221/376 941.

**Ghana:**
Australian High Commission, Milne Close, Off Dr Amilcar Cabral Road, Airport Residential Area, Accra, tel. 77 972.

**Greece:**
Australian Embassy, 15 Messogeion St., Ambelokipi, Athens, tel. 360 4611 or 360 4615.

**Grenada:**
No Resident Representative—see Jamaica.

**Guatemala:**
No Resident Representative—see Mexico.

**Guyana:**
No Resident Representative—see Jamaica.

**Hongkong:**
Australian Commission, Connaught Centre, Connaught Road, Hongkong, tel. 522 7171 or 522 7178.

**Hungary:**
No Resident Representative—see Austria.

**India:**
Australian High Commission, Australian Compound, No. 1/50-G Shantipath, Chanakyapuri, New Delhi, tel. 690 336 or 690 339.
Bombay: Australian Consulate-General Maker Towers, E Block, Colaba, tel. 211 071 or 211 072.

**Indonesia:**
Australian Embassy, Jalan Thamrin 15, Jakarta, tel. 323 109.
Bali: Australian Consulate, 1 Jln. Raya Sanur 146, Denpasar, Bali, tel. 0361/5997.

**Iran:**
Australian Embassy, 123 Shadid Khalid Al-Islambuli Ave., Abassabad, Tehran, Iran, tel. 833 1719.

**Iraq:**
Australian Embassy, Masbah 141/377, Baghdad, tel. 92 356.

**Ireland:**
Australian Embassy, Fitzwilton House, Wilton Terrace, Dublin 2, tel. 761 517 or 761 519.

**Israel:**
Australian Embassy, 185 Hayarkon St., Tel Aviv, tel. 243 152.

**Italy:**
Australian Embassy, Via Alessandria 215, Rome 00198, tel. 841 241.
Milan: Australian Consulate-General, Via Turati 40, Milan 20121, tel. 659 8727 or 659 8729.
Messina: Australian Consulate, Via Mario Aspa 7, Messina, tel. 090/63 263.

**Ivory Coast:**
No Resident Representative—see Ghana.

**Jamaica:**
Australia High Commission National Life Bldg., 64 Knuftsford Blvd., Kingston 5, tel. 92/63 551.

**Japan:**
Australian Embassy, No. 1-14 Mita 2 Chome, Minato-ku, Tokyo, tel. 453 0251
Osaka: Australian Consulate-General, Osaka International Bldg., Azuchimachi 2-Chome, Higashi-ku, Osaka, tel. 06/271 7071.

**Jordan:**
Australian Embassy, Between 4th and 5th Circles, Wadi Sir Road, Jabel Amman, tel. 43 246 or 43 2247.

**Kenya:**
Australian High Commission, Development House, Moi Avenue, Nairobi, tel. 334 666 or 334 672.

**Kiribati:**
Australian High Commission, Tarawa, tel. 316

**Korea, Republic of:**
Australian Embassy, Kukdong-Shell Bldg., 58-1 Shinmoonro 1-Ka, Chongro-ku, Seoul, tel 706 490.

**Kuwait:**
Australian Embassy, Al-Rashed Bldg., Fahd Al-Salem Street, Kuwait, tel. 415 844.

**Laos:**
Australian Embassy, Rue J Nehru, Quartier Phone Xay, Vientiane, tel. 2477.

**Lebanon:**
Australian Embassy, Farra Building, 463 Bliss St., Ras Beirut, tel. 803 340.

**Lesotho:**
No Resident Representative—see S. Africa.

**Luxembourg:**
No Resident Representative—see Belgium.

**Madagascar:**
No Resident Representative—see Tanzania.

**Malaysia:**
Australian High Commission, 6 Jln. Yap Kwan Seng, Kuala Lumpur, tel. 423 122.

**Maldives, Republic of:**
No Resident Representative—see Sri Lanka.

**Malta:**
Australian High Commission, Airways House, Gaiety Lane, Malta G.C., tel. 38 201.

**Mauritius:**
No Resident Representative—see Tanzania.

**Mexico:**
Australian Embassy, Paseo de la Reforma, 195, 5° Piso, Mexico 5, D.F. Mexico City, tel. 566 3055.

**Mongolia:**
No Resident Representative—see USSR.

**Morocco:**
No Resident Representative—see France.

**Nauru:**
Australian High Commission, Civic Centre, Nauru, tel. 5130.

**Nepal:**
No Resident Representative—see India.

**Netherlands, The:**
Australian Embassy, Koninginnegracht 23, 2514 AB The Hague, tel. (070) 630 983.

**New Caledonia:**
Australian Consulate-General, 18 Rue de Marechal Foch, Noumea, tel. 272 414.

**New Zealand:**
Australian High Commission, 72-78 Hobson St., Thorndon, Wellington, tel. 736 411 or 736 412.
Auckland: Australian Consulate-General, 7th & 8th floors, 32-38 Quay St., Auckland, tel. 32 429.

**Nigeria:**
Australian High Commission, 16 Adeola Hopewell St., Victoria Island, Lagos, tel. 618 875.

**Norway:**
No Resident Representative—see Sweden.

**Oman:**
No Resident Representative—see Jeddah.

**Pakistan:**
Australian Embassy, Plot 17, Sector G4/4, Diplomatic Enclave No. 2, Islamabad, tel. 22 115 or 22 111.

**Panama:**
No Resident Representative—see Mexico.

**Papua New Guinea:**
Australian High Commission, Waigani, Hohola, tel. 259 333.

**Paraguay:**
No Resident Representative—see Argentina.

**Peru:**
Australian Embassy, Edificio Plaza, 6th floor, Natalio Sanchez 220, Lima, tel. 288 313.

**Philippines:**
Australian Embassy, China Banking Corporation Bldg., Paseo de Roxas (Corner Villar Street), Makati Commercial Centre, Makati, tel. 874 961.

**Poland:**
Australian Embassy, Estonska 3/5, Saska Kepa, Warsaw, tel. 176 081.

**Portugal:**
Australian Embassy, Avenida de Liberdade 244-40, Lisbon 2, tel. 538 511.

**Qatar:**
No Resident Representative—see Saudi Arabia.

**Romania:**
No Resident Representative—see Yugoslavia.

**Saudi Arabia:**
Australian Embassy, Off Hamra Road, Jeddah, tel. 665 1303.

**Senegal:**
No Resident Representative—see Ghana.

**Seychelles:**
No Resident Representative—See Kenya

**Singapore:**
Australian High Commission, 25 Napier Rd., Singapore 10, tel. 737 9311.

**Solomon Islands:**
Australian High Commission, Hongkong & Shanghai Bank Bldg., Mendara Avenue, Honiara, tel. 561 or 563.

**South Africa:**
Australian Embassy, 302 Standard Bank Chambers, Church Square, Pretoria, tel. 37 051.
Capetown: Australian Consulate, 1001 Colonial Mutual Bldg., 106 Adderley St., Capetown, tel. 221 576.

**Spain:**
Australian Embassy, Paseo de la Castellano 143, Madrid 16, tel. 279 8501.

**Sri Lanka:**
Australian High Commission, 3 Cambridge Place, Colombo, tel. 98 767.

**Sudan:**
No Resident Representative—see Egypt.

**Swaziland:**
No Resident Representative—S. Africa.

**Sweden:**
Australian Embassy, (Sergels Torg 12), Stock-

holm C. Tel. 244 660.

**Switzerland:**
Australian Embassy, 29 Alpenstrasse, Berne, tel. 430 143.
Geneva: Australian Consulate, 56-58 Rue de Moillebeau, Petit Saconnex, 1211 Geneva 19, tel. 346 200.

**Syria:**
Australian Embassy, 128Á Farabi St., Mezzeh, Damascus, tel. 664 317.

**Tanzania:**
Australian High Commission, NLC Investment Bldg., Independence Avenue, Dar-Es-Salaam, tel. 20 244 or 20 246.

**Thailand:**
Australian Embassy, 37 South Sathorn Road, Bangkok 12, tel. 286 0411.

**Tonga:**
Australian High Commission, Salote Road, Nuku'Alofa, tel. 21 411.

**Trinidad & Tobago:**
No Resident Representative—see Jamaica.

**Tunisia:**
No Resident Representative—see Algeria.

**Turkey:**
Australian Embassy, 83 Nenehatun Caddesi, Gazi Osman Pasa, Ankara, tel. 275 318.

**Tuvalu:**
No Resident Representative—see Fiji.

**Uganda:**
No Resident Representative—see Kenya.

**Union of Soviet Socialist Republics:**
Australian Embassy, 13 Kropotkinsky Pereulok, Moscow, tel. 246 5011.

**United Arab Emirates:**
Australian Consulate-General, Sayed Mahamed Glass Tower Bldg., Tourist Club Area near Tourist Club Gates, Abu Dhabi, tel. 821 800.

**United States of America:**
Australian Embassy, 1601 Massachusetts Ave. N.W. Washington DC 20036, tel. 202/797 3000.
Los Angeles: Australian Consulate-General, Suite 1742, 3550 Wilshire Blvd., Los Angeles CA 90010, tel. 213/380 0980.
Chicago: Australian Consulate-General, 1 Illinois Centre, Suite 2212, 111 East Wacker Dr., Chicago 60601, tel. 312/329 1740.
Honolulu: Australian Consulate-General, 1000 Bishop St., Honolulu, Hawaii 96813, tel. 808/524 5050.
New York: Australian Consulate-General, International Bldg., 636 Fifth Ave., NY 10111, tel. 212/245 4000.
San Francisco: Australian Consulate-General, Qantas Bldg., 360 Post St., San Francisco 8, tel. (415) 362 6160.

**Vanuatu:**
Australian High Commission, Melitco House, Vila, tel. 2777.

**Venezuela:**
Australian Embassy, Centro Plaza, Avenida Francisco de Miranda, Caracas, tel. 283 7177.

**Vietnam, Socialist Republic of:**
Australian Embassy, 66 Ly Thuong Kiet, Hanoi, tel. 52 763.

**Western Samoa:**
Australian High Commission, Fea Gal Ma Leata Bldg., Beach Road, Tamaligi, Apia, tel. 23 411.

**Yugoslavia:**
Australian Embassy, 13 Cika Ljubina, Belgrade, tel. 624 655.

**Zambia:**
Australian High Commission, 3rd floor, Memaca House, Sapele Road, Lusaka, tel. 219 001 or 219 003.

**Zimbabwe:**
Australian High Commission, Throgmorton House, Corner of Samora Machel Avenue and Julius Nyerere Road, Salibsbury, tel. 794 591 or 794 592.

# Embassies in Canberra

**Argentina**
12 Daly St, Deakin.

**Austria**
107 Endeavour St, Red Hill.

**Bangladesh**
43 Hampton Crct, Yarralumla.

**Belgium**
19 Arkana St, Yarralumla.

**Brazil**
11th floor, Canberra House, Marcus Clarke St, Canberra City.

**Britain**
Commonwealth Ave, Yarralumla.

**Burma**
85 Mugga Way, Red Hill.

**Canada**
Commonwealth Ave, Yarralumla.

**Chile**
93 Endeavour St, Red Hill.

**China**
247 Federal Highway, Watson.

**Cyprus**
37 Beagle St, Red Hill.

**Denmark**
24 Beagle St, Red Hill.

**Egypt, Arab Republic of**
125 Monaro Cres, Red Hill.

**Fiji**
9 Beagle St, Red Hill.

**Finland**
10 Darwin Ave, Yarralumla.

**France**
6 Darwin Ave, Yarralumla.

**German Democratic Republic**
12 Beagle St, Red Hill.

**Germany, Federal Republic of**
119 Empire Crct, Yarralumla.

**Ghana**
44 Endeavour St, Red Hill.

**Greece**
22 Arthur Circle, Forrest.

**Holy See**
2 Vancouver Ave, Red Hill (office and residence of the Apostolic Pro-nuncio).

**Hungary**
79 Hopetoun Crct, Yarralumla.

**India**
135 Monaro Cres, Red Hill.

**Indonesia**
8 Darwin Ave, Yarralumla.

**Iran**
14 Torres St, Red Hill.

**Ireland**
Second floor, Bank House, Civic Square, Canberra City.

**Israel**
6 Turrana St, Yarralumla (Embassy and residence).

**Italy**
12 Grey St, Deakin.

**Japan**
112-114 Empire Crct, Yarralumla (Embassy and residence).

**Jordan**
20 Roebuck St, Red Hill.

**Korea, Republic of**
113 Empire Crct, Yarralumla.

**Laos**
113 Kitchener St, Garran.

**Lebanon**
1 Arkana St, Yarralumla.

**Malaysia**
71 State Circle, Yarralumla.

**Malta**
261 La Perouse St, Red Hill.

**Mauritius**
16 National Crct, Barton.

**Mexico**
1 Beagle St, Red Hill

**Netherlands, The**
120 Empire Crct, Yarralumla.

**New Zealand**
Commonwealth Ave, Yarralumla.

**Nigeria**
27 State Circle, Deakin.

**Norway**
3 Zeehan St, Red Hill.

**Pakistan**
59 Franklin St, Forrest.

**Papua New Guinea**
97 Endeavour St, Red Hill.

**Peru**
94 Captain Cook Cres, Griffith.

**Philippines**
1 Moonah Pl, Yarralumla (Embassy and residence).

**Poland**
7 Turrana St, Yarralumla (Embassy and residence).

**Portugal**
13 Charlotte St, Red Hill

**Romania**
3 Tyaparah St, O.Malley (Embassy and residence).

**Singapore**
81 Mugga Way, Red Hill.

**South Africa**
Cnr State Circle and Rhodes Pl, Yarralumla.

**Spain**
54 Norman St, Deakin.

**Sri Lanka**
35 Empire Crct, Forrest.

**Sweden**
Turrana St, Yarralumla (Embassy and residence).

**Switzerland**
7 Melbourne Ave, Forrest (Embassy and residence).

**Thailand**
111 Empire Crct, Yarralumla (Embassy and residence).

**Turkey**
60 Mugga Way, Red Hill (Embassy and residence).

**Union of Soviet Socialist Republics**
78 Canberra Ave, Griffith.

**United States of America**
State Circle, Yarralumla (Embassy and residence).

**Uruguay**
Adelaide House, Suite 5, Woden.

**Vietnam**
92 Endeavour St, Red Hill (Embassy and residence).

**Yugoslavia**
11 Nuyts St, Red Hill.

## Accommodations Guide

Australia hotels are widely classified into three categories: Premier, Moderate and Budget. Premier establishments offer a good range of services and many of them are of international standard. Moderate types are well-kept and pleasantly furnished with comfortable accommodations providing most of the amenities usually required by visitors. Budget properties are simple and modest, catering to the needs of budget travellers. In Australia, a distinction is also made between hotels and motels. While a hotel must provide a public bar amongst its other facilities, a motel may not have bar areas. If they choose to have such facilities, they are usually only for their guests and not the public.

Below is a random presentation of accommodations available in Australia. Motels are indicated by (M). Charges, though accurate at time of publication, are subject to fluctuations and unless otherwise indicated, constitute cost of room only.

## SYDNEY, NSW

### Premier

**Cosmopolitan Motor Inn**(M), Knox St., Double Bay 2028, tel. 02/366 871, tlx. AA 21187 COSIN. Single A$54-63, double A$65-77

**Gazebo**, 2 Elizabeth Bay Rd., Kings Cross 2011, tel. 02/358 1999, tlx. AA 21569 GAZEBO. Single A$72-79, Double A$79-85

**Hyatt Kingsgate**, Kings Cross Rd., Kings Cross 2011, tel. 02/357 2233, tlx. AA 23114 HYATT. Single A$93, Double A$103

**Menzies Sydney Hotel**, 14 Carrington St., Sydney 2000, tel. 02/20 232, tlx. AA 20443 MENZHO. Single A$89, Double A$99

**New Crest**, 111 Darlinghurst Rd., Kings Cross 2011, tel. 02/358 2755, tlx. AA 21352 CRESTEL. Single A$55-61, Double A$61-66

**Noahs Northside Gardens** (M), 54 Mclaren St., North Sydney 2080, tel. 02/922 1311, tlx. AA 24796 NOANG. Single A$78, Double A$89.

**North Sydney Travelodge** (M), Blue Street, North Sydney 2080, tel. 02/920 499, tlx. 26644 TRA. Single A$79-87, Double A$85-90

**Sebel Town House**, 23 Elizabeth Bay Rd., Kings Cross 2011, tel. 02/358 3244, tlx. AA 20067. Single A$85, Double A$94

**Sheraton Wentworth Hotel**, 61 Philip St., Sydney 2000, tel. 02/230 0700, tlx. AA 21227. Single A$97-105, Double A$105-115

**Sydney Hilton**, 259 Pitt St., Sydney 2000, tel. 02/266 0610, tlx. AA 25208 HILTELL. Single A$99, Double A$114

**The Boulevard**, 90 William St., Sydney 2000, tel. 02/357 2277, tlx. AA 24350 BLBD. Single A$85-98, Double A$94-103

**The Regent Sydney**, 199 George St., Sydney 2000, tel. 02/238 0000, tlx. Aa 73023 REGSYD. Single A$95, Double A$120

**Wynyard Travelodge** (M), 3 York St., Sydney 2000, tel. 02/20 254, tlx. AA 26690 TRAVLOJ. Single A$85, Double A$92

## Moderate

**Airport Hotel Hilton**, 20 Levey St., Arncliffe 2005, tel. 02/597 0122, tlx. AA 70795 AHISYD. Single A$79-71, Double A$92-106

**Cambridge Inn**(M), 212 Riley St., Sydney 2010, tel. (02)212 1111, tlx. AA 23813 TOPINN. Single A$68, Double A$78

**Cliveden**, 4 Bridge St., Sydney 2000, tel. 02/235 1333, tlx. AA 27750. Single A$60, Double A$60 (Self-contained units serviced regularly).

**Chevron**, Macleay St., Potts Point 2011, tel. 02/358 0433, tlx. AA 20489 CHEVRON. Single A$63, Double A$70-82

**Commodore Chateau** (M), 14 Macleay St. Potts Point 2011, tel. 02/358 2500, tlx. AA 22490. Single A$75-90, Double A$80-95

**Corban International** (M), 183 Coogee Bay Road, Coogee 2034, tel. 02/665 2244, tlx. AA 24112. Single A$40, Double A$45

**Florida Motor Inn**, 1 McDonald St., Kings Cross 2011, tel. 02/358 6811, tlx. AA 21128. Single A$50, Double A$54

**Hampton Court**, 9 Bayswater Rd., Kings Cross 2011, tel. 02/357 2711, tlx. AA 27456. Single A$43, Double A$54

**Hyde Park Plaza Motor Inn**, 38 College St., Sydney 2000, tel. 02/331 6933, tlx. AA 22450 CURTINN. Single A$56, Double A$60

**Koala Oxford Square** (M), Oxford & Pelican streets, Sydney 2000, tel. 02/269 0645, tlx. AA 21868. Single A$65, Double A$71 (Cooking facilities avaiable)

**Koala Park Regis** (M), Castlereagh & Park streets, Sydney 2000, tel. 02/267 6511, tlx. AA 21318. Single A$60, Double A$66

**Macleay Street Travelodge** (M), 26 Macleay St., Potts Point 2011, tel. 02/358 2777, tlx. AA 23752 TRAVLOJ. Single A$67, Double A$73

**Marquee Sheraton** (M), 40 Macleay St., Potts Point 2011, tel. 02/358 1955, tlx. AA 21174. Single A$58, Double A$64. (Cooking facilities available)

**Motel Lodge** (M), 68 Roslyn Gardens, Kings Cross 2011, tel. 02/358 6611, tlx. AA 22375 KINGSX. Single A$47, Double A$51 (Cooking facilities available)

**Rushcutter Travelodge** (M), 110 Bayswater Rd., Rushcutters Bay 2011, tel. 02/331 2171.' Single A$80, Double A$85

**Sunset Motor Inn** (M), 14 Roslyn Gardens, Kings Cross 2011, tel. 02/358 1944, tlx. AA 23017 SUNKYX. Single A$38, Double A$43. (Cooking facilities available)

**Telford Lodge Motor Inn**(M), 79 Oxford St., Bondi Junction 2022, tel. 02/389 9466, tlx. AA 22147 TELOG. Single A$41, Double A$47 (Cooking facilities available)

**The New Barclay Hotel** (M), 17 Bayswater Rd., Kings Cross 2011, tel. 02/358 6133, tlx. AA 24112 CORIN. Single A$34, Double A$39

**The Russell**, 143a George St., Sydney 2000, tel. 02/241 3543, tlx. AA 23891. Single A$33-44, Double A$47-57

**The Whitehall Hotel**, 85 New South Head Rd., Rushcutters Bay 2011, tel. 02/328 7044, tlx. AA 21829. Single A$46.50, Double A$52

**The Wiltshire**, 339 Kent St., Sydney 2000, tel.

02/264 8099, tlx. AA 27344 SYDAPT. Single A$62, Double A$69 (Self-contained units serviced regularly)

**Top of the Town Holiday Inn**, (M), 110 Darlinghurst Rd., Kings Cross 2011, tel. 02/33 0911, tlx AA 59121. Single A$55, Double A$65

**Victoria Towers**, 145 Victoria St., Potts Point 2011, tel. 02/357 3400, tlx. AA 72792 VICTOW. Single A$44-49, Double A$49-54 (Self-contained units serviced regularly)

**Zebra Hyde Park** (M), 271 Elizabeth St., Sydney 2000, tel. 02/264 6001, tlx. AA 25304. Single A$58, Double A$62 (Cooking facilities available)

To make advance reservations at any of the youth hostels, write to the correct Youth Hostel Association office:

**National Office**: 118 Alfred St., Milsons Point, NSW 2061, Australia, tel. 02/929 3407.

**Western Australia**: Perry Lakes Stadium, Wembley W.A. 6014, P.O. Box 59, tel. 09/387 5355.

**Victoria**: 122 Flinders St., Melbourne Victoria 3000, tel. 03/635 421.

**Tasmania**: 133 Elizabeth St., Hobart Tasmania 7000, tel. 002/349 617.

**South Australia**: 72 South Terrace, Adelaide S.A. 5000, tel. 08/515 583.

**Queensland**: 462 Queen St., Brisbane Queensland 4000, tel. 07/221 2022.

**Northern Territory**: Darwin Youth Hostel, Hidden Valley Road, Berrimah, N.T. 5789, tel. 089/843 107.

**New South Wales**, 355 Kent St., Sydney NSW 2000, tel. 02/295 068.

If you wish to stay at a farm during your holidays, write to any one of the following for more details:

**Australian Home Accommodation**, P.O. Box 42, Hawksburn, Victoria 3142, tel. 03/509 1962, tlx. AA 32235 BLADN.

**Bed & Breakfast International**, 18-20 Oxford St., Woollahra, Sydney, NSW 2025, tel. 02/334 236, tlx. AA27229, cable: VACSAM, Sydney.

**Farm Holidays**, P.O. Box 307, Avalon, NSW, tel. 02/918 2446.

**Tourex Development Co Ltd.**, 21 & 22 Piccadilly Arcade, 222 Pitt St., Sydney NSW 2000, tel. 02/267 5777, tlx. AA70899.

**Group Farm Tours**, 8 Kalang Rd., Camberwell Victoria 3124, tel. 03/297 662.

## Budget

**Aldon**, 354 Edgecliff Rd., Woollahra 2027, tel. 02/328 6156. Single A$18-25, Double A$28-35 (Charges include bed-and-breakfast. Cooking facilities are also available)

**Bokhara**, 41 Cremorne Rd., Cremorne Point 2090, tel. 02/907 121, tlx. AA 27956 ENERGX. Single A$23, Double A$32 (Charges include bed-and-breakfast)

**Canberra Oriental**, 233 Victoria St., Kings Cross 2011, tel. 02/358 3155. Single A$45. Double A$55 (A private hotel with no permit to serve liquor)

**CB Private Hotel**, 417 Pitt St., Sydney 2000, tel. 02/211 5115. Single A$12, Double A$18 (Not licensed to serve liquor)

**Coronation**, 7 Park St., Sydney 2000, tel. 02/267 8362. Single A$27-30, Double A$37-42 (Charges include bed-and-breakfast)

**Gladswood Hotel**, 11 Gladswood Gardens, Double Bay 2028, tel. 02/361 091, tlx. AA 20149. Single A$35. Double A$42 (A private hotel with no permit to serve liquor)

**Grand Hotel**, 30 Hunter St., Sydney 2000, tel. 02/232 3755. Single A$32, Double A$44 (charges include bed-and-breakfast)

**Grantham Lodge**, 1 Grantham St., Kings Cross, tel. 02/357 2377, tlx. AA 71092. Single A$45 (A$200 weekly), Double A$54, (A$275 weekly). (Self-contained units serviced regularly)

**The Imperial**, 221 Darlinghurst Rd., Kings Cross NSW 2011, tel. 02/331 4051, tlx. AA 25718 IMPHTL. Single A$23, Double A$34. (Private Hotel with no permit to serve liquor. Charges include bed-and-breakfast)

**Manhattan**, Greenknowe Ave., Potts Point 2011, tel. 02/358 1288, tlx. AA 24910. Single A$29.50, Double A$49.50 (Charges include bed-and-breakfast. Private hotel with no permit to serve liquor.)

**Mansions**, 18 Bayswater Rd., Kings Cross 2011, tel. 02/358 6677. Single A$24, Double A$40 (Charges include bed-and-breakfast)

**Monterey**, 1 Avenue Rd., Mosman 2088, tel. 02/960 2177. Single A$26

**Westend**, 412 Pitt St., Sydney 2000, tel. 02/211 4822. Single A$44, Double A$49

**Sydney Youth Hostel** (for members only), 28 Ross St., Forest Lodge 2037, tel. 02/692 0747. A$7 per person.

# CANBERRA, ACT

## Premier

**Canberra International Motor Inn**, Northbourre Avenue, Dickson, Canberra ACT 2602, tel. 062/476 966, tlx. AA 62154 CIMIHO. Single A$69, Double A$75.

**Canberra Rex**, Northbourne Avenue, Braddon 2601, tel. 062/485 311, tlx. AA 62363 CANREX. Single A$64, Double A$70

**Noah's Lakeside International**, London Circuit, Canberra City 2600, tel. 062/476 244, tlx. AA 62374. Single A$88, Double A$102

## Moderate

**Embassy** (M), Hopetoun Circuit & Adelaide Avenue, Deakin 2600, tel. 062/811 322, tlx. AA 62171. Single A$42, Double A$54

**Ethos**, Northbourne Avenue, Dickson 2602, tel. 062/486 222, Single A$28-50, Double A$38.50

**Forrest Lodge Motor Inn** (M), 30 National Circuit, Forrest 2603, tel. 062/953 3433, tlx. AA 62272. Single A$35, Double A$40

**Kythera** (M), 100 Northbourne Ave., Braddon 2601, tel. 062/487 611, tlx. AA 62055 KYTHERA. Single A$35.75, Double A$38

**Manuka Motor Inn**(M), Canberra Avenue & Burke Crescent, Griffith 2603, tel. 062/950 481. Single A$37, Double A$41

**Parkroyal** (M), 102 Northbourne Ave., Braddon

2601, tel. 062/491 411, tlx. AA 61516. Single A$71, Double A$80

**Town House Motel** (M), 12 Rudd St., Canberra City 2600, tel. 062/488 011, tlx. AA 62057 TOWNCAN. Single A$42, Double A$49.50

**Travelodge Canberra City** (M), Northbourne Avenue, Canberra City 2600, tel. 062/496 911, tlx. AA 62052. Single A$78, Double A$85

**Wellington**, National Circuit & Canberra Avenue, Forrest 2603, tel. 062/953 884, tlx. AA 62150. Single A$36. Double A$42

## Budget

**Ainslie**, Ainslie Avenue, Braddon 2601, tel. 062/485 511, Single A$33-45, Double A$33-45 (Charges include bed-and-breakfast)

**Civic**, Northbourne Avenue, Canberra City 2600, tel. 062/487 622. Single A$16, Double A$28

**Gowrie**, 210 Northbourne Ave., Braddon 2601, tel. 062/496 033. Double A$27.10. (Private hotel does not serve liquor. Charges include bed-and-breakfast)

**Macquarie Private Hotel**, 18 National Circuit, Barton 2600, tel. 062/732 325. Single A$16.90, Double A$27.10 (Does not serve liquor. Charges include bed-and-breakfast)

**Tall Trees**, 21 Stephen St., Ainslie 2602, tel. 062/491 731. Single A$16-29, Double A$19-32. (Private hotel with no license to serve liquor)

**National Memorial Youth Hostel**, Dryandra St., O'Connor 2601, tel. 062/489 759. Single A$7 (Cooking facilities available)

## MELBOURNE, VICTORIA

## Premier

**Chateau Commodore**, 131 Lonsdale St., Melbourne 3000, tel. 03/663 3161, tlx. AA 31483. Single A$75, Double A$80

**Hotel Australia**, 266 Collins St., Melbourne 3000. tel. 03/630 401, tlx. AA 30988 AUSTMEL. Single A$50, Double A$65

**Melbourne Hilton**, 192 Wellington Parade, East Melbourne 3002, tel. 03/419 3311, tlx. AA 33057. Single A$94, Double A$108

**Noahs Hotel Melbourne**, Exhibition Street, Melbourne 3000, tel. 03/662 0511, tlx. AA 32779. Single A$74, Double A$85

**Old Melbourne Hotel**, 5 Flemington Rd., North Melbourne 3051, tel. 03/329 9344, tlx. AA 32057. Single A$65, Double A$75

**St. Kilda Road Travelodge** (M), Corner of St. Kilda Road and Park Street, South Melbourne 3205, tel. 03/669 4833, tlx. 30869. Single A$87, Double A$94

**Southern Cross**, Corner of Bourke & Exhibition streets, Melbourne 3000, tel. 03/630 221, tlx. AA 30193. Single A$82, Double A$94

**The Melbourne Regency Hotel**, Corner of Lonsdale & Exhibition streets, Melbourne 3000, tel. 03/662 3900, tlx. AA 38890 REGEM. Single A$79, Double A$89

**Travelodge Melbourne Airport** (M), Melbourne Airport 3045, tel. 03/338 2322, tlx. AA 34263.

Single A$71, Double A$79

**Regent Melbourne**, 25 Collins St., Melbourne 3000, tel. 03/630 321, tlx. AA 37724 WENMEL. Single A$92, Double A$103

**Windsor Hotel**, 115 Spring St., Melbourne 3000, tel. 03/630 261, tlx. AA 30437 WINOTEL. Single A$80, Double A$90

## Moderate

**Centre City Motor Inn**, 500 Flinders St., Melbourne 3000, tel. 03/625 015, tlx. AA 36475 CENCIT. Single A$45, Double A$49 (Self-contained units serviced regularly. Cooking facilities available)

**Commodore Queens Road** (M), 4 Queens Rd., Melbourne 3004, tel. 03/262 411, tlx. AA 30853. Single A$55, Double A$60

**Crossley Lodge** (M), 51 Little Bourke St., Melbourne 3000, tel. 03/662 2500, tlx. AA 31980 CROSLY. Single A$51, Double A$56

**Downtowner** (M), 66 Lygon St., Carlton 3053, tel. 03/347 7733, tlx. AA 31025 COMOTEL. Single A$48, Double A$53 (Charges include bed-and-breakfast)

**Flagstaff City Motor Inn**, 45 Dudley St., Melbourne 3000, tel. 03/329 5788, tlx. AA 36928. Single A$39, Double A$44 (Cooking facilities available)

**Innkeepers Lygon Lodge** (M), Lygon Street, Carlton 3053, tel. 03/347 7033, tlx. VIA AA 32048. Single A$39, Double A$42 (Cooking facilities available)

**Koala Queenslodge** (M), 81 Queens Rd., Melbourne 3004, tel. 03/518 581, tlx. AA 31100. Single A$55, Double A$60 (Cooking facilities available)

**Marco Polo Inn**(M), Harker & Flaemington roads, North Melbourne 3051, tel. 03/328 164, tlx. AA 31093. Single A$45-50, Double A$50-55

**Melbourne Town House** (M), 701 Swanston St., Melbourne 3000, tel. 03/347 7811, tlx. AA 31271. Single A$45-52, Double A$53-60

**Palm Lake** (M), 52 Queens Rd., Melbourne 3004, tel. 03/510 231, tlx. AA 30813. Single A$50-55, Double A$59-62

**Parkroyal** (M), 441 Royal Parade, 3052, tel. 03/380 9221, tlx. AA 37080. Single A$71-74, Double A$77-80

**President** (M), 63 Queens Rd., Melbourne 3004, tel. 03/518 411, tlx. AA 30987 PRESMOT. Single A$60, Double A$65

**Rathdowne Hotel**, 49 Rathdowne St., Carlton 3053, tel. 03/662 1388, tlx. AA 39528 RATHON. Single A$64, Double A$69 (Charges include bed-and-breakfast)

**City Limits Inn**(M), 20 Little Bourke St., Melbourne 3000, tel. 03/662 2544, tlx. AA 39503 CITLIM. Single A$49, Double A$55 (Charges include bed-and-breakfast)

**Sheraton** (M), 13 Spring St., Melbourne 3000, tel. 03/639 961, tlx. AA 31021 SHERTEL. Single A$50-52, Double A$55-60

**Treasury Motor Lodge** (M), 179 Powlett St., East Melbourne 3002, tel. 03/415 281, tlx. AA 32052. Single A$32, Double A$37

## Budget

**London**, 99 Elizabeth St., Melbourne 3000, tel. 03/676 201, tlx. AA 676201 LONMEL. Single A$16, Double A$24

**Magnolia Court**, 101 Powlett St., East Melbourne 3002, tel. 03/419 4530. Single A$22, Double A$32 (Private hotel with no permit to serve liquor)

**The George Powlett** (M), 30 Powlett St., East Melbourne 3002, tel. 03/416 408. Single A$29, Double A$35

**The Spencer** (M), 44 Spencer St., Melbourne 3000, tel. 03/626 991, tlx. AA 37544 SPENCR. Single A$27, Double A$30

**The Victoria**, 215 Little Collins St., Melbourne 3000, tel. 03/630 441, tlx. AA 31264. Single A$22-37, Double A$27-44

**YWCA Family Motel**, 489 Elizabeth St., Melbourne 3000, tel. 03/329 5188. Single A$18, Double A$26

**Melbourne Youth Hostel** (for members only), 500 Abbotsford St., North Melbourne 3051; also at 76 Chapman St., North Melbourne 3051. A$5.50 per person.

## PERTH, W.A.

### Premier

**Ansett Gateway Hotel**, 10 Irwin St., Perth 6000, tel. 09/325 0481, tlx. AA 92999 MOPER. Single A$70, Double A$75

**Parmelia Hilton International**, Mill Street, Perth 6000, tel. 09/322 3622, tlx. AA 92365. Single A$78-90, Double A$90-103

**Riverside Hotel**, 150 Mounts Bay Rd., Perth 6000, tel. 09/321 4721, tlx. AA 92750 RIVERSIDE. Single A$54-69, Double A$73-91

**Sheraton Perth**, 207 Adelaide Terrace, Perth 6000, tel. 09/325 0501, tlx. AA 92938 SHER-ACO. Single A$80-98, Double A$86-104

**Transit**, 37 Pier St., Perth 6000, tel. 09/325 7655, tlx. AA 92739 TRANSIN. Single A$67, Double A$72

### Moderate

**Airways Hotel Apartments**, 195 Adelaide Terrace, Perth 6000, tel. 09/323 7799, tlx. AA 93113 AIRAPT. Single A$40, Double A$45 (Cooking facilities available but not licensed to serve liquor)

**Cheteau Commodore** (M), Corner of Victoria Avenue and Hay Street, Perth 6000, tel. 09/325 0461, tlx. AA 92872 COMETEL. Single A$60, Double A$65

**Freeway**, 55 Mill Point Rd., South Perth 6151, tel. 09/367 7811, tlx. AA 92483 FREEWAY. Single A$39, Double A$47

**Inn Town**, 70 Pier St., Perth 6000, tel. 09/325 2133, tlx. AA 93267 ITPMBL. Single A$35, Double A$48 (Charges include bed-and-breakfast. Not licensed to serve liquor)

**Miss Maud**, 97 Murray St., Perth 6000, tel. 09/325 3900, tlx. AA 93176 MSMAUD. Single A$39.50-50, Double A$53-59

**Mounts Bay Lodge** (M), 166 Mounts Bay Rd., Perth 6000, tel. 09/321 8022, tlx. AA 93251 MBL. Single A$41, Double A$46

**Kings Perth** (M), 517 Hay St., Perth 6000, tel. 09/325 6555, tlx. AA 92616 KINGS. Single A$60, Double A$65

**New Rhodes**, 292 Mill Point Rd., South Perth 6151, tel. 09/367 5711, tlx. AA 92900 RHODES. Single A$39, Double A$44

**Perth Travelodge** (M), 54 Terrace Rd., Perth 6000, tel. 09/325 3811, tlx. AA 92316 TRAV-LEX. Single A$49, Double A$57

**Swanview** (M), 1 Preston St., Como 6152, tel. 09/367 5755, tlx. AA 92181 SWANVW. Single A$28, Double A$32

**The New Esplanade**, 18 The Esplanade, Perth 6000, tel. 09/325 2000, tlx. AA 93327 ESPLEN. Single A$53, Double A$59

**Town House**, 776 Hay St., Perth 6000, tel. 09/321 9141, tlx. AA 92419 HIMOPER. Single A$53, Double A$60

**Town Lodge**, 134 Mill Point Rd., South Perth 6151, tel. 09/367 5655, A$29-32 per person. (Self-contained units serviced regularly. Cooking facilities available.)

## Budget

**The Adelphi**, 130A Mounts Bay Rd., Perth 6000, tel. 09/321 9751. Single A$30-35, Double A$35 (Self-contained units serviced regularly.)

**Criterion**, 560 Hay St., Perth 6000, tel. 09/325 5155, Single A$15.50-24.50, Double A$25.50-30 (Charges include bed-and-breakfast)

**CWA House**, 1174 Hay St., Perth 6000, tel. 09/321 6081, Single A$24, Double A$31.50 (Private Hotel with no permit to serve liquor.)

**Pacific** (M), 111 Harold St., Highgate 6000, tel. 09/328 5599, tlx. AA 92068 FLAG. Single A$21.50, Double A$30

**Perth Youth Hostel**, 60 Newcastle St., Perth 6000, tel. 09/328 1135. A$4 per person. (Cooking facilities available)

**Southway Lodge**, 35 Angelo St., South Perth 6151, tel. 09/367 5273. Single A$23, Double A$25 (Self-contained units serviced regularly. Cooking facilities available)

**YWCA**, Jewell House, 180 Goderich St., Perth 6000, tel. 09/325 2744. Single A$9.50, Double A$14

## DARWIN, NT.

### Premier

**Telford International**, Dashwood Crescent, Darwin 5790, tel. 089/815 333, tlx. AA 85309. Single A$57, Double A$67

**Travelodge** (M), 122 The Esplanade, Darwin 5790, tel. 089/815 388, tlx. AA 85273. Single A$69

**Mindil Beach Federal**, Gilruth Avenue, Mindil Beach, Darwin 5794, tel. 089/817 755, tlx. AA 825214 FEDDAR. Single A$75, Double A$90

### Moderate

**Asti** (M), Smith St., Darwin 5790, tel. 089/818 200, tlx. AA 81503 MULTICO. Single A$40-

47, Double A$45-52

**Cherry Blossom** (M), 108 The Esplanade, Darwin 5790, tel. 089/816 734. Single A$32, Double A$42

**Darwin**, Herbert Street, Darwin 5790, tel. 089/819 211, tlx. AA 85194 HODAR. Single A$42, Double A$66

**Darwin Motor Inn** (M), 97 Mitchell St., Darwin 5790, tel. 089/813 901, tlx. AA 85090 MOTRINN. Single A$44, Double A$49

**Don Hotel Casino**, Cavanagh Street, Darwin 5790, tel. 089/815 311, tlx. AA 85405. Single A$50, Double A$60

**Poinciana** (M), McLachlan Street, Darwin 5790, tel. 089/818 111, tlx. AA 85104 POINC. Single A$44, Double A$50

**Telford Top End Hotel**, Daly Street, Darwin 5790, tel. 089/816 511. Single A$55, Double A$63

**Tiwi Lodge** (M), Cavanagh Street, Darwin 5790, tel. 089/816 471. Single A$27, Double A$33

## Budget

**Esplanade Lodge**, 88 The Esplanade, Darwin 5790, tel. 089/819 733, tlx. AA 85118 LANROO. Single A$22, Double A$32 (Charges include bed-and-breakfast).

**Windsor Tourist Lodge**, 35 Cavanagh St., Darwin 5790, tel. 089/819 214. Single A$25, Double A$30

**YMCA Doctor's Gully**, Darwin 5790, tel. 089/818 377. Single A$14 (A$59 weekly), Double A$22, Dormitory A$10

**YMCA**, 117 Mitchell St., Darwin 5790, tel. 089/818 644. Single A$14 (A$70 weekly), Double A$23 (A$115 weekly). Charges include bed-and-breakfast.

**Darwin Youth Hostel**, (Tracy Village), Lee Point Road, Wanguri 5790, tel. 089/843 107. A$4 per person.

# HOBART, TASMANIA

## Premier

**Four Seasons Downtowner**, 96 Bathurst St., Hobart 7000, tel. 002/346 333, tlx. AA 58074. Single A$42.50, Double A$55

**Four Seasons Westside**, 156 Bathhurst St., Hobart 7000, tel. 002/346 255, tlx. AA 58228 FSLHWS. Single A$50, Double A$57.50

**Innkeepers Lenna**, 20 Runnymede St., Hobart 7000, tel. 002/232 911, tlx. AA 58190. Single A$62, Double A$73

**Wrest Point Hotel-Casino**, 410 Sandy Bay Rd., Hobart 7000, tel. 002/250 112, tlx. AA 58115. Single A$52.75. Double A$65-90

## Moderate

**Blue Hills**(M), 96A Sanday Bay Rd., Hobart 7000, tel. 002/232 861, tlx. AA 58165 PANRAMA. Single A$31, Double A$37

**Four Seasons Town House**, 167 Macquarie St., Hobart 7000, tel. 002/344 422, tlx. AA 58087 FSLHTH. Single A$25-30, Double A$35-42.50

**Hadleys**, 3 Murray St., Hobart 7000, tel. 002/234 355. Single A$27, Double A$34

**Hobart Pacific Motor Inn** (M), Kirby Court, West Hobart 7000, tel. 002/346 733, tlx. AA 58129. Single A$45, Double A$50

**Innkeepers Hobart** (M), Fountain Roundabout, Hobart 7000, tel. 002/342 911, tlx. AA 58010 INNKHOB. Single A$44, Double A$49

**Innkeepers St. Ives**, 86 Sandy Bay Rd., Hobart 7000, tel. 002/301 801, tlx. AA 58377 STIVE. Single A$46, Double A$52 (Cooking facilities available)

**Marquis of Hastings**, 209 Brisbane St., Hobart 7000, tel. 002/343 541. Single A$27, Double A$40 (Charges include bed-and-breakfast)

## Budget

**Bay Inn**, 646 Sandy Bay Rd., Hobart 7000, tel. 002/251 161. Single A$18, Double A$28

**Barton Cottage**, 72 Hampden Rd., Hobart 7000, tel. 002/236 808. Single A$27, Double A$37 (Charges include bed-and-breakfast)

**Cromwell Cottage**, 6 Cromwell St., Hobart 7000, tel. 002/342 453. Single A$20, Double A$30 (Charges include bed-and-breakfast)

**Hobart Youth Hostel**, 52 King St., Bellerive 7018, tel. 002/442 552. A$3 per person.

# ADELAIDE, SA

## Premier

**Adelaide Parkroyal** (M), 226 South Terrace, Adelaide 5000, tel. 08/223 4355, tlx. AA 82156. Single A$65-73, Double A$73-81

**Ansett Gateway Hotel**, 147 North Terrace, Adelaide 5000, tel. 08/217 7552, tlx. AA 88325. Single A$69, Double A$75

**Hilton International**, 233 Victoria Square, Adelaide 5000, tel. 08/217 0711, tlx. AA 87173. Single A$86-96, Double A$99-110

**Meridien Lodge** (M), 21 Melbourne St., North Adelaide 5006, tel. 08/267 3033, tlx. AA 88018. Single A$56, Double A$60

**Oberoi Hotel**, 62 Brougham Place, North Adelaide 5006, tel. 08/267 3444, tlx. AA 82174. Single A$72, Double A$77

**Town House** (M), Hindley & Morphett streets, Adelaide 5000, tel. 08/211 8255, tlx. AA 82941 THOUSE. Single A$70, Double A$75

## Moderate

**Adelaide Travelodge** (M), 208 South Terrace, Adelaide 5000, tel. 08/223 2744, tlx. AA 89232. Single A$42-59, Double A$48-65

**Ambassadors**, 107 King William St., Adelaide 5000, tel. 08/514 331, tlx. AA 88680 AMBHOI. Single A$31, Double A$40

**City Central Motel** (M), 23 Hindley St., Adelaide 5000, tel. 08/514 040. Single A$24, Double A$30-32

**Earl of Zetland**, 158 Gawler Place, Adelaide 5000, tel. 08/223 5500. Single A$30, Double A$44

**Flinders Lodge Motel** (M), 27 Dequetteville Terrace, Kent Town 5067, tel. 08/332 8222, tlx. AA 82376. Single A$34, Double A$38 (Cooking facilities available)

**Grosvenor**, 125 North Terrace, Adelaide 5000, tel. 08/512 961, tlx. AA 82634 HILTON. Single A$40-60, Double A$45-65

**Hilton Adelaide Motor Inn** (M), 176 Greenhill Rd., Parkside 5063, tel. 08/271 0444, tlx. AA 82037. Single A$38, Double A$42

**Newmarket**, Corner of North & West terraces, Adelaide 5000, tel. 08/513 836. Single A$24, Double A$34

**Parkway** (M), 204 Greenhill Rd., Eastwood 5063, tel. 08/271 0451, tlx. AA 82034 PARKWAY. Single A$30, Double A$32

**Patawalonga Motor Inn** (M), 13 Adelphi Terrace, Glenelg North 5045, tel. 08/294 2122, tlx. AA 82824. Single A$36-40, Double A$40-44

**Princess Lodge** (M), 73 Lefevre Terrace, North Adelaide 5006, tel. 08/267 5566, tlx. AA 82419 PRINAD. Single A$26, Double A$35.50

**Regal Park** (M), 44 Barton Terrace, North Adelaide 5006, tel. 08/267 3222, tlx. AA 82526 REPARK. Single A$40, Double A$45

**Royal Coach** (M), Dequetteville Terrace, Kent Town 5067, tel. 08/425 676, tlx. AA 825614 ROYALCO. Single A$37, Double A$41 (Charges include bed-and-breakfast)

**South Terrace Travelodge** (M), 208 South Terrace, Adelaide 5000, tel. 08/223 2744, tlx. AA 89232. Single A$42-59, Double A$48-65

**Telford Old Adelaide** (M), O'Connell St., North Adelaide 5006, tel. 08/267 5066, tlx. AA 89271. Single A$55, Double A$62

## Budget

**Hanson**, 437 Putney St., Adelaide 5000, tel. 08/223 2442. Single A$17, Double A$29

**Plaza Hotel**, 85 Hindley St., Adelaide 5000, tel. 08/516 371. Single A$17-26, Double A$27-35

**Powell's Court Motel** (M), 2 Glen Osmond Rd., Parkside 5063, tel. 08/271 7995. Single A$28, Double A$34 (Cooking facilities available)

**Strathmore**, 129 North Terrace, Adelaide 5000, tel. 08/514 456. Single A$19.50, Double A$31

**YMCA**, 76 Flinders St., Adelaide 5000, tel. 08/223 1611, Single A$9, Double A$7 per person

**Adelaide Youth Hostel**, 290 Gillies St., Adelaide 5000, Single A$5 (senior), or A$4 (junior)

## BRISBANE, QUEENSLAND

### Premier

**Crest International Hotel**, King George Square, Brisbane 4000, tel. 07/229 9111, tlx. AA 41320. Single A$75, Double A$85

**Ansett Gateway Hotel**, 85 North Quay, Brisbane 4000, tel. 07/221 0211, tlx. AA 41335 MOBRIS. Single A$73, Double A$79

**Gazebo Terrace Hotel** (M), 345 Wickham Terrace, Brisbane 4000, tel. 07/221 6177, tlx. AA 41050 MYHOST. Single A$73, Double A$77

**Lennons Plaza Hotel**, 66 Queens St., Brisbane 4000, tel. 07/320 131, tlx. AA 40252. Single A$75-81, Double A$81-89

**Brisbane Parkroyal** (M), Corner of Alice & Albert streets, Brisbane 4000, tel. 07/221 3411, tlx. AA 40186. Single A$94, Double A$98

### Moderate

**Albert Park Motor Inn** (M), 551 Wickham Terrace, Brisbane 4000, tel. 07/221 3111, tlx. AA 42801 ALBRIS. Single A$44, Double A$48

**Brisbane Travelodge** (M), 355 Main St., Kangaroo Point 4169, tel. 07/391 5566, tlx. AA 42620 TLODGE. Single A$66, Double A$72

**Embassy Hotel**, Corner of Edward & Elizabeth streets, Brisbane 4000, tel. 07/221 7616. Single A$45, Double A$55 (Charges include bed-and-breakfast)

**Metropolitan Motor Inn** (M), Corner of Upper Edward & Leichardt streets, Brisbane 4000, tel. 07/221 6000, tlx. AA 42099 METEL. Single A$56, Double A$63 (Cooking facilities available)

**Parkview Motel** (M), 128 Alice St., Brisbane 4000, tel. 07/312 695, tlx. AA 40270 FLAGPAV. Single A$44, Double A$48

**Regal** (M), 132 Alice St., Brisbane 4000, tel. 07/311 541, tlx. AA 40321 REGAL. Single A$39-43, Double A$45-49

**The Ridge Motor Inn** (M), Corner of Leichardt & Henry streets, Brisbane 4000, tel. 07/221 5000, tlx. AA 41566 RIDGE. Single A$69, Double A$75

**Tower Mill Motor Inn** (M), 239 Wickham Terrace, Brisbane 4000, tel. 07/311 421, tlx. AA 40382 TOWRMIL. Single A$54, Double A$62

**Zebra Motor** (M), 103 George St., Brisbane 4000, tel. 07/221 6044, tlx. AA 41057 ZBRABRS. Single A$62, Double A$68

### Budget

**Dorchester Holiday Flats**, 484 Upper Edward Street, Brisbane 4000, tel. 07/221 2967. Single A$30, Double A$30 (Private hotel with no permit to serve liquor. Cooking facilities available.)

**Marrs Town House**, 391 Wickham Terrace, Brisbane 4000, tel. 07/221 5388. Single A$19-23, Double A$32-37 (Private hotel with no permit to serve liquor. Charges include bed-and-breakfast.)

**Mornington Private Hotel**, 527 Gregory Terrace, Brisbane 4000, tel. 07/524 204. Single A$14, Double A$22 (Private hotel with no permit to serve liquor.)

**The Canberra**, 192 Ann St., Brisbane 4000, tel. 07/320 231, tlx. AA 40586 CANBRA. Single A$18-38, Double A$32-46

**Ruth Fairfax House CWA**, 89 Gregory Terrace, Brisbane 4000, tel. 07/221 8188. Single A$25, Double A$48 (Private hotel with no permit to serve liquor.)

**Soho Budget Hotel**, 333 Wickham Terrace, Brisbane 4000, tel. 07/221 7722. Single A$31, Double A$37 (Private hotel with no permit to serve liquor.)

**The Tourist**, 555 Gregory Terrace, Brisbane 4000, tel. 07/524 171. Single A$12, Double A$21 (Cooking facilities available)

**Brisbane Youth Hostel** (for members only), 15 Mitchell St., Kedron 4031, tel. 07/571 245. A$5 per person, A$2.50 per junior.

# GLOSSARY

| | |
|---|---|
| ABC | Australian Broadcasting Commission |
| ACT | Australian Capital Territory (Canberra) |
| ACTU | Australian Council of Trade Unions |
| ALP | Australian Labor Party |
| ASIO | Aussie CIA |
| Abo | Aboriginal (impolite) |
| Across the ditch | Across the Tasman Sea: New Zealand |
| Air fairy | Flight steward |
| Alf | Stupid person |
| Alice, The | Alice Springs |
| Amber | Beer |
| Anzac | Member of the Australian and New Zealand Army Corps in World War I |
| Arse | Ass, bum, bottom |
| Arvo | Afternoon |
| | |
| BHP | Broken Hill Proprietary, a mining corporation |
| Babbler | Babbling brook-cook |
| Back of Bourke | Far Outback |
| Back of beyond | The Outback |
| Bail up | To rob, hold up |
| Banana bender | Queenslander |
| Barby | Barbecue |
| Barrack | To cheer at a sporting event |
| Bastard | Term of endearment (when it's not a term of dislike) |
| Battler | Person who struggles hard for a living |
| Beaut | Short for "beautiful" (Very good) |
| Beaut | Great, fantastic |
| Beergut | Self explanatory |
| Bible basher | Minister |
| Bikey | Biker |
| Billabong | Water hole in semi-dry river |
| Billy | Tin container used for boiling water to make tea |
| Bitser | Mongrel dog ("Bits a this and bits a that") |
| Black Stump, The | Where the back of Bourke begins (way beyond Bulamakanka) |
| Blacktracker | Aboriginal bush tracker |
| Blind Freddie could have seen it | Great incompetence |
| Bloke | Man, used like "guy" in the U.S. |
| Bloody | Universally undeleted expletive, as in "up at Tumba-bloody-rumba shootin' kanga-bloody-roos" |
| Blowie | Blowfly |
| Bludger | Sponger, ne'er do well |
| Blue | A fight. Also a redhead |
| Bonzer | Terrific |
| Bookie | Bookmaker |
| Boot | Trunk of a car |
| Buckley's Chance | One chance in a million |
| Bugs Bunny | Money |
| Bulamakanka | Mythical, far distant place |
| Bumper crop | Good harvest |
| Bunch of fives | A fist |
| Bunyip | Australia's yeti/Loch Ness monster |
| Bush | Countryside outside cities and towns |
| Bushranger | Bandit, outlaw |
| | |
| Cacky hander | Left hander |
| Chemist | Pharmacist |
| Chips | French fried potatoes |
| Chook | Chicken |
| Chuck | Throw |
| Chuck a Uey | Do a U-turn |
| Chunder | Vomit |
| Clap trap | Useless talk |
| Cobber | Friend |

| | |
|---|---|
| Cockie | Small farmer |
| Come a gutser | Make a bad mistake |
| Coolabah | A type of box eucalyptus tree |
| Cop it sweet | To take the blame or the loss agreeably |
| Corker | A good one |
| Corroboree | Aboriginal ceremonial gathering |
| Crissie | Christmas |
| Crook | Broken, sick or no good |
| Cropper, to come a | To come undone |
| Cuppa | Cup of tea |
| | |
| Dag/daggy | Dreadful looking |
| Daks | Trousers |
| Damper | Unrisen bread (bush tucker q.v.) |
| Dead 'orse | Meat pie and sauce |
| Deli | Delicatessen |
| Demo | Demonstration (political or practical) |
| Dero | Derelict; drunkard |
| Didgeridoo | Aboriginal droning instrument |
| Digger | Australian soldier, but used by foreigners meaning any Australian (Australians prefer "Aussie") |
| Dill | Idiot |
| Dingo | Wild Australian native dog |
| Dinkie die | The whole truth |
| Dinkum | Genuine or honest |
| Do yer block | Lose your temper |
| Don't come the raw prawn | Don't try and fool me |
| Drongo | Worthless person |
| Dumper | A heavy surf wave |
| Dunny | Toilet ("Useless as a glass door on a dunny") |
| | |
| Eau de cologne | Phone |
| | |
| Fair dinkum | Same as "Dinkie die" above |
| Flash as a rat with a gold tooth | Showing off |
| Flat out | As fast as one can go |
| Flog | Sell or hock |
| Footpath | Pavement or sidewalk |
| Footy | Football |
| Funnel web | Poisonous spider |
| | |
| G'day | Good day |
| Galah | Fool or idiot (after the parrot of same name) |
| Garbo | Garbageman |
| Get stung | To be overcharged |
| Getting off at Redfern | Coitus interruptus (Redfern being the last railway station before Sydney Central) |
| Gift of the gab | The gift of persuasive speech |
| Give it the flick | Get rid of it |
| Gloria Soame | Glorious home (Strine) |
| Gong, The | Wollongong |
| Grade A | Grey day (Strine) |
| Greenie | A conservationist |
| Grizzle | To complain |
| Grog | Any alcoholic drink |
| Gurgler, down the | Down the drain, wasted |
| | |
| Heart starter | First drink of the day |
| Hoon | Lumpen prole |
| Humpy | Aboriginal shack |
| | |
| Job | To punch |
| Joey | Baby kangaroo (in the pouch) |
| Journo | Journalist |
| Jumbuck | Sheep |

| | |
|---|---|
| Kangaroos in his top paddock | A bit crazy |
| Kick | Pocket or wallet |
| Kick the bucket | To die |
| Kip | To sleep. Also term for instrument used to toss pennies in two-up |
| Kiwi | New Zealander |
| Knackered | Tired |
| Knee trembler | Sexual intercourse standing up. Coitus verticalis |
| Knock | To criticise |
| Knuckle | To hit with the fist |
| Knuckle sandwich | A punch |
| | |
| Lair, Larrikin | Street tough or hoodlum |
| Lingo | Language |
| Loaf | To do nothing (He's just loafing about these days) |
| Lob | Arrive |
| Loo | Brit/Aust. slang for toilet |
| Lousy | Mean |
| Lucky Country, The | Name for Australia coined by author Donald Horne |
| Lurk | A racket, a dodge or an illegal scheme |
| | |
| Mate | Your best buddy or comrade (does not mean spouse) |
| Mick | A Roman Catholic |
| Middy | Ten-ounce beer glass (in N.S.W.) |
| Mob | A group of persons or things (not necessarily unruly, etc) |
| Mozzie | Mosquito |
| Mug | A gullible fool. A fool who thinks he is being smart is a 'Mug Alec' |
| | |
| Neck oil | Beer |
| Never never | Desert land far away in the outback |
| New chum | Newly arrived immigrant |
| Nick | Steal |
| Nip | Nickname for Japanese. Also, a bar measure for spirits |
| Nipper | Small child |
| Nit | Fool, idiot |
| No hoper | Same as above, but worse |
| Nong | Fool |
| | |
| O.S. | Overseas |
| Ocker | Quintessential Aussie bumpkin-loudmouth |
| Oodles | Plenty of |
| Outback | The bush, uncivilized, uninhabited country |
| Oz | Australia or Australian (ironic term) |
| | |
| Panic merchant | Chronic anxiety case |
| Penguin | A nun |
| Perve | To watch a woman with admiration (does not mean "perverted") |
| Piddle in the pocket | To flatter |
| Pie-eyed | Drunk |
| Pinch | Arrest |
| Pissed | Drunk |
| Plonk | Cheap wine |
| Point Percy at the porcelain | To urinate (men only!) |
| Poker machine | Slot machine |
| Pom or Pommy | Englishman |
| Poof, poofter | Male homosexual |
| Postie | Mailman |
| Prang | Accident, crash |
| Pseud | Poseur, pseudo-intellectual |
| Pub | "Public house," bar, drinking establishment |
| | |
| Quack | Slang for any kind of doctor |
| | |
| RSL | Abbreviation for Returned Servicemen's League |
| Ratbag | Eccentric character. Also Friendly term of abuse |
| Ratshit | Lousy |
| Red-back | Poisonous spider |
| Ripper | Good |

| | |
|---|---|
| Roo | Kangaroo |
| Roof rabbits | Possums or rats in the ceiling |
| Root | Euphemism for sexual intercourse |
| Running round like a chook with its head cut off | Self explanatory if you see "chook" |
| | |
| Sack | To fire, dismiss from employment (also as in "get the sack"—be fired) |
| Salvo | Member of the Salvation Army |
| Schooner | Large beer glass |
| Scrub | Bushland |
| Scunge | A dirty, untidy person; a serious confusion or mess; |
| Semi-trailer | Articulated truck |
| Septic, Seppo | American |
| Shandy | Beer and lemonade mix ("Two shandies off the horrors"—close to Delirium Tremens) |
| She'll be apples | It'll be right |
| She's sweet | Everything is all right, has many equivalents, e.g. she's jake |
| Sheila | Young woman |
| Shoot through | Leave unexpectedly |
| Shout | Buy round of drinks (as 'it's your shout') |
| Shove off | To depart |
| Sidekick | A friend, companion |
| Silly as a cut snake | Self explanatory |
| Silvertail | Member of high society |
| Slats | Ribs |
| Sly drool | Slide rule (Strine) |
| Smoke-o | Tea break |
| Snags | Sausages |
| Speedos | Gents nylon swimming trunks |
| Sprog | Baby |
| Spunky | good-looking boy or girl |
| Squatter | Large landholder |
| Station | Large farm or ranch |
| Stickybeak | Busy body |
| Sting | To charge |
| Stockman | Cowboy, station hand |
| Strides | Trousers |
| Strine | Vernacular Australian |
| Stubby | Small bottle of beer |
| Swagman | Vagabond, rural tramp |
| Sydney or the bush | All or nothing |
| | |
| TAB | Abbreviation for Totalisator Agency Board, legal offtrack betting shop |
| Tall poppies | Achievers, what knockers like to cut down |
| Tazzie | Tasmania |
| Technicolour yawn | Vomit |
| Telly | The TV, also the Sydney Daily Telegraph |
| Thingo | Thing, whatchamacallit |
| Tin lid | Kid |
| Togs | Swimming suit (sometimes called a "bathing costume," too) |
| Toot | A lavatory |
| Trendy | Middle class trend follower |
| Trouble n' strife | Wife |
| Tube | Can of beer |
| Tucker | Food |
| Turps | Any form of alcohol. On the turps, to be drinking |
| Two pot screamer | Person unable to hold their drink |
| Two up | Popular gambling game involving two pennies thrown in the air |
| | |
| Uni | University |
| Up the creek | In trouble |
| Ute | Short for utility truck—a pickup track |
| | |
| Vegemite | Vile brown yeast sandwich spread which Australians grow up on |
| | |
| Walkabout | Travelling on foot for long distances, an Aboriginal tradition |
| Walloper | A policeman |

| | |
|---|---|
| Whinge | Complain |
| Whip-round | A collection of money for the benefit of another or for some celebration |
| Wog | Minor disease, also an Arab |
| Wop | Southern European (again impolite) |
| Wowser | Bluenose, prude, killjoy |
| | |
| Yabber | Chatter |
| Yack | To talk |
| Yahoo | An unruly type |
| Yakka | Work |
| Yobbo | Hoon, loudmouth |

# Further Reading

## General

*Australian Dreaming: 40,000 Years of Aboriginal History*. Compiled and edited by Jennifer Isaacs. Sydney: Lansdowne Press, 1980.

*The Heritage of Australia: The Illustrated Register of the National Estate*, Melbourne: Macmillan, 1981.

Baglin, Douglass and Wilson, Robert. *Great Houses of Australia*. Sydney: Lansdowne Press, 1984.

Isaacs Jennifer. *Australia's Living Heritage: Arts of the Dreaming*. Sydney: Lansdowne Press, 1984.

Morcombe, Michael and Irene. *Discover Australia's National Parks and Naturelands*. Sydney: Lansdowne Press, 1983.

Morrison, Reg and Grasswill, Helen. *Australia, A Timeless Grandeur*. Sydney: Lansdowne Press, 1981.

Morrison, Reg and Lang, Mark. *The Colours of Australia*. Sydney: Lansdowne Press, 1982.

Raymond, Robert. *Australia, The Greatest Island*. Sydney: Lansdowne Press, 1982.

Wilson, Robert. *The Book of Australia*. Sydney: Lansdowne Press, 1982.

## History

Barnard, Marjorie Faith. *A History of Australia*. Sydney: Angus and Robertson, 1962.

Blainey, Geoffrey. *A Land Half Won*. Melbourne: Macmillian, 1980.

Cameron, Roderick. *Australia: History and Horizons*. London: Weidenfeld and Nicolson/Hicks Smith, 1971.

Carter, Jeff. *In the Steps of the Explorers*. Sydney: Angus and Robertson, 1969.

Casey, Maie. *An Australian Story, 1937–1907*. London: Joseph 1962.

Crowley, F.R. *A New History of Australia*. Melbourne: William Heinemann, 1974.

Dunlop, Eric W. *Australia: Colony to Nation*. Melbourne: Longmans, 1965.

Gordon, Harry. *An Eyewitness History of Australia*. Adelaide: Rigby 1976.

Horne, Donald. *The Australian People; Biography of a Nation*. Sydney: Angus and Robertson, 1972.

Kepert, L. *History as It Happened*. Melbourne: Nelson 1981.

Menzies, Robert Gordon, Sir. *The Measure of the Years*. Melbourne: Cassell, 1970.

Page, Michael. *Turning Points in the Making of Australia*. Adelaide: Rigby, 1980.

Wannan, Bill. *Legendary Australians*. Adelaide: Rigby, 1974.

## Natural History

Hill, Robin. *Bush Guest*. Melbourne: Lansdowne, 1968.

Morcombe, Michael. *Australia, the Wild Continent*. Sydney: Lansdowne, 1980.

Serventy, Vincent. *Nature Walkabout*. Sydney: Reed, 1967

Woldendrop, Richard and Slater, Peter. *The Hidden Face of Australia*, by R. Woldendorp and Peter Slater. Melbourne, Nelson, 1968.

Worrell, Eric. *Australian Wildlife: Best-Known Birds, Mammals, Reptiles, Plants of Australia and New Guinea*. Sydney: Angus and Robertson, 1966.

## Social History

Conquest, R. *Dusty Distances: Yesterday's Australia*. Adelaide: Rigby, 1978.

Dufty, David and others. *For Better or for Worse: Australian People in Charge*. Sydney: Hicks Smith, 1975.

Fabian, Sue. *The Changing Australians*. Adelaide: Rigby, 1978.

Kepert, L. *History as it Happened*. Melbourne: Nelson. 1981.

Stone, Derrick I. *Life on the Australian Goldfields*. Sydney: Methuem, 1976.

Young, C. *The New Gold Mountain: The Chinese in Australia*. Richmond: S.A. Raphael Arts, 1977.

## Australian Language

*The Macquarie Dictionary*, Sydney: Macquarie University, 1982.

Hornadge, Bill. *The Australian Slanguage*. Sydney: Cassell, 1980.

Lauder, Afferbeck. *Strine*. Sydney: Lansdowne Press, 1982.

McAndrew, Alex. *The Language We Speak in Australia*. University of Sydney, 1979.

McCarthy, F.D. *New South Wales Aboriginal Place Names*. Sydney: Australian Museum, 1971.

Wilkes, G.A. *Dictionary of Australian Colloquialisms*. Sydney: University Press, 1978.

# ART/PHOTO CREDITS

# INDEX